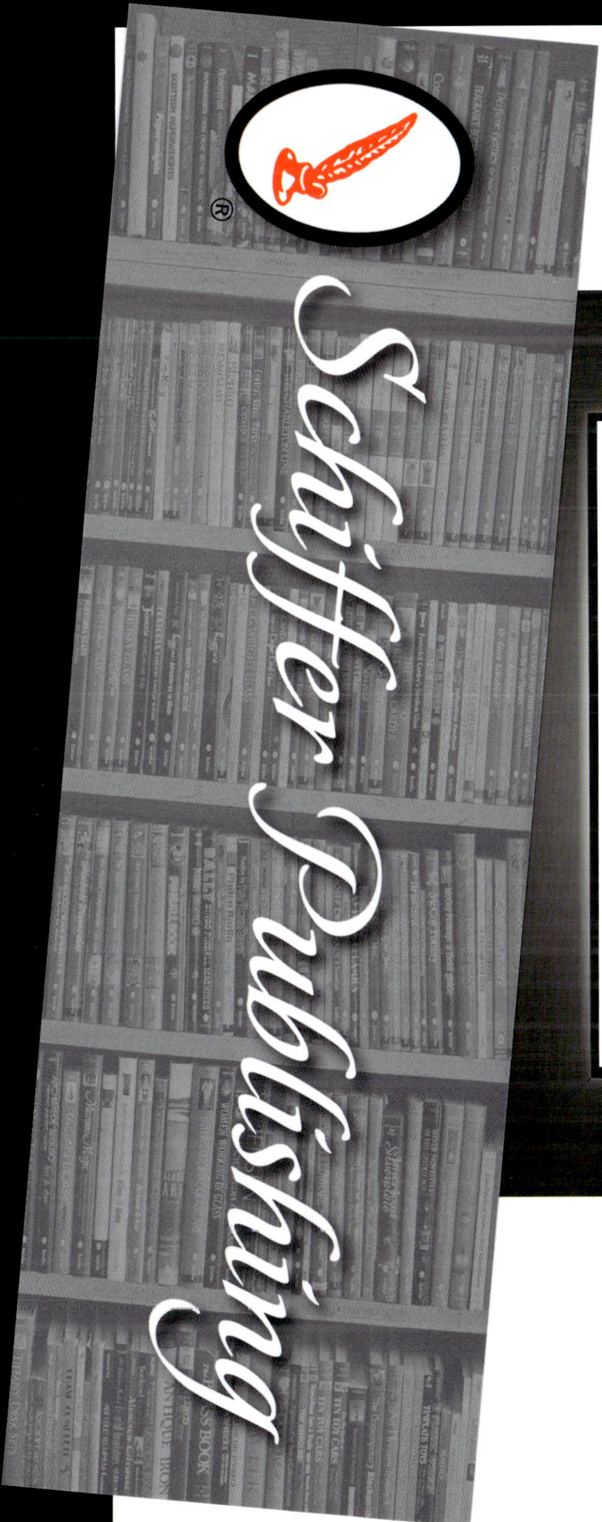

Artists' Homes & Studios

E. Ashley Rooney

Foreword by Rob Evans

Schiffer Publishing Ltd

4880 Lower Valley Road • Atglen, PA 19310

Library of Congress Control Number: 2014947257

Front cover photo: Keith Berr
Back cover photos: Terrence Coffman, Karla Matzke (Jack Gunter), Florence Putterman (Kerry Shirk), and Barton Rubenstein

Designed by Brenda McCallum
Cover design by RoS
Type set in heading font Credit Valley/Amplitude/Agenda
ISBN: 978-0-7643-4692-7
Printed in China

Published by Schiffer Publishing, Ltd.
4880 Lower Valley Road
Atglen, PA 19310
Phone: (610) 593-1777; Fax: (610) 593-2002
E-mail: Info@schifferbooks.com

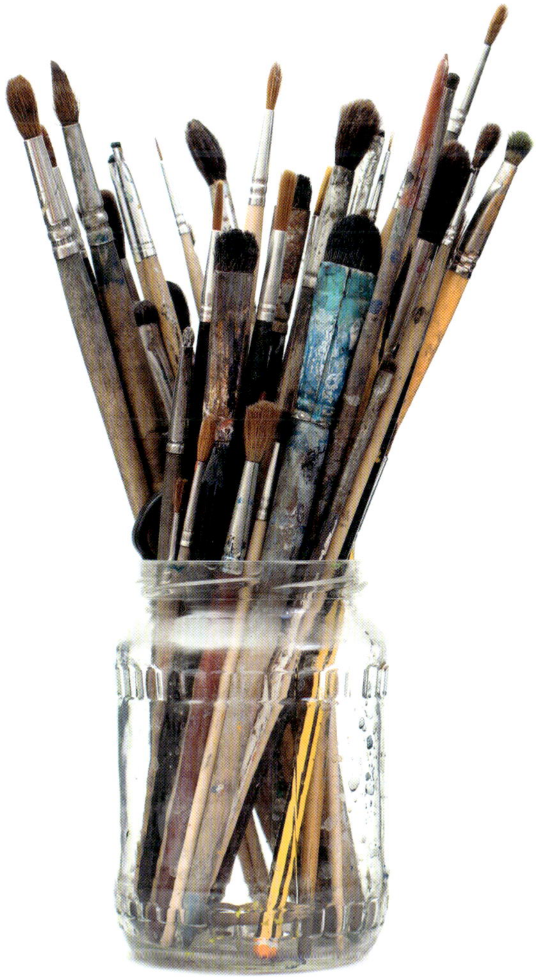

Contents

FOREWORD

The Artist's Studio: Creative Hub and Sorcerer's Kitchen

Rob Evans

Throughout the ages, the artist's studio has held a certain intrigue and fascination for those who wish a glimpse into the creative magic worked by artists. The studio is the sorcerer's kitchen, where creative energy and ideas are magically transformed into works of art, a *wunderkammer* of painting materials, sketchbooks, fascinating and unusual props or costumes, still life objects, and artworks in various states of progress. It can be a social gathering space for the artist's circle of friends, patrons, and colleagues, where thoughts and creative ideas are exchanged; or it can serve as an atelier where apprentices or students are trained. It is also the place where collectors or patrons often are allowed exclusive access, perhaps having the opportunity to be the first to see a new masterpiece or trendsetting body of work, or strike a backroom deal with the artist on the purchase of a work of art. Yet it can also serve as the artist's most private inner sanctum—a place of retreat from the pressures or temptations of the art world or the interruptions of day-to-day life—a most secretive getaway where the artist can escape into the Zen of creating.

This dichotomy the studio often presents, between public and private space, is perhaps best exemplified by the studios of two great twentieth century American masters: Andrew Wyeth and Andy Warhol. For Wyeth the studio was a place of complete escape from the spotlight of fame and popularity—a place of deep contemplation, concentration, and extreme privacy. Wyeth once famously stated that allowing visitors into the studio to watch him work would be "like somebody watching you have sex—painting is that personal to me." His studio, now preserved after his death as part of the Brandywine Conservancy, still has the sign he placed on the door which reads "I am working so please do not disturb."

Warhol's studio, on the other hand, functioned at the complete opposite end of the spectrum. Warhol embraced his celebrity status as a Pop Culture icon, and his massive New York City studio (known as the "Factory") was entirely accessible, becoming famous as a hip hangout for artsy types, adult film performers and movie stars, rock stars and musicians, poets and writers, drug addicts, drag queens, as well as many other visitors and groupies. His working process was very public and social, and he employed a menagerie of his followers (known as the "Warhol Superstars") to help him create his paintings, star in his films, and create the openly communal and sensational atmosphere for which the Factory became legendary.

The vast majority of all other artist studios fall somewhere between these two extremes, depending on each artist's working style and methods, temperament, and desire to engage with the public. Located in every conceivable rural, suburban, or urban setting, in a vast array of attics, bedrooms, basements, garages, warehouses, adaptively reused commercial buildings and barns, or designated arts centers, each studio is a fascinating measure of that particular artist's unique artistic identity. Often surrounded by materials and tools of their trade, cabinets and shelves filled with objects of personal significance and inspiration, conceptual studies and sketches, works in progress or in development, books, catalogs, and other visual cues, artists' personal workspaces give insight into their creative process, work procedures and technique, and the conceptual nature of their artistic work.

The studio environment itself can even have a strong impact on the work an artist creates there—its furniture or window views, location, family history, or specific lighting becoming integral to the artist's imagery or emotional content. The great American realist painter Bo Bartlett recently purchased his former childhood home in Georgia, transforming it into a studio where he was able to mine a wealth of early family memories and associations to create a specific and powerful body of work based on these recollections.

Having painted in various studios over the years, it has been fascinating for me to see the influence of each space on the work I created within them. After graduating from art school in 1981, I set up my very first studio in an unfinished home on family property overlooking the Susquehanna River in Pennsylvania. The insects, animal bones, rocks, and other natural artifacts collected on daily excursions roaming the surrounding wooded hills figured prominently in subsequent paintings. A few years later, I moved into the nearby farmhouse, once owned by my maternal grandparents, and set up a studio in the upstairs bedroom. The series of interior drawings and paintings I created in that studio, inspired by the spare rooms in that mid-nineteenth century home, eventually launched my career as an artist. My current studio, located in the large, renovated bank barn on that same property, includes a conference room, gallery, and bed and breakfast loft, and accommodates not only my studio working needs but also a desire to connect with patrons, friends, and fellow artists. This access to my workspace and environment, allowing visitors to view my creative process and the objects and places that inspire my work, provides a level of engagement and insight they might not have otherwise, building lifelong friendships and support from collectors who, as a result, will likely continue to purchase works through various phases of my career.

The success of this business approach, of allowing and encouraging private studio access, inspired me a number of years ago to found and develop the Pennsylvania Arts Experience, an artist trail in the scenic river valleys of southeastern Pennsylvania. Its mission is specifically to market and promote the wealth of talented artists and artisans working in this region by providing exclusive access to their studios through coordinated visits and tours. This concept has been successfully implemented in other regions across the country, such as the highly successful "Handmade in America" trail in the mountains of North Carolina, and has been a powerful tool in attracting cultural tourism to the regions they serve. Artist trails can have a significant economic impact on the local arts community, not only by connecting artists with patrons, but also by directing visitors to galleries, museums, and other cultural destinations.

Through its intriguing artist profiles and lush illustrations, this book serves as a unique and engaging "artist trail" in print, providing the reader exclusive visual access to a geographically diverse and rich array of fascinating and alluring studio spaces. It is hoped that this book will also inspire and entice the readers to go out and visit artist studios in person, either individually or through an artist trail or open studio event, allowing them to witness firsthand the creative process and gain insight into the artists' work—and, who knows, perhaps the experience might even lead to a long-term patronage or friendship with an artist.

Rob Evans is an artist, independent curator and founder of the Pennsylvania Arts Experience artist trail. His work has been exhibited widely throughout the United States and abroad and can be found in numerous public collections including the Metropolitan Museum of Art, the National Gallery of Art, and the Corcoran Museum of Art. His work has been featured inside and on the covers of many magazines, newspapers, books, and on public radio and television. Evans recently curated the exhibit "Visions of the Susquehanna: 250 Years of Paintings by American Masters," which traveled to six museums in the mid-Atlantic region. More about the artist can be found online at www.robevansart.net.

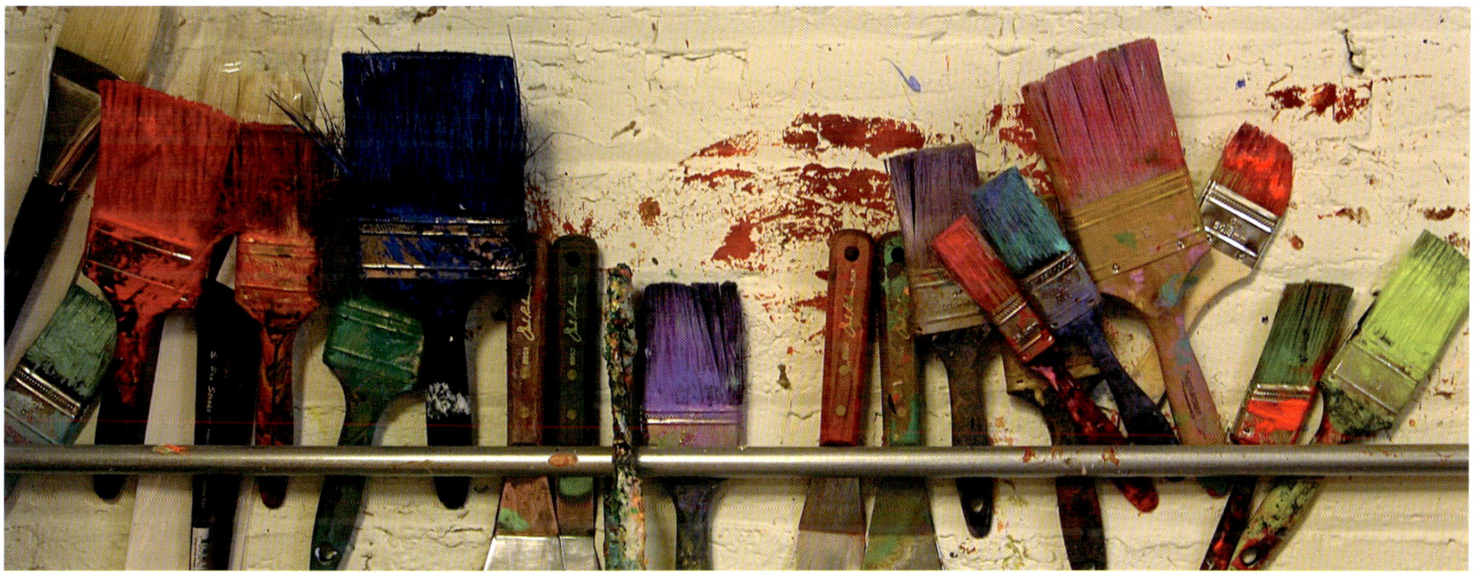

Terrence Coffman hates cleaning brushes so he uses cheap house painting brushes that he throws away. Sometimes while working he places them between the old brick walls and exposed conduit lines. He like the contrast of texture of roughly used bristles and 125 year-old brick.

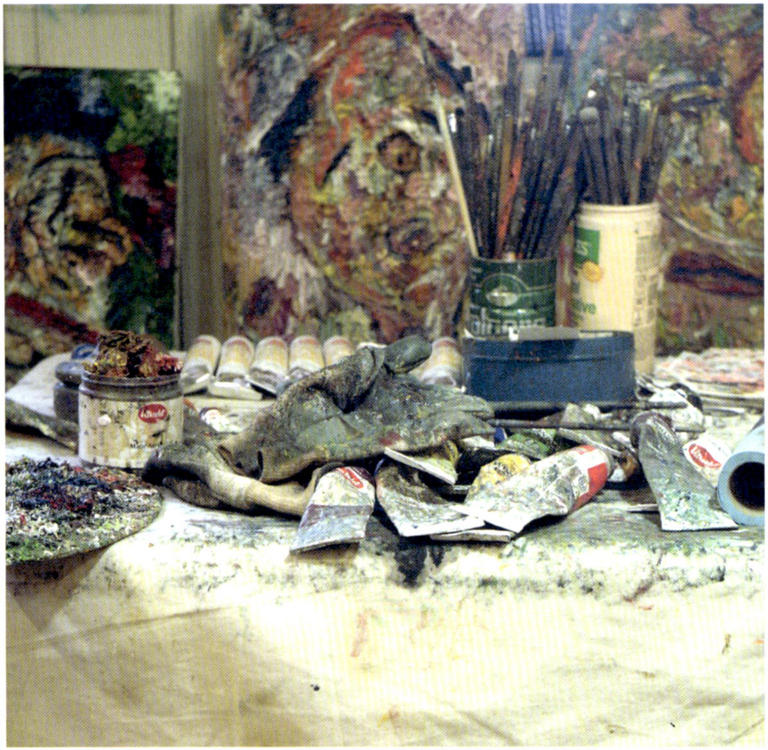

Acknowledgments

The creative act never ceases to amaze me; each new book is a novel experience, an adventure, and a challenge. There is a reason why I selected these artists for this book. Their work is exciting; they look to the future; and I learn from them.

Many other artists have exciting studios. I couldn't fit them all in the book, but I do suggest you look for them.

Rob Evans, an artist, independent curator, and founder of Pennsylvania Arts Experience, drew on his own experience in writing the Foreword. I chuckled out loud on reading it. Barbara Purchia proofread the manuscript, and my friend Renee Sage reviewed my Introduction.

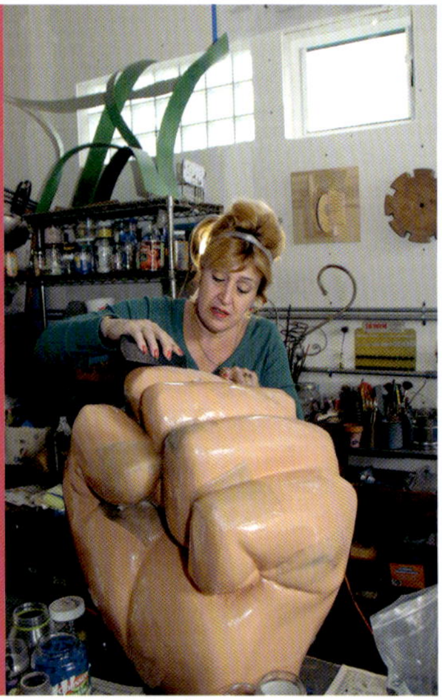

Notice the differences between these two artists. In the first image, Tom Block's studio table groans under the tools of the trade, while his frosting-thick oil paintings slowly dry. Courtesy of Julie Wolsztynski. *In the second, Nicole Beck's studio, which sees plenty of welding, grinding, woodworking, cementing, mosaic, and what have you, is amazingly tidy, although she is punching out some fiberglass details on **Fistacuffs**.*
Photo: www.ericcraigstudios.com

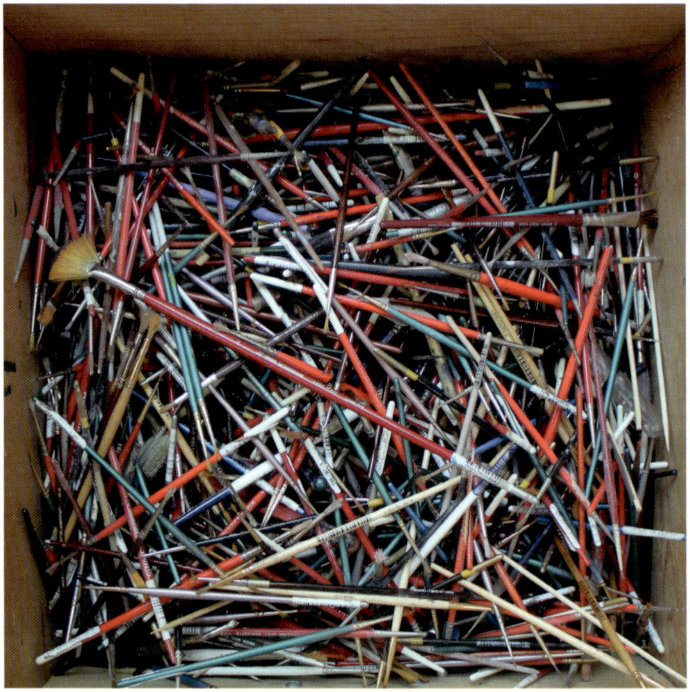

When Scott Fraser's brushes start breaking down, he discards them in this drawer.

Behind the Scenes of Making Art

The famous Dutch artist Rembrandt van Rijn initially shared a studio in Leiden with his colleague Jan Lievens. Around 1626, Rembrandt painted a charming small piece of Lievens in his studio. The studio was quite barren; the work, which cannot be seen by the viewer, looms large.

Rembrandt was far from the only artist who painted his studio. In 1855, Gustav Courbet exhibited his monumental oil on canvas, *The Artist's Studio, a real allegory summing up seven years of my artistic and moral life.* Figures in the painting represent various influences on Courbet's artistic life. Immediately recognizable in the center, Courbet is studying a landscape that he is working on.

Who doesn't enjoy peeking into another artist's creative space, to see where and how they paint? For many artists, it is a very personal space. Claude Monet, who lived in his home at Giverny for forty-three years, added a wooden floor to the barn and turned it into his studio. Above the studio, Monet had his own apartment, with a large bedroom, and a bathroom. He is known for his open-air painting, but he still needed a place to store and finish his canvases.

Situated on the outskirts of Aix-en-Provence, France, is Paul Cézanne's final studio on Les Lauves hill, built to his specifications in 1902. It is spacious and light. Like today's artists, he surrounded himself with familiar objects: a table, a short ladder, a high easel, a potbellied stove, a sofa, a few chairs, bottles, vases, and other bits and pieces.

The Musée Rodin was originally a French mansion that was sold to the Society of the Sacred Heart of Jesus to be used as a girls' school. Ultimately, the school was closed and the mansion, known as the Hotel Biron, was rented out to artists, such as Jean Cocteau, Isadora Duncan, Henri Matisse, and August Rodin, who rented four south-facing rooms on the main floor. When the property was sold to the French government in 1911, Rodin proposed that he would leave all of his works to the French State in exchange for residing in the mansion the rest of his life. It was a deal, and after he died, the mansion became the Musée Rodin, opening in 1919.

In the United States, Georgia O'Keeffe moved from New York City to Abiquiu, New Mexico, and lived and worked in a home dating from the Spanish Colonial era. The 5,000-square-foot compound was in ruins when she purchased it in 1945, and, for the next four years, O'Keeffe supervised its restoration. The home's sparse furnishings represent the big names in mid-century design. Works by Herman Miller, Charles Eames, and Eero Saarinen are mixed in with O'Keeffe's collection of rocks and skulls.

When Jackson Pollack and Lee Krasner moved to East Hampton, New York, they converted a small barn on the property to his studio. There, he laid his canvas on the floor and walked around it, applying paint from all four sides. After his death in 1956, Krasner began to use the studio. She liked to tack her canvases on the walls.

Having worked with so many artists for my books on regional artists, I thought it would be of interest to see where they work. Perhaps we could understand better how this geographically and artistically diverse group of artists transform an idea or feeling into a work of art.

Leonardo da Vinci once said, "An artist's studio should be a small space because small rooms discipline the mind and large ones distract it." A thought to ponder, but is it necessarily true? Some studios are large, with lovely high ceilings and oversized skylights. Others are modest, even cramped. Some are amazingly pristine and carefully ordered with drawing, painting gallery and meditation zones and some are a study of chaos, but in all of them the artists appear to create.

Today's studios range from chicken coops to entire islands, from extra bedrooms to horse barns. We see that artists feel strongly about how they organize their studios, where they store their canvases and other works of art, how they keep their brushes and tools, and hang their art. One of the primary differences seems to be whether the artist likes the hubbub of other people and artists about. Some talk about the need for company, while others enjoy the freedom of padding down the hall in their slippers late at night to work on a piece. They want the peace and quiet and the quiet retreat. Florida artist, Tere Pastoriza, comments that her studio is a "Blissful refuge from chaos, and sometimes it is chaos itself. It is where I draw, paint, read, and listen to music and to myself." Others like to be part of a community.

Many artists talk about their music systems and gardens. Dogs appear to be faithful companions. Many collect natural objects to inspire them. Big or small, tidy or messy, the artist studio is obviously a sanctuary—"a place for creative incubation," as Joseph Campbell would say.

1

Studios Plus

Studios Plus are those studios that contain galleries, living space, or something else. Some are downtown, while others may reside in a lovely pastoral scene or even on islands! Some have fireplaces; others have gardens; and a few even offer sculpture parks.

Kathleen Kinkopf at work.

Karen Hibbs loves the light in her studio.

Keith Berr hosts events for the ASMP and Cleveland arts group in his gallery.

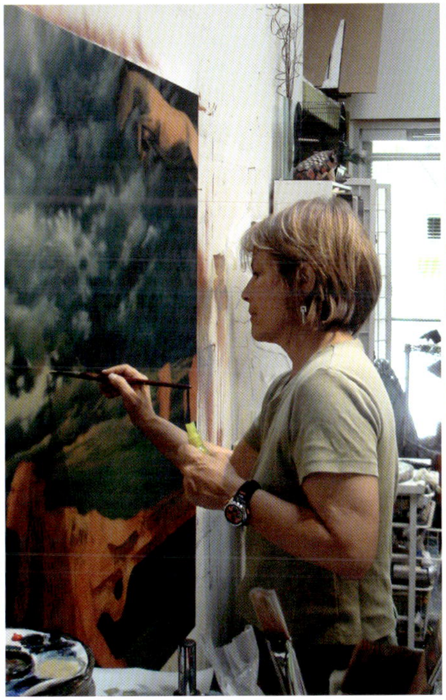

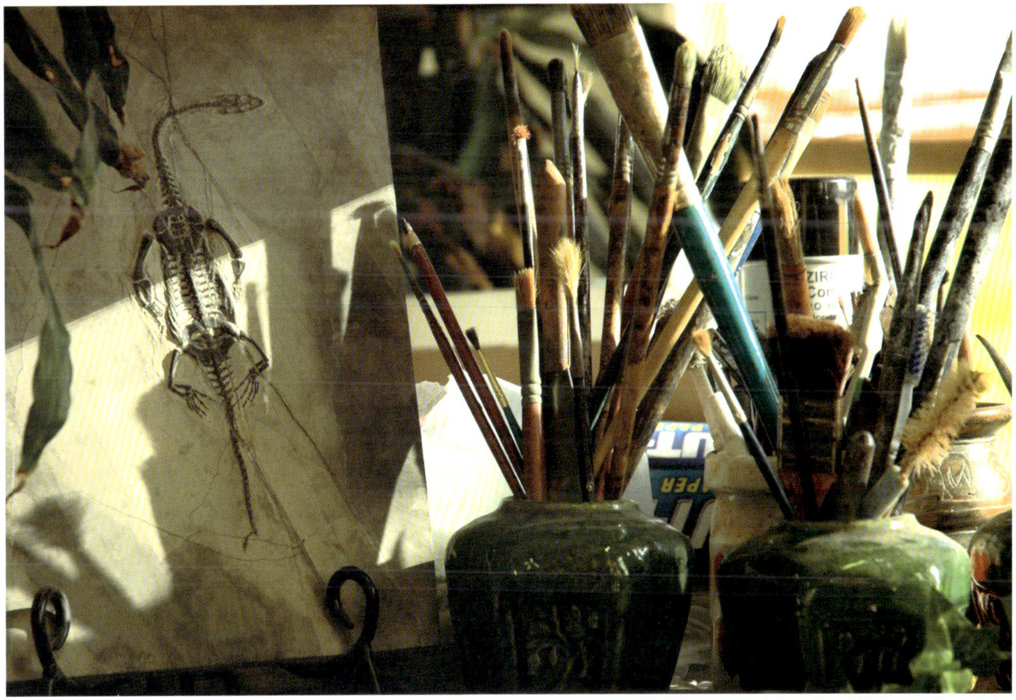

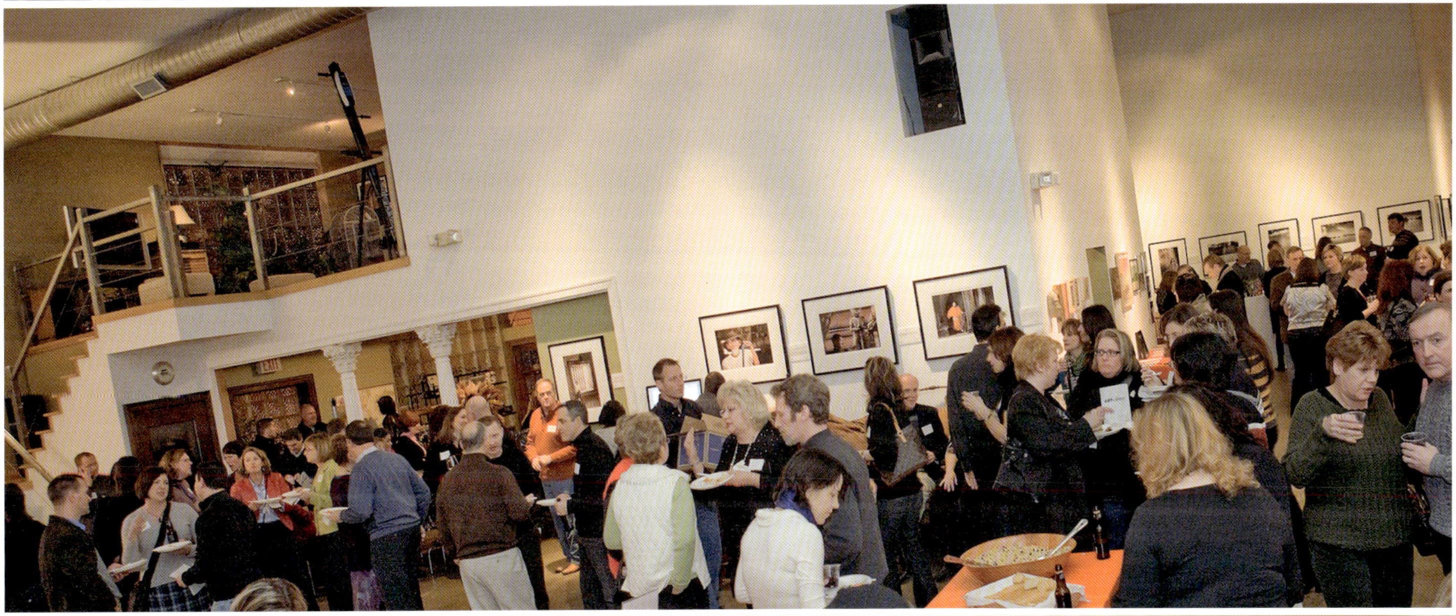

Keith Berr

Cleveland, Ohio

I am a commercial and fine art photographer living and working in a 6,500 square-foot, custom-built facility that was specifically designed for photographic and gallery use. My partner and producer, Linda Barberic, and I travel worldwide, on commercial and personal projects, for clients ranging from resort shoots in the Fiji Islands to people in steel mills, chefs and their food, CEOs from Fortune 500 companies, brain surgeons and their surgeries, rodeo stars, race drivers and their cars on the Bonneville Salt Flats, and to the culture and people of Bhutan. My scope of work is large, and I enjoy having a camera in my hand every day to create images that are a memorable part of life.

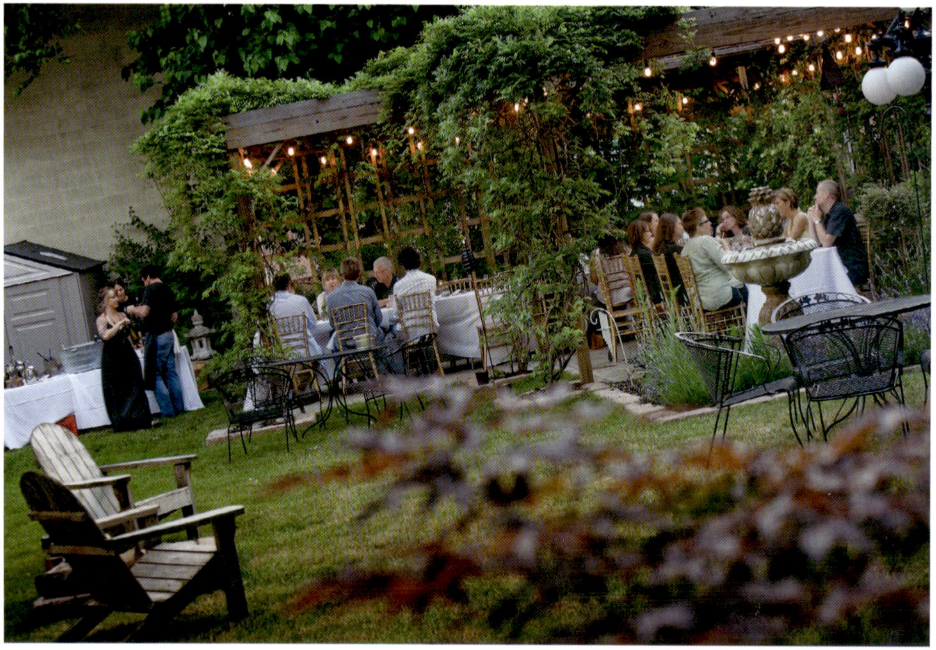

We often host gallery and fund-raising events, including dinner parties, in our inner-city garden space.

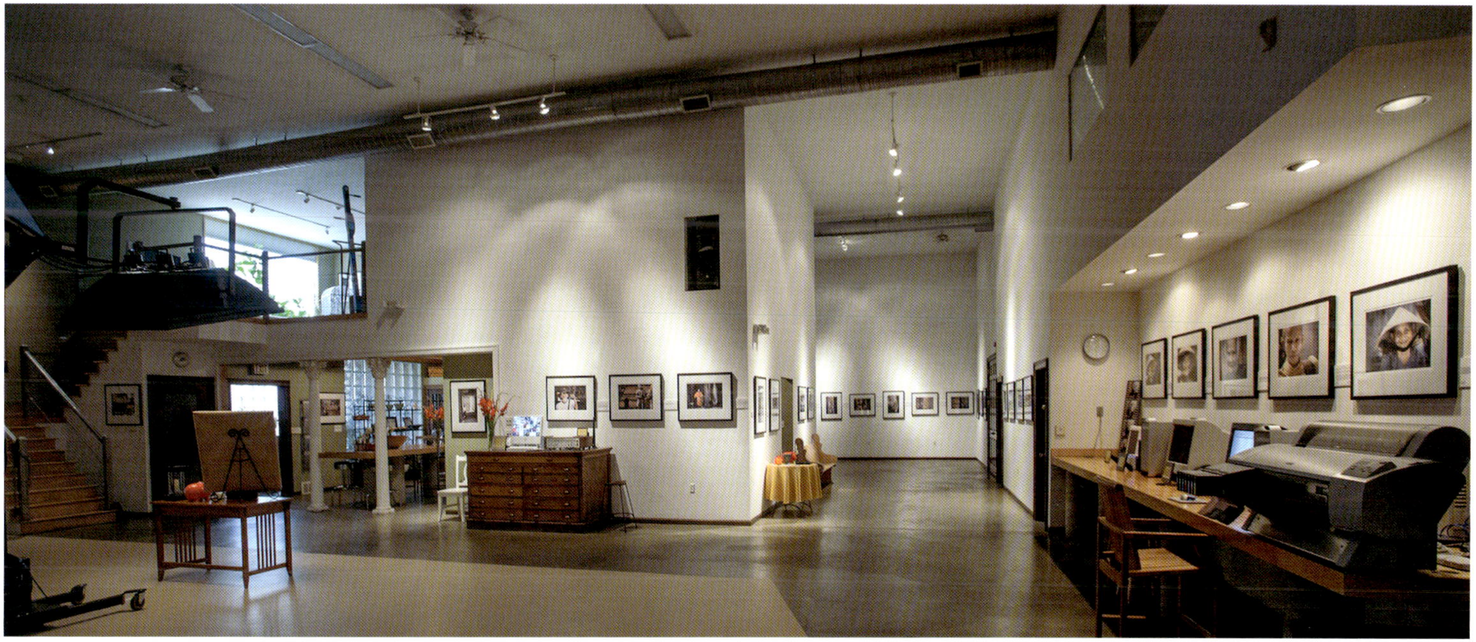

I've been honored with numerous awards for my work and recently named one of the country's top twenty photographers with the American Society of Media Photographers (ASMP) and also inducted into the American Advertising Federation Hall of Fame.

We back the artists in our city and host events for the ASMP and Cleveland arts groups. It's important for those of us who live in the city to support and build the art culture around us.

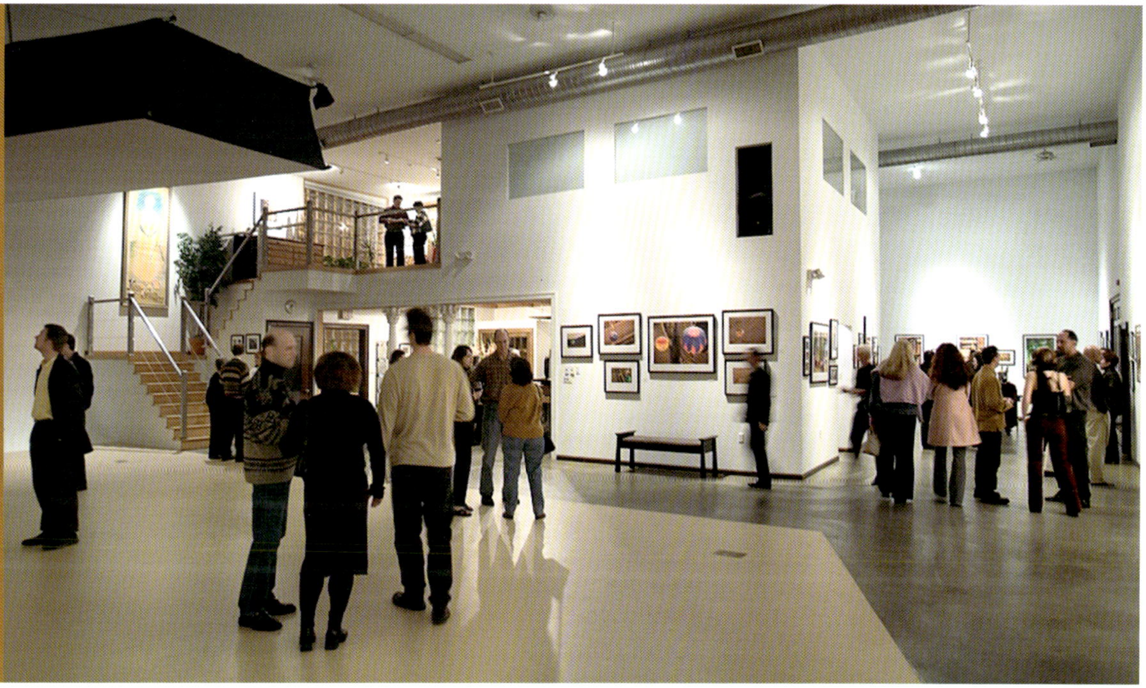

Terrence James Coffman

Jefferson, Wisconsin

I bought and renovated my home and studio nine years ago. It's a warehouse that, for over 130 years, served as a blacksmith shop and brewery bottle house. The brick walls and concrete floors are perfect for me. My studio needs to be more like a factory where floors and walls can be splattered with paint. A pristine environment can intimidate creativity. I want a place where paint can fly!

My paint surfaces are applied with large silkscreen squeegees and house painter's brushes. The colors are forced together without conscious thought or control. For me control is arrogant. I approach painting as opening myself to visions that are caught rather than conceived. I don't stand before a subject and copy it. I breath it in, consume it, and let it flow out of me onto canvas.

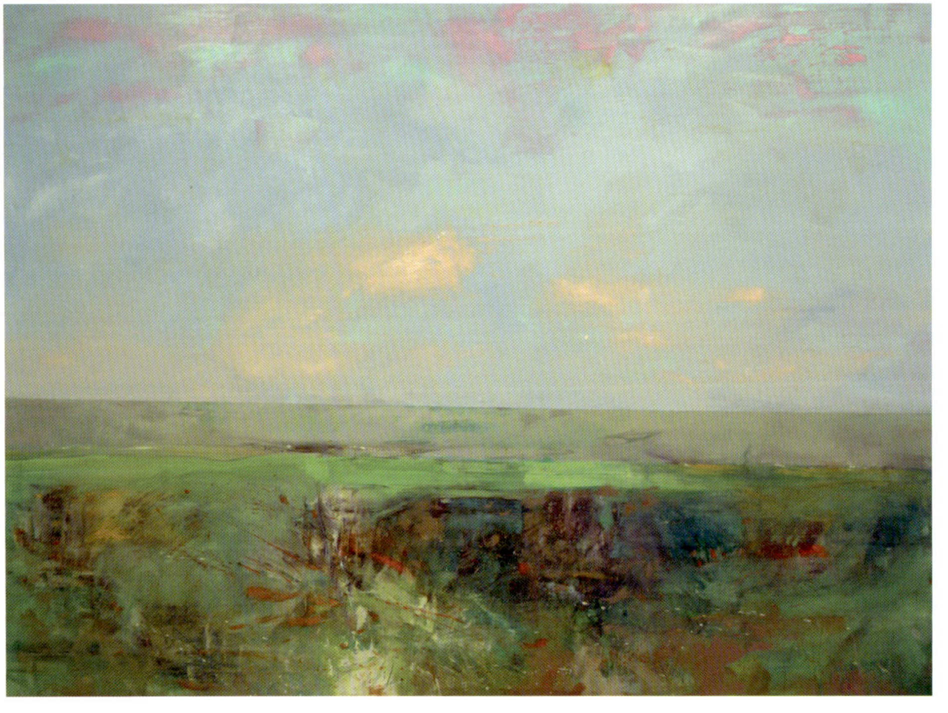

Flaggy Shore #2. *Oil on linen. 72 x 96". 2012.*

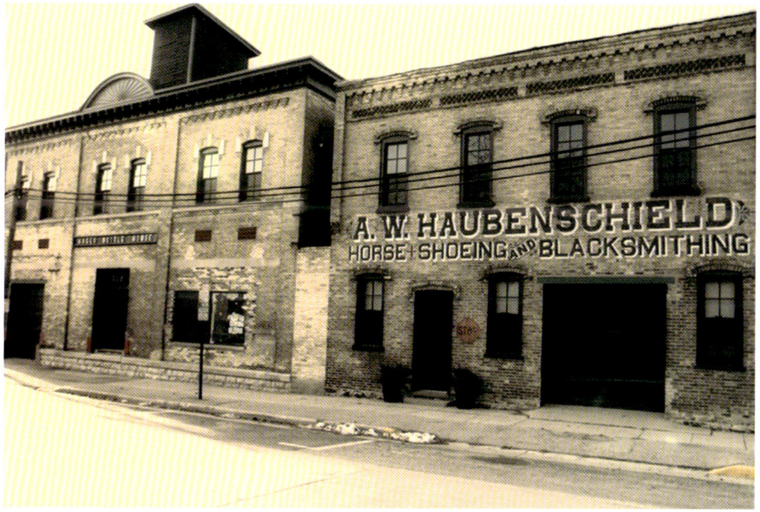

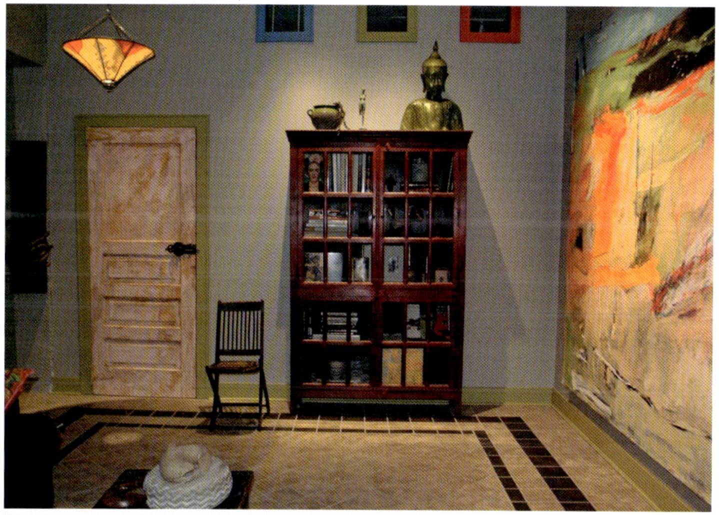

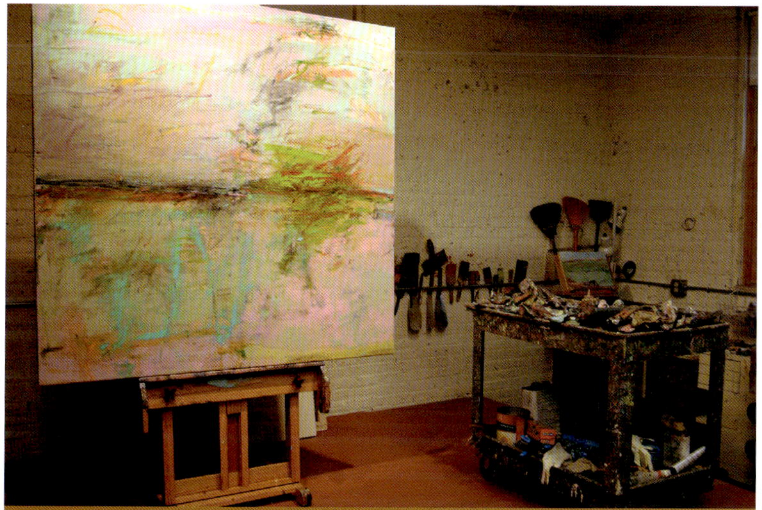

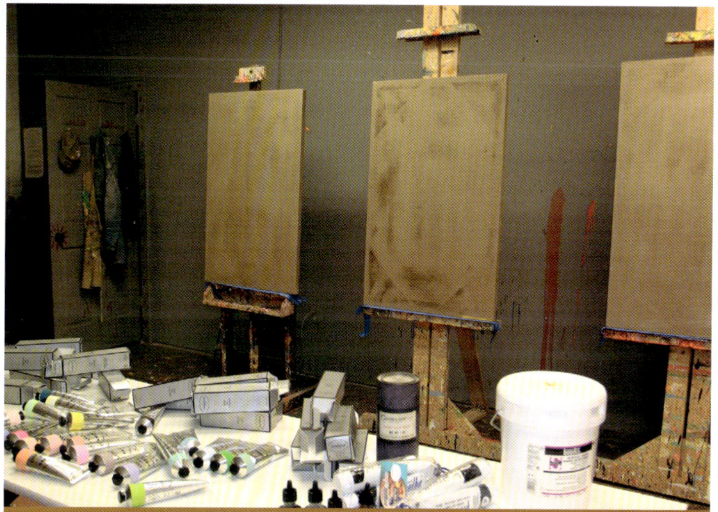

My Center Avenue studio and home are two old buildings joined together in the late 1940s. The ground floor of the blacksmith shop is where I paint; above are the studios of four other artists. The brewery bottle house is where I reside.

My working studio is 400 square feet with 14-foot high ceilings, which allows me to do large paintings. I work on three or four paintings at a time. I use a large rolling palette, one traditional easel, and three wall-mounted easels.

The lobby of my building separates the studio wing from the loft living space. I painted the door much in the same way that I paint my large canvases.

Because my working studio is 25 feet long, I am able to work on several paintings at the same time. Here I'm working on three panels for a client in Chicago.

Clark Ellefson

Columbia, South Carolina

The current Lewis+Clark studio is in an old brick warehouse in Columbia, South Carolina, across from an old train station in an historic district built in the early 1900s. There is an old garage door in front from when it was a liquor warehouse in the 1930s. I purchased this building in 1989 and used half for my woodworking shop and half for office space and a gallery. I am now making lamps, tin robots, and robot heads. I live in the back in a space I call "The Bunkhouse." Simple, rough, alive.

I studied fine arts in college; sculpture and ceramics were my favorites. After school and a stint working for the South Carolina State Arts Commission, I supported my sculpture endeavors with carpentry and woodworking. This led to furniture making, which I pursued for twenty years. I became interested in lighting, and I am now making lamps and furniture and working with tin.

I am now almost finished with a studio space in a metal building about five blocks away, which I share with the glass blowers of One Eared Cow Glass. We have more space and opportunity there, but I will miss my old brick building in this turn-of-the-century neighborhood.

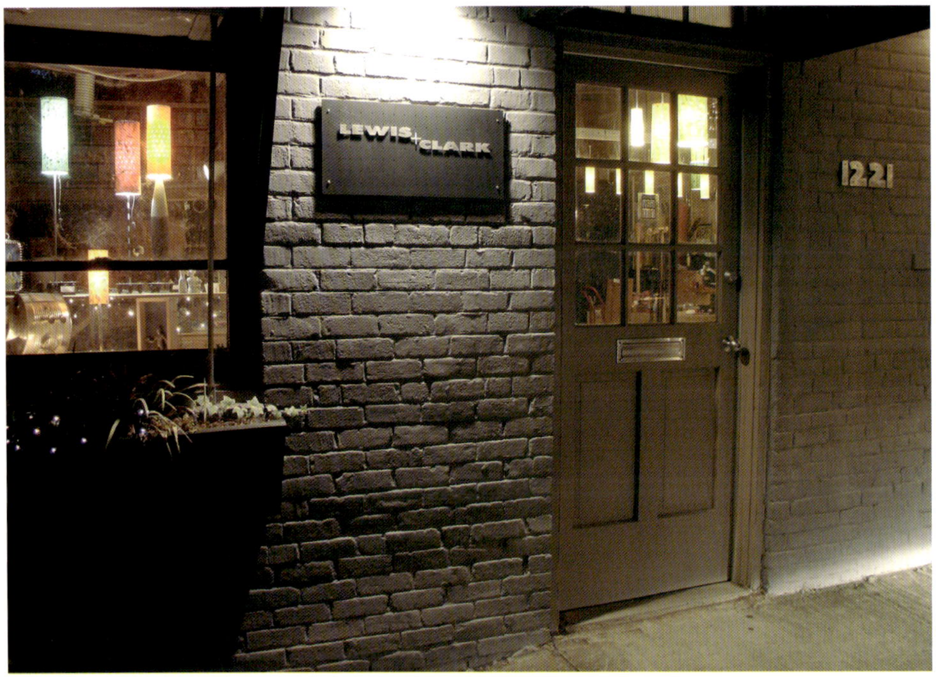

My studio at night welcomes viewers to the bright clutter within.

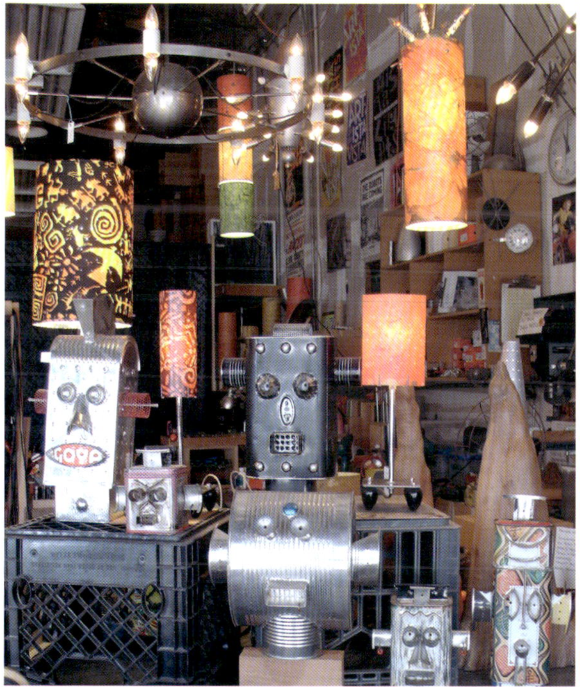

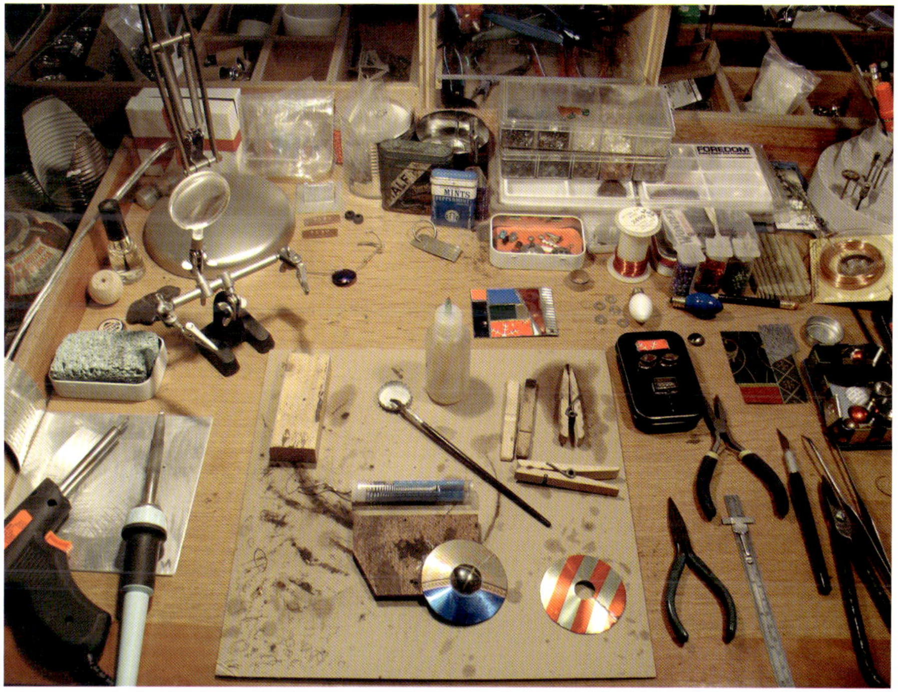

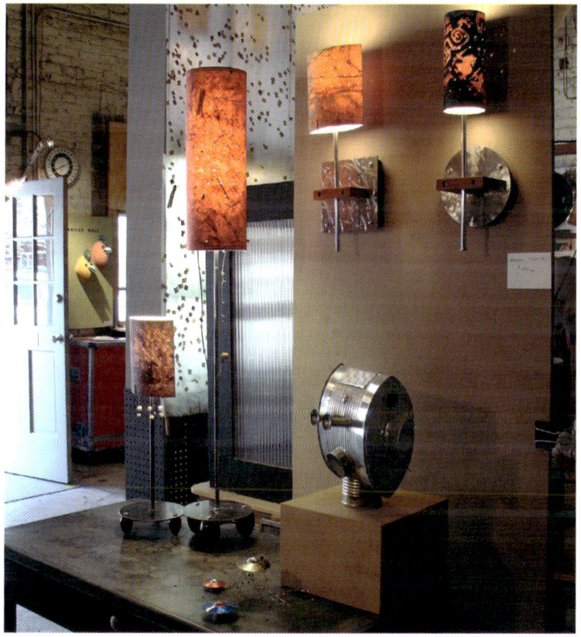

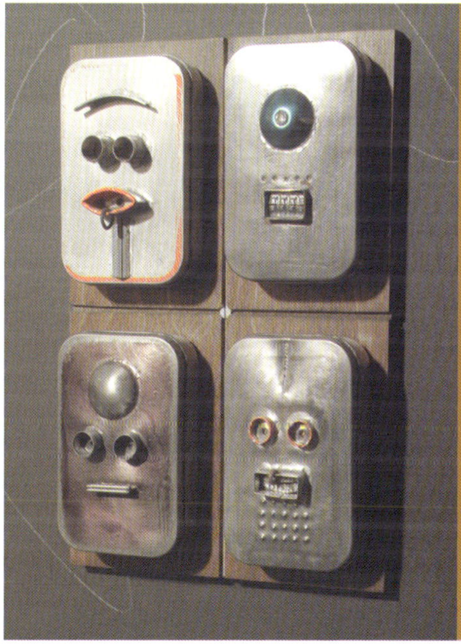

My new studio space has a more modern uncluttered feel—for now!

Lamps, sconces, and a tin robot head create a neo-rustic collection.

Tin working bench, a small space with ideas in every scrap.

Altoid tin robot heads, the usual suspects.

Rob Evans

Wrightsville, Pennsylvania

In 1994 my wife, Renee, and I purchased a nineteenth century farm perched on a hillside overlooking the Susquehanna River in southeastern Pennsylvania. Once owned by my grandparents, this farm has a magnificent bank barn with a stone foundation and an upper structure that had been significantly refurbished in the mid-1940s.

Seeing great potential in this building, we immediately set about making our own renovations, putting in a large studio for me, a studio/classroom for Renee, a spacious conference room and gallery (available for exhibitions, meetings, and events), and a loft bedroom with a spectacular skylight view of the river (offered as a bed and breakfast rental). My studio has a large workspace with a balance of spotlights and natural north light coming from skylights. In addition to the usual shelves and drawers filled with art supplies, the studio also includes a large library of art books and numerous "cabinets of curiosity" filled with collections of natural artifacts such as bones, seashells, insects, and fossils, which inspire my work.

The studio has served me well not only as workspace but as a venue for exhibiting and selling my work. In addition to annual open studios held there, my studio is available to visit by appointment and is a stop on the Pennsylvania Arts Experience, an artist trail I helped found several years ago.

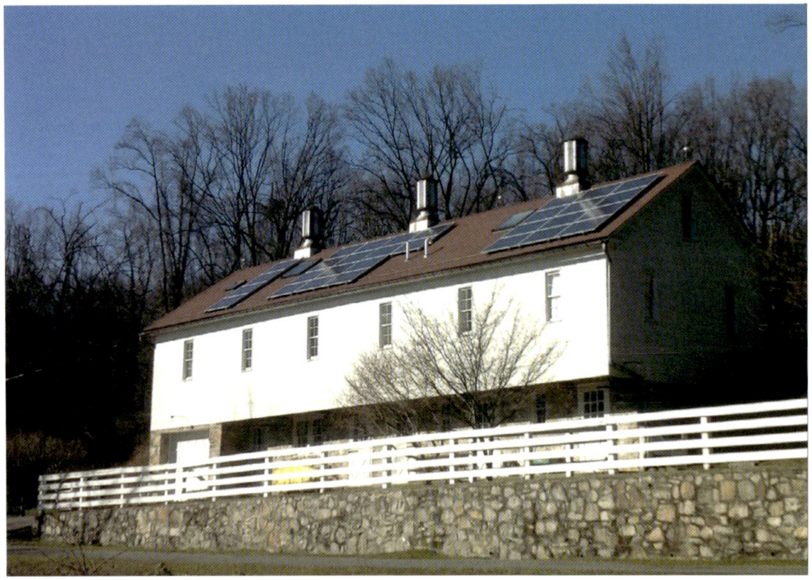

The exterior of the barn/studio. We are strong supporters of going "green" and recently installed thirty solar PV panels on the roof.

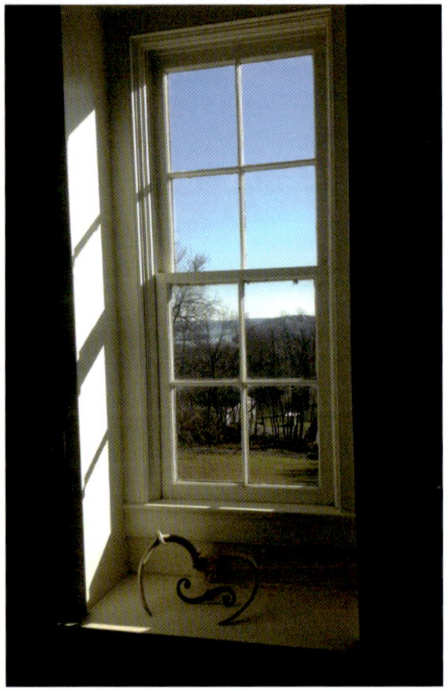

The Susquehanna River can be seen from the studio library window.

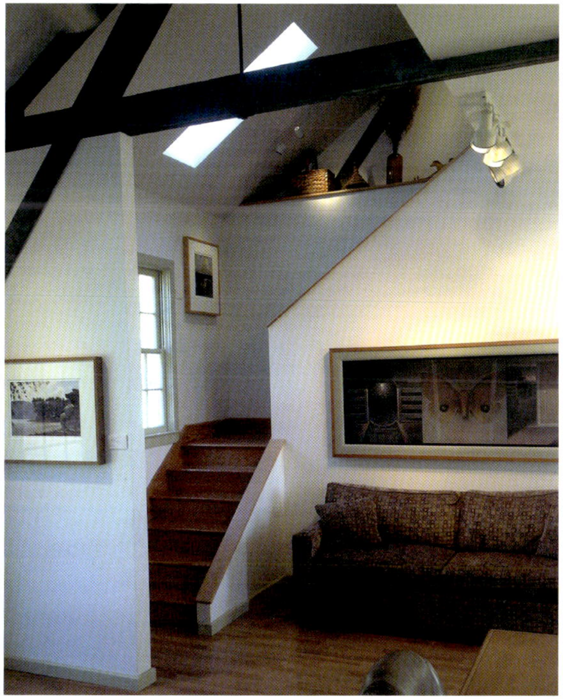

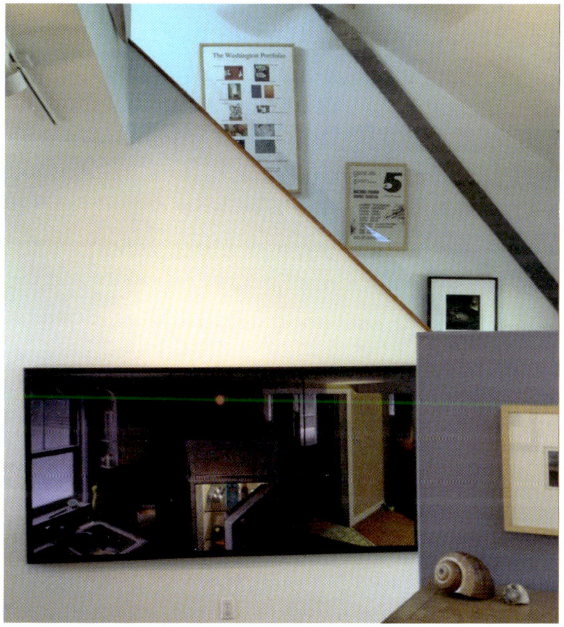

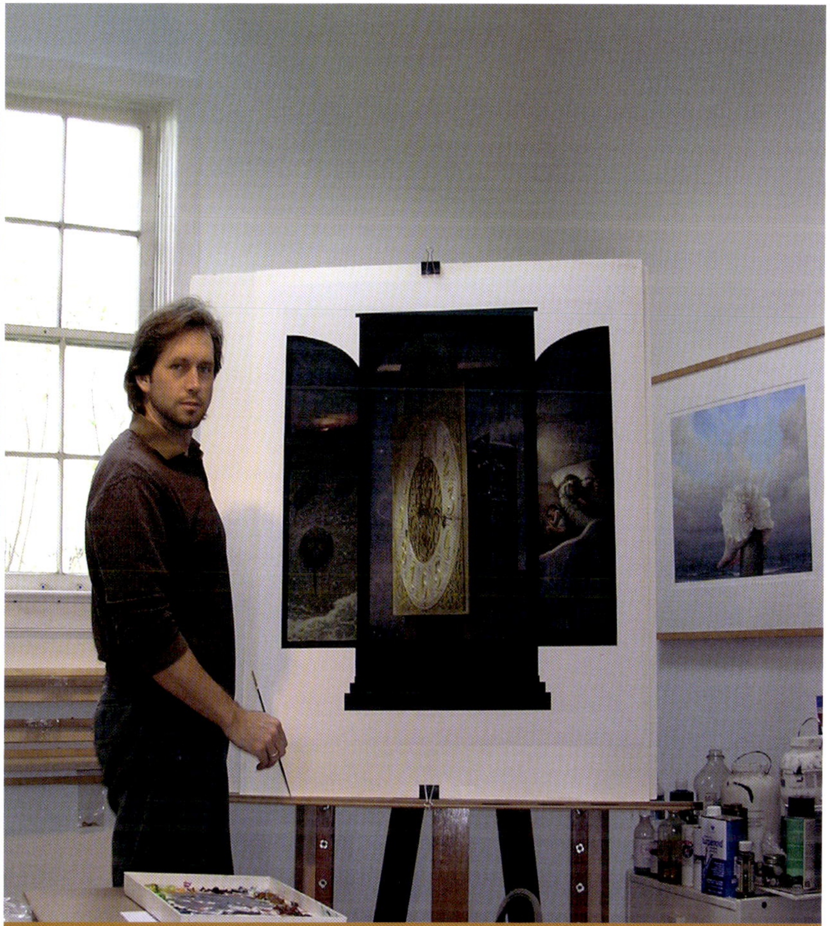

The stairs lead from the studio gallery/conference room to the loft B&B bedroom. On the wall from left to right: **Otter Creek** (pigment print, 2008), **Arch** (pigment print, 2005), and **Moth** (acrylic on panel, 1993).

My studio space has a cabinet of seashells in the foreground and the stairs leading to my office loft. Posters on the stair wall are from my exhibits in Moscow and Washington, D.C. The painting on the wall is **Evening Ritual** (oil on panel, 1989).

At work in the studio. **Study for Movement** (mixed media, 2010) is on the easel; **Storm Surge** (pigment print, 2005) in the background on the wall.

Hanrahan Meyers Architects (hMa)

New York, New York

hMa is a progressive, design-oriented firm focused on the creation of exceptional buildings and cities. For 25 years, hMa's commitment to quality building goes back to the firm's roots, designing unique, award-winning projects based on the principles of nature, innovative materials and details, and cutting edge technologies.

The firm designed Bridge-Studio, a new artist studio building in Easton, Pennsylvania, which contains a painting studio on the east side and a writing studio on the west. The new studio is entered by walking up a bridge, into the open breezeway, overlooking the Delaware River, approximately 100 feet below the edge of the site.

In addition to producing their own bodies of work, Joe Amrhein and Susan Swenson own Pierogi Gallery in Williamsburg, New York, and regularly entertain artists from their New York gallery at their home in Pennsylvania. The couple's desire for an appropriate setting to entertain artist friends created part of the program for the new studio building.

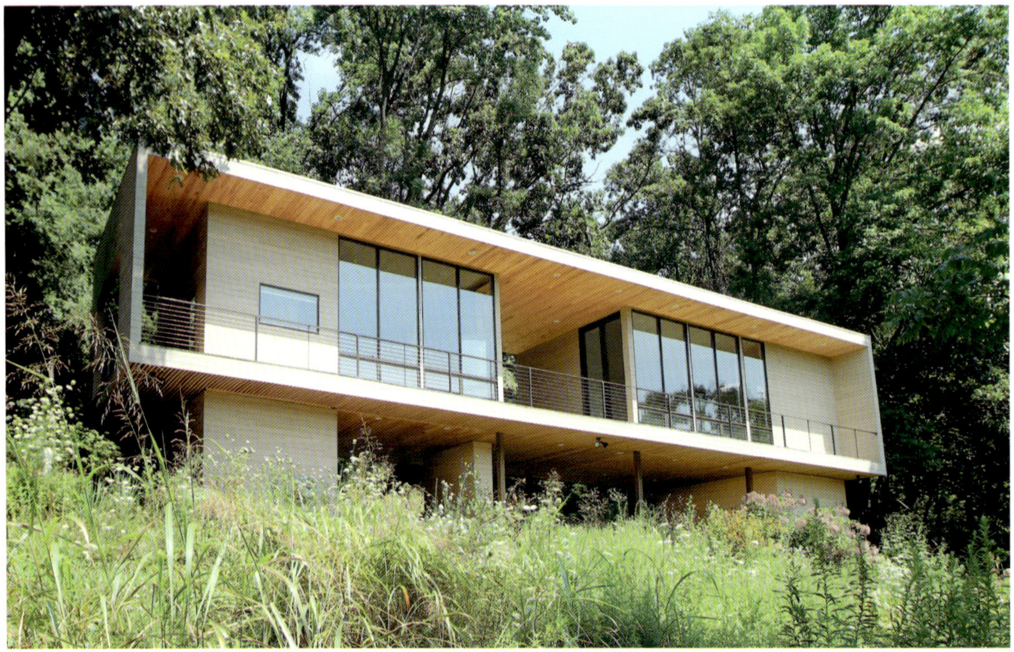

Southwest view of Bridge Studio. Bridge Studio features a breezeway in the center, between the two studios, with an outdoor fireplace. The outdoor fireplace hearth houses a flue for a second fireplace in the writing studio and for a third fireplace in the open outdoor area below the Bridge.

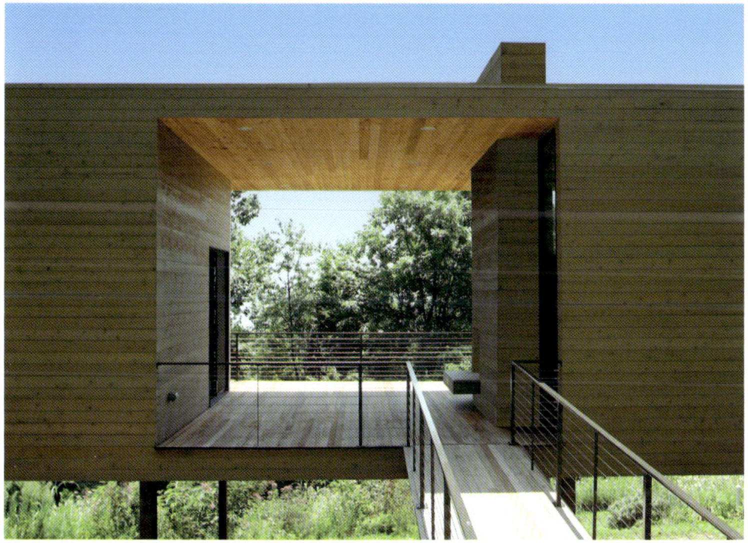

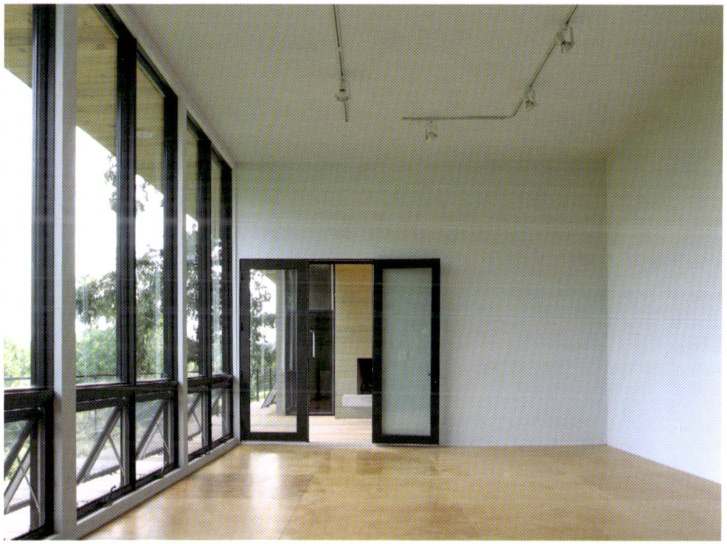

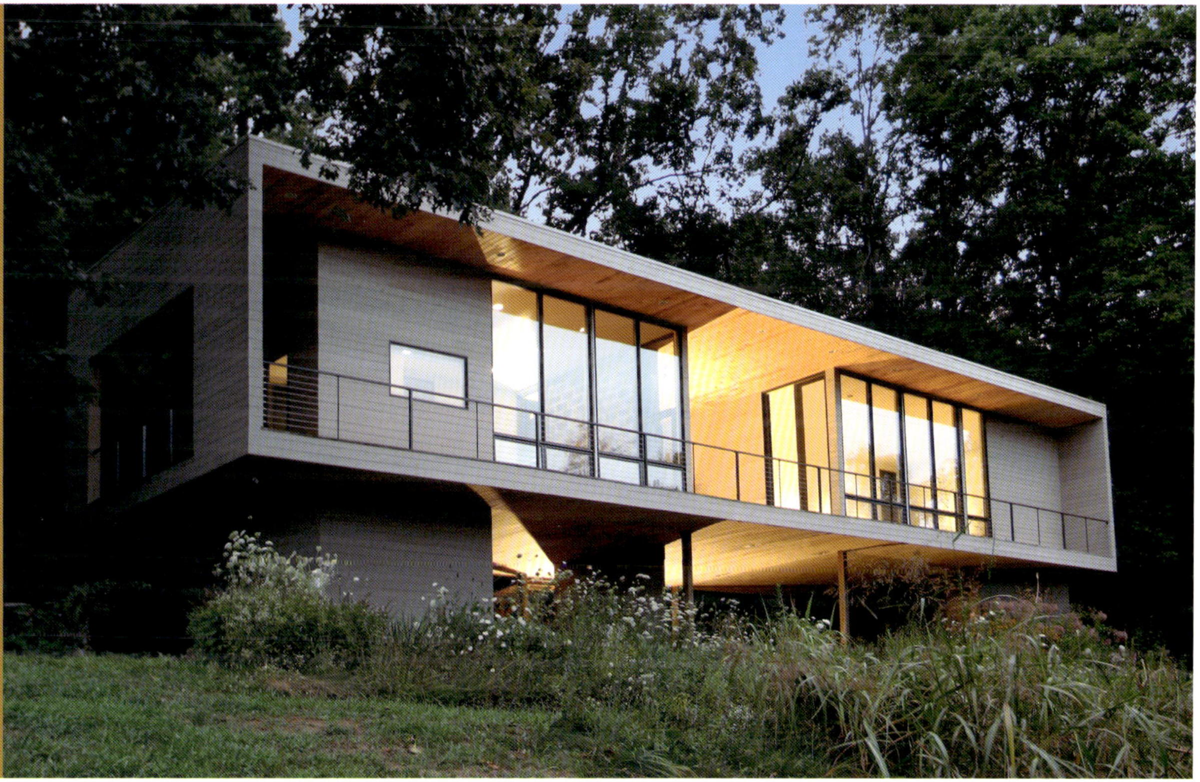

Looking up entry ramp through breezeway toward the Delaware River.

Interior of painting studio.

Southwest view at night.

Kathleen Kinkopf

Albuquerque, New Mexico

I've had a variety of studios during my career, ranging from spare bedrooms to garages, but my current studio is a dream, built specifically for creating art. Some features include 18-foot ceilings, three oversized skylights, privacy, and ample storage. It's wonderful to paint all day with natural, filtered light overhead.

The building itself and its extraordinary setting are what make my studio unique. It was designed and built specifically to house our custom studios, storage, and workshop, in addition to six commercial office spaces (with a grand entry and hall to display our work), as well as our contemporary living quarters on the second floor. Perched above the city of over one million residents, we have 360 degrees of unobstructed views of Albuquerque to the west, and hundreds of square miles of unspoiled open space and our beloved Sandia Peak to the east. While I spend most waking hours in my studio creating art, I love having the balance of this expansive open space literally outside my studio door. My creativity and inspiration are fueled and nurtured not only by my vast research library and the culture and activities the city offers, but also by the proximity to wildlife, desert smells and sounds, and hard-packed running trails. There is no doubt I have the best of many worlds without having to wander too far from home.

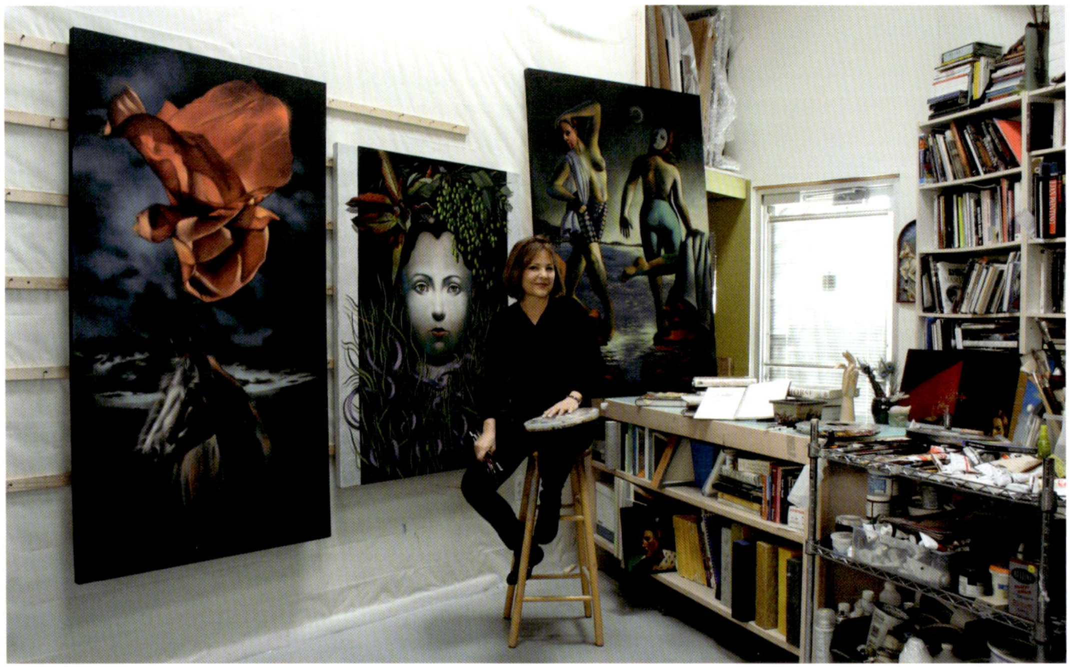

My studio is a real workhorse space. I rarely sit for too long (except for this shot) or have the opportunity to put things away neatly or completely, because of multiple projects that continually overlap.

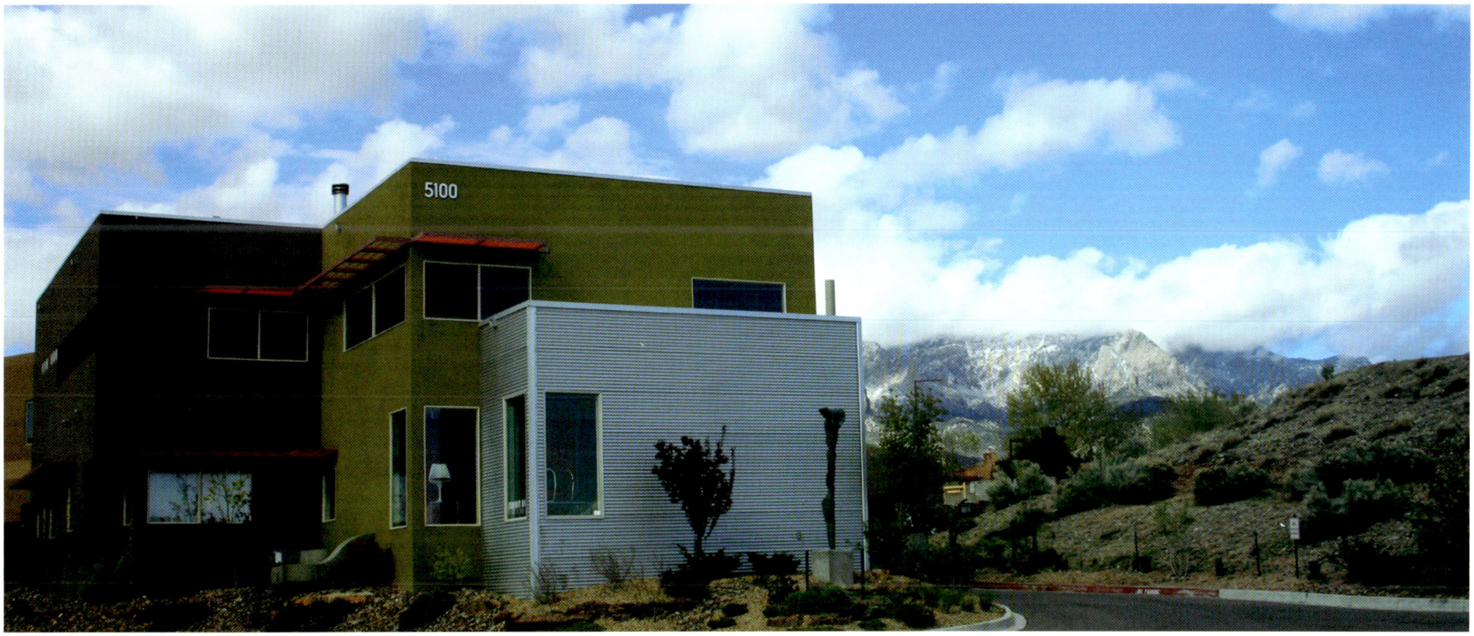

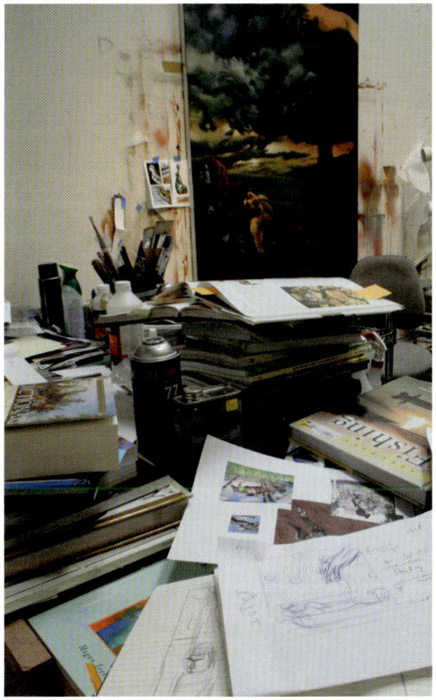

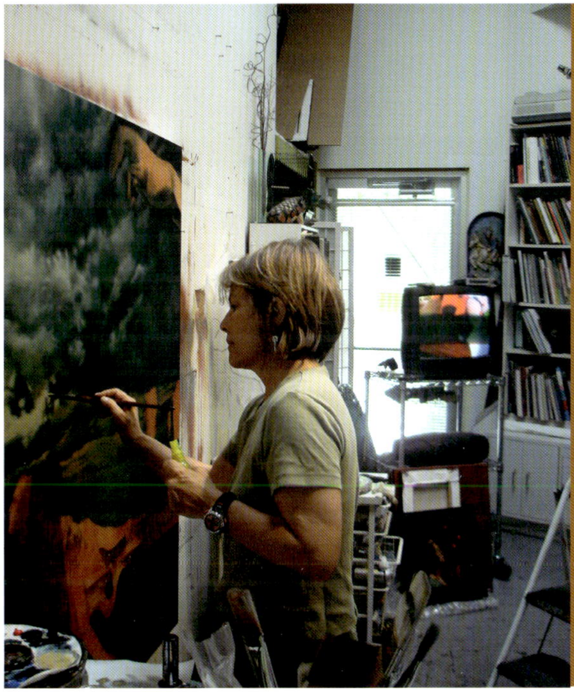

We designed and built this mixed-use concept in an urban setting, adjacent to high desert open space, near the base of Sandia Peak. The first floor is office and studio space, and our residence occupies the entire second floor.

A great painting starts with inspiration, but many of mine require extensive research. I use the Internet, but my own library still serves me well. My collection totals well over a thousand books and periodicals.

I prep my canvas surfaces in the adjacent workshop and paint them in the studio on the wall, rarely using an easel. The studio with its generous ceilings and oversized skylights can accommodate very large works.

Karla Matzke

Camano Island, Washington

Several years ago I found the perfect property to build my dream gallery, personal art studio, home, and sculpture park. I wanted to use sustainable and recycled materials and build a "green" structure that incorporated industrial design and a mid-century modern style. The first floor encompasses a 3000 square-foot art gallery with 10-foot ceilings, movable walls, and large glass garage doors that provide an abundance of light, as well as facilitate the moving of large artworks.

Upstairs, I designed my studio spaces to include a resource library, framing, storage, and a painting studio. The other half is my living quarters. The third story is dedicated for a guest artist in residence. A sky bridge links their sleeping quarters with their studio, which has a northern view of Mt. Baker.

Nestled among evergreen trees, the gallery and sculpture park currently exhibits seventy-five artists whose works are of world-class significance. My 10-acre landscaped setting exhibits much of the natural flora of the Northwest and sculptures by prominent and emerging American artists.

The park is a remarkable work of art itself. The graceful site embodies "a geometry of playfulness," as trees, walls, lawns, and flowers come together to form a brilliant frame for outdoor sculptures. New seasons and different times of day make the park an ever-changing background for art and a welcoming destination for visitors. I expect that this magical acreage will nurture my career and provide a place for other artists to expand their horizons as well.

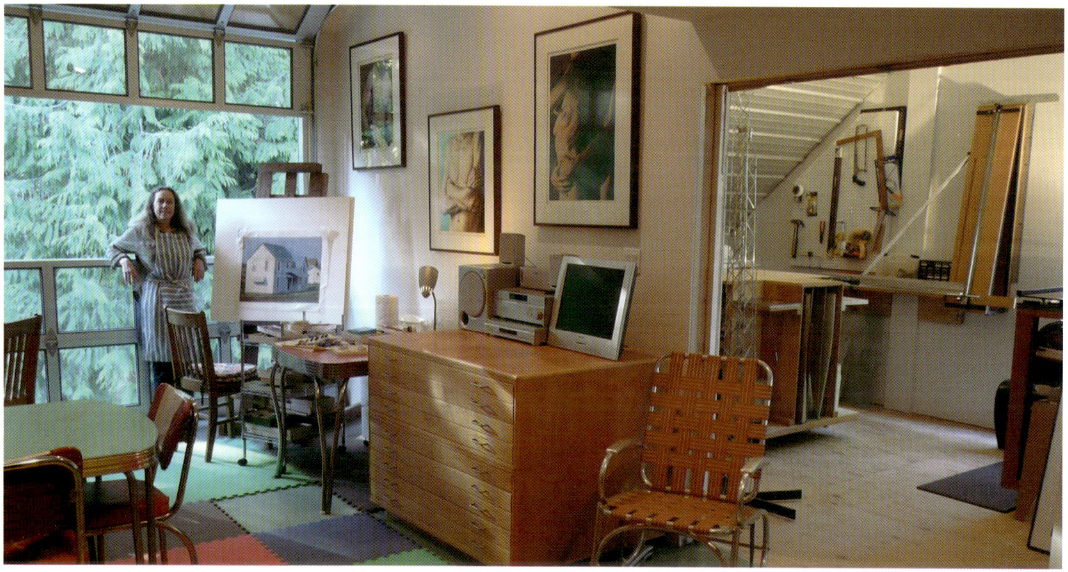

Matzke Fine Art Gallery, studio, and residence. My painting studio is on the second floor. Courtesy of Jack Gunter.

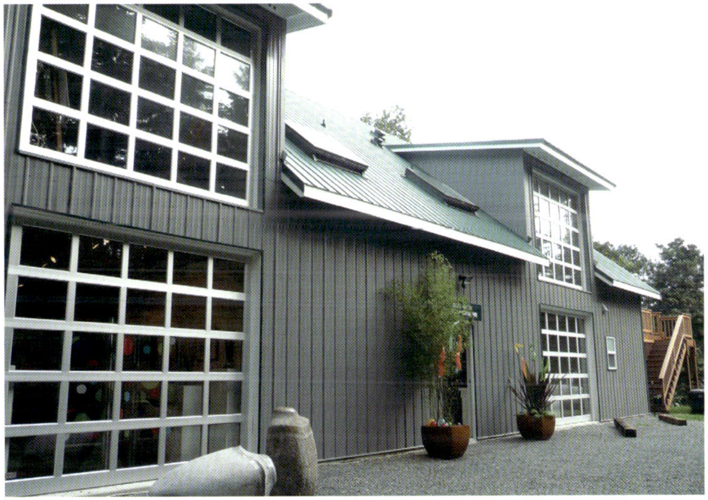

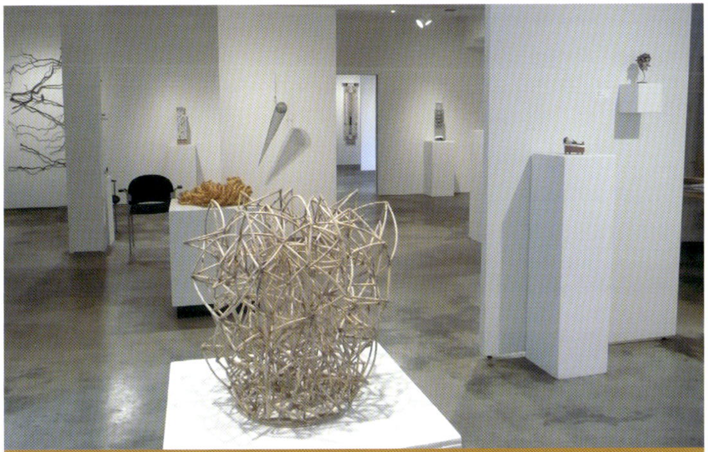

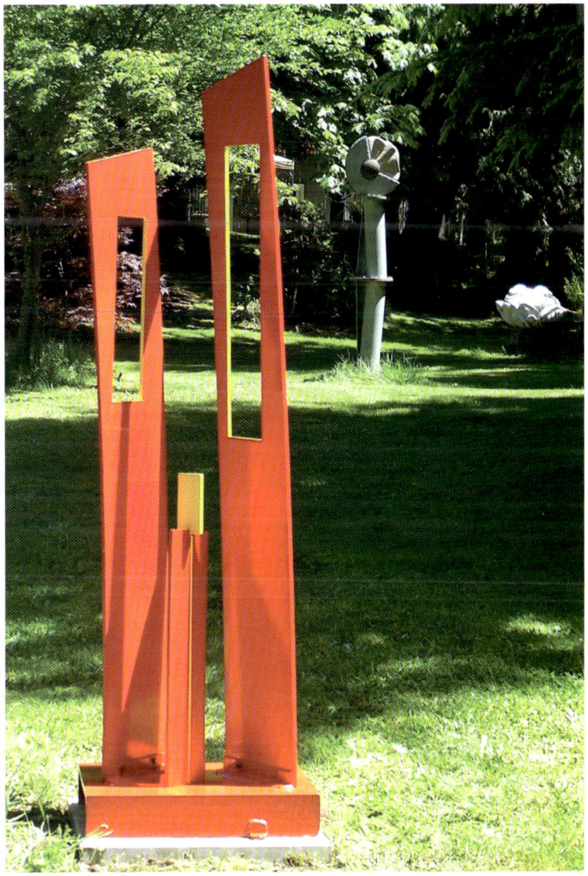

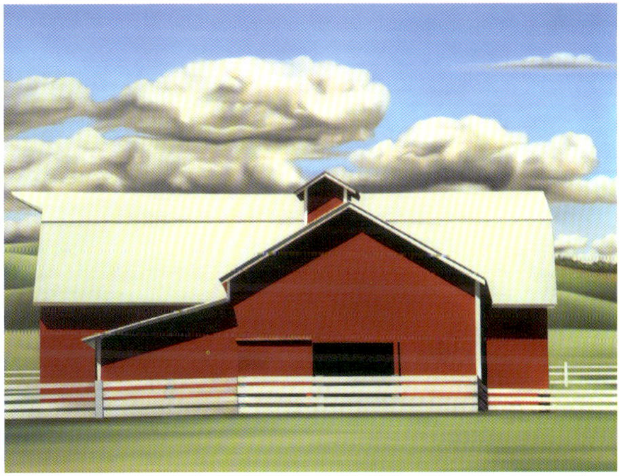

Painting and framing studios. Courtesy of Jack Gunter.

Detail of the gallery space with changing monthly exhibits.

Detail of the 10-acre sculpture park. Sculpture in the foreground, ***Tete'a Tete****, painted steel by Arno Zielke; mid ground* ***Red Sun****, granite and steel by Reg Akright; and background marble sculpture,* ***Blossom*** *by Tracy Powell. Courtesy of Arno Zielke.*

Summer Wheat*. Pastel on paper. 35 x 49".*

Ann Morris

Lummi Island, Washington

I built my studio on forested property overlooking the Rosario Straits and San Juan Islands. The location is perfect for me, as all the flora and fauna of the island, which serve as the materials for my work, surround me. At the time of constructing my studio, I was creating my life-size figurative pieces, so the studio was built large to allow for that scale of work. The doors open wide to transport the bronzes in and out, and the carport accommodates delivery trucks. The surrounding wooded grounds are home for the sixteen pieces, where nature and art enhance each other.

Since 2001, I have been making smaller works for which a former mold-making space serves as a gallery. Of late, my work has shifted from small bronzes to crafting boats of cane, twigs, seaweed, and grasses. On my daily walks, I gather materials for these boats that hang from the rafters and float in air.

The studio is ideal for me, as it is on the way to nowhere. This space is very quiet and excellent for reflective work. Here, I am nourished.

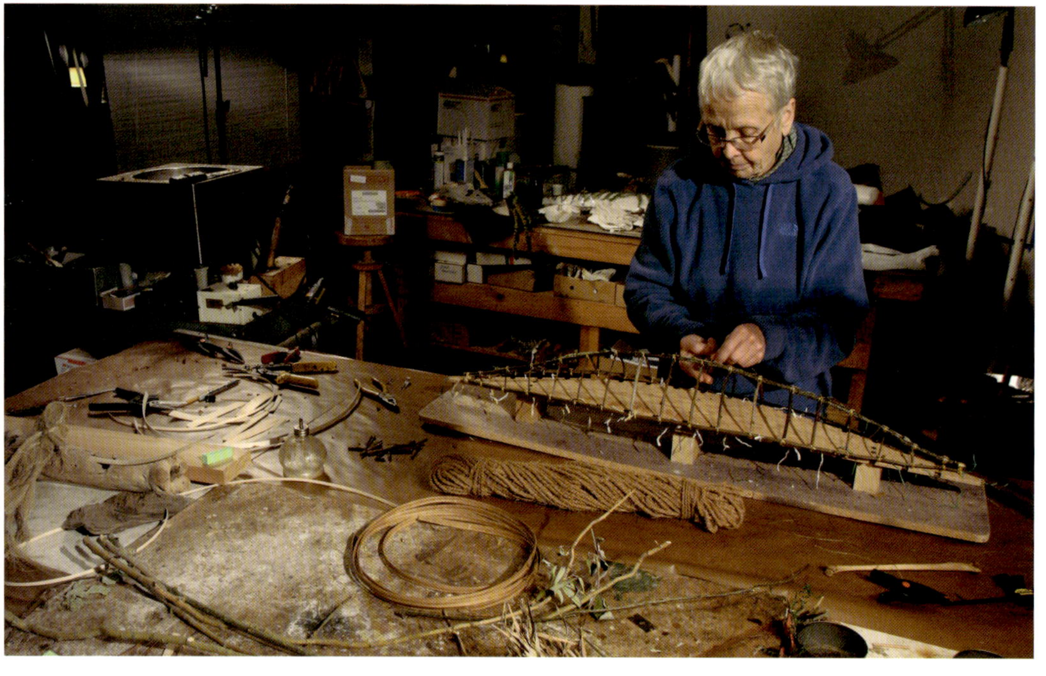

The good thing about a large workspace is having room to lay out lots of materials to choose from as inspiration urges. Here, I work my wax and weave my materials. Courtesy of Dal Neitzel.

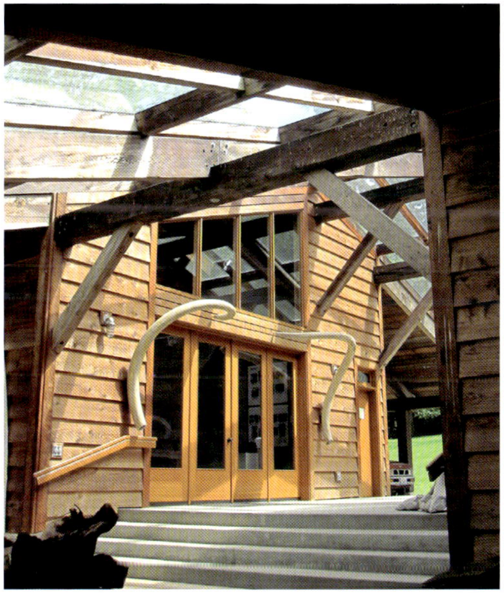

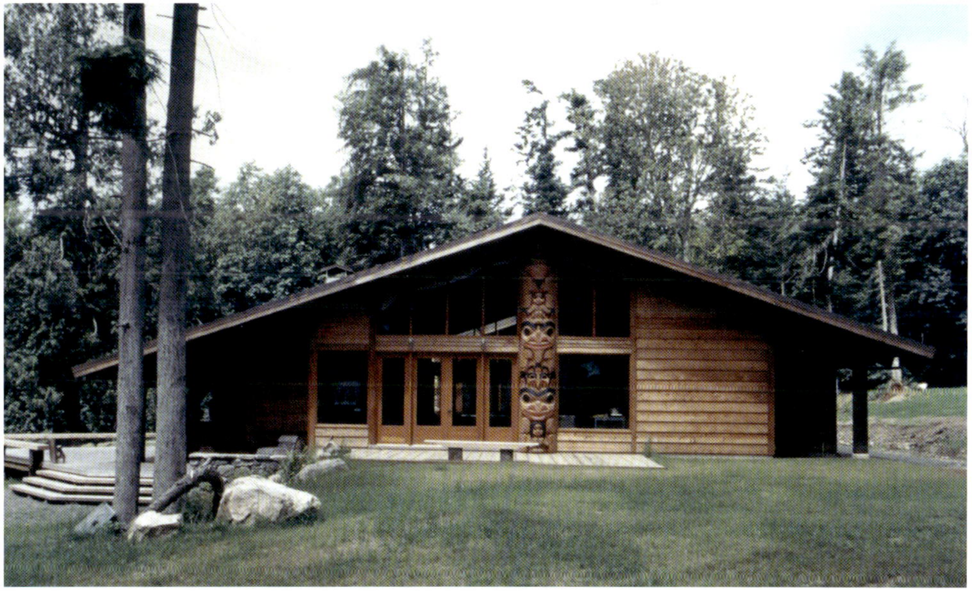

Mammoth tusks cast from fiberglass guard the entrance of my studio gallery where all of my smaller pieces are housed for show. Courtesy of Alex Moseley.

The south-facing wall of my studio is adorned with a totem carved by Scott Jensen. Within these doors are my worktables where I melt and work the wax forms of my pieces. Courtesy of Alexander Moseley.

The central hearth, built from local river rock, grounds my space. Here, contemplation, reading, writing, and warmth await my attention. Courtesy of R. Allen Jensen.

Sculpture Woods and ***Double Dream***. *Bronze. 6.5 x 6 x 5.5'. 1993. Courtesy of Rob Vinnedge.*

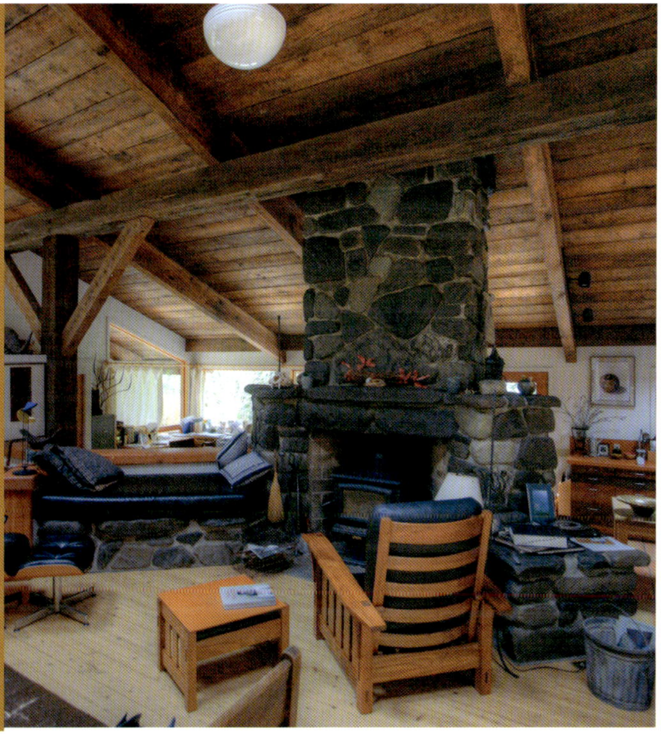

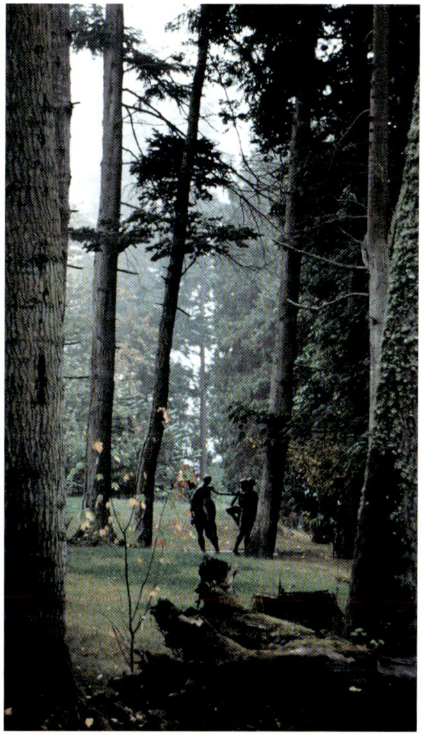

Barton Rubenstein

Chevy Chase, Maryland

When I purchased this 1906 house in 2001, I decided to renovate it and build a large, 25-foot-high structure in the back yard, which is now the main studio space. In addition, there is a conventional garage and office space that is semi-attached to the house. The exterior features of the house were not allowed to be altered because it is a registered historic home. In order for the county to approve my plans, I had to design and build the studio space in keeping with the architectural style of the original bungalow-style home.

The main studio is 650 square feet with ample electricity to allow for multiple welding machines and plasma cutters, as well as other machines. The studio has a 1-ton hoist that rolls along an I-beam, which can be used either inside or outside of the studio. There are four wall fans that can replace the air inside the studio with new air in approximately two minutes. The studio has a bathroom. Although the studio has air conditioning and heating, I typically work in a temperature that is the same as the outdoor weather because I need to continuously remove the toxic welding fumes and grinding particulates from the studio with the fans.

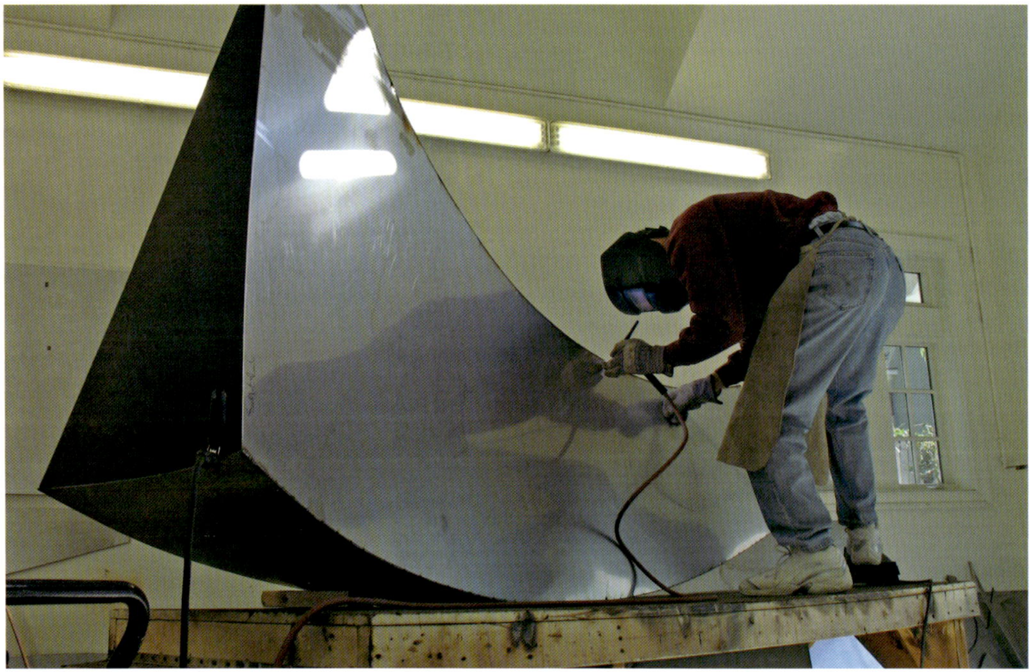

Standing on a table, I am welding ***Arch****, a stainless steel water sculpture. I use a Miller Econotig welding machine, which gives me the capability to weld very precise edges. Most sculptures are fabricated on wooden tables with rollers; that way I can move and transfer elements of a sculpture to different parts of the studio. I have a 1-ton hoist on a large beam in the ceiling.*

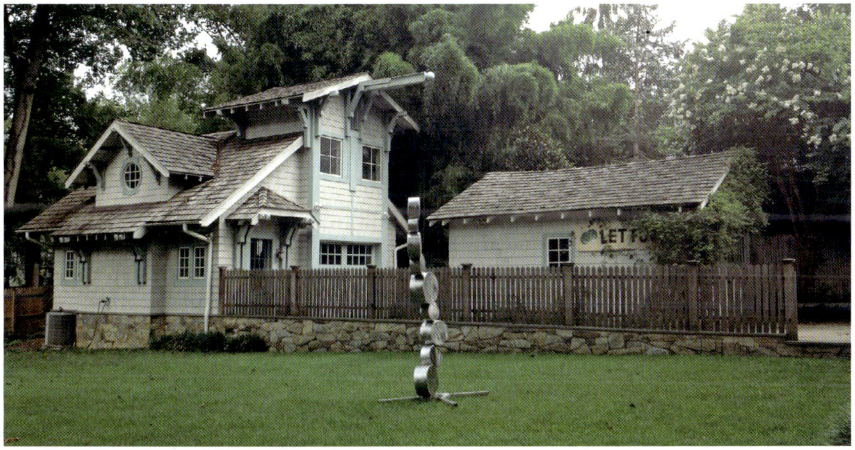

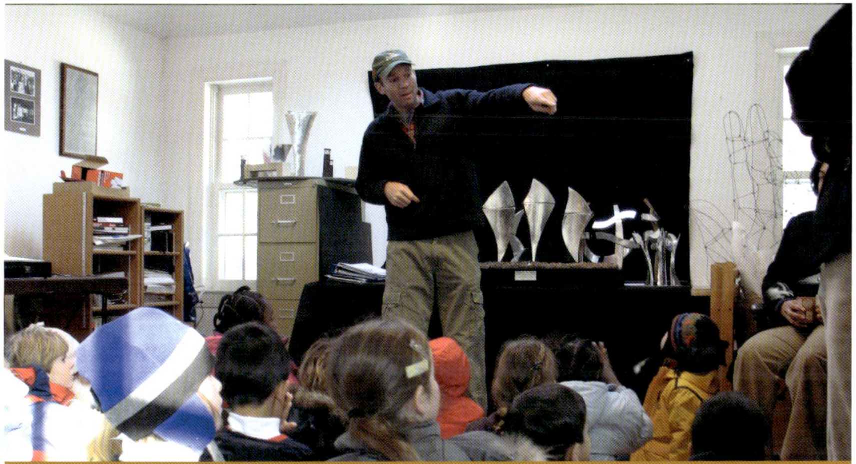

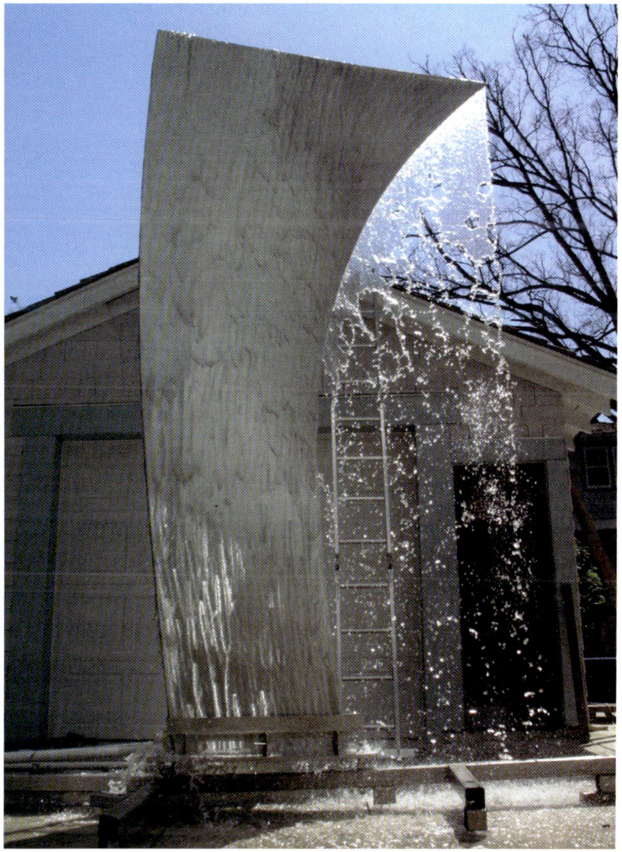

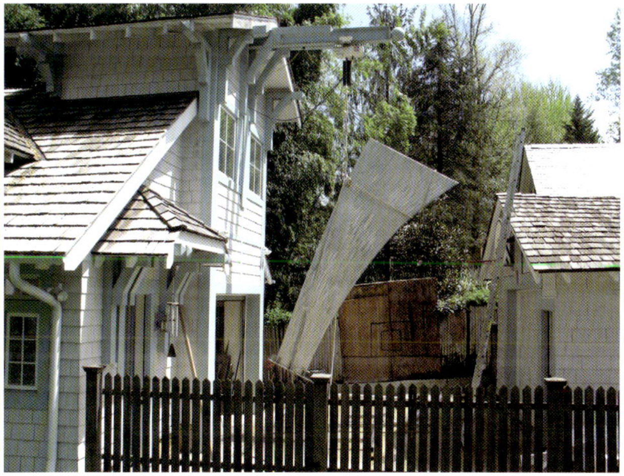

*Rubenstein Studios and one of my newest creations, **Breathe**.*

I have had a number of groups come to the studio, both children and adults. I like to balance the time between the studio and office spaces, so that everyone can have the opportunity to understand all aspects of being an artist.

In front of the studio, I have a water sculpture experiment area, which allows me to erect sculptures using the hoist and connect plumbing to a reservoir built into the ground. The system recycles water indefinitely and allows me to test the water sculptures for proper flow and operation. The goal is that the water must flow the same way every time the pump is turned on.

Robert Swedroe

Surfside, Florida

When I found what became my future home, it was actually a gated compound built in 1946. It incorporated a 1200 square foot, three-car garage and a bathroom with a large utility sink that every artist needs. I transformed the garage into an air-conditioned studio with glass doors. As a result, ambient north and south light illuminate the space, which also offers a view of the entry courtyard fountain.

Having the convenience of a studio across the courtyard from my home provides comfortable access for me to work any time of day or night. It also allows me to exhibit and show my work without disturbing the functions of the household. Most importantly, I love the studio environment with its views of the courtyard and greenery and the sounds of my birds singing from my nearby aviary.

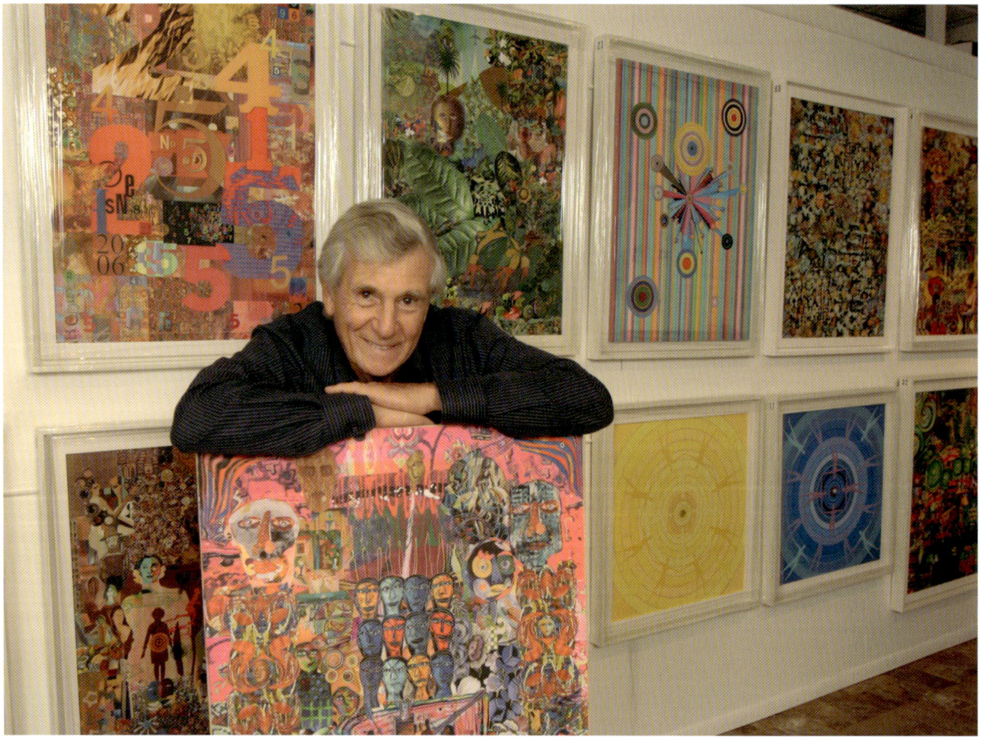

*I devised a wall to exhibit my collage work and built racks of metal file folders to store my art. I am holding **Harlem Nights**.*

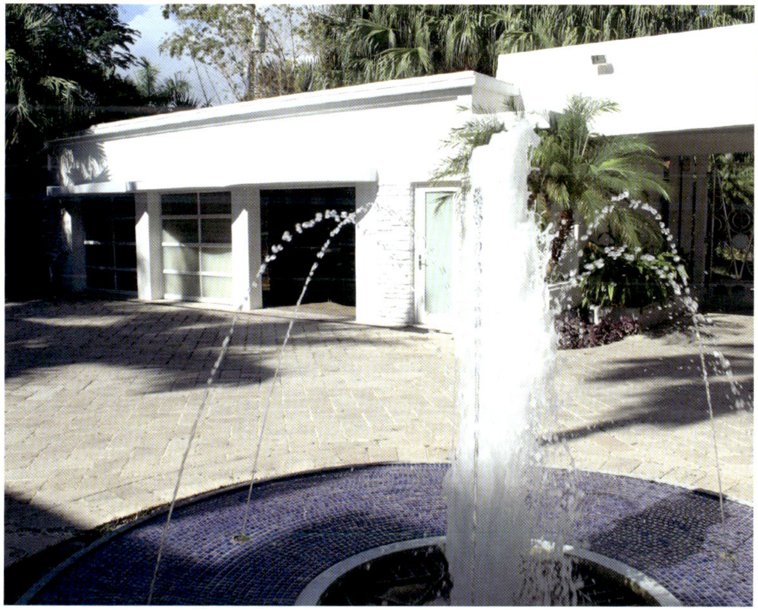

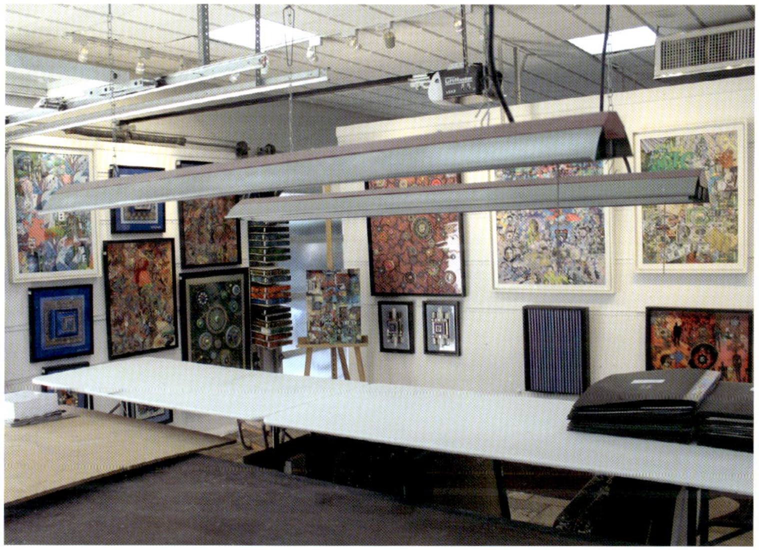

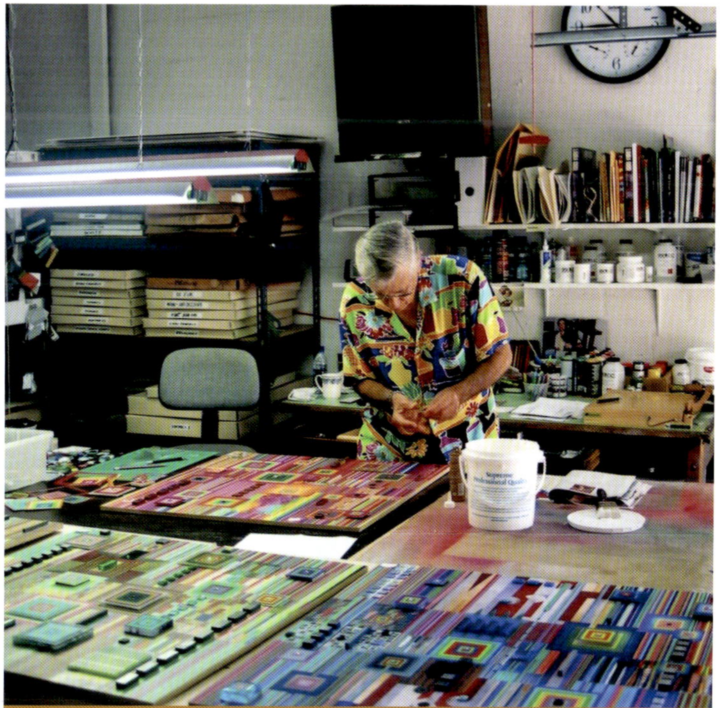

My studio and the courtyard fountains. The garage door openings allow me to move collages with various types of coating to the courtyard for sun drying.

My collage work requires abundant collecting, cutting, and filing preparatory to creating each piece of art. I designated file boxes and storage areas readily accessible to my working space, which is primarily an eight-seat dining table augmented by foldable party tables.

At work in the studio.

Jeanie Gooden

San Miguel de Allende, Mexico

My home and studio in Central Mexico are separate but feel integrated in terms of design. The architect, Luis Sanchez Renero, once asked why I would consider working at home when I could walk through a city like San Miguel de Allende to begin my day. With the city's beautiful Colonial architecture, rich color, and texture, I agree.

The design of our home integrates the age and texture of the historic city streets into very modern interior spaces. Sections of wood, concrete, glass, and stone translate so authentically that guests often ask if they are inside or out when they enter the house. The house inspired my first large-scale paintings. With 35-foot ceilings and concrete walls that welcome art, I often rotate paintings in and out of the house to explore how a painting feels in a space.

Only a mile away, my studio also has a sense of being outdoors. Open areas above a large metal door and clear panels in the roof allow natural light to fill the space. I often feel that I should switch off the lights as I end my day—only to remember that everything I see is natural. Everything about the space is raw and durable, and splatters and clutter are welcome and additive. Music and voices float through the space from the street. It is not uncommon for people in the neighborhood to knock on the door or stop me on the street to visit. Those moments have proven to be very special opportunities to practice Spanish and learn more about the Mexican culture.

My American friends and cohorts help me live this life. For example, Scott Johnson of Hawks Photography helped me put these images together for submission.

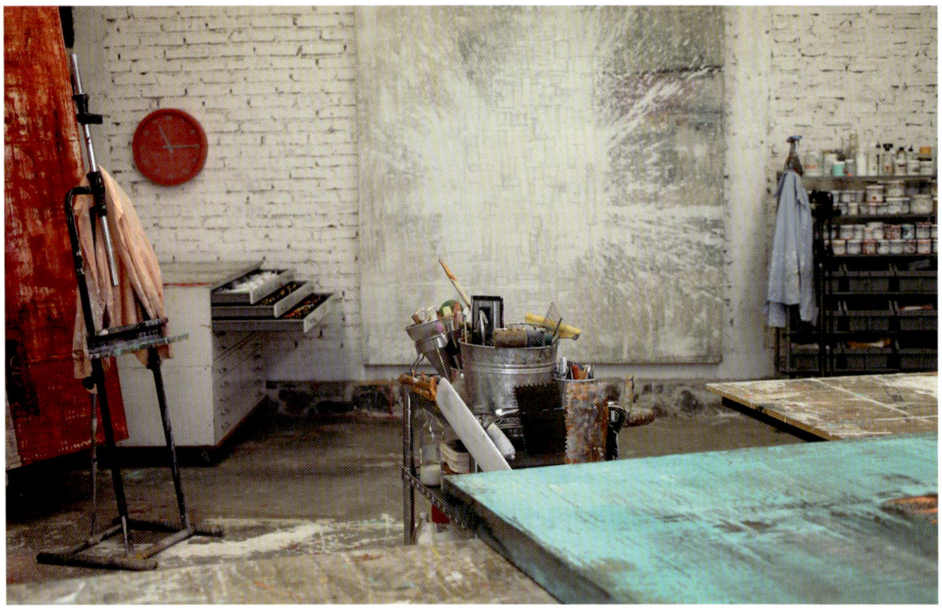

Weathered walls are part of my inspiration. I like to see my work shown on surfaces that have been kissed by time. I find the best test for my paintings is to hang them in my space and feel how they live. The mixed media painting is ***A Better Way to Live*** *(84 x 86").*

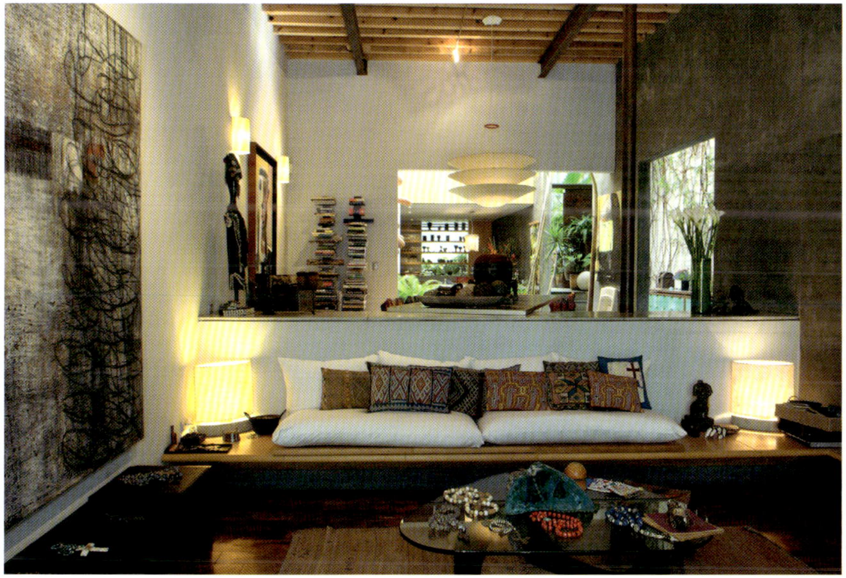

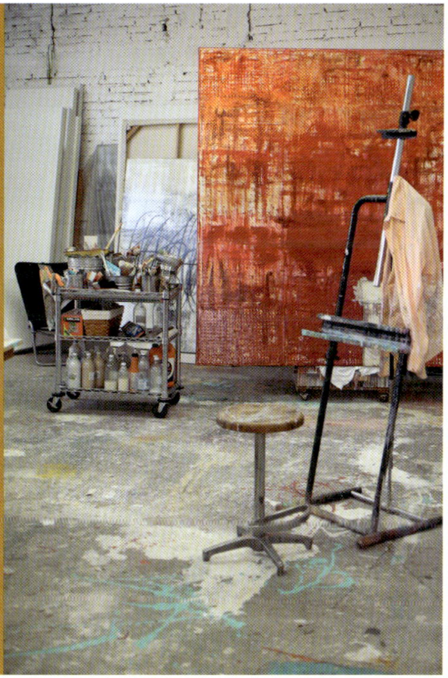

From the garden, you can enter the living room and see all the way through the house. The living room welcomes art. If I allow one of my paintings to hang in my living room for more than a week, it is considered finished. The mixed media painting on the left is ***Knock Knock Secret Is That You?*** Courtesy of Lander Rodriguez.

One could say that I live in a concrete box with a glass lid that welcomes light and plants. This 35-foot ivy-covered wall is fed by natural light flooding in through a glass ceiling. Courtesy of Lander Rodriguez.

Paint tables translate my days in color and whisper titles while I work. The mixed media painting on the easel is ***Find the Red and Breathe in It.***

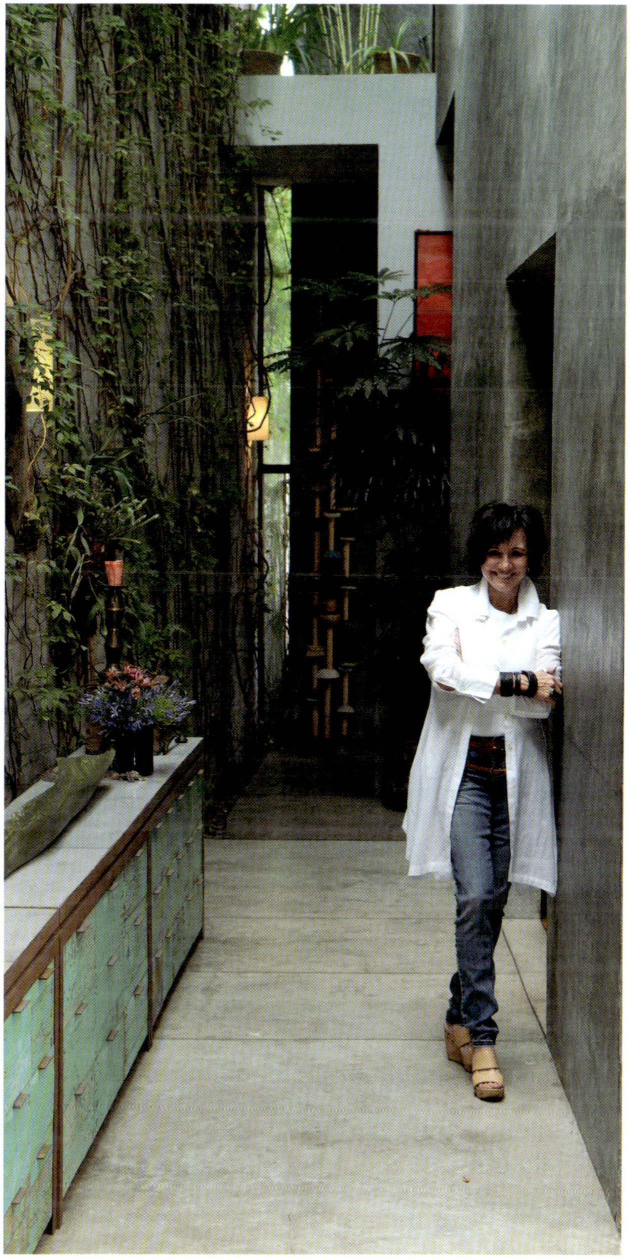

2

In-House Studios

Many artists have been fortunate to site their studio within their existing home, whether it be in a former bedroom or the basement. Some have undertaken substantial work to renovate the space so it works as a studio. Generally, these in-home studios are crammed with equipment, frames, and finished work. In this chapter, we show both studios in existing space and in especially designed spaces.

The tropical milieu of Barbara Krupp's home has an impact on her art.

A space is set apart in Mel Rea's studio for for watercolor and works on paper. Courtesy of Chris Langer.

Allison Gildersleeve's studio is the first floor of her brick storefront. Photo courtesy of Joel Bach.

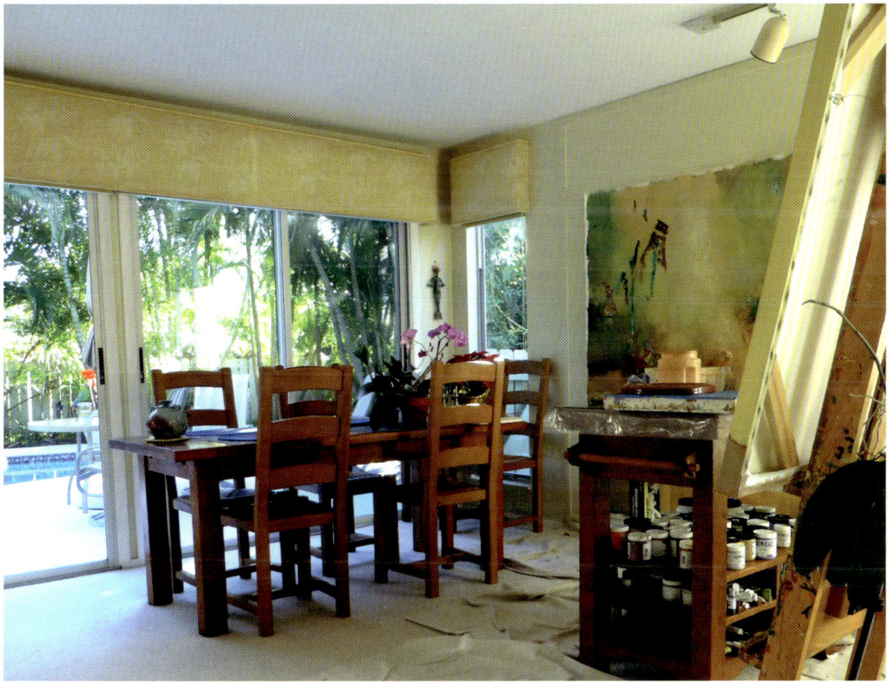
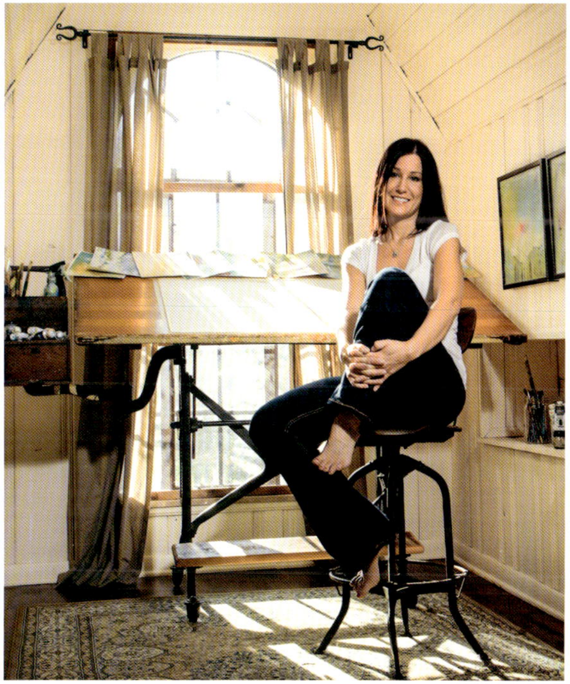
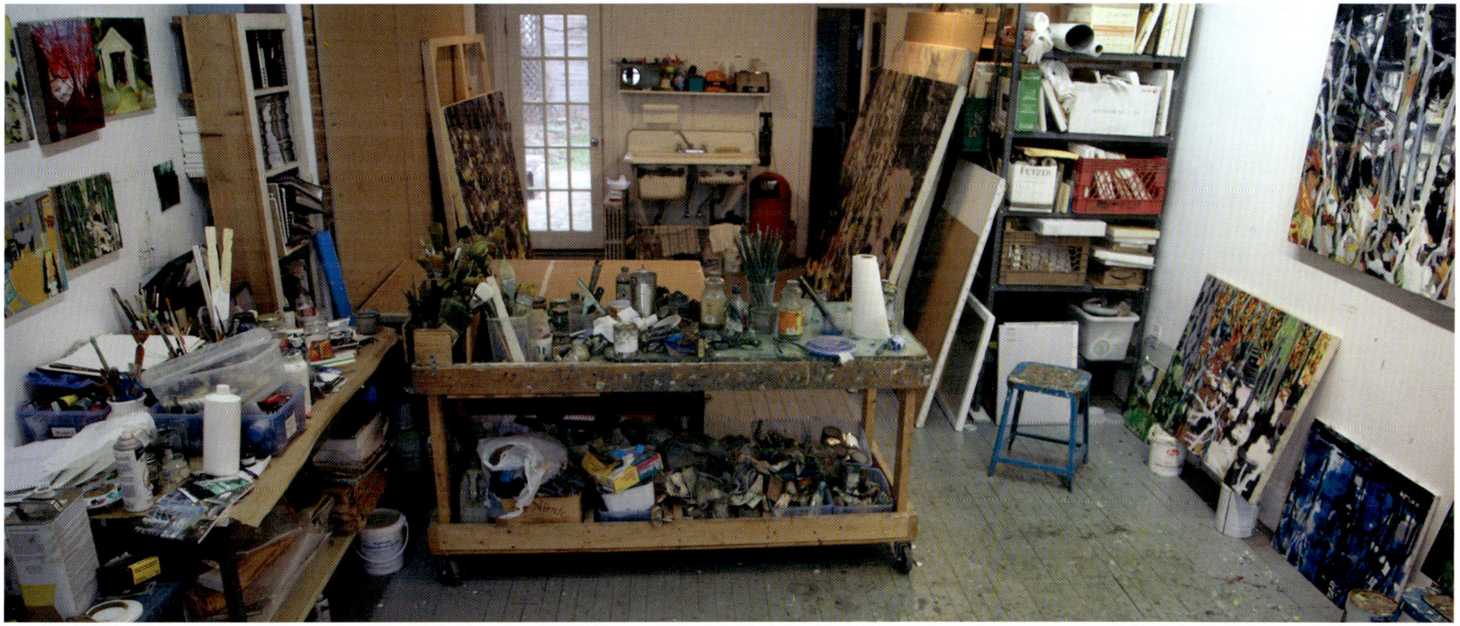

Joan Danziger

Washington, DC

My sculptures combine an interplay of the animal strength and beauty of nature with the human spirit. They are reaching into the heart of nature to evoke mysterious and secret worlds, which draws upon my fascination with dream imagery and metamorphosis.

The use of animal imagery as a metaphorical or psychological subject has great potency for me. It gives my sculptures a life of their own and creates a magical world.

Recently, I have been exploring the Order of Coleoptera or spectactular beetles.

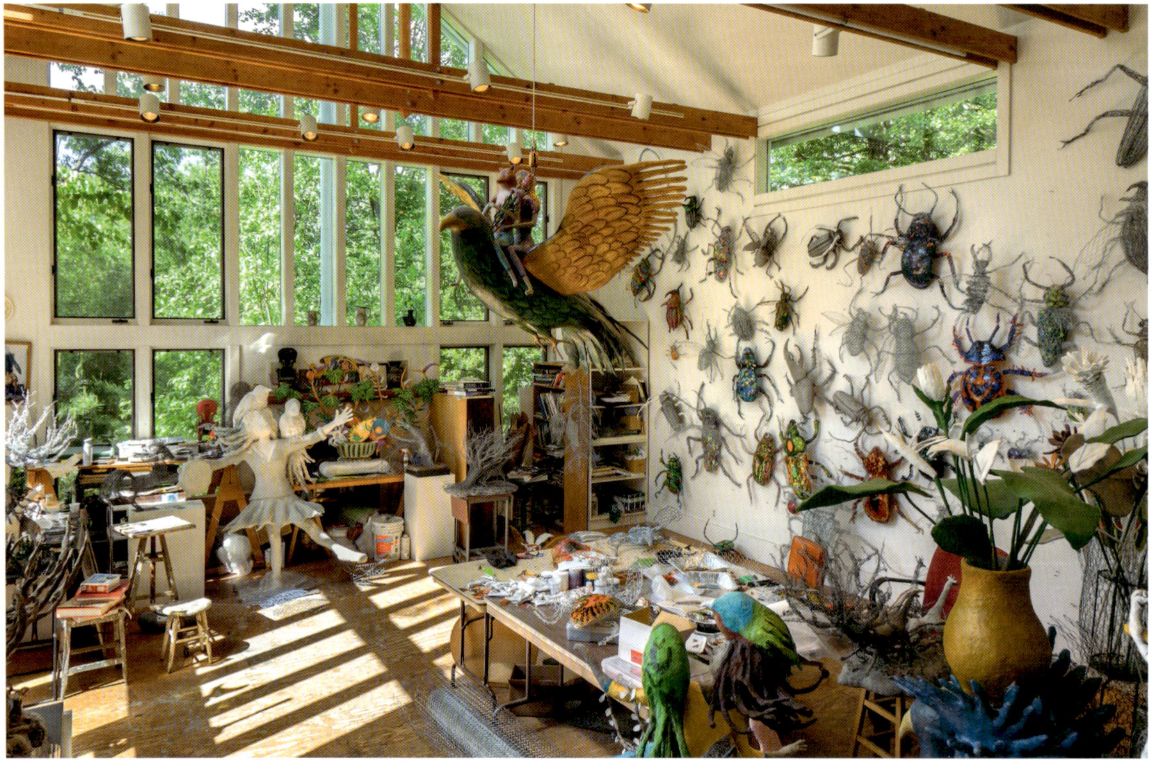

Working in a magical studio full of light from all directions and amazing colors is an aesthetic experience. My studio, with its vast space and high walls, has influenced the direction of my work and encouraged me to make sculptures on a grand scale. The materials I have used are mixed media: metal armature, fused glass, frit, and acrylic paint. Art ranges in size from 12 inches to 6 feet. Courtesy of Neil Greentree.

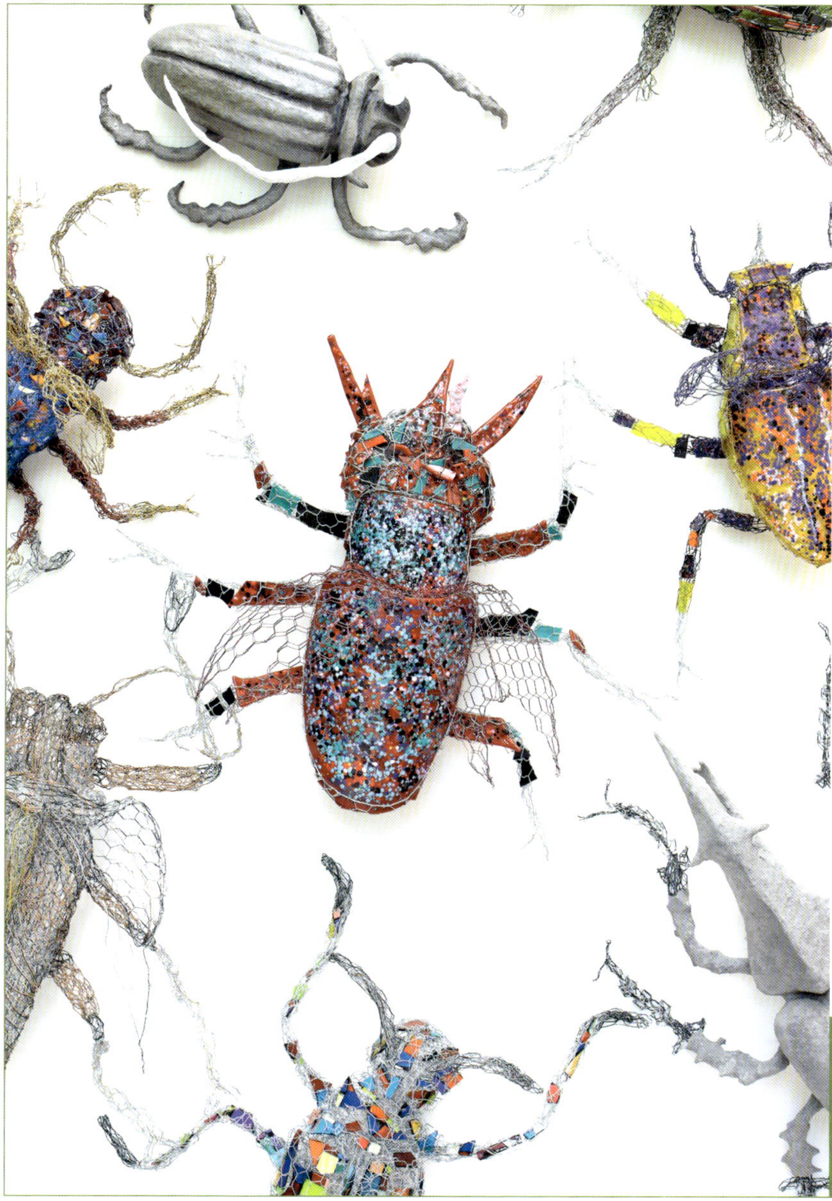

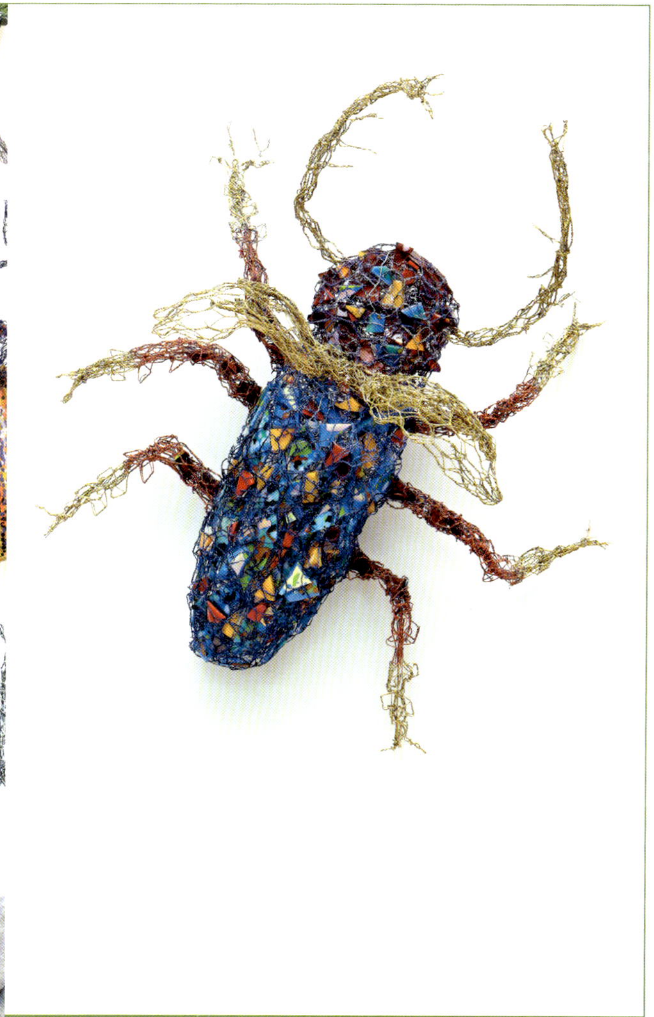

Red Devil Group. Courtesy of Neil Greentree.

Blue Mosaic Beetle. Courtesy of Neil Greentree.

Jamie Allen

Kailua, Hawaii

In June 2010, I moved from Green Pond, New Jersey, to the island of Oahu, Hawaii. My current studio is located on the second floor of my grandmother's house, which used to be her own art studio for many years. Because of its open space, natural light, and high ceilings, this studio provides both an ideal working and living environment. It is surrounded with large mango and banyan trees, lush vegetation, and an active canal that runs from the Pacific Ocean. My work is a direct reflection of these natural elements as well as my daily life experiences. Essentially, I build imaginary environments on paper that are a collection of the items and colors I have both seen and sensed. As an artist, I am dedicated to exploring how the natural and artificial world shapes one's life—both directly and indirectly. I find this to be true with every wash, splash, spill, and mark I make.

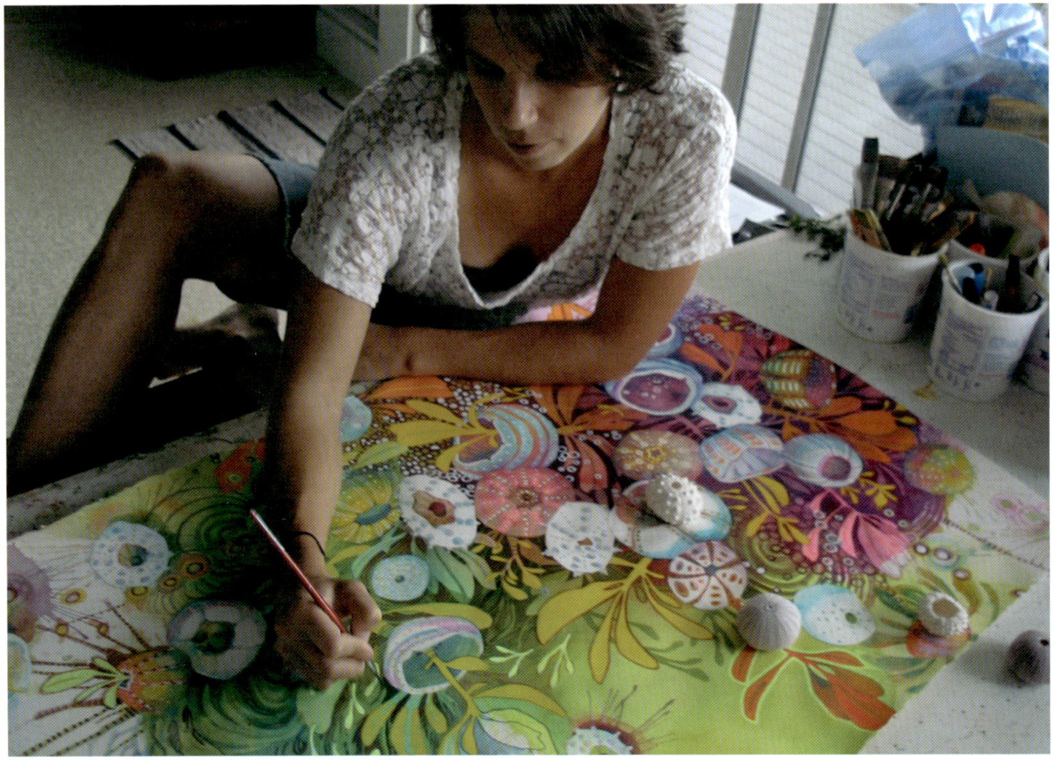

My studio relies on natural light coming from my lanai, which overlooks the canal in Kailua, Hawaii. When I work on fine detail, I work at my table. Here I am painting ***Celebrating,*** *a commission by a wife for her husband.* Courtesy of Mark Osman.

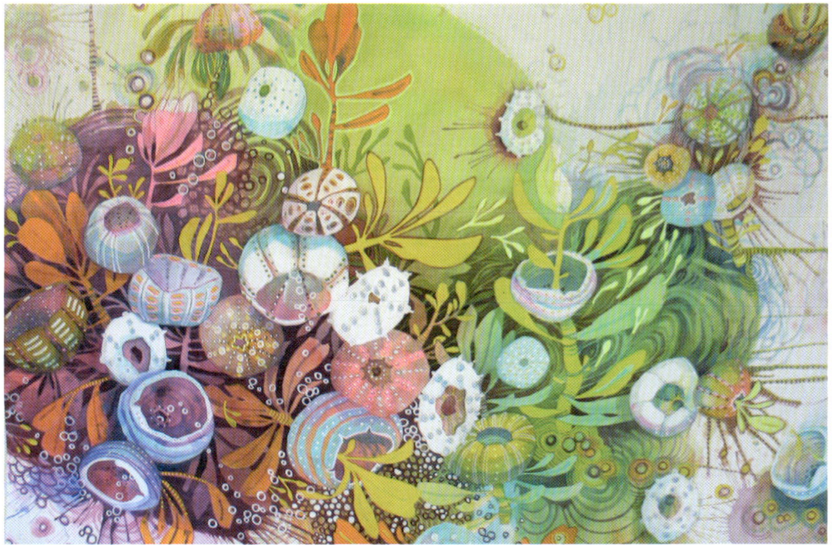

When I first start my painting process, I work on the floor and pour large pools of watercolor and acrylic paint in an abstract manner influenced by the Color Field Painters. Drawings from my grandmother's orchid garden are used for inspiration for the painting, ***And the Heart Says*** *(mixed media, 37 x 45"). Here are my "well" used paintbrushes, palette, and sketchbook containing drawings and pressed foliage. Courtesy of Mark Osman.*

This is an example of the beginning stages of my work: large fluid organic washes that blend and drip together. The next step is drawing collected objects. Again, the natural light is seeping into my studio through an open door. The doors and windows in my studio are always open to let in the natural light and wind.

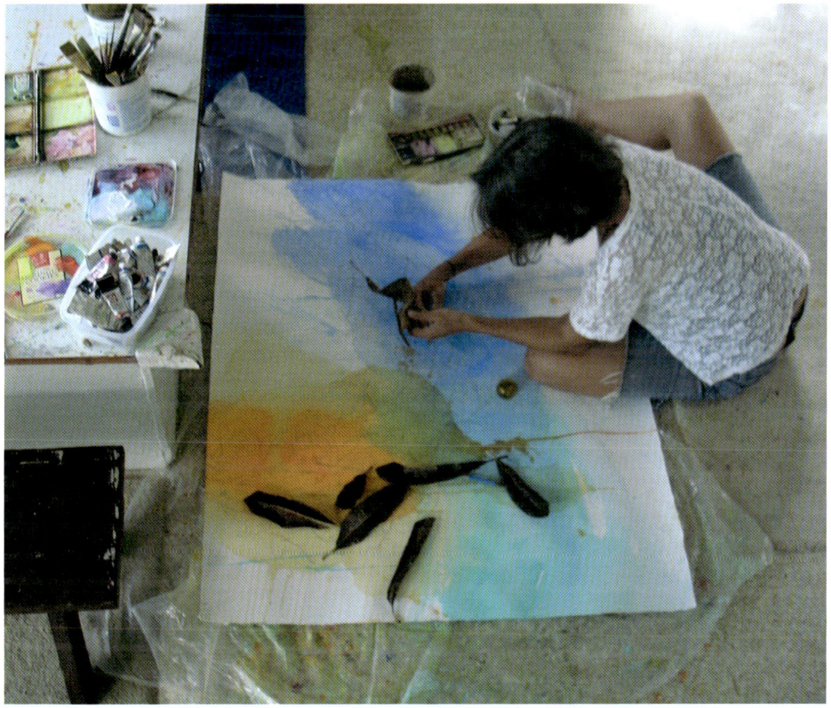

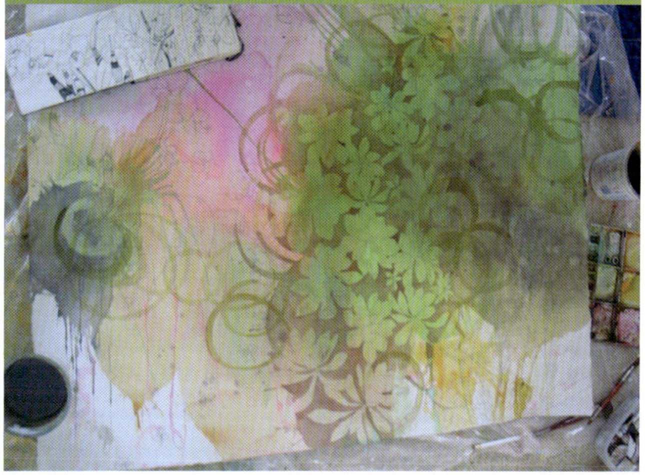

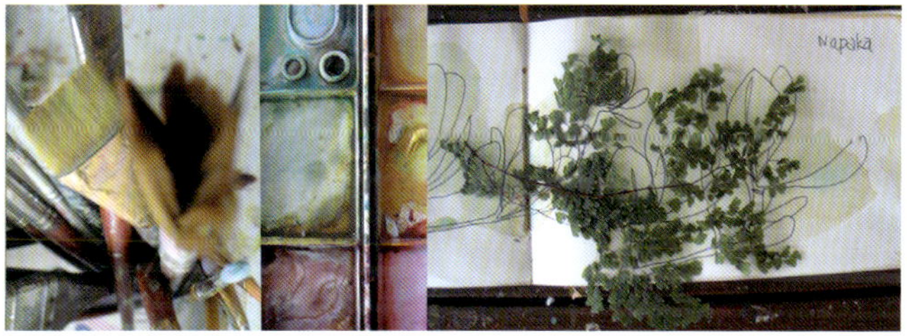

Sandy Askey-Adams, PSA

Churchville, Pennsylvania

I work in soft pastels and oils, but mainly pastels. My studio, which is off my kitchen, suits my needs with natural north light, artificial lighting, storage, shelving, and a back door leading out to a creek, which I have painted many times. I also have a garden.

I love hiking and walking through woods alongside side creeks, streams, and rivers. The creek outside my studio seems perfect for me. I have a deep appreciation for nature, which is my inspiration and influence for painting.

I can forget about time and the happenings of the world around me while painting and listening to classical music.

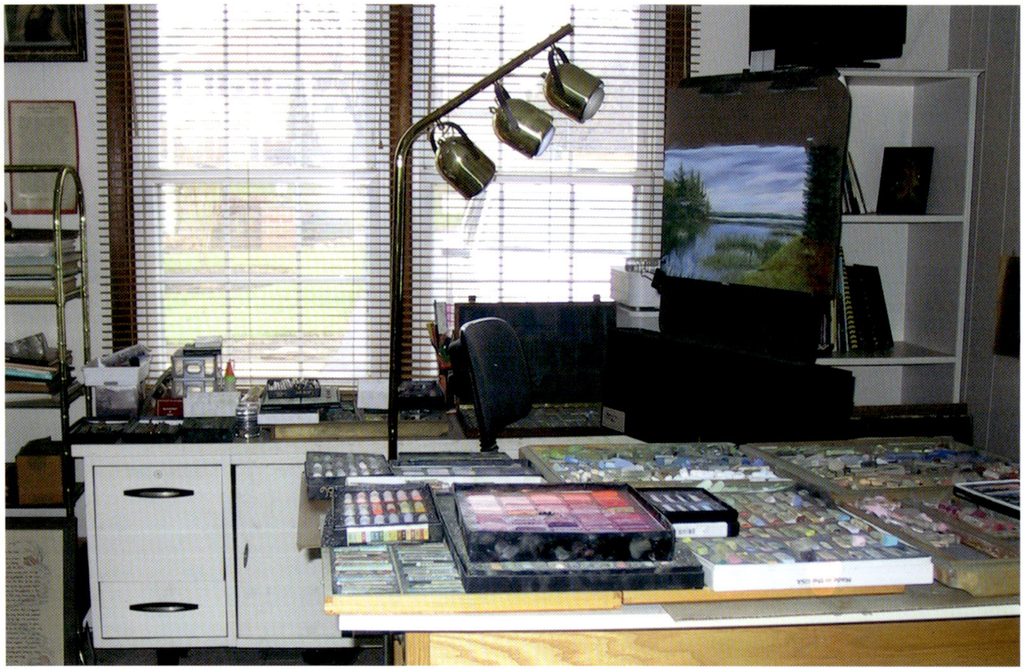

There are two air filtering machines set up in my studio, and an "Artists Air" filtering system is attached under the easel because pastel is a dusty medium. It pulls the pastel dust down and out of the air while I am working at the easel. As a safety precaution, I wear gloves and a mask while working with the pastels. A mat is on the floor to catch any pastel sticks that drop while working.

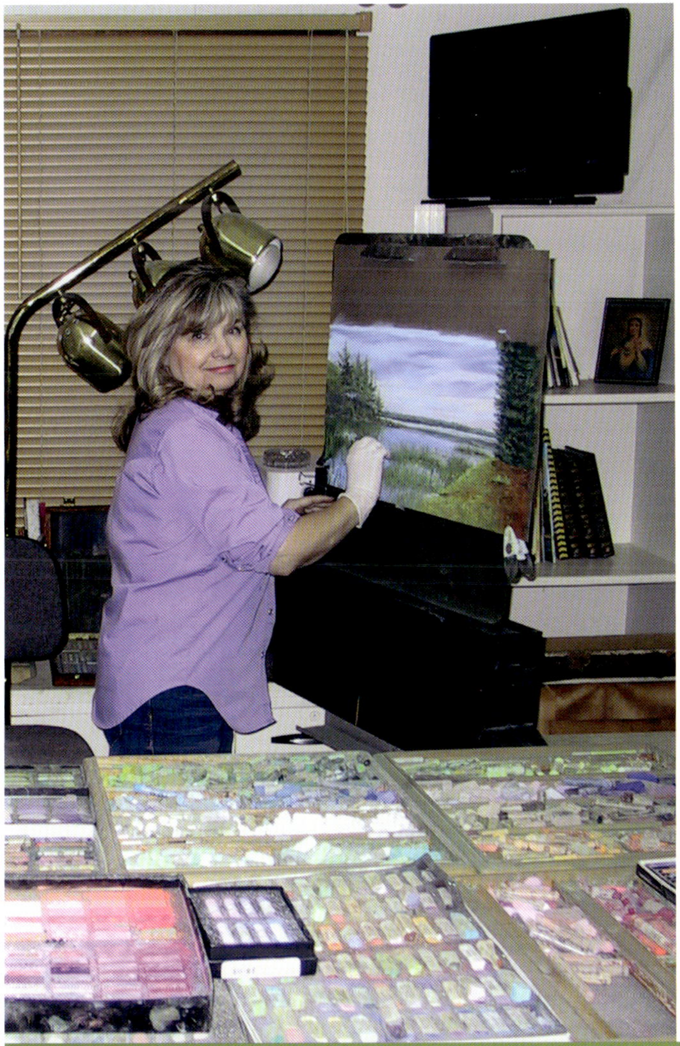

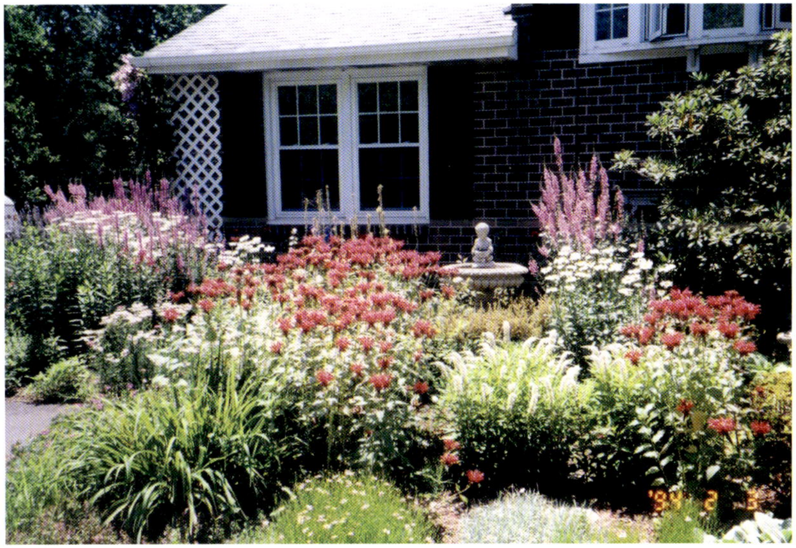

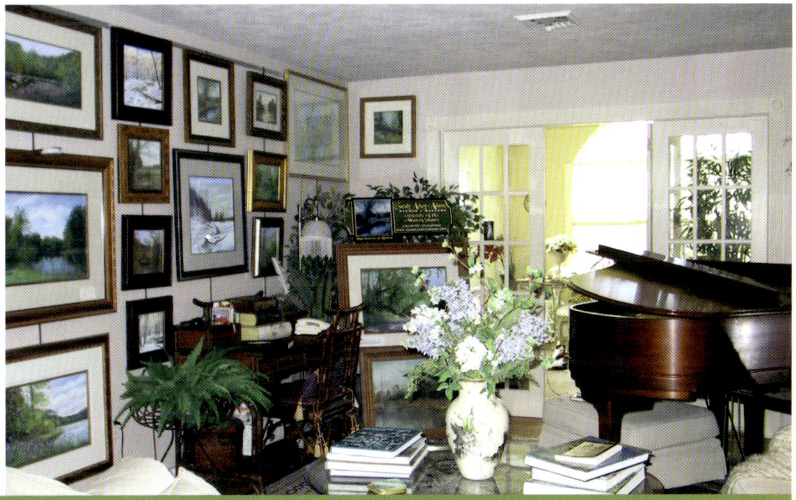

The windows to the left of the garden are the windows of my studio. It is especially nice to be able to work inside at my easel with the garden right outside my windows; then there are times I will be outside in the garden drawing or painting the flowers.

The Walker Wall System allows me to have an art gallery in my home. My art gallery contains a baby grand piano, comfortable seating, coffee table, and a desk.

Sheryl Budnik

Comstock Park, Michigan

My painting studio is a large room upstairs in the 1955 Cape Cod brick home I purchased in 1985. A hallway leads to an adjoining room that I made into a gallery. Once the kids were gone and I was retired from thirty years of art teaching and creative work at a newspaper, I had the rooms repainted and new windows, air, and track lights installed. I kept the original carpet, and my art friends remark about the color with each visit — for me, it's perfect. I am a visceral palette knife oil painter, and the colors can fly!

A studio in your home is wonderful and ultimately convenient: no driving to a studio in poor weather, or rent to pay. It is quiet—no annoying music or chitchat from other artists. Meals can be cooking downstairs. I dress in painting clothes in the morning, then head upstairs, often painting barefoot. As an intuitive contemporary landscape and waterscape painter, I can tape images to the wall or line them up on the floor. All of my art books are there. TV and boring movies can play downstairs for some background noise. Collectors can call and come to the gallery and see the studio. At day's end, I often head upstairs for a final look at my work, often seeing a solution for the next day.

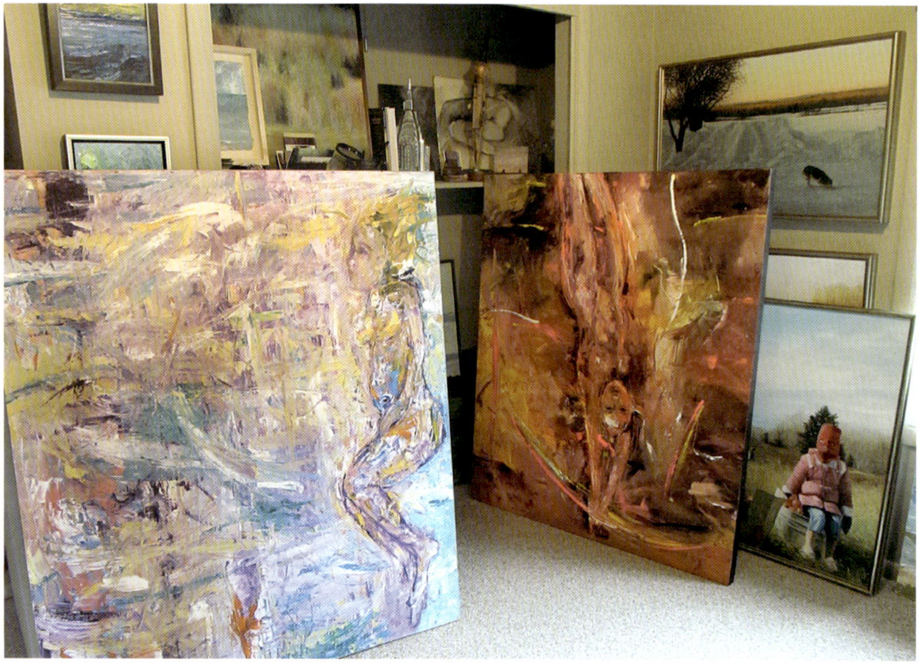

This viewing room is an annex to my working studio.

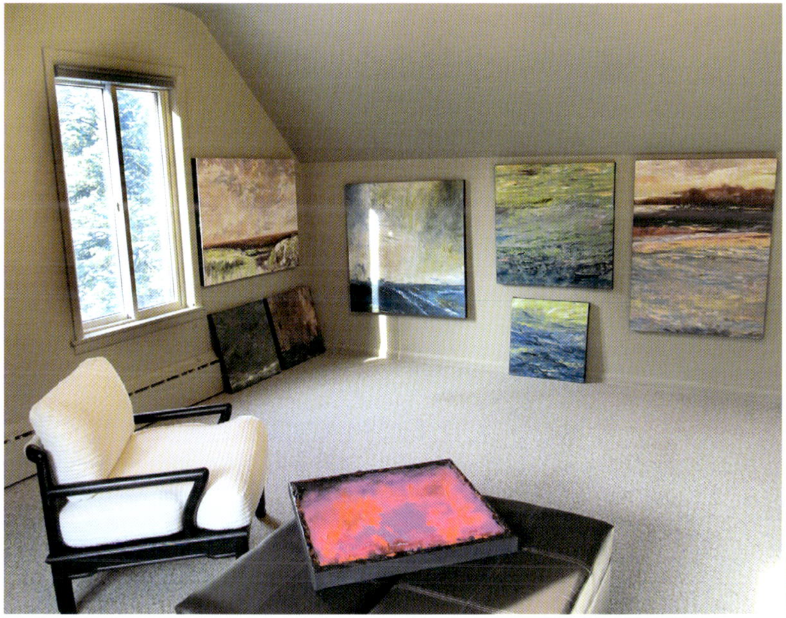

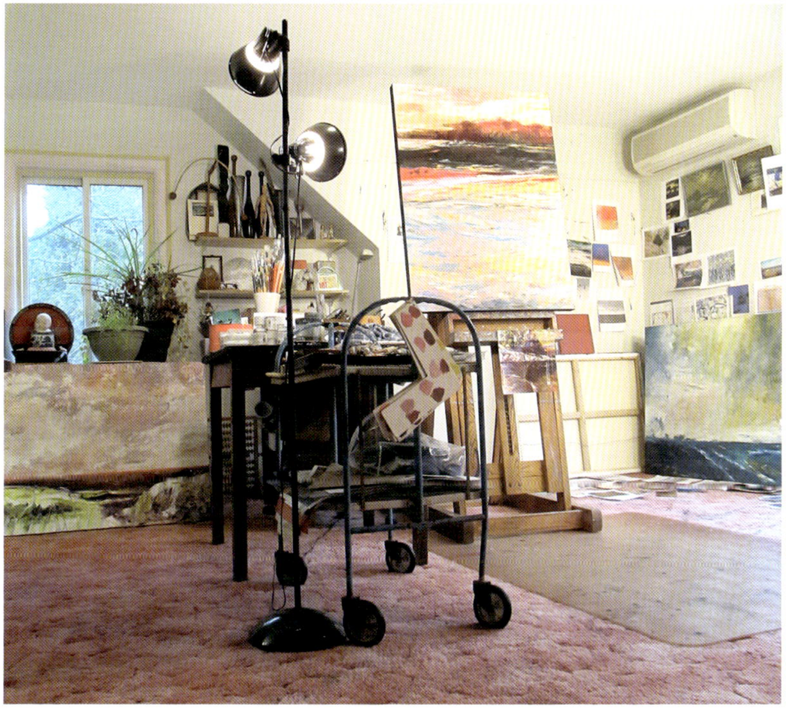

This 15 x 18-foot room, next to my studio, has new paint, carpet, windows, and track lights. ***Painting Setting Itself on Fire*** *is on the bench. Paintings on the wall, left to right, are* ***Flying Point Beach, Ocean Storm, Shimmer Blue, Emerald Blue****, and* ***Shoreline.***

My oak easel can hold a canvas to the ceiling. Paint table and cart are finds.

The business end of the studio contains a chair from a friend "to match your ugly carpet." The shelf unit holds boxes of pictures, hanging supplies, tools, and stuff. Doors off the closet provide storage space for drawings, prints, rags, and old paintings. The collage is ***Grand Rapids in the Pink*** *(Thai papers and foils, and shredded money on the map of Grand Rapids).*

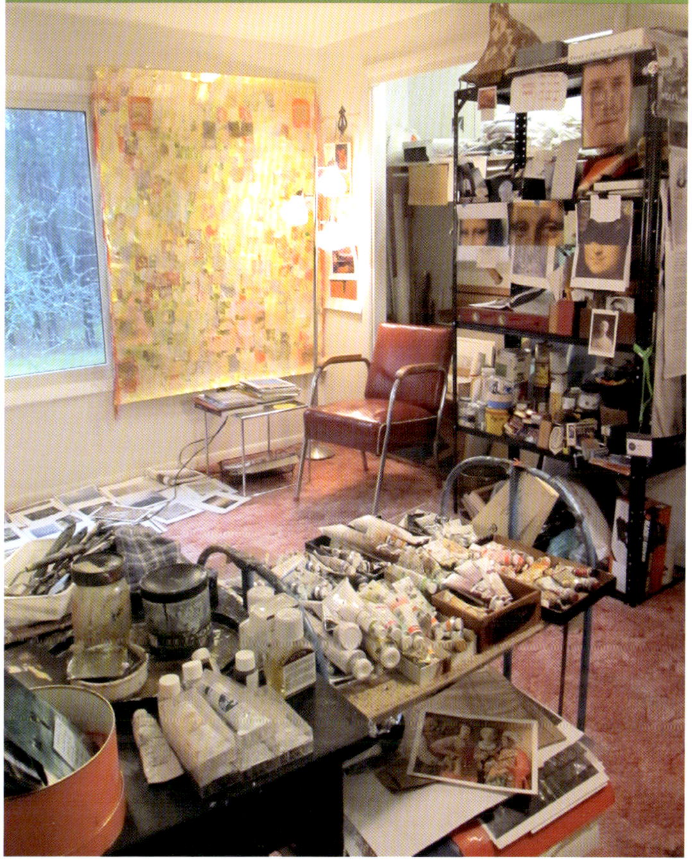

Michelle DeMarco

Three Rivers, Massachusetts

My studio is one-quarter of my 700 square foot condominium. It suits my artwork because it's small, minimal, and an essential part of my living space. Whether I call it "green living" or having a small eco-footprint, it is a reflection of my interconnectedness with all of life. Its very smallness spurs me to actively seek the world. Then the entire world becomes my actual studio.

My walks and hikes connect me to this earth and allow me to perceive and understand that nature wavers between the divine and the material. Globalization and technology connect me to the world at large. My artwork is formed in both of these relationships. This living engagement is my aesthetic practice and encourages my capacity to dream, wonder, imagine, create, and love. This, with the infusion of the art of living into the heart of every exchange, is my reference point pointing to the magic in the world. This is ecomimesis—an existential beauty and free delight.

My studio atmosphere creates a womb for my sustained dialogue with and about our world.

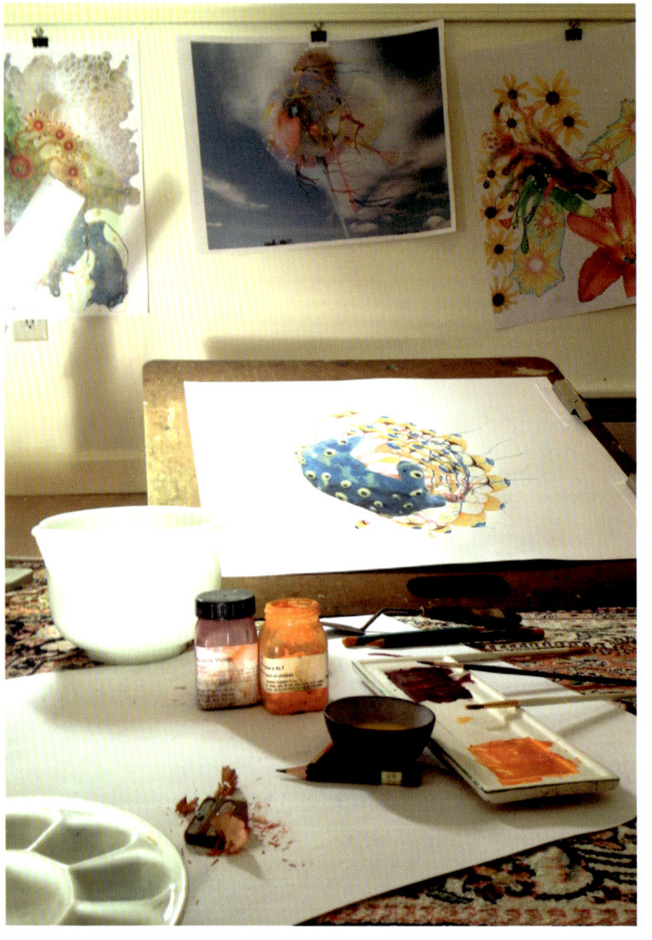

A moist media work in progress, which is a digital image fused with egg tempera. On the wall are several works for the new book. I find it comfortable to work on the floor lying down.

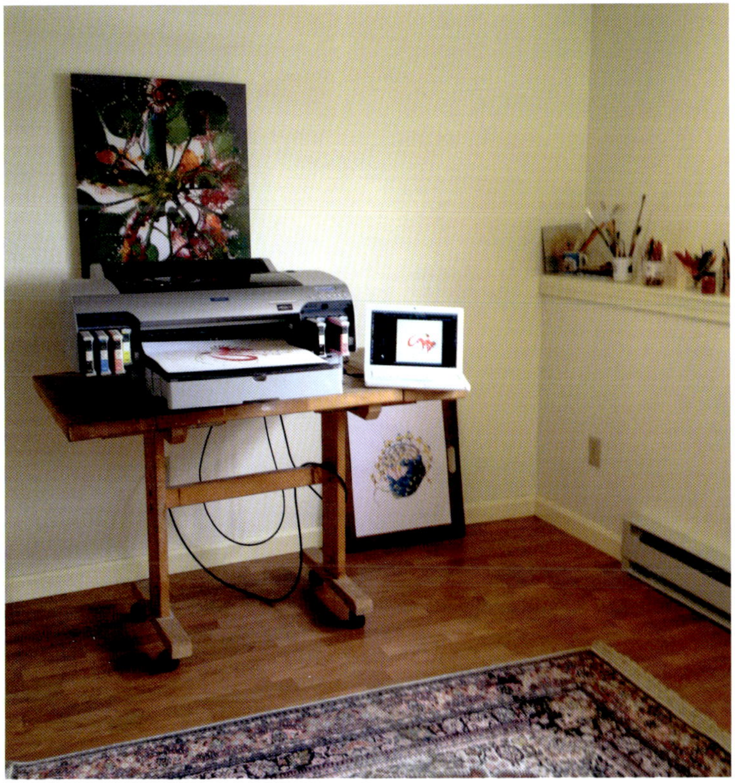

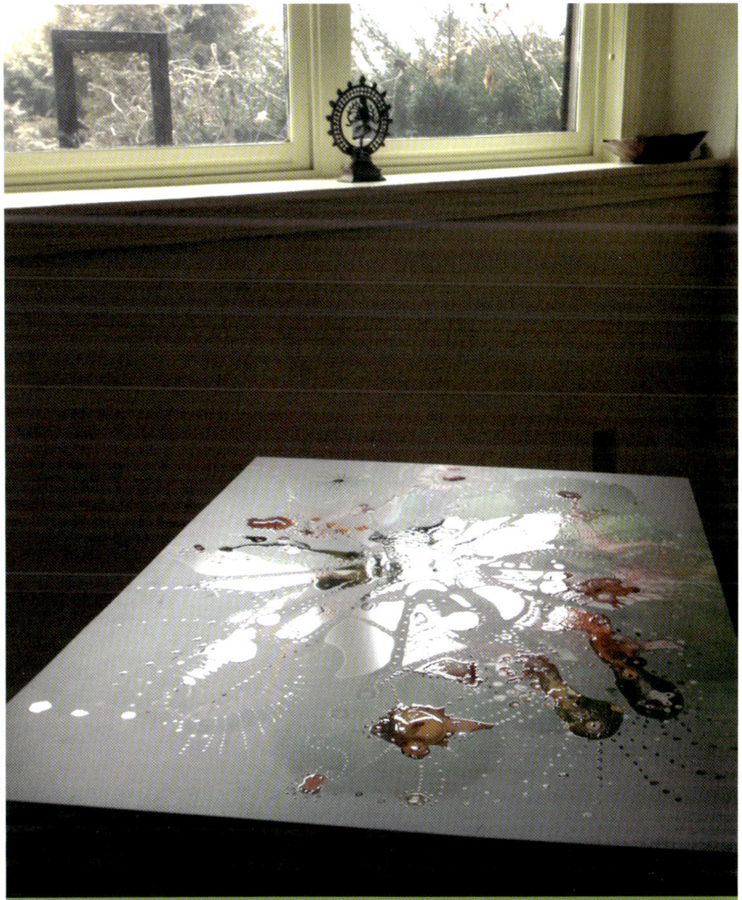

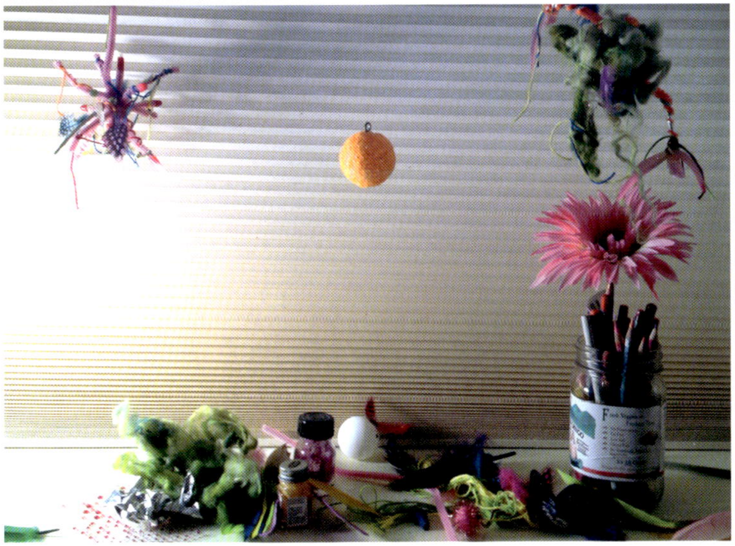

My MacBook and Epson 4000 inkjet printer with Starflower 2.2 on the wall and a book drawing in progress on the floor. The Epson allows me to print on varied substrates like aluminum and plexi-glass.

The late afternoon sun in the studio is exceptional for the large aluminum works. The poured varnish and pigments light up in the late day glow.

The custom blinds across the double windows serve to allow filtered light for quiet little sculpture works.

Allison Gildersleeve

Brooklyn, New York

My studio is in a brick storefront in Brooklyn that was built in 1899; our family of four, plus one black cat, lives upstairs. I'm a messy and impatient painter—tables are piled high with photos and drawings, works in progress lean against the walls. My children come in, making all sorts of creations alongside me while I work. My husband wanders through and spins off his thoughts, like sparks, as the paintings evolve. Being a painter feels as if I'm subject to a sort of centrifugal force that I can't avoid. I spiral around one focal point: the impact of accumulated histories on the perception of place. All the chaos of life, space, and family gets funneled into that vortex and congeals on the canvas.

I think the contrast of living and raising children in this industrial, gridded setting compared to my own childhood setting (acres of wooded land crisscrossed by rambling stone walls) has pushed a tension into my work that wouldn't occur if I still lived in a rural area. The paint strokes cluster and fight with each other, colors vibrate, and everything is crammed without room to breathe. However, somewhere in that chaos exists a hint of escape, a promise of a place uncluttered, a respite that matches the longing I feel for a pause from the constant buzzing of city life.

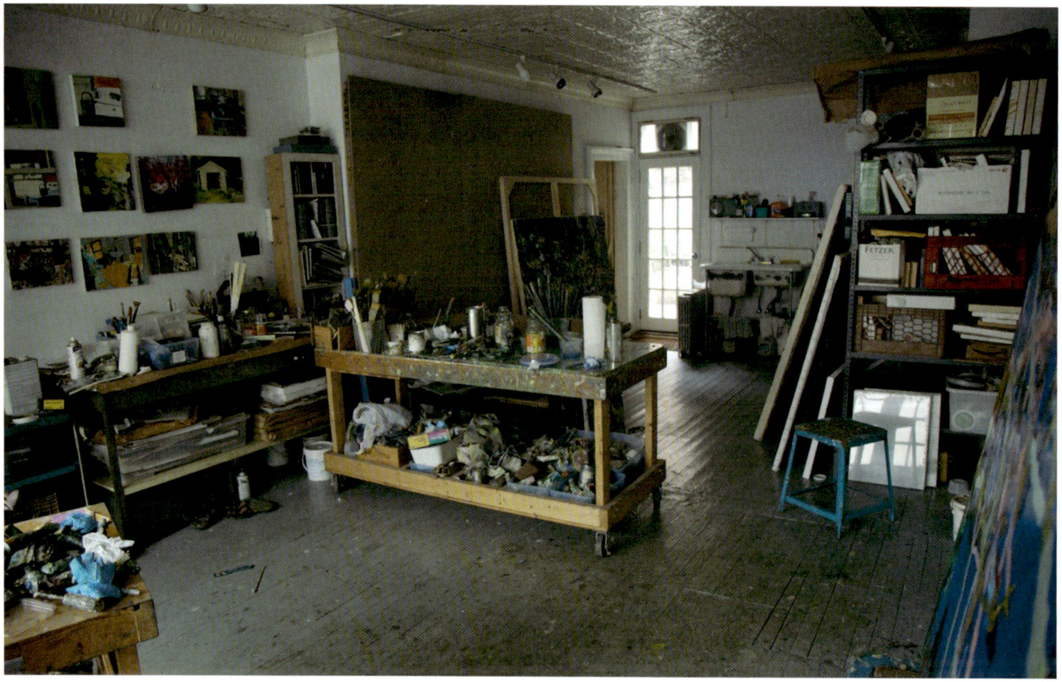

Overview of the studio, looking out towards the door to our back garden, Courtesy of Joel Bach.

This is our two-story brick building in Williamsburg, Brooklyn; my studio is on the first floor and we live on the second. Courtesy of Joel Bach.

My drawing tables with a collection of small paintings on the wall above. Courtesy of Joel Bach.

We retrofitted the facade this past summer with a factory-style window to restore the building's character and add more light to the studio. Courtesy of Joel Bach.

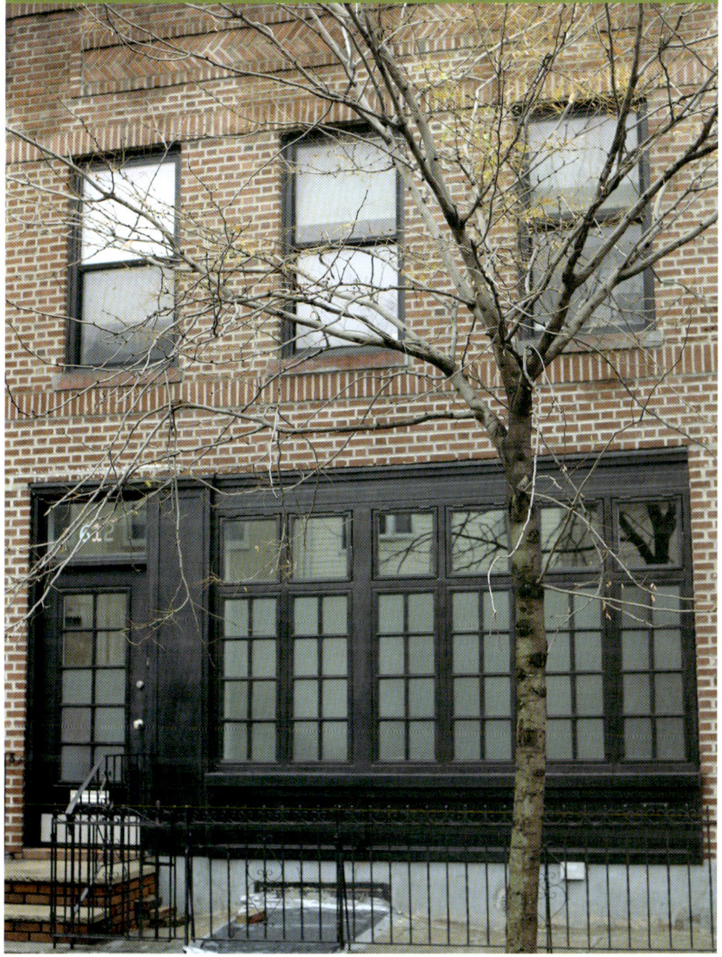

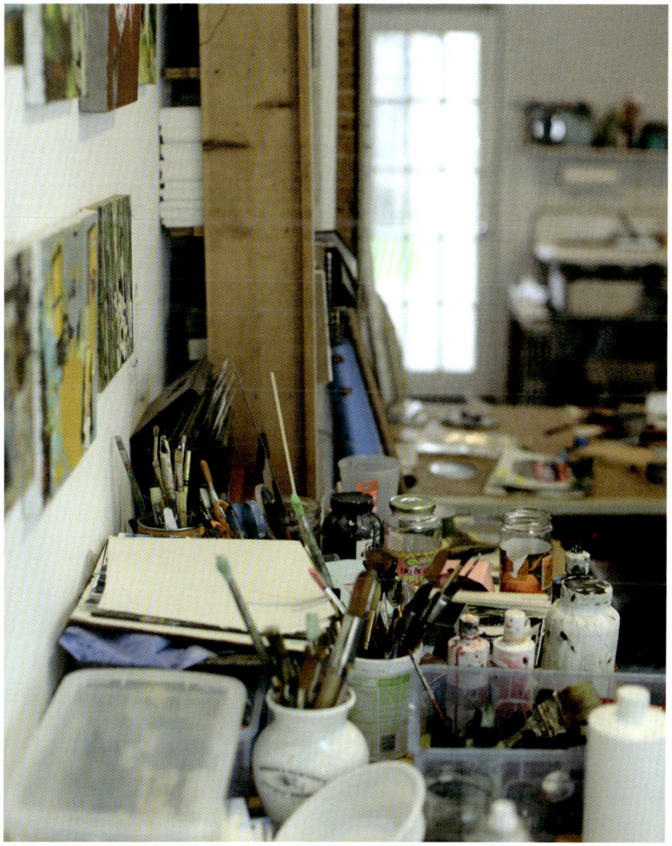

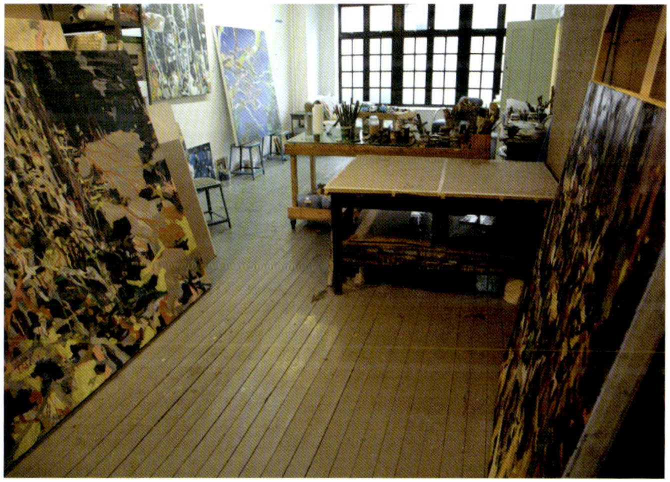

Ann Harwell

Wendell, North Carolina

With a career teaching pre-school and two very active teenage sons, making fabric art was an avocation until 1997 when I moved to an open art studio in downtown Raleigh, North Carolina. The studio allowed interaction with the public and other artists in the building. It was flattering to receive the response of the public, and the support and camaraderie of my fellow artists were wonderful. However, I was on display with constant interruptions and distractions.

By 2012, my sons had homes of their own, so we converted our master bedroom into a studio and moved my work home. The quiet of our home in the country, with garden, flowers, woods, and fields outside the window, is an inspirational change from the busy city streets. There is no drive to and from work. I have a comfortable and intimate studio that I can get to in two seconds and work whenever I want. It is spacious enough to have supplies, equipment, and inventory close at hand. With a palette of thousands of neatly folded fabric pieces, organization by color and pattern is necessary. I have control over the distractions and can hyper-focus. When I am at work, the world falls away and I am in "the zone." The quality and quantity of my work have increased greatly. I am so glad to be home.

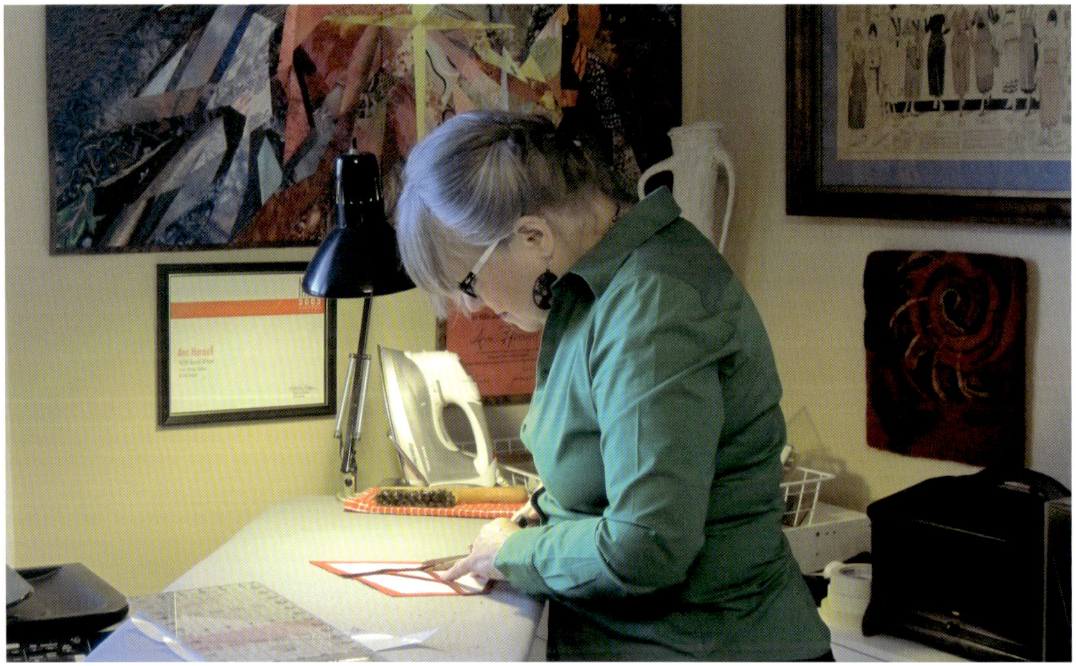

*Ironing with **Orion Nebula** on the wall over my shoulder.*

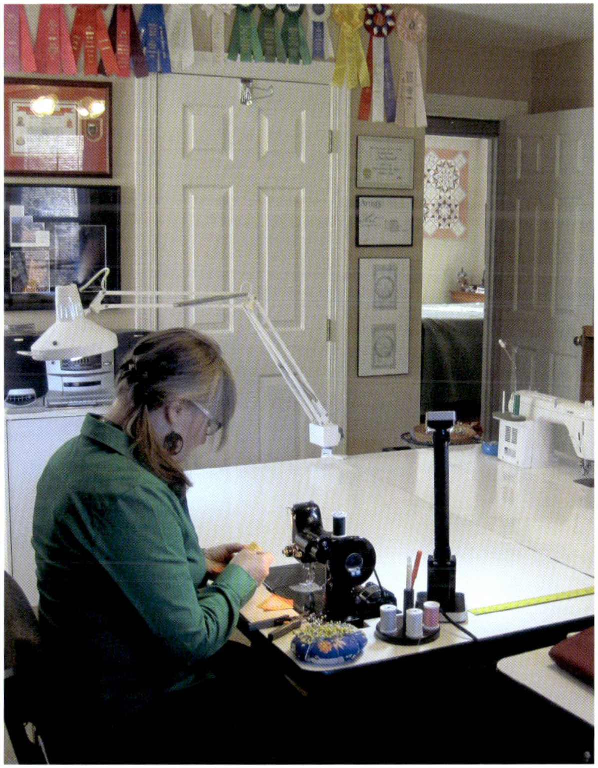

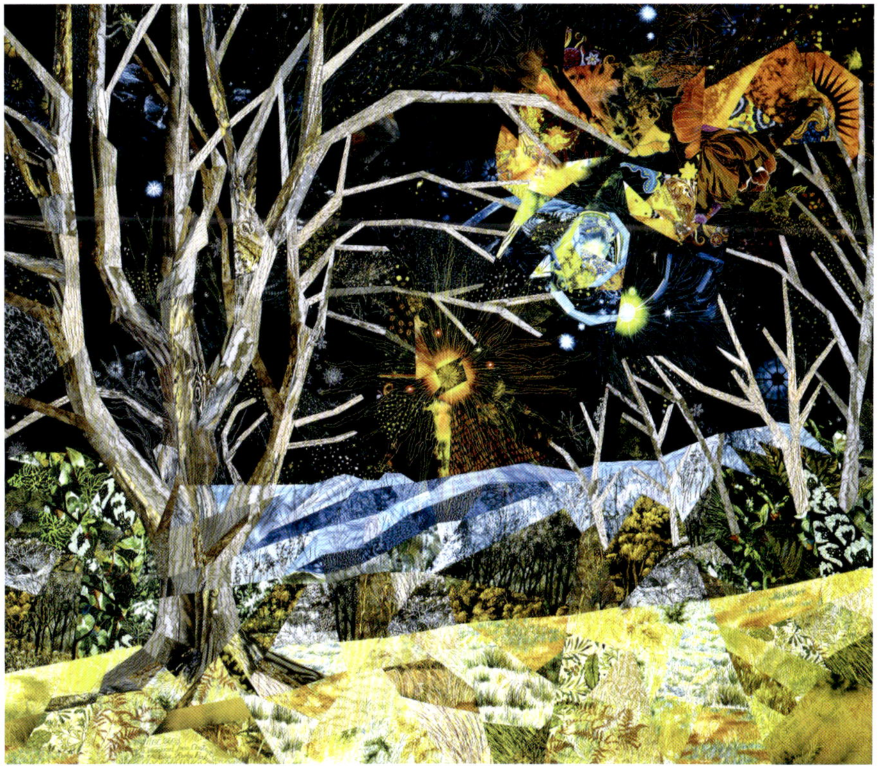

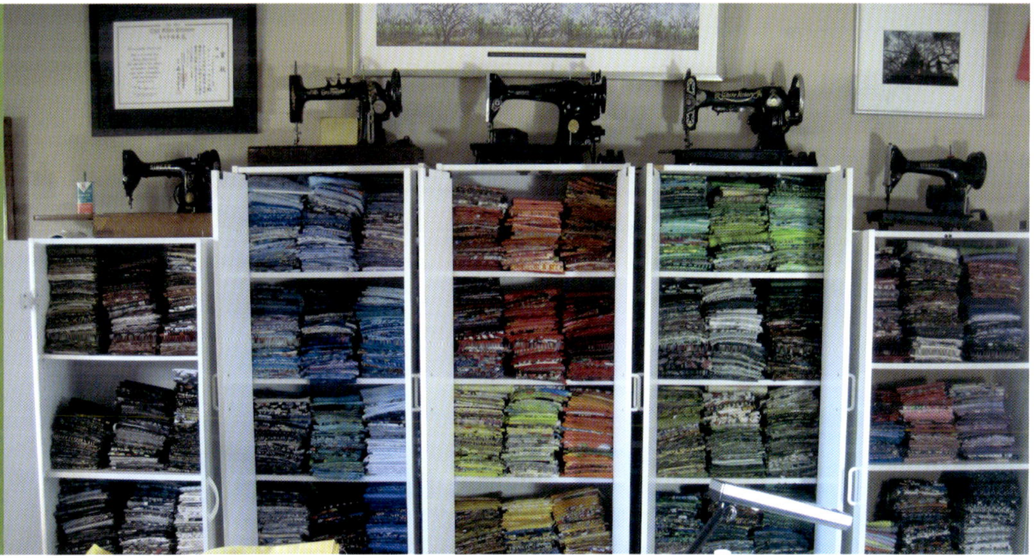

Sewing machines embedded into 30 x 60" tables provide plenty of workspace.

From Whence Heaven? *Fiber. 48 x 57". 2007. Courtesy of Dick Cicone, Raleigh, NC.*

My palette with antique sewing machines on top.

Barbara Krupp

Vero Beach, Florida

My studio is in my home, my own space surrounded by my life. Within a few feet of my easel are my eating, cooking, gardening, and swimming areas. I could not ask for anything better. My large paintings hang on the wall and can be seen in progress by family members and friends alike. I share my life with Allan Teger. Together we have Sunday brunches, dinners, garden tours, art openings, and everyday life. I walk through my gardens each day for inspiration. When painting is finished for the day, I walk to my office where my view is of the pergola garden. I am half way between the Indian River lagoon and the ocean. The soothing sounds of the sea surround me. Next to my office is my storage area where I keep my extra canvas, paint, and brushes.

I work on several paintings at a time. The large ones are usually viewed in the living room until it is time to ship them to the many galleries in which I exhibit.

I have been living in Vero Beach, Florida, for ten years. Although I am a morning painter, I occasionally paint right through the day. A walk to the beach or to the lagoon to watch the sunset is a lovely ending to the painting day. A day of painting, for me, is a labor of love.

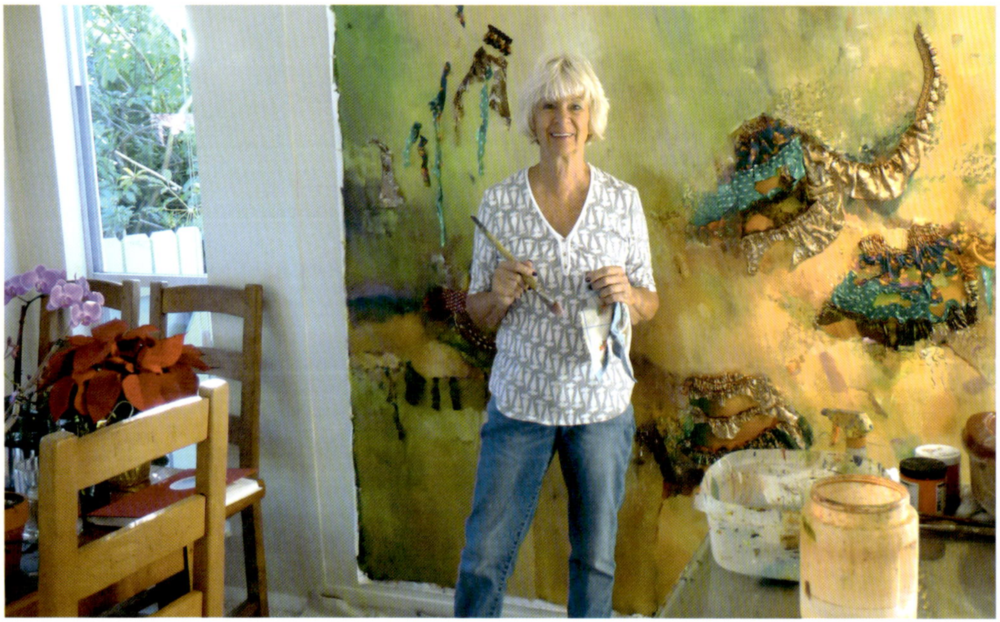

My artwork is painted either on the easel or tacked on the wall. This enables me to work on more than one piece at a time and to be studying them while they are in progress. This painting includes clothing and found objects.

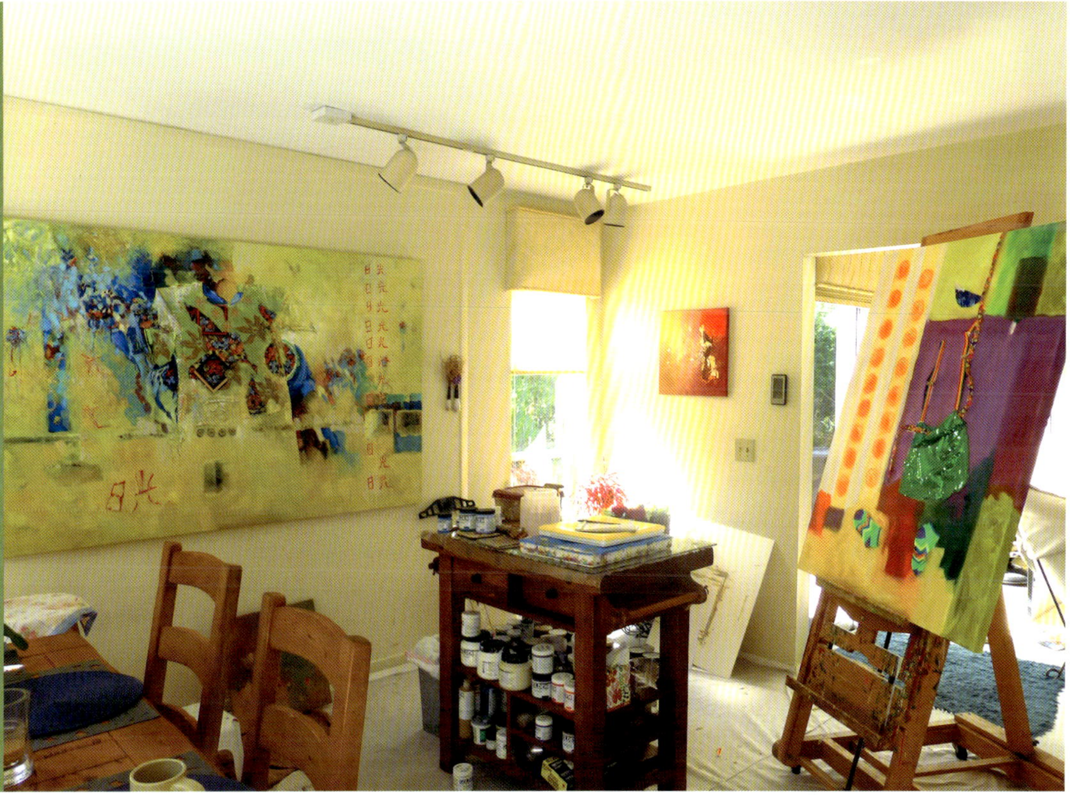

My studio is a shared space with the dining room. I have Sunday brunches, dinners, and everyday meals with friends and patrons next to the place where the art is done. It is an exciting place. Courtesy of Allan Teger.

I think living in the tropics can give your art a more magical tilt, a warm movement, and a colorful touch that cannot be reached when painting in other climates.

I designed the pergola. I wanted a Frank Lloyd Wright look— very simple. I spend time gathering flowers so I can be surrounded by beauty while I paint.

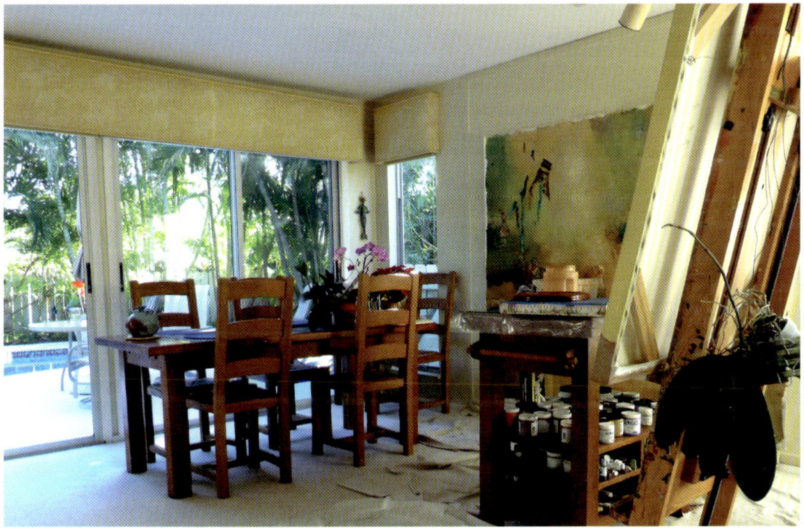

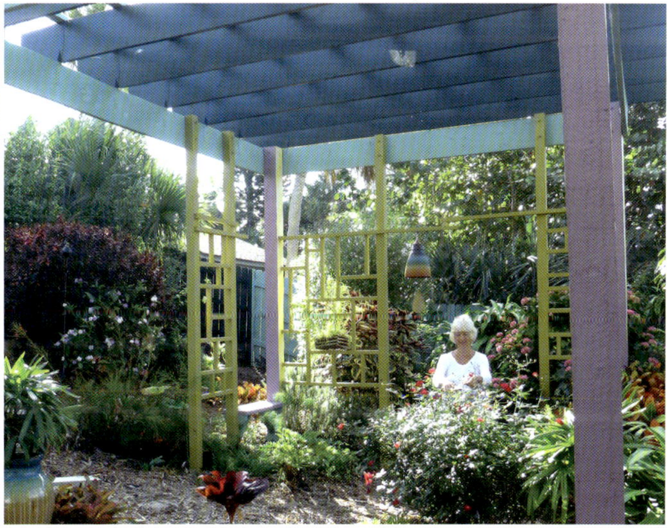

Dorothy Netherland

Charleston, South Carolina

I've worked in several different studios over the years, including one at an art center shared by many artists and a more commercial space with another artist. Now, I am using a space inside my home, and while there are benefits to the other types of studios I've had in the past, my home studio suits me very well these days. Although it's a small space, it gets good light, and I'm grateful that we have an extra room for me to use. Not only is it more convenient to be here at home, it is not a rented space; therefore, it is completely mine. This little blue room is an extension of me!

There are so many advantages to being able simply to go upstairs at any hour to get in some work, but it does require self-discipline to avoid becoming distracted. In the past, I really loved the sense of community one gets in a shared space, but while I think it's still important to regularly have contact with other artists, I no longer feel the need to work around other people. Maybe it came with age, or time, or simply with the understanding, deep down in the bones, that making art is what I do.

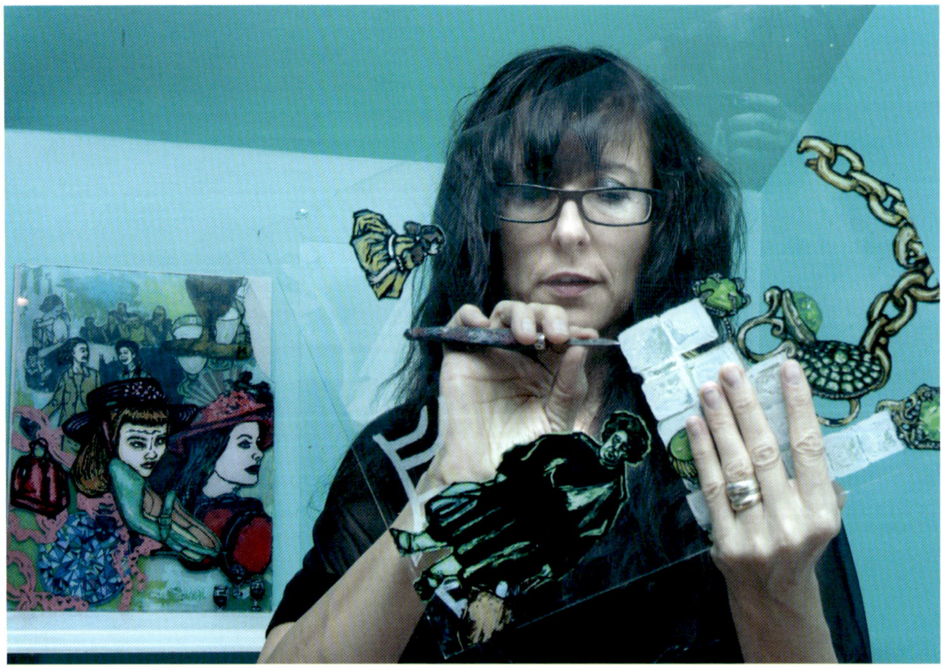

Re-working a pane from ***The Sweet Life****. On the shelf is a broken painting,* ***Twin Set****, 2011.*
Courtesy of Nancy Santos.

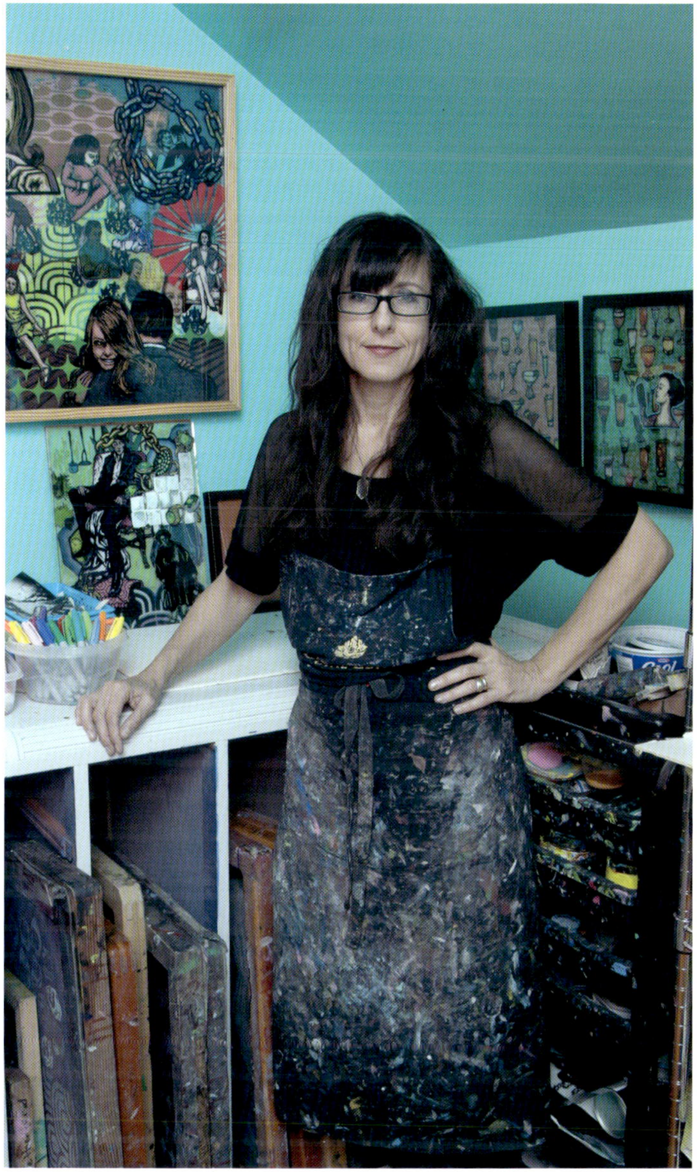

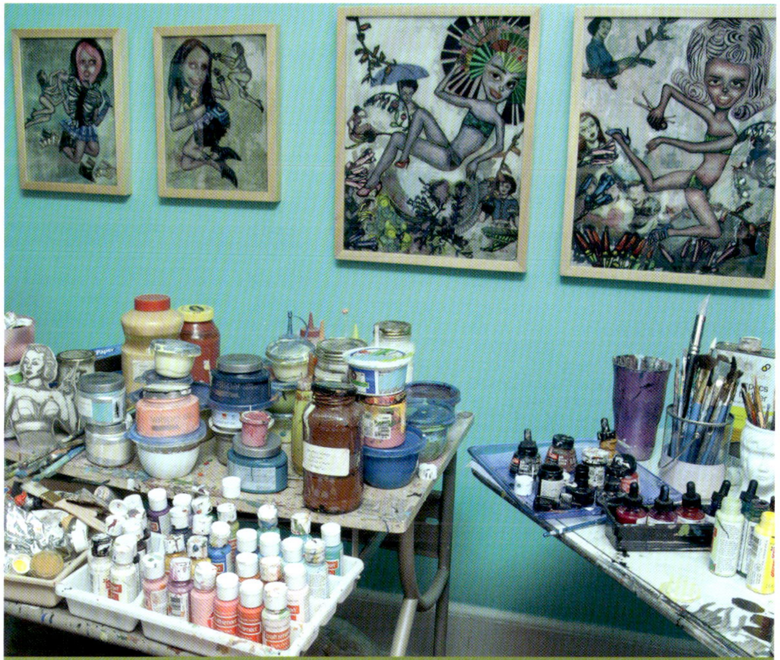

In this corner is the dresser I converted into a table, which holds my screen-printing screens. ***Cry Baby****, 2012, and* ***The Sweet Life****, 2011, are on the wall. Behind me are* ***Happy Hour 1 and 2****. Note: all my paintings seen here are mixed media on glass.* Courtesy of Nancy Santos.

Paint, ink, and other supplies on tables in another corner. On the wall are ***Violent Femme 1*** *and* ***2****, and* ***Velveteen 2*** *and* ***3****.* Courtesy of Nancy Santos

Lynn O'Brien

Cleveland Heights, Ohio

I work in a studio that was added on to the back of my 1924 home by a previous owner. I prefer having my studio at home because it allows me to work on my art whenever I want. I don't have to drive anywhere or have big chunks of time available. I just walk down a few steps from the living room or kitchen, and I'm there, ready to go. I think my art is more a part of my daily life than if my studio were somewhere else.

The studio is lower than the rest of the house. It was built on a slab of concrete rather than on a foundation, so, to me, it has a feeling of being separate from the house even though it is not physically separate. The previous owners used the space as a recreation room, but I learned that it was originally built as a home studio space for a well-known local sculptor. I like knowing this, because I feel that I've brought the studio back to its intended purpose. My studio isn't huge so it can get pretty messy when I have a deadline, but it's my space, dedicated solely for making art, and I love hanging out in there, even on a bad day.

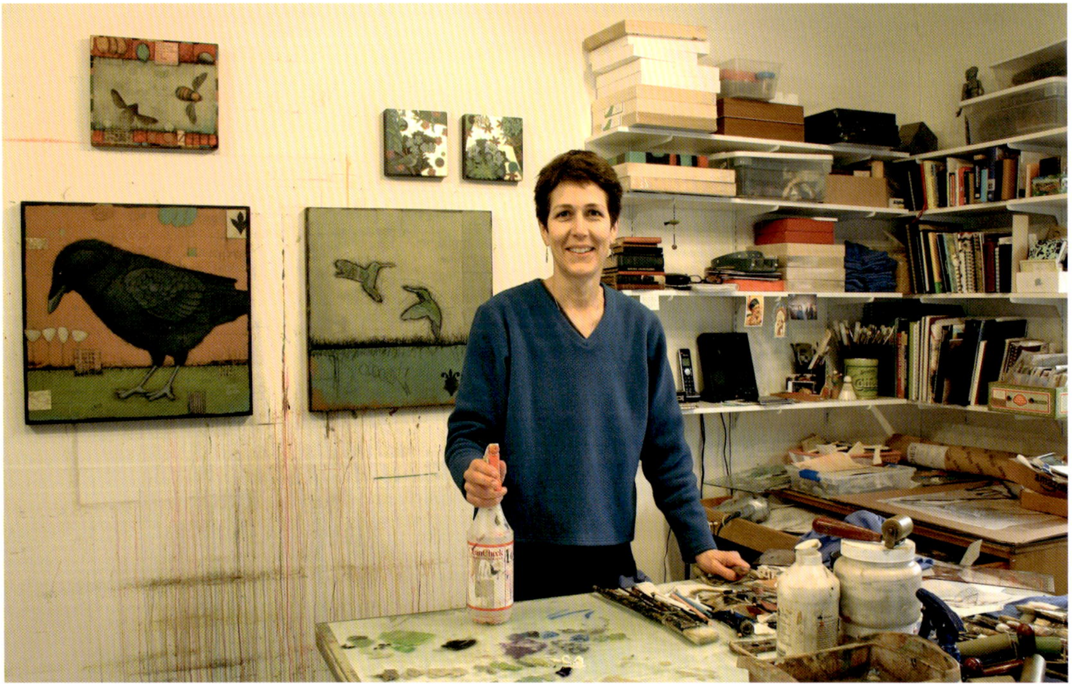

I use the wall behind me as an easel. I put rows of nails in the wall at different heights so I can hang differently sized panels and move things around easily. ***Raven with Flowers*** *(left) is a mixed media piece recently completed. Shelves in the back corner store unused panels, my laptop, small books, and plastic bins with natural objects I have collected.* Courtesy of Mark Willis.

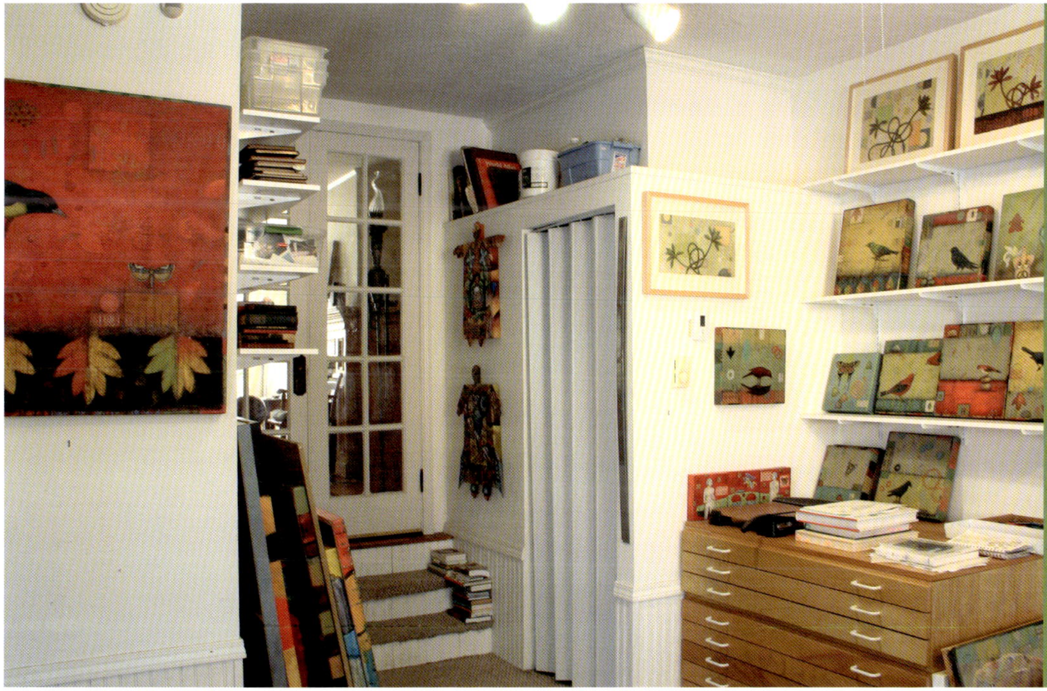

My studio has a mostly glass exterior doorway that lets in light and makes it easy for me to load my car. I installed shelving for storing and displaying smaller finished pieces (shown are various pieces from my ***Garden*** *and* ***Forms from Nature*** *series). I stack and hang larger current works against the walls (left). My mixed media painting,* ***Forms from Nature #20****, is shown on the wall. Flat files store paper, collage and reference material, and finished paper pieces.*

My work area sits between two large windows on the left and the exterior studio door on the right. I store and use my larger reference books at this table and develop preliminary drawings here. The shelves hold multiple bins with drawers that store and organize smaller collage materials and tools.

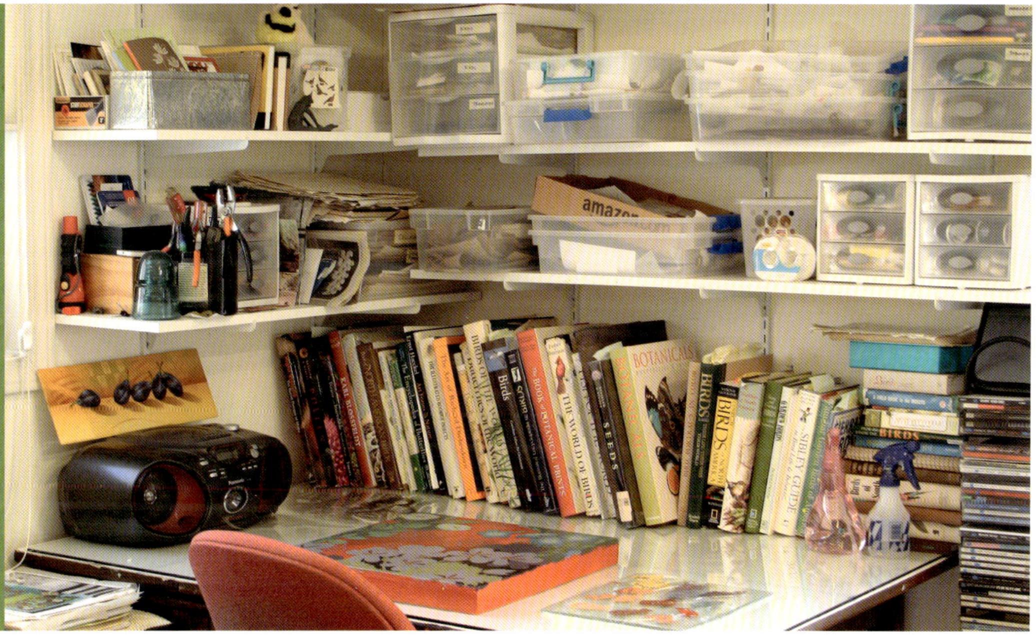

Mel Rea

Cleveland Heights, Ohio

I'm often asked if I find it difficult working out of my house. My typical response is, "No, I love it. Don't you find it difficult leaving the house to get to work!" My home is a charm-filled brick bungalow in northeast Ohio. I tend to work throughout the day in waves of inspiration. Between the waves, I re-center myself with quiet tasks such as walking my dog, tending my garden, re-inventing a soup recipe, or flipping through my many beautiful art books that are a constant source of inspiration.

I work in different rooms depending on the medium. When seeking new ideas and color combinations, I often work things out on paper in my upstairs studio. I acquired a huge antique drafting table that I visualize being filled with memories of artistic creations from years past. I find I'm most inspired around mid-morning, just after 10 a.m., when light spills in from the large picture window.

When flipping between oil paints or encaustics, I morph into a "basement troll." With the windows opened, fans whirring, and the beeswax warming, I fill my jars with turpentine and squeeze pigment-filled oils from their tubes. It's time to loosen up. I feel complete freedom to splash, drip, squeeze, burn, scrape, or whatever my work is calling out to me.

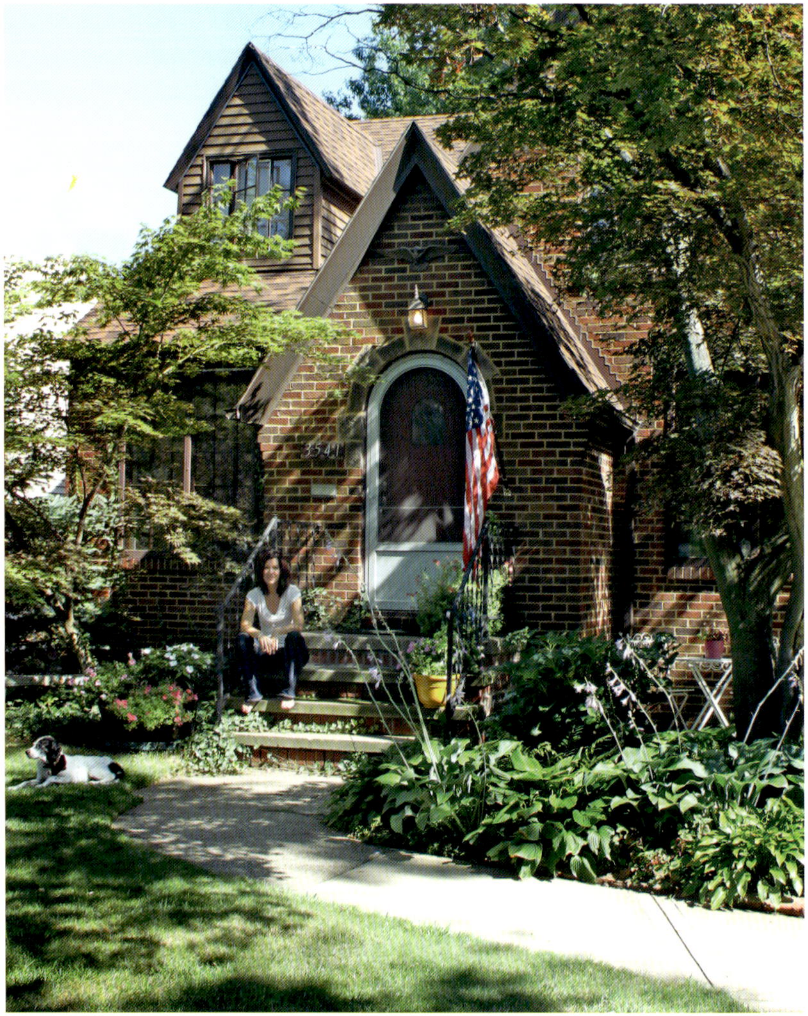

My 1939 brick bungalow home and studio.
Courtesy of Carrie Reagh.

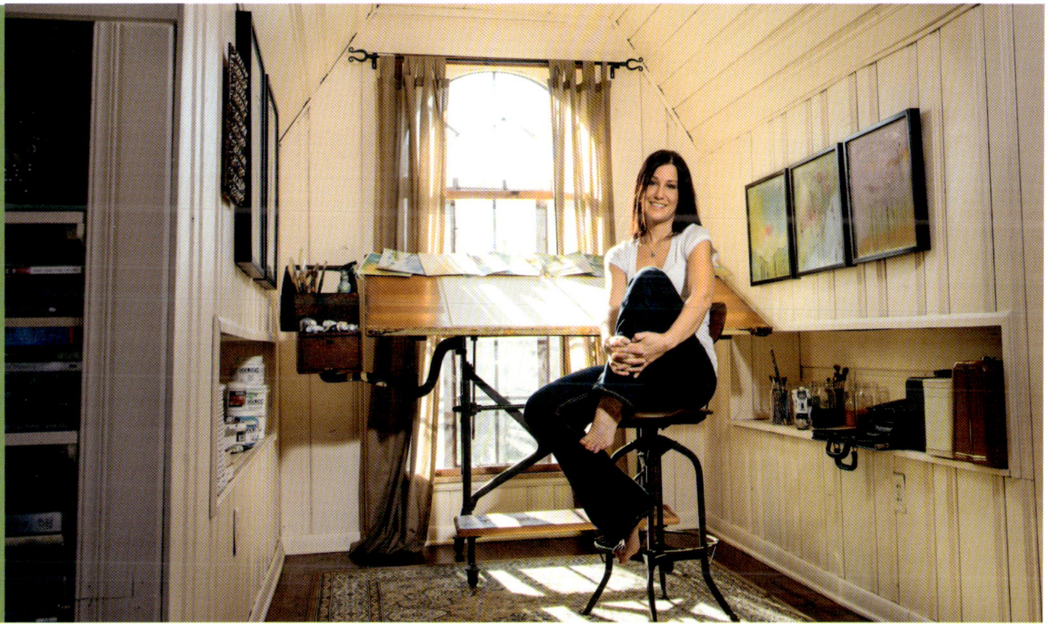

My room for watercolor and works on paper. Courtesy of Chris Langer.

My encaustic and oil painting studio. Courtesy of Chris Langer.

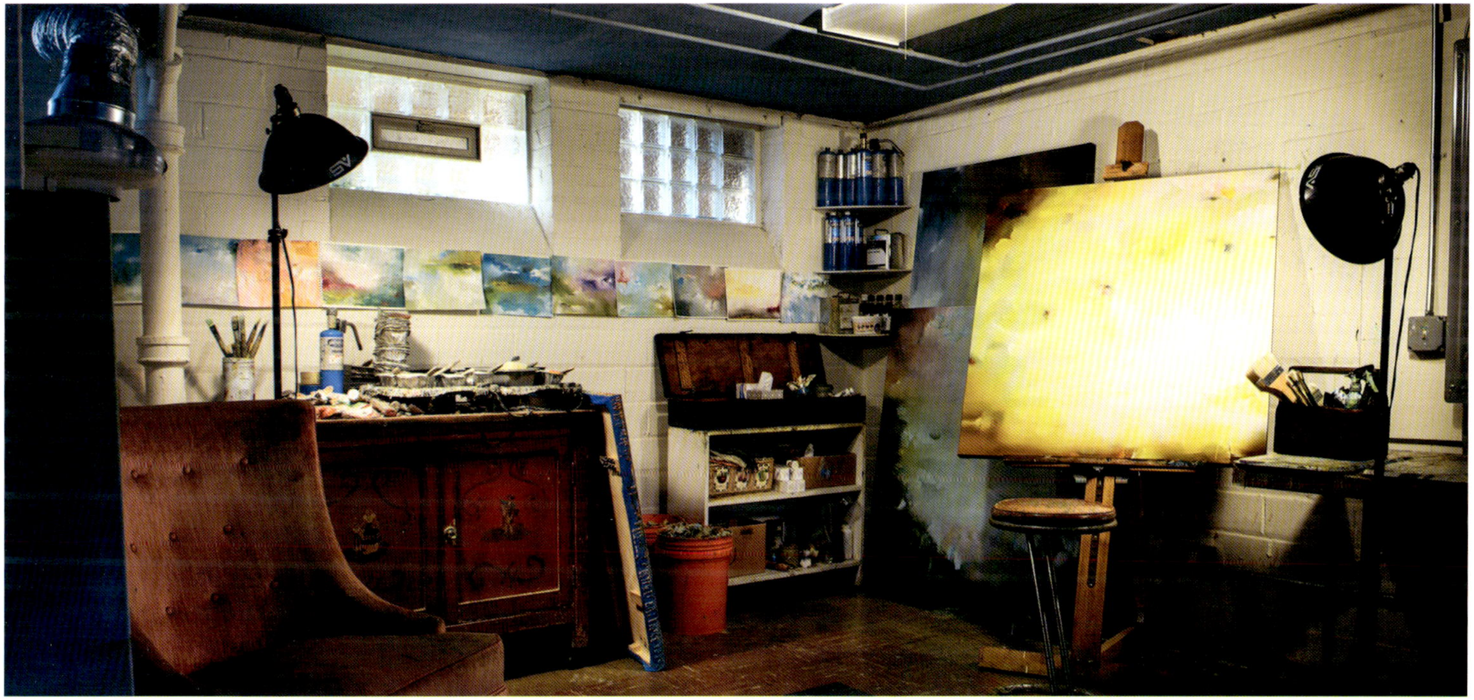

Paul Santolieri

Philadelphia, Pennsylvania

My Philadelphia home is an old structure from the 1820s, where I also keep my studio, in what was once a row of four workers houses. Each of these is called a "trinity" because of the layout of three rooms, one on top of the other. Its cottage-like feel and simple masonry structure provide a support for my work as an artist. Inside I use the walls and rooms like a collage, a shifting arrangement of color and objects I'm working on. In the backyard, a glass mosaic and relief are progressively creeping up the brick exterior, emerging from the garden floor, fabricated from leftover materials from projects and collected from my travels. There's an overall design for the walls, and I work on it in between travels. I also invite collaborators to add small portions of their work to the piece, to create an assortment of gestures and responses from other minds, adding color, light, and reflections to the building. Inside, I use the sunlit attic and cave-like basement as a workspace. Although it is small, I make the most of every inch I can use. A lot of my work is installation, site-specific, and public pieces, and I use the home space as my point of departure.

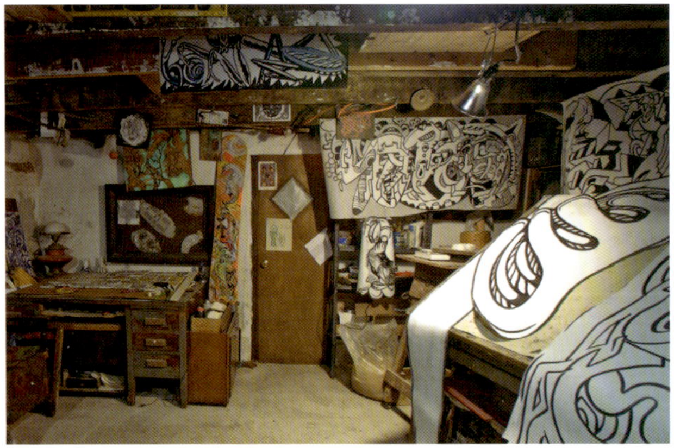

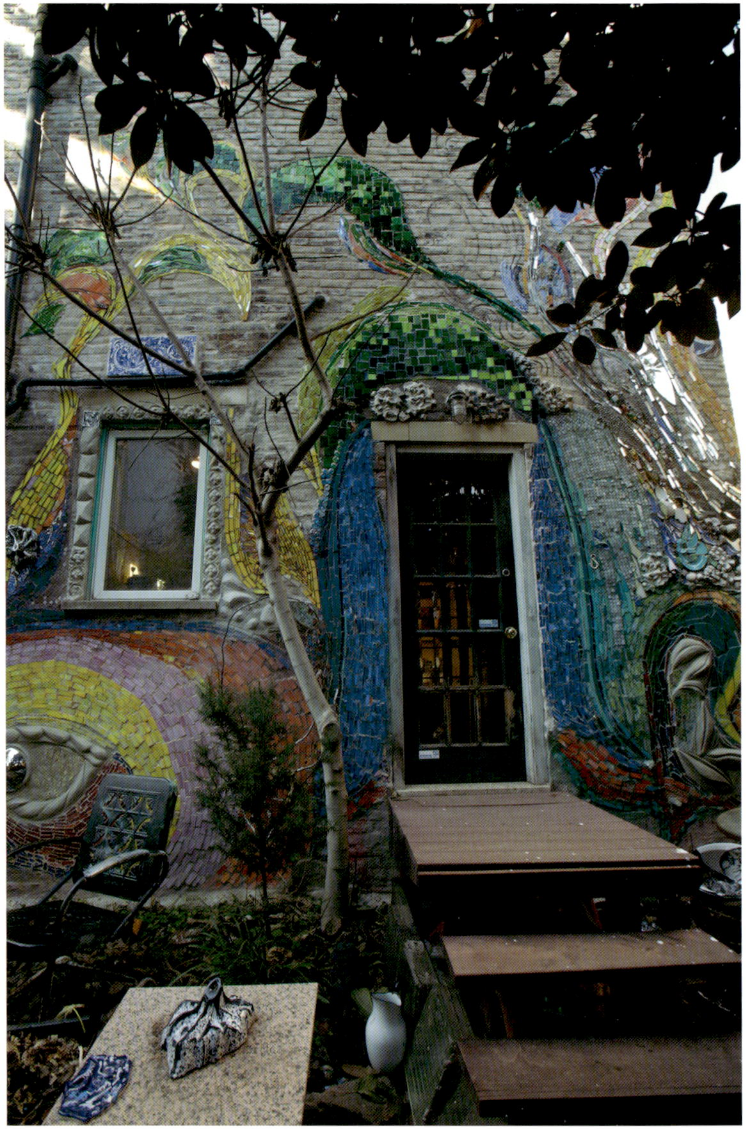

*Garden with **Headtree** mosaic.*

Basement with various black and white ink drawings on cloth.

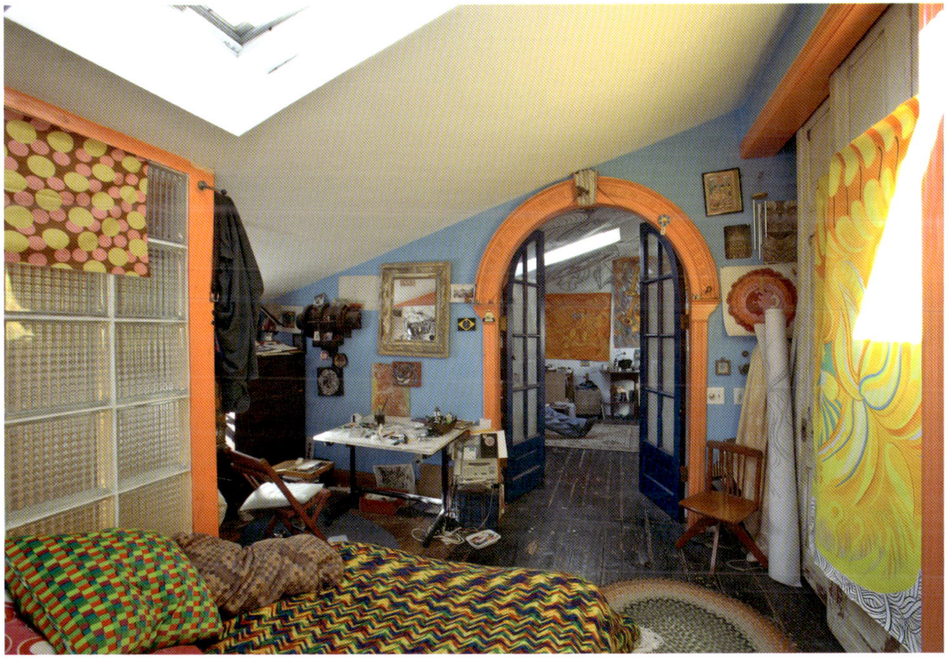

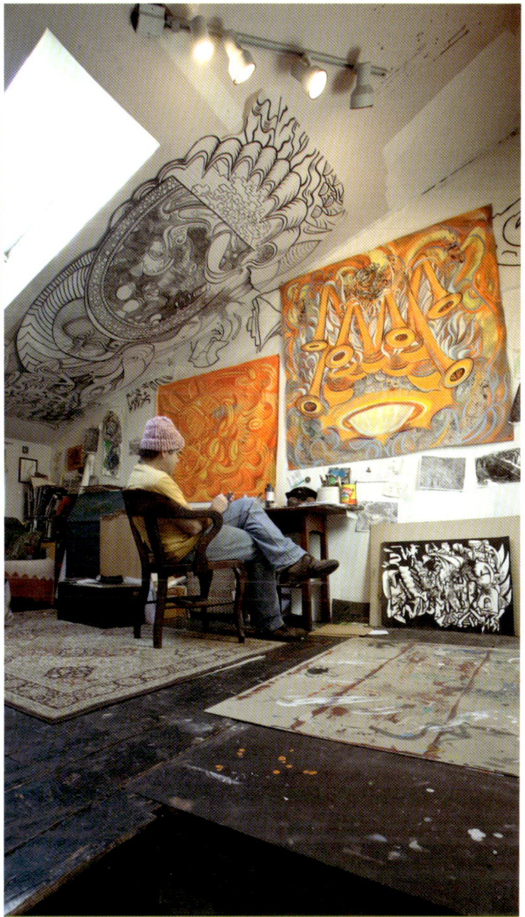

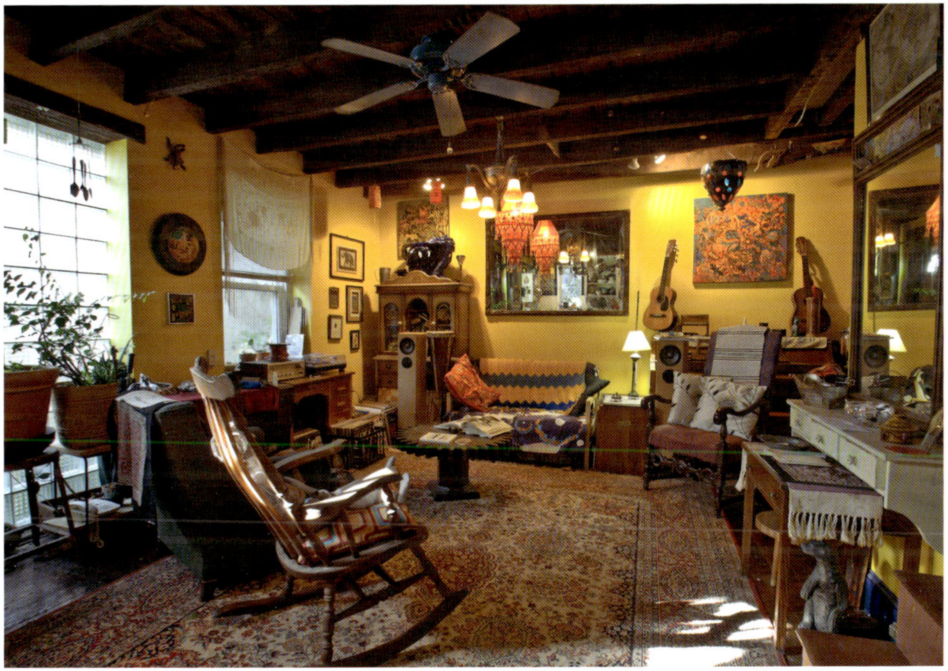

Arched doors separate the two rooms in my attic studio. This room is for sleeping and working on desktop drawings.

The first floor with ***Dragonflor****, acrylic on canvas, on wall.*

The other room contains larger works on the wall such as ***Trumpet Flower****, acrylic on polytab, and* ***Left Brain****, ink on polycloth, on the ceiling.*

W. Gerome Temple

Savannah, Georgia

Set in an 1890s historic home in Savannah, Georgia, the view from my drafting table looks onto hundred-year-old live oak trees dripping with Spanish moss. The interior of my studio epitomizes the maximum usage of a small space; I have filled every inch of my studio with inspiration, from a large carnival puppet looming over one corner of the room to shelves covered with antique toys, figurines, and ancient relics from the past. As an illustrator who works with pen and ink on paper, my studio needs are minimal: a clean work surface and ample light.

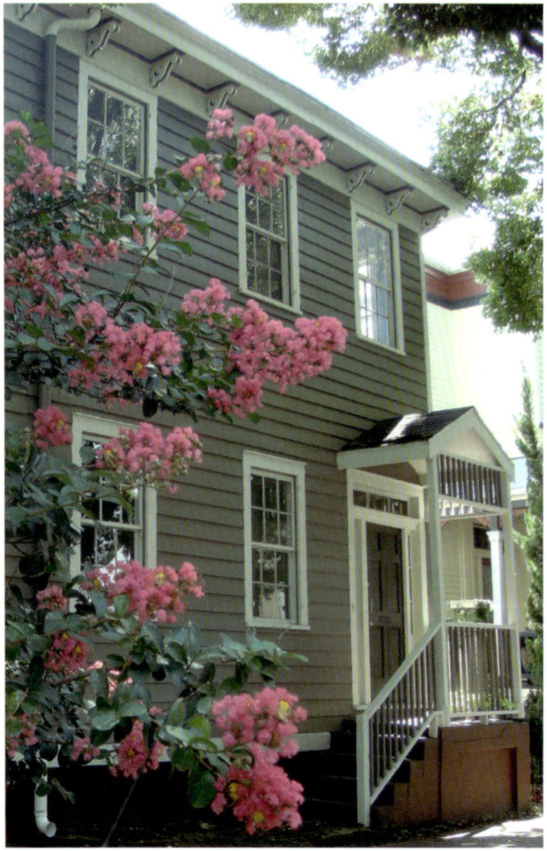

My studio is housed in my Colonial-style, 1890s townhome, located in the historic district of Savannah, Georgia.

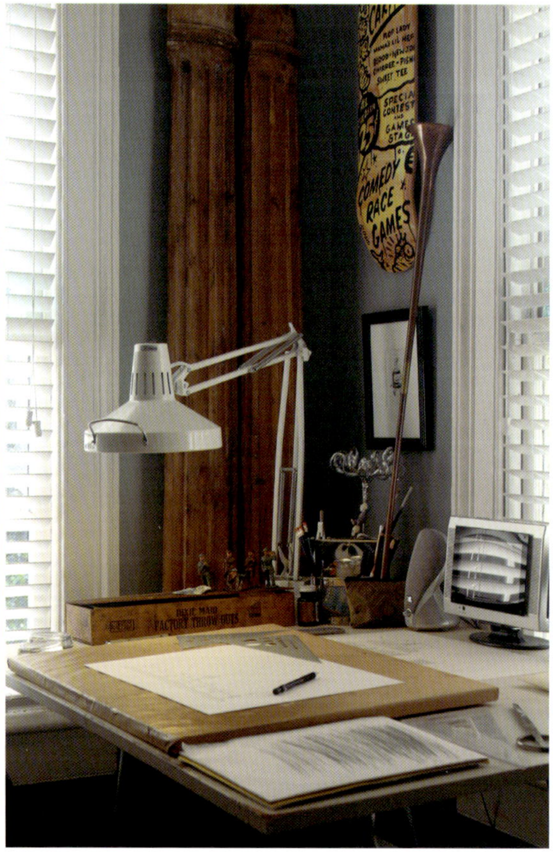

Saturated by light, my drawing table sits next to salvaged pillar fragments. Drawing tools are laid out for quick access.

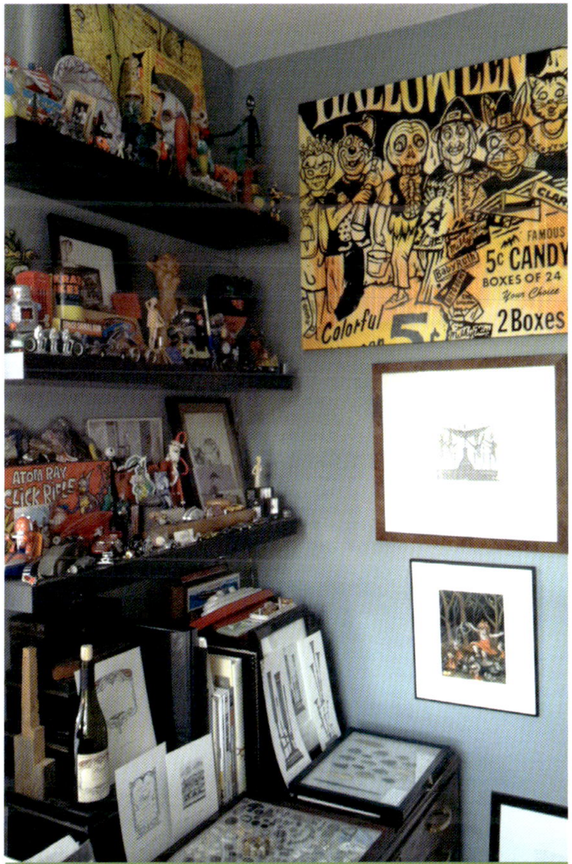

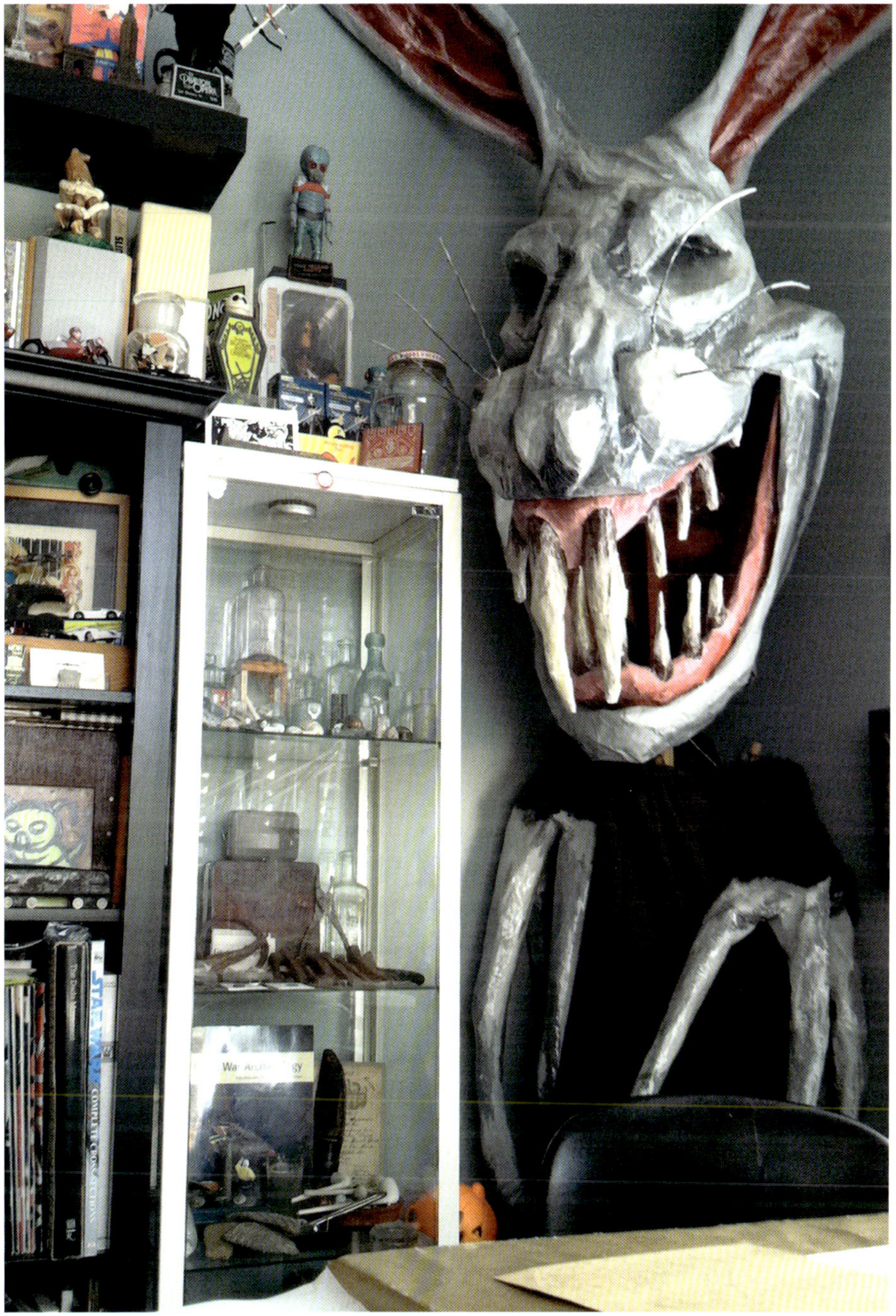

On the flat file are cases of artifacts. Above are shelves filled with inspiration. Many of these collectable toys are from my childhood or from my grandparent's collection. On the wall are works of art by fellow illustrators and myself (top to bottom) ***Halloween Candy*** *by R. Land,* ***Puppet Parade*** *by W. Gerome Temple, and a gouache painting by Benji Williams.*

Big Wig*, my first 14-foot tall giant carnival puppet, looms over my shoulder while I draw. The cabinet next to the puppet is filled with artifacts excavated from my yard and pieces found throughout Europe. The back of my studio door features work by Gary Baseman and R. Land.*

Claudia G. Thomas

Winter Park, Florida

I live in a condo and have converted my second bedroom into a working studio. I can paint at night or on overcast days because of two cool and two warm daylight florescent bulbs suspended from the ceiling. Without proper lighting, the colors in the finished painting would not reflect those in the natural world. I use stackable, heavy-duty plastic shelving all the way to the ceiling to hold unused canvases and smaller finished paintings. Standard-sized frames are stored on steel racks. Bottles of varnish, mediums, and solvents are kept in a corner space on a steel mesh shower caddy. I use rubber floor runners from Home Depot over the carpet around my easel to protect the floor from paint splatters. I utilize two of the plastic shelves stacked as a taboret, where I have my palette, mineral spirits, palette knives, and brushes. Tubes of paint are stored in dividers and are easily accessible in a storage box near the easel. Large Tupperware storage bins against the wall hold finished unframed paintings. Paintings are everywhere in various stages of drying.

The balcony overlooks a canal that connects two lakes, so I have plenty of fresh air and north light through my studio window. In the cooler months (eight months of the year), I move my equipment out onto the balcony. I paint plein air landscapes, so most of the year I am outdoors at various local sites, but finish the paintings in the studio.

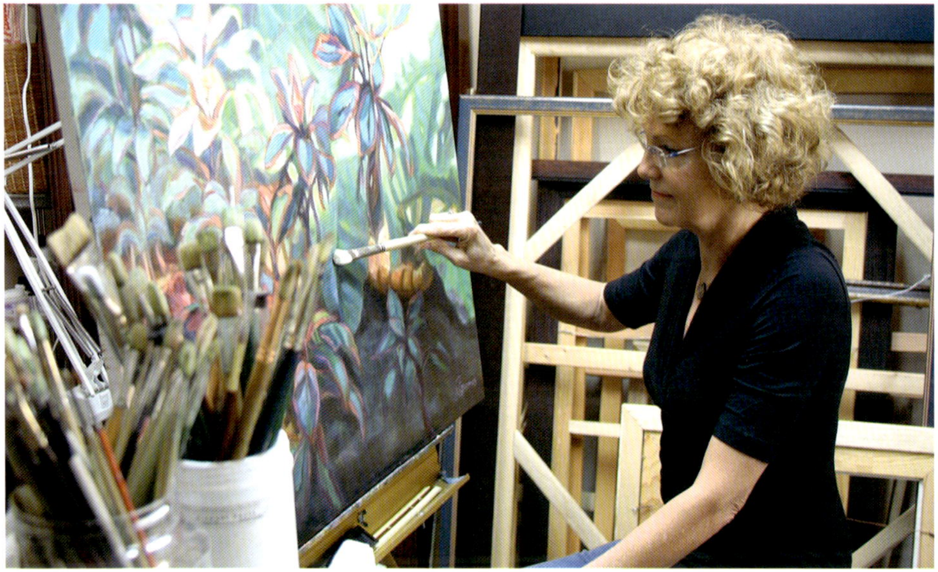

Here I am working on ***Red Lilies****. 2012.*

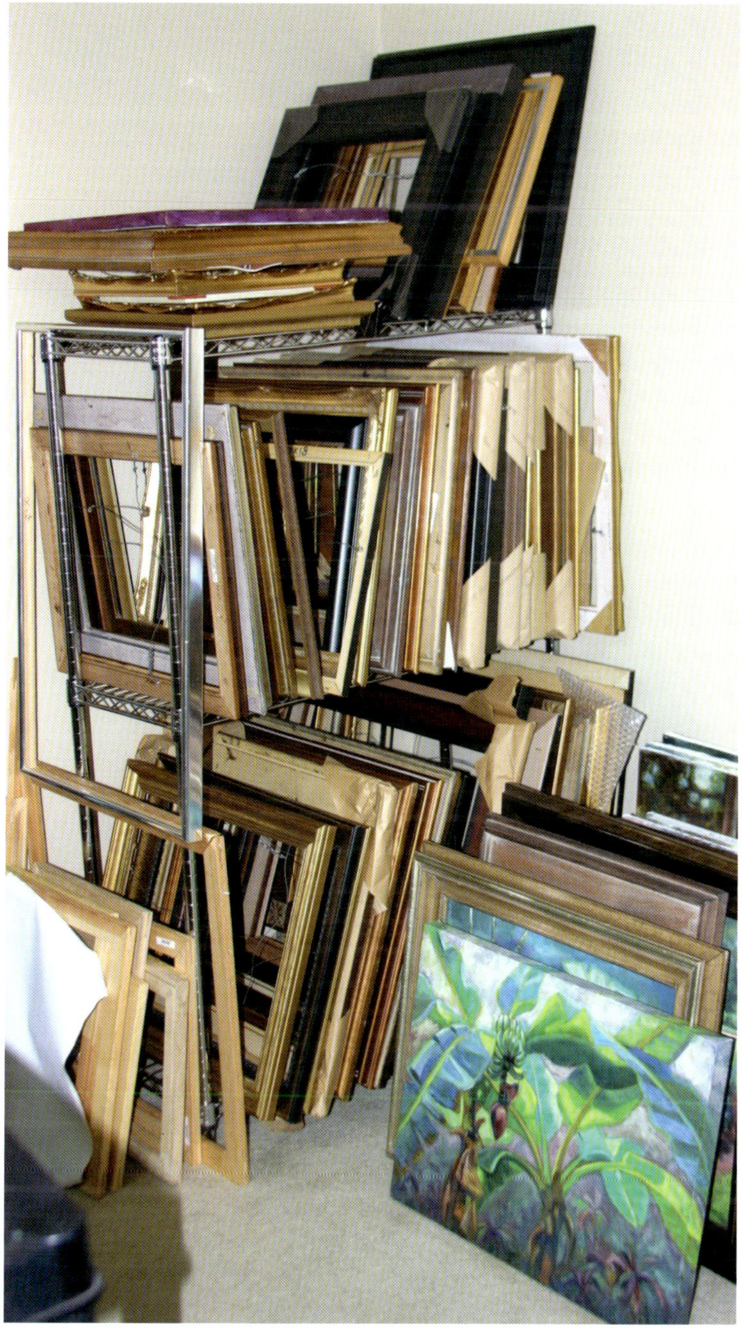

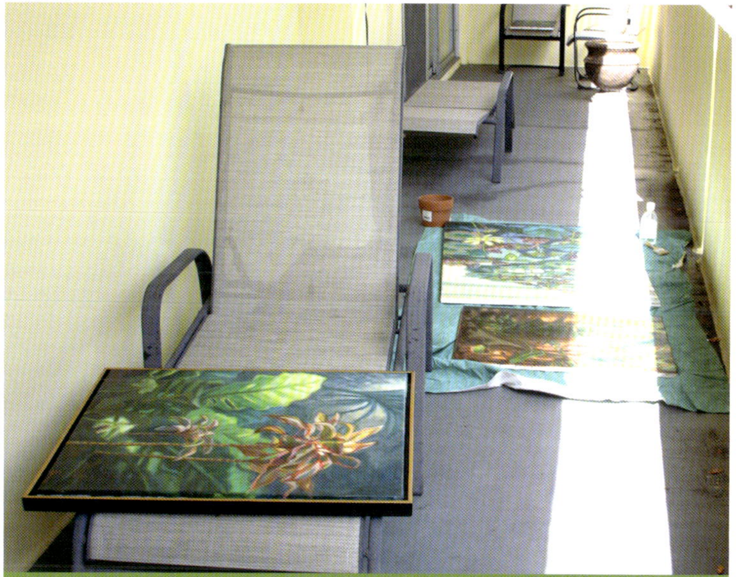

Frames stored on stainless steel racks purchased at Home Depot. ***Banana Palms****, 2011, on the floor.*

Varnished paintings drying on my fourth floor balcony, which overlooks the canal that connects two lakes.

Mary Lou Alberetti

New Fairfield, Connecticut

My studio, which is part of my home, is a wonderful space for inspiration and creation. This 50-foot-long studio has grown over the years. Skylights and walls of windows punctuate the recent addition, with its granite worktable and large showroom. It provides me with the perfect space and light for creating my unique ceramic sculpture, ceramic reliefs, and mixed-media collage pieces. A separate area holds my slab roller, kilns, clay mixer, and glaze materials. An outdoor shed and gas kiln extend the working space.

My shelves are heavy with books on architecture and the hundreds of photos collected from my travels in Italy, Turkey, France, Spain, and other countries where architectural gems have inspired and challenged me. My walls are filled with photos of textures, colors, stones, arches, columns, ancient walls, and sketches of incubating ideas. Many tables are filled with works in progress.

Forms imagined and perceived begin to evolve in the atmosphere of my studio. My sculptures, reliefs, and collages (multilayered textured pieces) attempt to capture light, color, and atmosphere. Through these works, I seek to evoke the depth and mystery of the human experience. It is my hope that the joy and passion of creating these works in my studio can elicit the same kind of joy for the viewer.

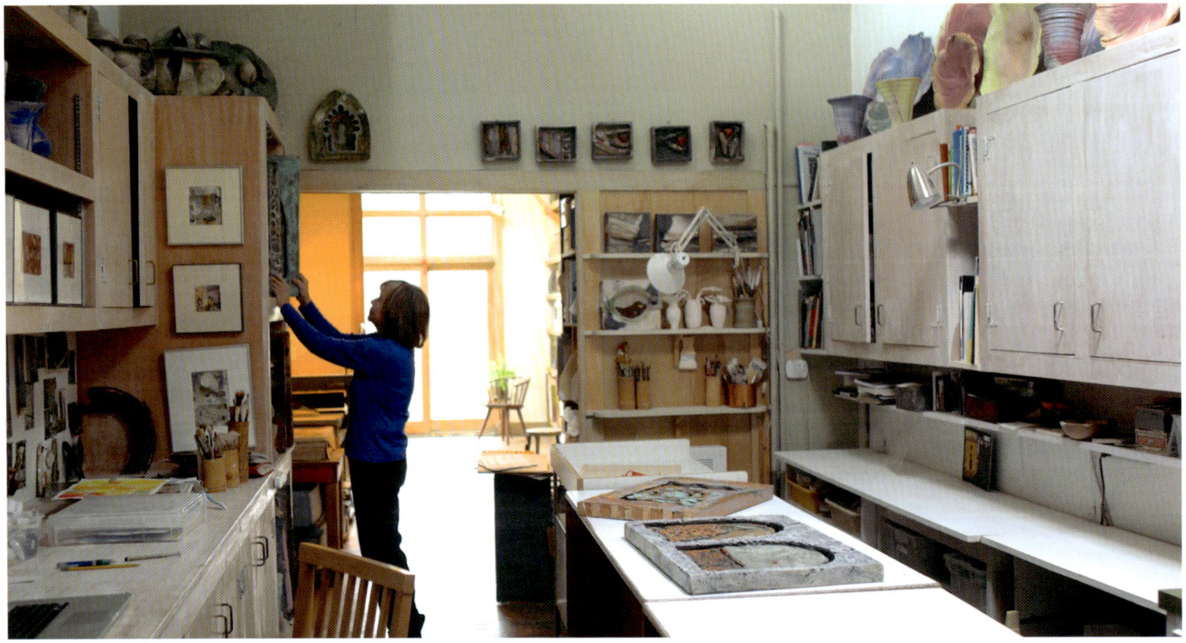

Many cabinets and shelves on both sides of the studio provide ample storage and display areas. This view in the primary work area looks into the equipment area, the exhibition area, and the doors leading to the outdoor kiln and storage shed. The walls and upper shelves are filled with examples of earlier work.

Under a large skylight is a perfect work area—one of several large worktables with built-in storage. I designed these tables with wheels so I can move them to reconfigure my workspace.

Ceramic reliefs are displayed on specially designed, custom-built, sturdy oak shelves with additional storage racks below.

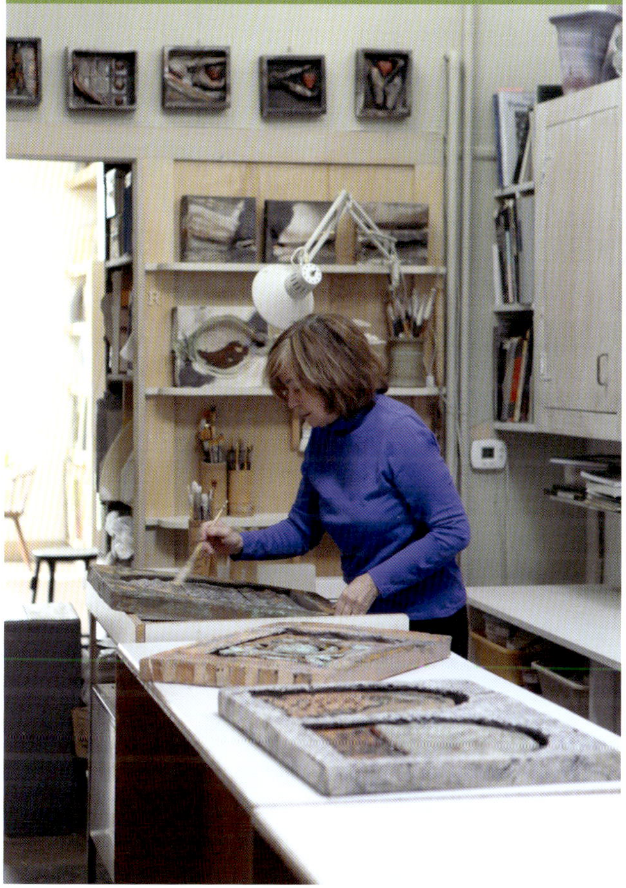

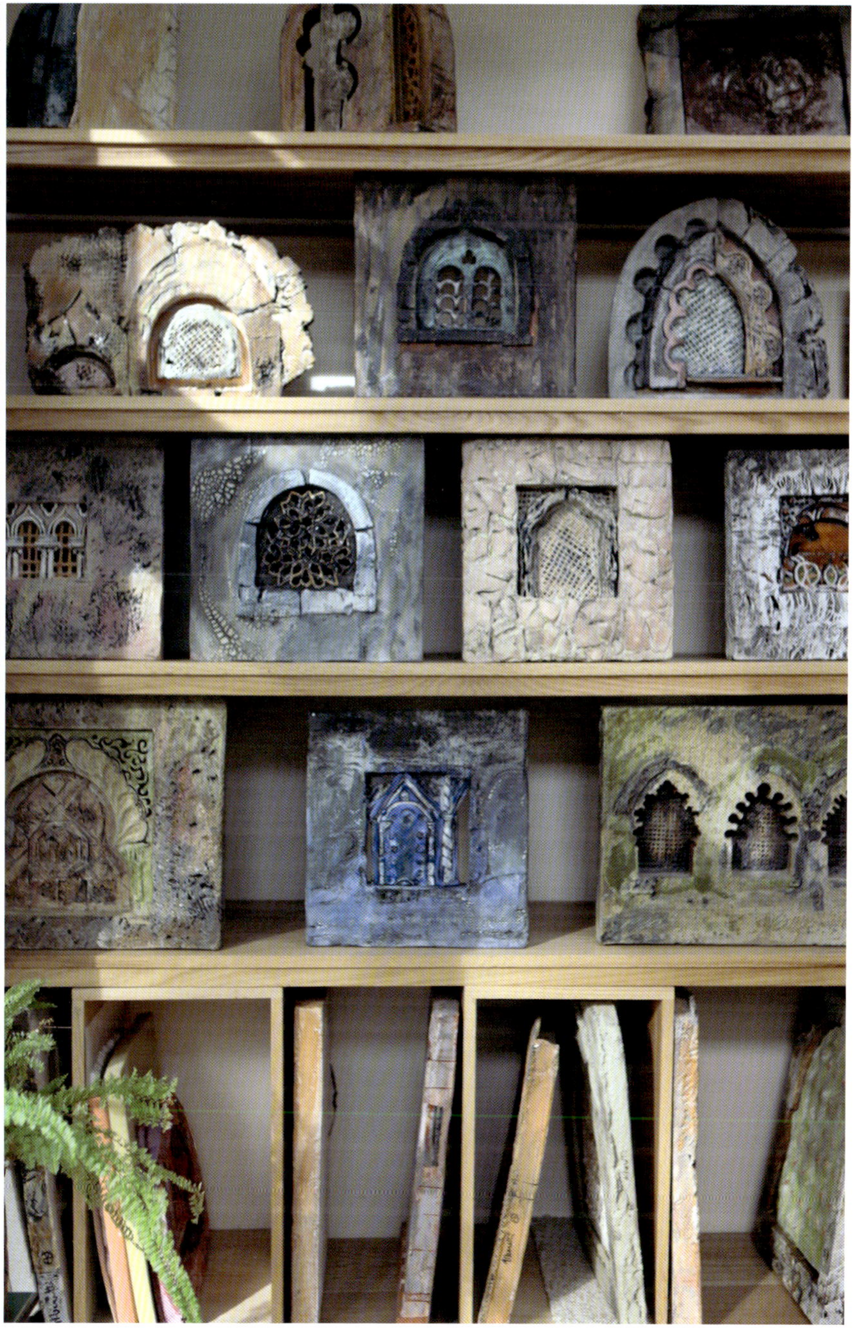

Steven Alexander

Dalton, Pennsylvania

In 2002, my wife, Laura, and I designed and built our home and studio on four rural acres in the hills of eastern Pennsylvania, about two hours west of New York City. To minimize our footprint, we stacked the spaces: studio on the first floor, living on the second floor, and sleeping on the third. The studio is about 1,000 square feet with an 11-foot ceiling, concrete floor, and natural light from numerous windows. The space is U-shaped with a central stairway that also contains storage racks.

This is the first time in many years that my studio and living spaces have been combined, and it has been a great solution. As we raised our two daughters, the convenience of proximity created a relatively seamless flow between work and life, allowing me to work in the spaces of time as they occurred. The space is wonderfully flexible, and I change the studio configuration constantly to accommodate the needs of each new project.

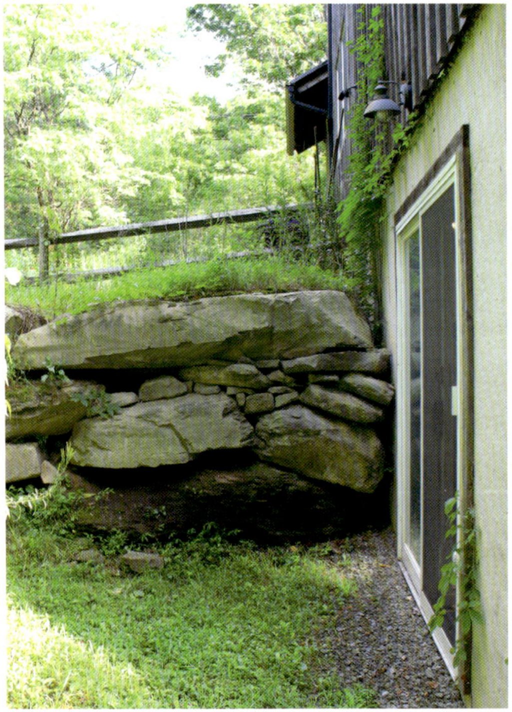

The inauspicious studio entrance is at the end of a curving path that leads downhill from the front of the house. Of course, there is also an interior studio entrance.

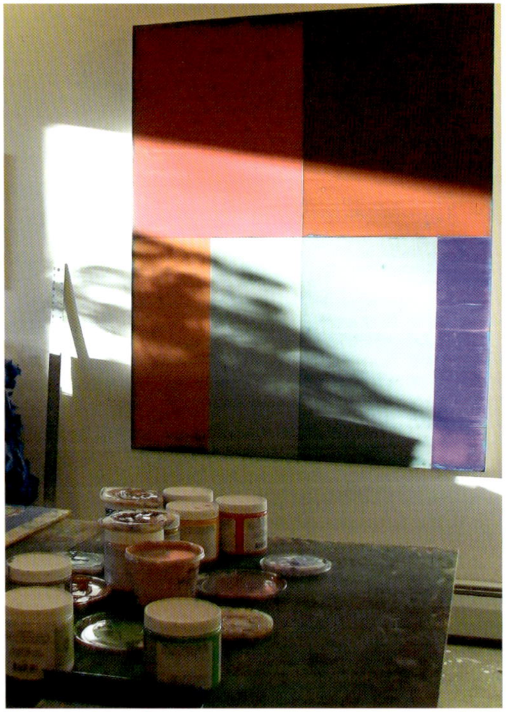

Early morning light illuminates ***Chronology,*** *surrounded by worktables and tools, including a big chunk of used masking tape.*

Body Double (72 x 54") leans on the studio's central column; beyond is a work area with the largest window.

You can see a corner of my primary worktable and a nice combination of natural and incandescent light.

Since I usually work on my paintings horizontally, the concrete floor has accumulated a beautiful patina. This painting, **Shift #5** (12 x 144"), composed of twelve separate canvases, is now in a private collection in Houston.

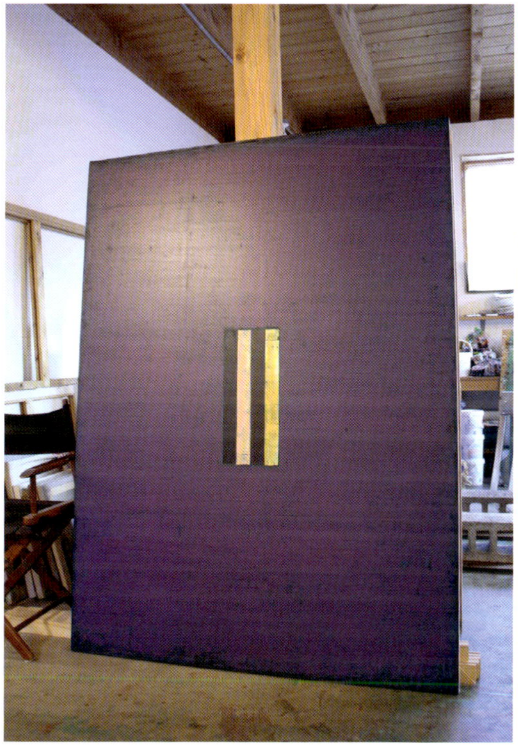

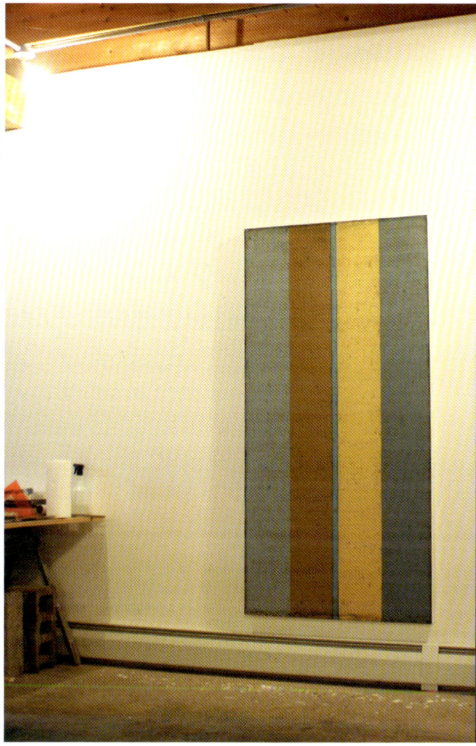

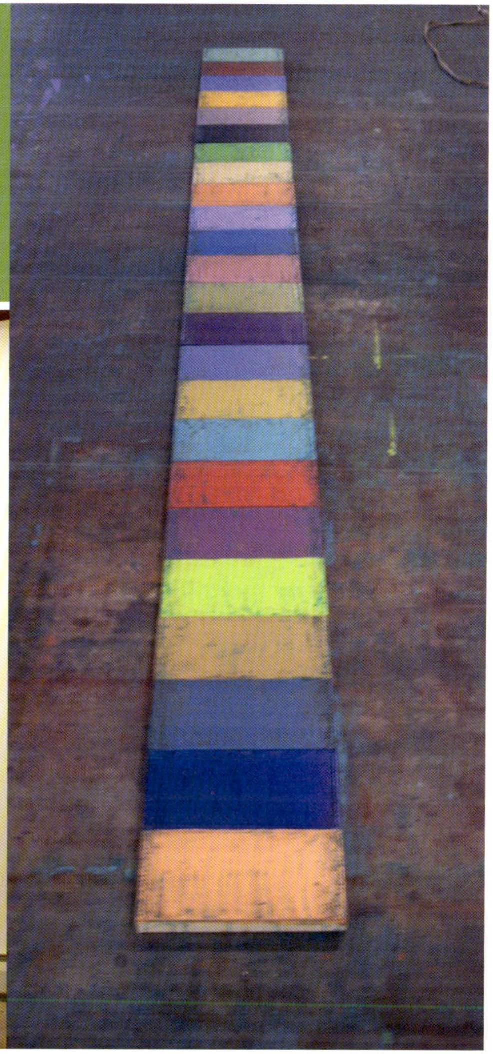

Alice Ballard

Greenville, South Carolina

Refuge. Gift. Inspiration. Creative cocoon. My studio is all these things to me. Its quiet, meditative space energizes and nurtures my creativity. It is where I balance the demands of teaching and of creating art.

I also cherish my studio as a special gift from my husband, Roger Dalrymple, an artist and architect. When we moved to South Carolina from Alaska, Roger designed and built our modern home renovation, transforming an older brick ranch into an open, contemporary home. My studio is part of an addition that looks out on our ever-evolving gardens. With its high ceilings, open beams, white walls, skylights, and numerous windows that invite the natural light of the changing seasons, my studio is a stimulating space for creating art.

The beauties of nature have intrigued me since childhood, when my grandparents taught me about gardening. As a painter, the landscape became my theme; today, I focus on nature's fascinating forms. In my studio, natural treasures sit alongside my ceramic sculptures. Working in clay now connects my two loves: gardening and art. The natural flow of working in my garden and my studio—often simultaneously—has become part of the rhythm of my daily life. It is there that I feel at one with life and the natural world.

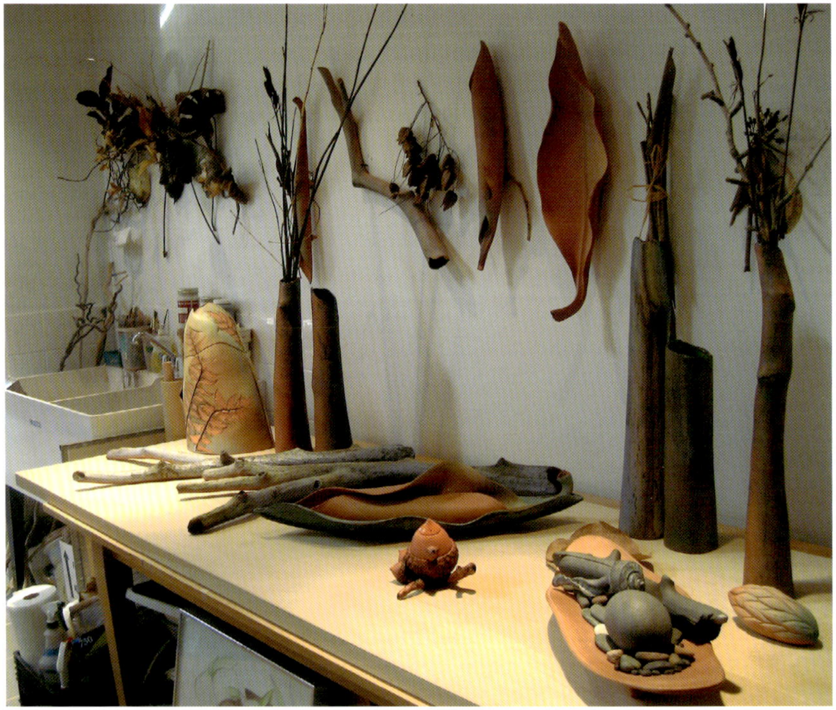

A wall graced with both collected natural treasures and my clay interpretations greets the visitor on entering the studio.

*Our home is an ideal extension of my studio. In front of the fireplace, is a daybed designed and fabricated by my husband, Roger Dalrymple, to complement a Bertoia chair. My **Pod Trio** is installed above the fireplace. A pair of crepe myrtle containers showcases fall grasses collected from our gardens.*

My chair gives me a view of our gardens. Through the windows, the afternoon sun lights everything with golden hues and long shadows.

*A forest of crepe myrtle containers covers a maple table in the center of my studio. Standing by my reading chair is **Tree Totem IX**. Wall niches contain examples of my white work sculpture series.*

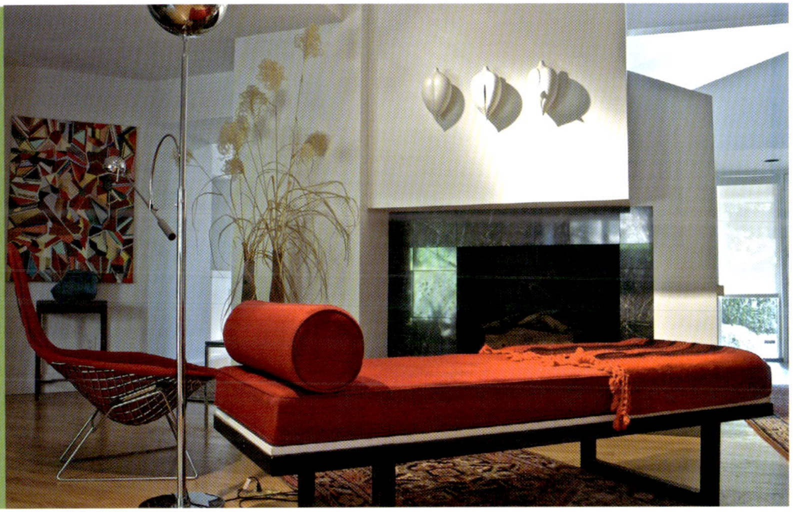

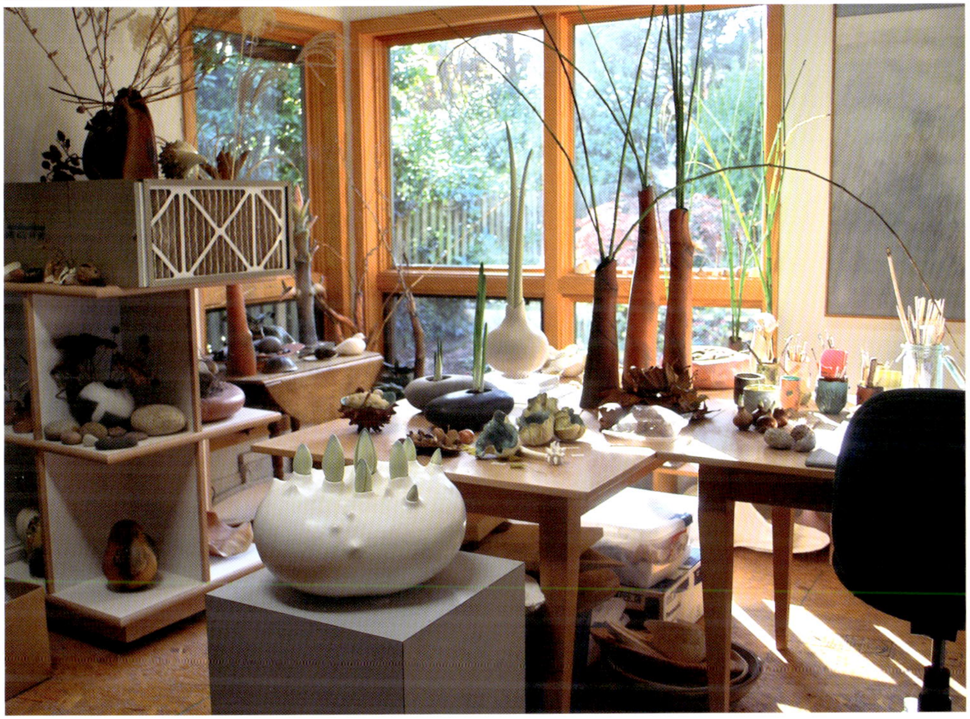

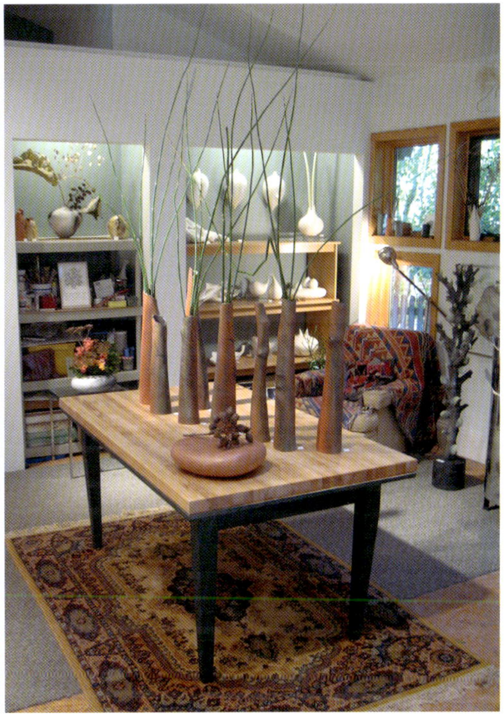

Helmut Barnett

Austin, Texas

Each work is an act of discovery. As the painting or drawing evolves from a series of random or deliberate shapes or lines, the process informs me and I delight in the possibilities. The infinite combinations, the accidental, the unexpected, all contribute to the conscious act of creating.

Some pieces are dashed off in a moment of decisive inspiration, while others demand a full measure of time and labor. For me, making art is a continuous process of building on my previous work.

And the finished piece? A modest assumption that one's work has contributed something to the vocabulary of art and has conveyed to others the same sense of wonder and delight experienced by the artist.

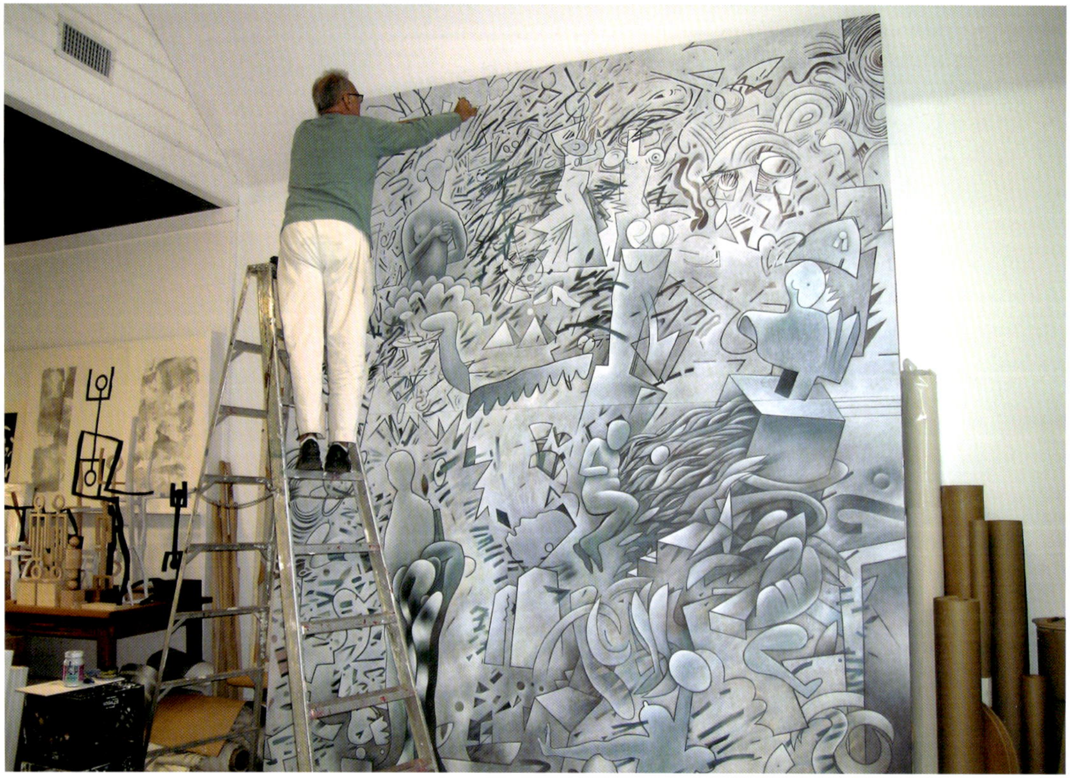

Here, I am working in the new addition to my studio, which was built with a 16-foot ceiling and has an 8-foot door for my large canvases. ***Ramses*** *is my largest painting yet at 11.5 feet tall; its linear aspects relate to my black and white drawings.*

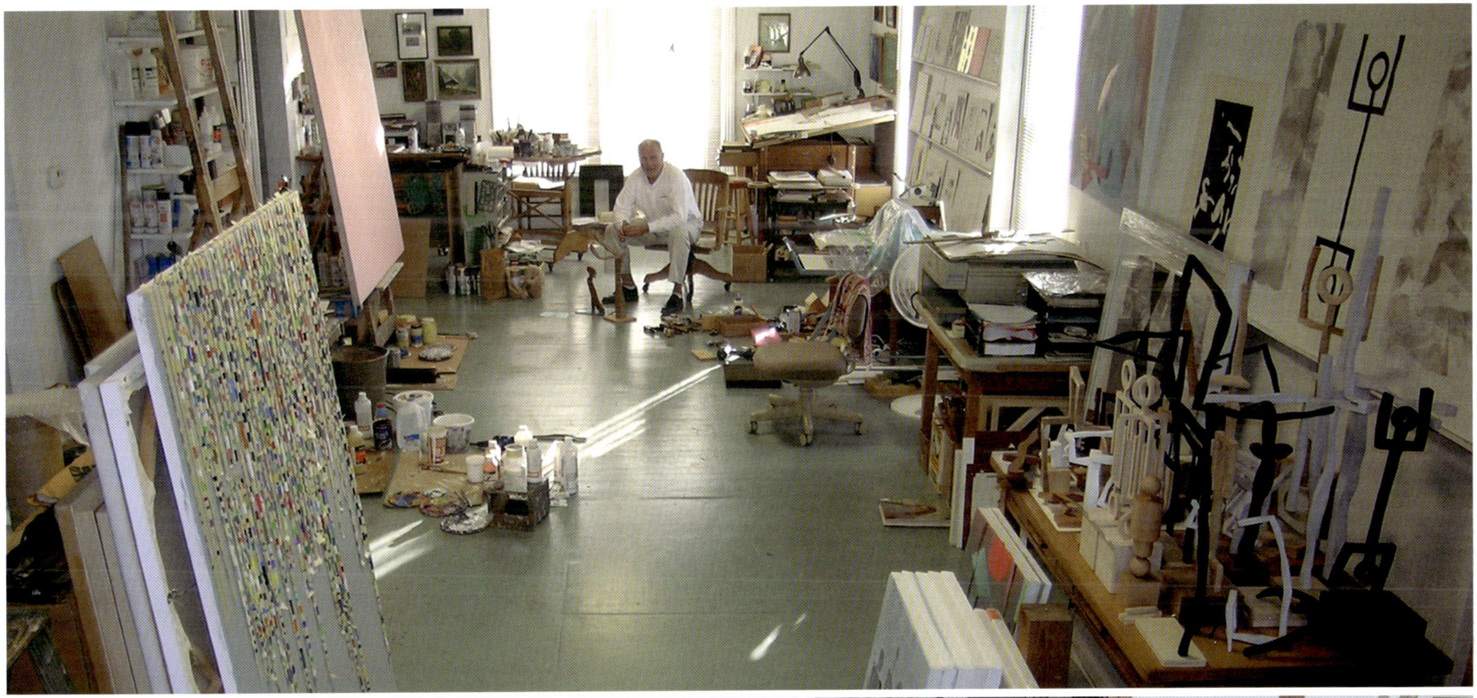

I built two display areas on the right wall to view my works on paper in progress. The table in the right foreground shows my wooden maquettes; I have always thought that many of my abstract shapes could be realized three-dimensionally.

My entire house is used as studio space. The restoration process for this 100-year-old structure, which included rebuilding the front porch, took eight months. In this view of the studio, you can see **Gray Scale** in progress (masking tape still in place) on my easel, which was homemade to accommodate large canvases.

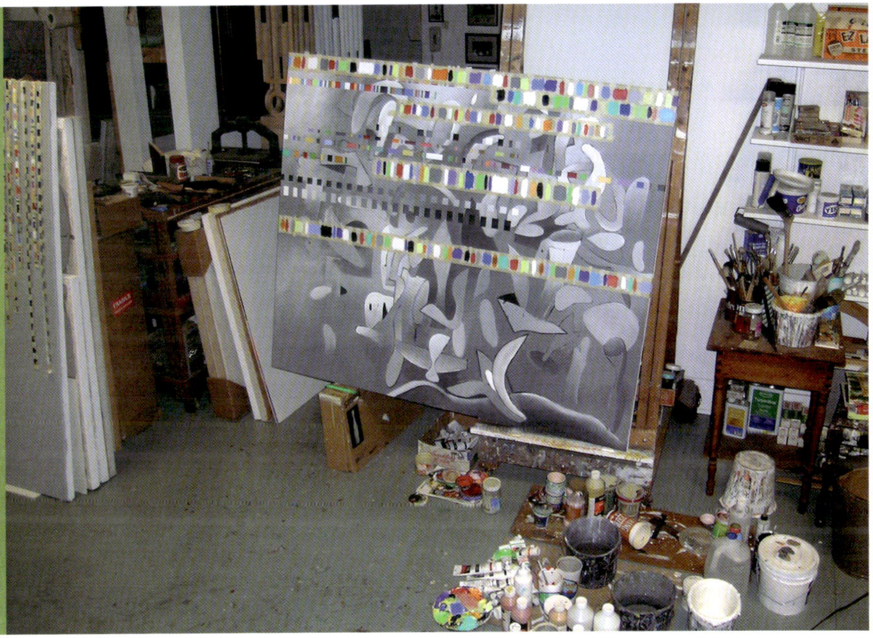

Maureen K. Brookfield

Marshfield, Massachusetts

I love the morning light in my studio, a large room off the back of my house, which was built for me by my supportive husband when we moved to Marshfield from New Jersey. No more painting on the kitchen table for me!

The studio looks out over my garden and pool area with big sliding glass doors and windows. The light streaming in always lifts my spirits and puts me in the mood to paint. I have a big drafting table right in the middle of the room where I paint my watercolors. It gives me plenty of elbow room. The table tilts up when needed to stop me getting too tight with my compositions, thus enabling me to stay loose and fluid when painting.

With space for shelves, a computer table, and a vertically divided shelving unit for my paintings, I have lots of storage available to me. Against the back wall, I have a desk and light table for drawing and illustration work. I have everything I need just a few steps away, plus plenty of wall space to display some of my paintings.

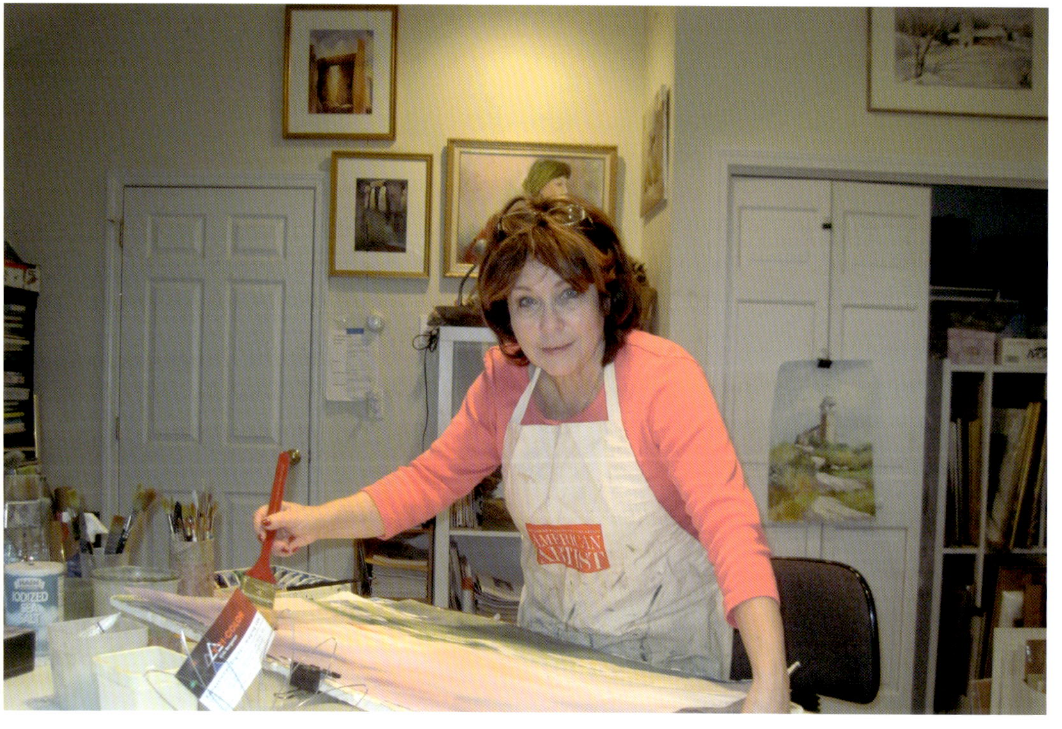

*Just started my **Star Island** painting. I have a big brush and like to splash around.*

My studio entrance from the pool patio provides easy access from outside.

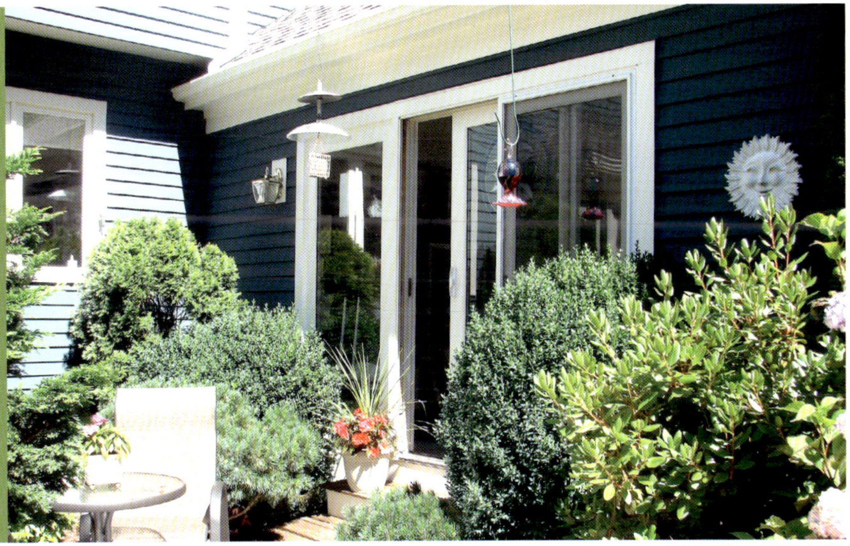

My drawing and illustration area and the back wall displaying some of my paintings.

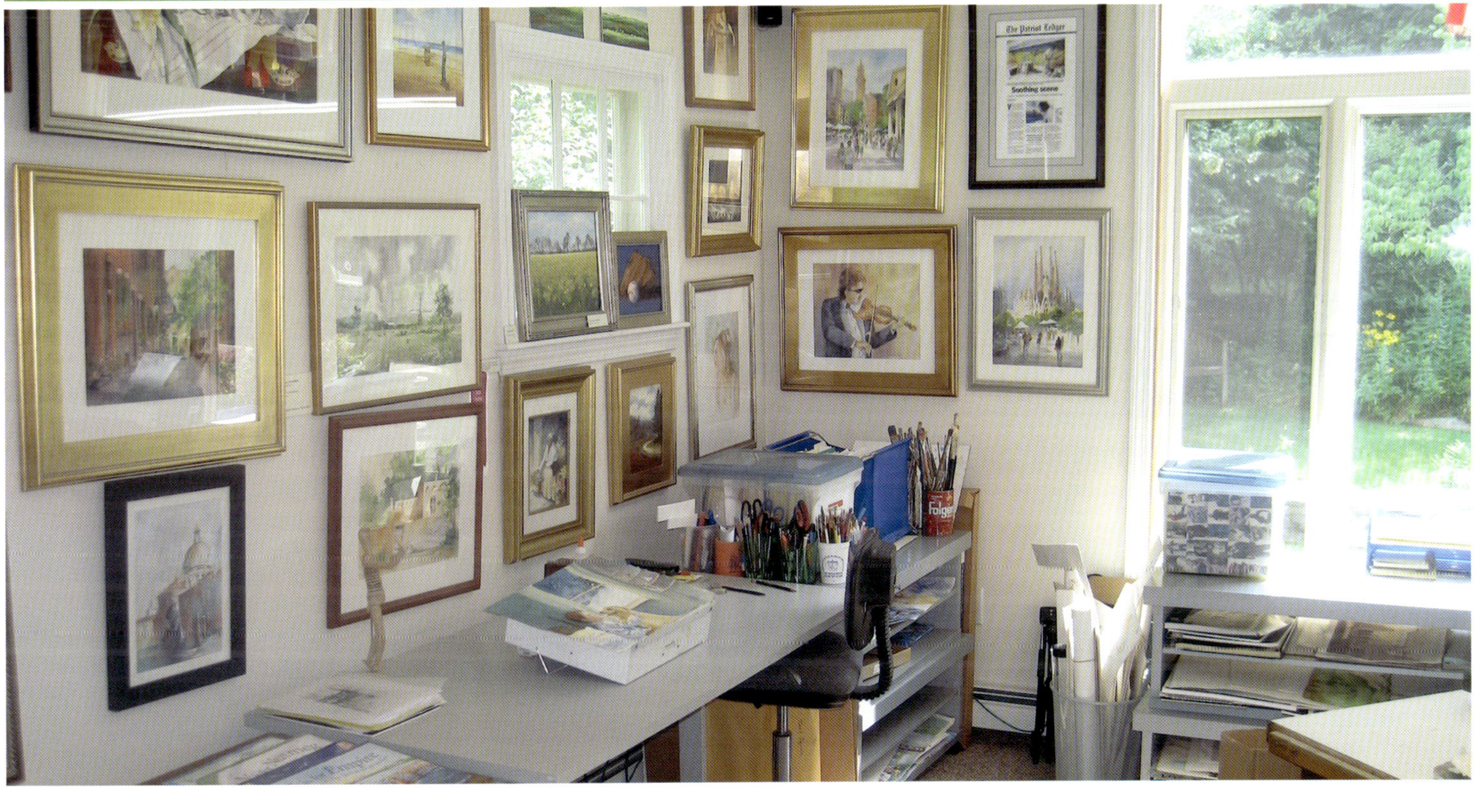

Cynthia F. Cooley

Durham, New Hampshire

We built a new garage at our summer home in Durham, New Hampshire, in 1994, and the upper floor became my studio. Here I have the chance to work on subjects that are different from my Pittsburgh paintings of steel mills and city scenes. I create the images I want to paint from my own photographs and sketches, but the colors of the water and trees from my studio windows definitely influence my palette. Looking out at the bay reinforces my love for painting water, especially in watercolor, whether it's the ocean, a river, a lake, or a swamp. I am a representational artist, but by using a vibrant palette, strong design, and active brushstrokes, I try to produce memorable works that refer to reality but have their own objective life as paintings.

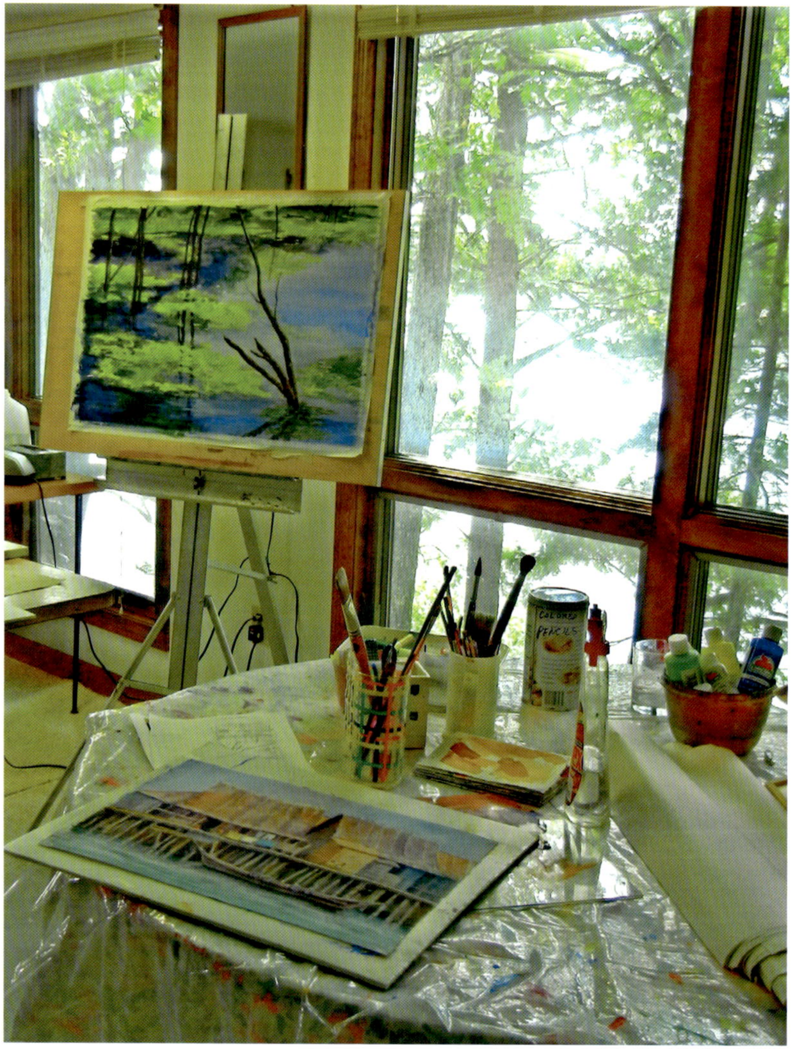

It's great to have room to work on several paintings at once. On the easel: ***Swamp Lilies****, a watercolor in progress. On the table is the watercolor* ***Malaysia Fishing Village****.*

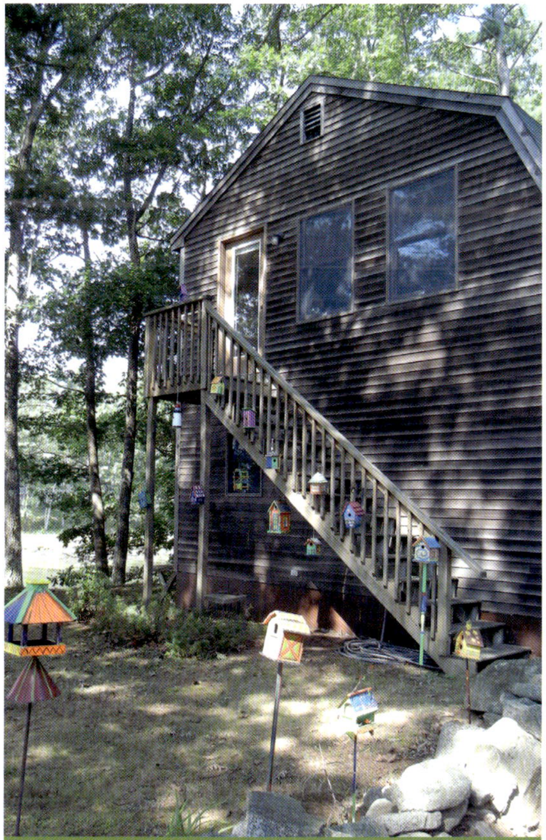

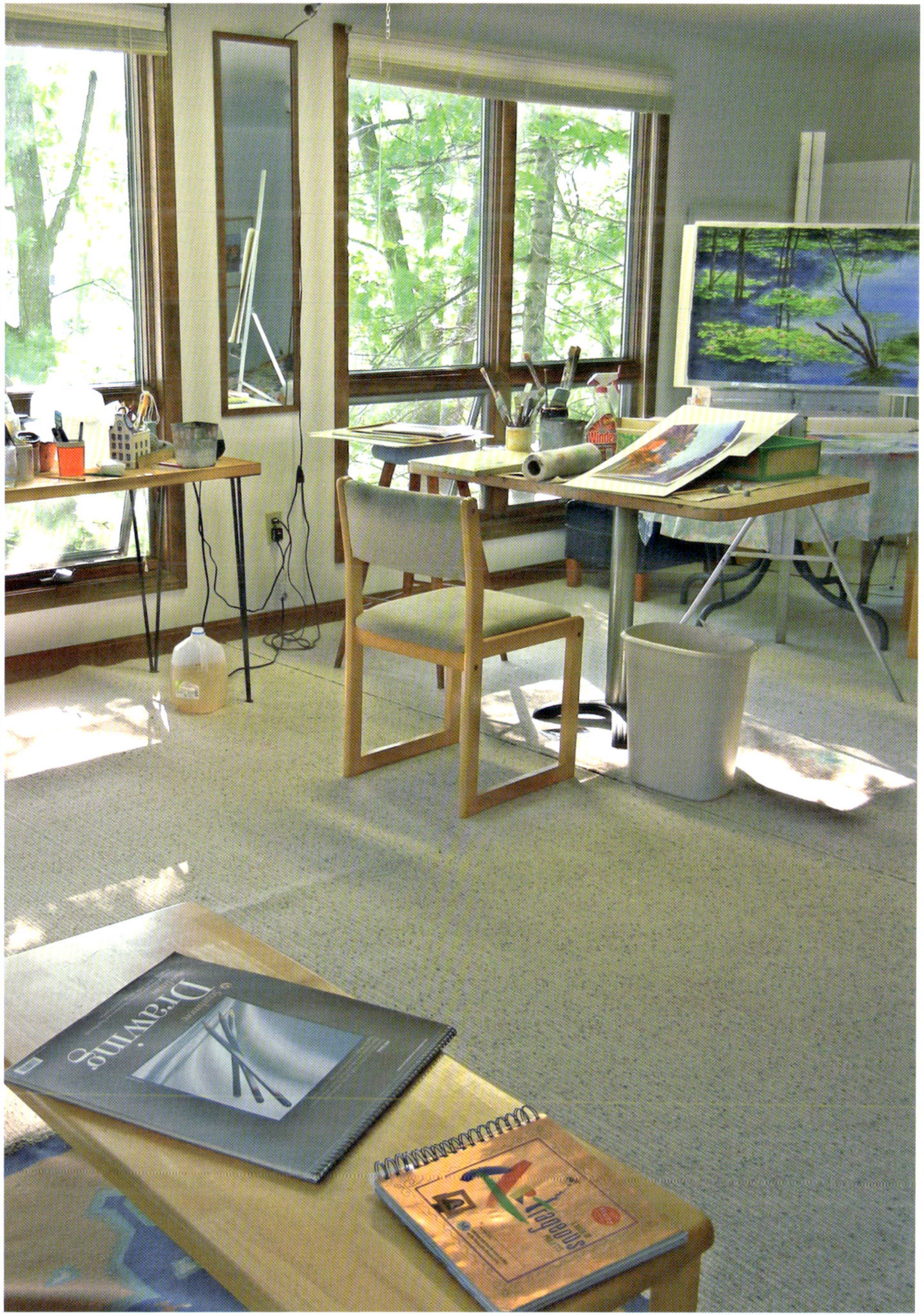

Birdhouses I've decorated over the years line the garden wall and the stairs to my summer studio.

The large windows of my summer studio overlook a saltwater bay. It's quiet here, away from a busy house usually filled with family and guests.

Wade Eldean

Macatawa, Michigan

I started messing around with paints and making art when I was ten years old; later, I received formal training and earned an MFA from the University of Idaho. Since then, I have exhibited my art internationally and taught art and design courses at Hope College, Baker College, and the University of Idaho.

Much of my artwork emphasizes children, popular culture, travel, and innovative creative techniques. I juxtapose childish qualities and imagery with hints of violence, compliance, stereotyping, and other societal pressures placed by mass media and public interaction upon children as they develop.

A few years ago, I rebuilt my studio, adding an exhibit space and choosing several building materials that reflect my personality. My studio has taken on a bowling alley flavor: more than 1000 square feet of pine and maple bowling lanes from a closed bowling alley were repurposed. The reclaimed floor includes beautiful dark walnut inlays, which previously directed the bowler where to aim. Dark walnut can be seen in the floor patterning and on the stairs and railings. Other bowling relics further this theme, as an outdated scorer's table (with built-in ashtrays) and random bowling pins make appearances.

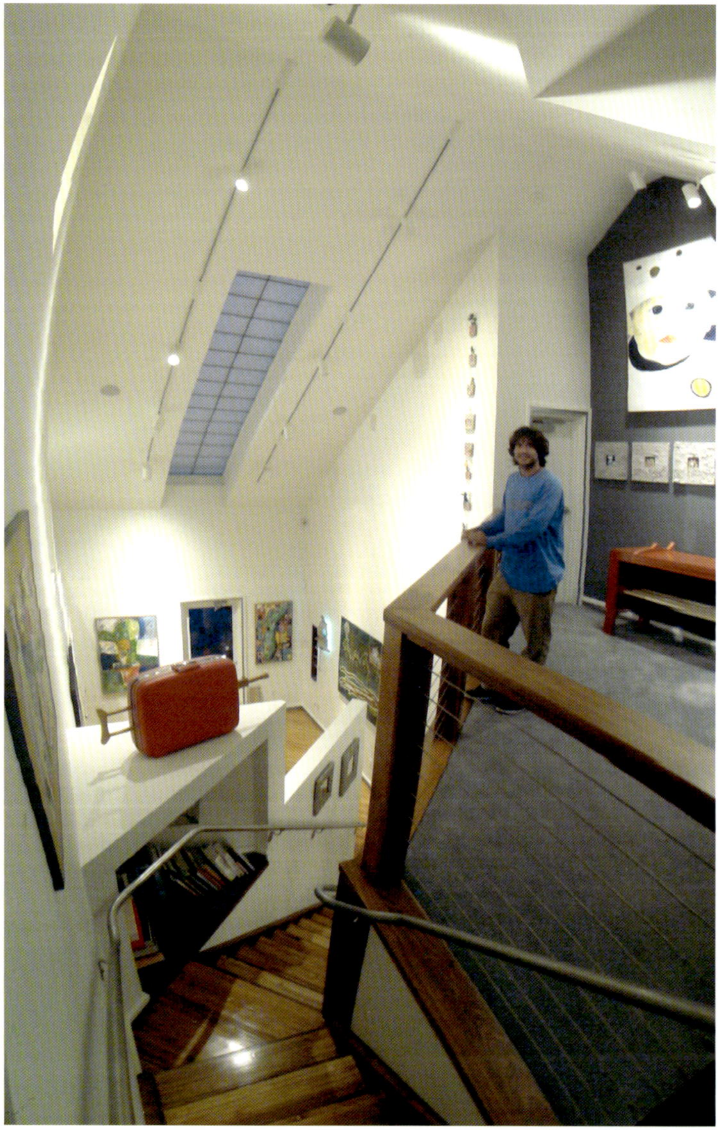

As I have a boating background, nautical influences and materials often make it into my artwork and are present in the studio. For example, nautical turnbuckles and stainless steel cabling complete the walnut railings, a painting created on a Lake Michigan chart is seen on the back wall (right of the door), and a desk, titled ***Double Header****, that I created with the profile of a Chinook salmon emerging from the desk's top, appears at right.* Courtesy of Kris Eldean.

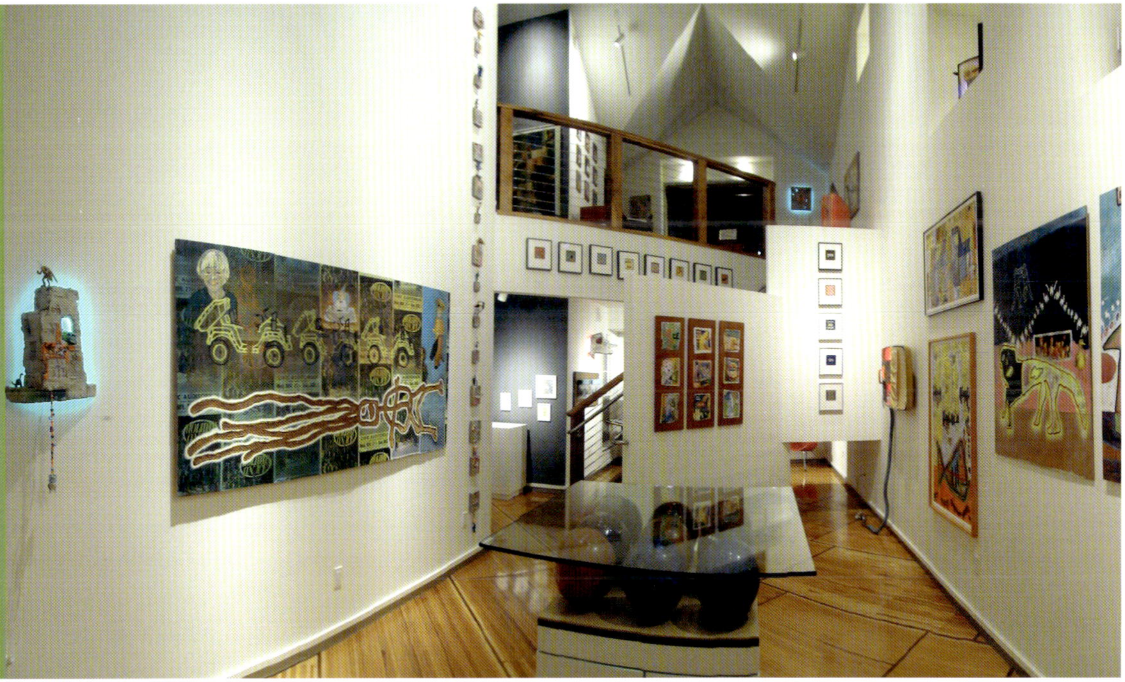

Continuing with the bowling theme, I created ***The Spare Table****, which mainly consists of a sculpture display pedestal, nine bowling balls, and a glass top. Large boxes built into the walls (upper right corner) give my sculptures their own unique niche.*

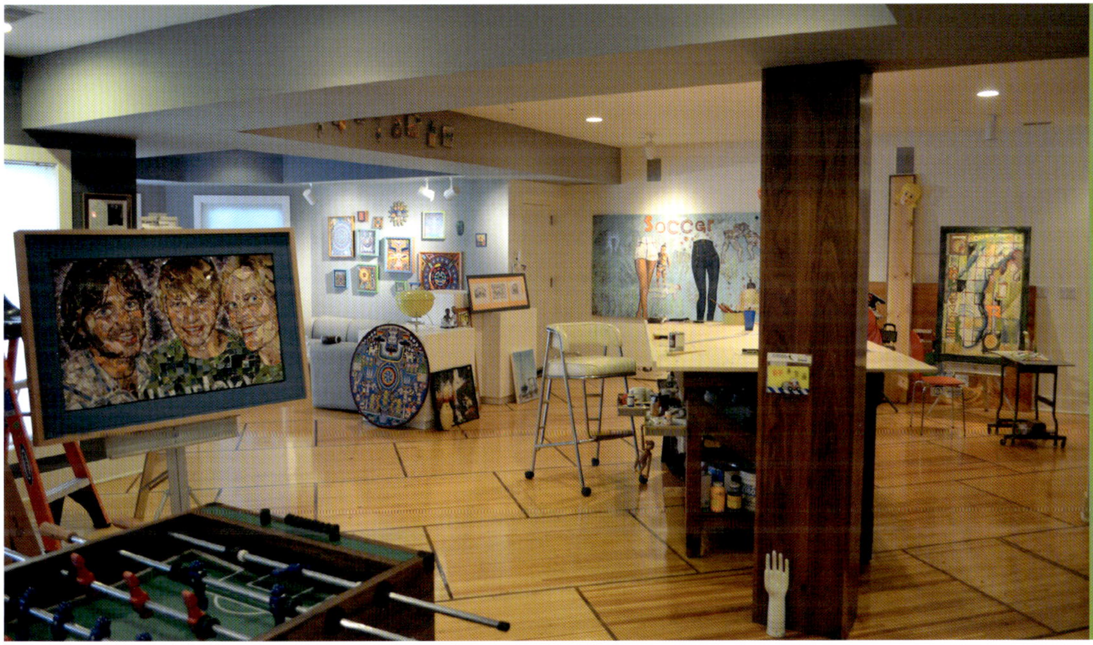

My paints and brushes are housed in a repurposed, cedar gardening table. I installed a new top on the table, which is hinged so it can be used like a drafting table or easel while stainless steel shelves slide out from below, giving easy access to paints and brushes. After hours, the table will accommodate ten poker players.

Catherine Eyde

Tucson, Arizona

I am a visual storyteller. My paintings are inspired by my heritage, a love of the folk and the surreal. I was fortunate to help design my current studio, which is part of my home and the core where I create and present my artwork to the public. Its architecture reflects my visual desires: high ceilings, warm wood beams adjoined to plaster walls, windows filled with light, and ancient carved doors that seem to tell a story. It has old charm with new art being made inside.

The Tucson light fills my workspace, offering a wonderful sense of spaciousness. Neutral tones in the room provide a subtle backdrop to the jewel-like colors that glow from my paintings. A Moorish keyhole entry to my office nook can be seen from the main room, illuminated by the sunlight that leaks through the courtyard trees and enters the room through a star-shaped window.

My favorite spot to create is on a vintage drafting table with a grand workspace. Low music often fills the room as I work quietly, alone and still, lost in "other worlds" uncovering new narratives and imagery from within. My studio inspires my aesthetics, stimulates my imagination, and coincides with elements seen in my work.

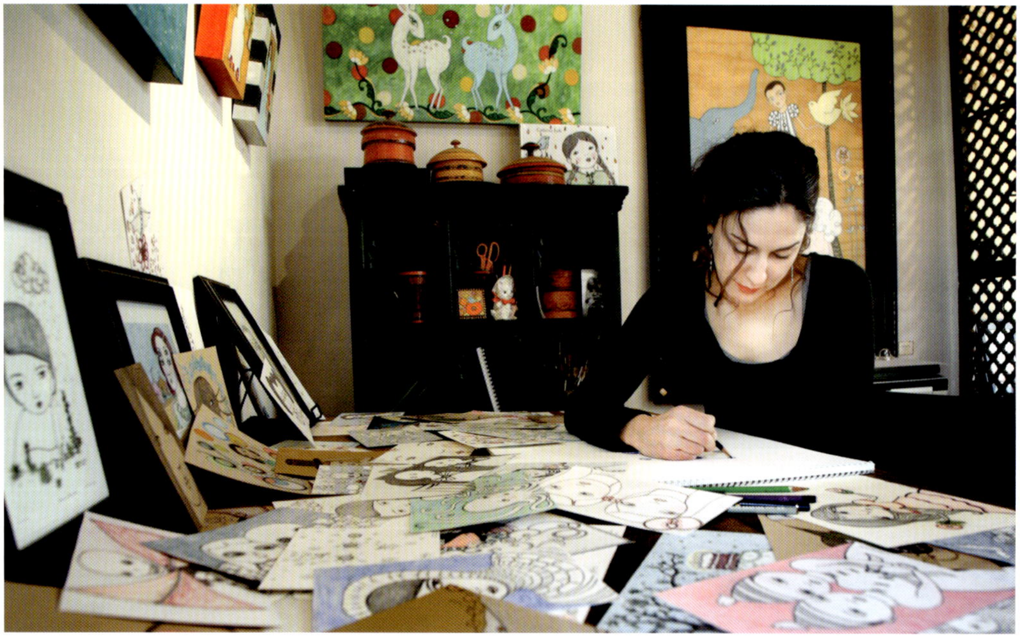

A mess of drawings covering my drafting table, back dropped above by my dots and deer painting, ***Flirt.*** Photo ©2013 Patricia Katchur.

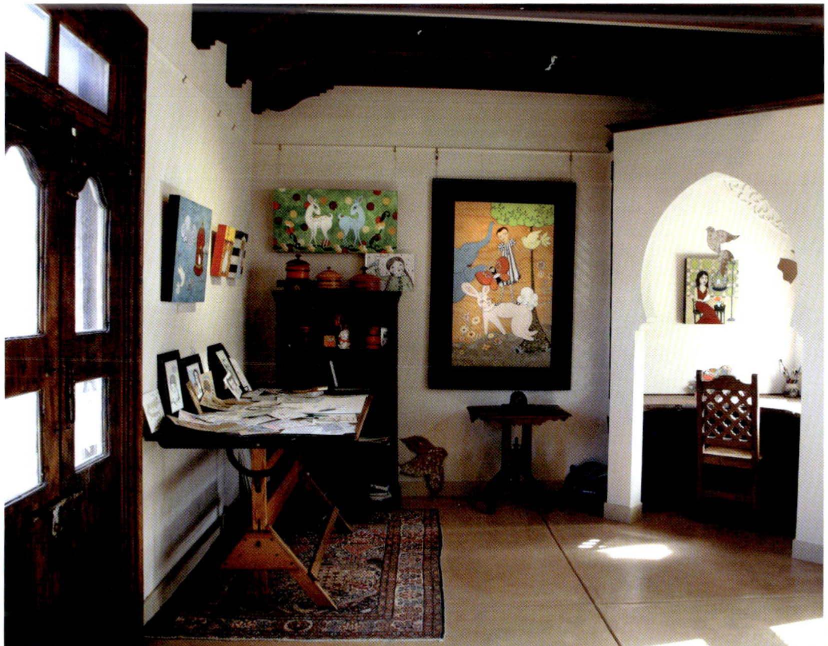

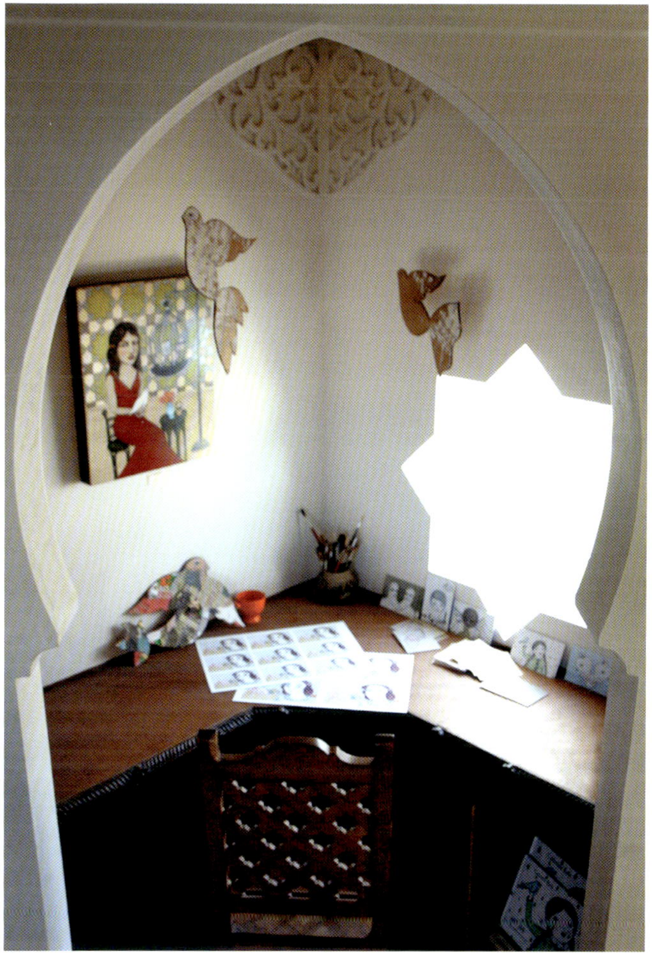

*Natural light enters my studio from the North and South. My painting, **Easter Opening,** 2008, hangs in a black frame on the back wall surrounded by several paintings from my series **Sweet Love**, 2010, on the left and **Art for the Imagination**, 2010, on the right.* ©2013 Patricia Katchur.

*Keyhole entry to my side office. On the left wall hangs **Valentine,** 2010, three of my **Cardboard/collage birds,** 2010, and scattered across the desk are prints from my project ART 365. I made a drawing for every day of 2011.* ©2013 Patricia Katchur.

Kat Fitzpatrick

Bay Saint Louis, Mississippi

My studio was a gift from Hurricane Katrina and a community of big-hearted volunteers with strong backs, some artisan woodworkers, and a friendly ex-husband. Once, there was another studio on this spot. Built in 1905, it was a charming cottage that was positioned to catch the breezes from the Bay of St. Louis, a block-and-a-half away. During Katrina, a 30-foot storm surge floated the building right off its piers and left it mired and full of mud. A small 600-square-foot addition to the original house remained standing after the old house was torn away. It was stripped to bare studs and rafters, rewired, re-plumbed, and new sheetrock was hung and floated. It became my home and studio combined. I used the tiny counter and the kitchen table to paint with encaustics (beeswax+damar crystals+ pigment, melted). I learned to give thanks for each small step forward. There were so many who had lost everything.

Katrina made us bolder and more inventive. A friend and my ex-husband figured out a way to save an historic house (also built in 1905) that was scheduled for demolition in the next town over. Through grants and volunteers, church groups, and paid workers, the house was dismantled, coded stick by stick, and transported in five containers to my property. The next two years were like playing pickup sticks, as the woodpiles were slowly transformed into a beautiful studio house.

I paint and teach in the old kitchen, except when I am giving workshops around the country. I use the central hallway as an exhibition space for openings or as an extension of the studio when we are using the "HotBox" for encaustic mono-printing.

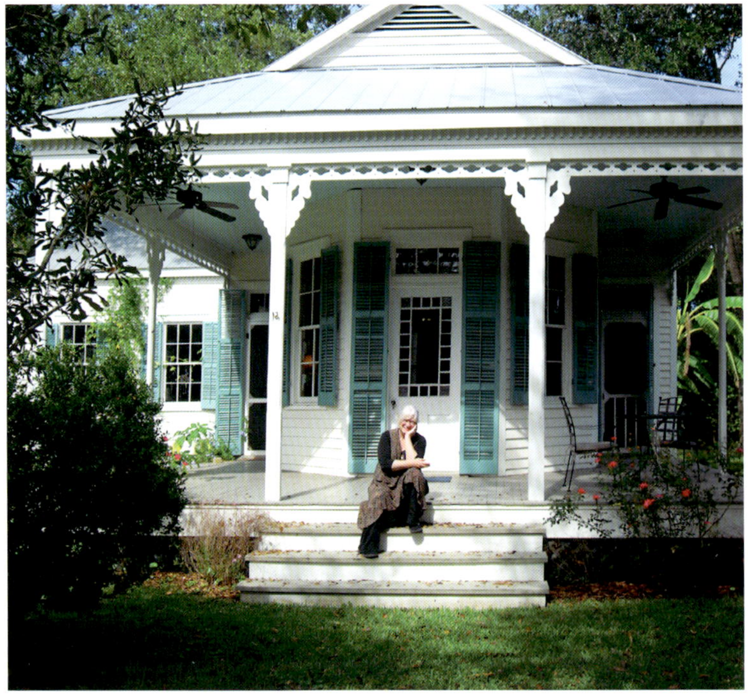

My beautiful studio house. Courtesy of Anna Macedo.

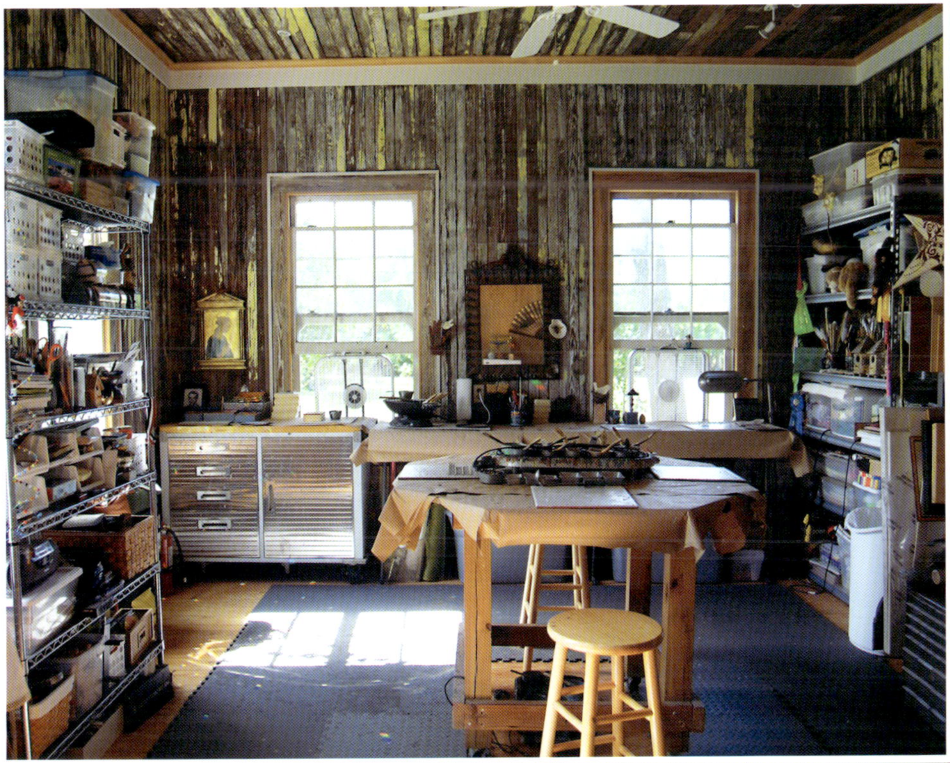

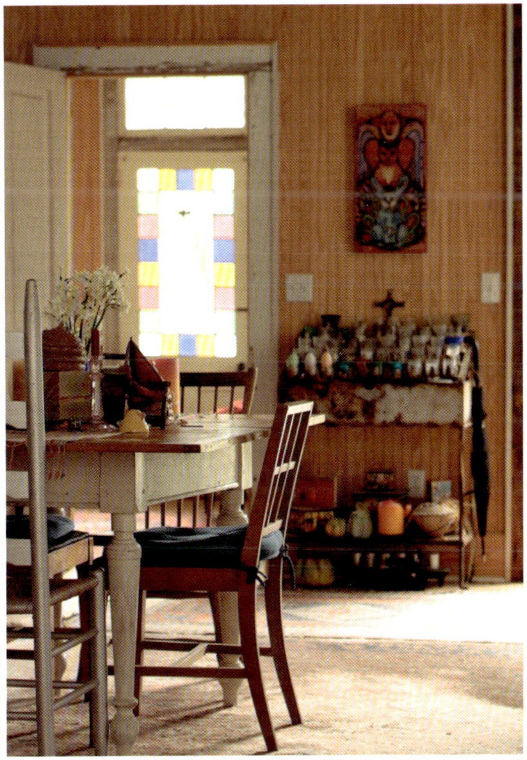

The tongue-and-groove painted pine is generally original to the house. The wainscoting is a diagonal, alternating pattern of panels that we used to call "wood-butcher style" in the 1970s. It is actually a great way to use short bits of wood creatively rather than throw them away. Wherever possible, we used the original multi-colored and Katrina-weathered wood with just a light sanding. Industrial restaurant carts and open shelving with casters are my main storage solutions with a "Space Rover" wheeled painting storage cart. Black cushioned mats cover the floor. We work around an octagonal wooden table on casters. Everything needs to be visible but not too chaotic for the comfort of my students. Courtesy of Anna Macedo.

This view is through the central gallery/work/teaching space (11 x 11 x 22') and beyond to the hexagonal room with front stained glass door. Courtesy of Anna Macedo.

Little Tree. *Encaustic on wood. 6 x 7".* Courtesy of Diane Chun.

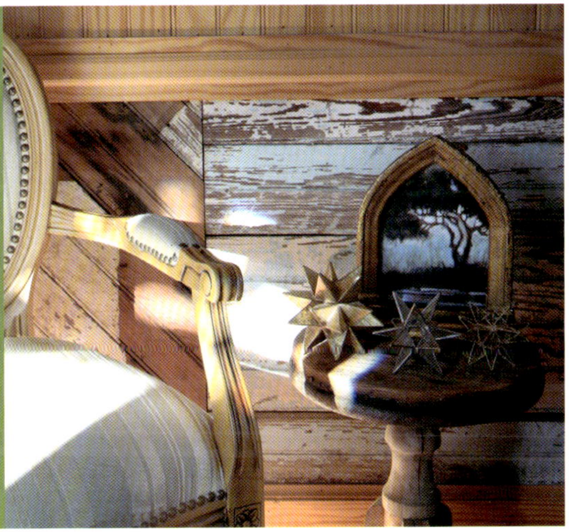

Scott Fraser

Longmont, Colorado

I am fortunate to have a good-sized studio attached to my home, with lots of north-facing windows and high ceilings. Here, I can spread out, get a lot of my objects out on tables and shelves, study them, and move them around. Sometimes I tinker around with a setup for years before I have the right composition for a painting. Being an indoor painter and painting from life, I'm at the mercy of the seasons and their weather patterns. In winter, the days are short and the light more variable, but summers are great because most of the days are sunny. Colorado's big blue sky at high altitude help me maintain a consistent bright light. There is a luminosity in my paintings that comes from the natural light I work with. I also have a sweet view of the garden outside my studio.

My custom easel, which can take large canvases, is motorized, so, with a touch of my foot, I can adjust it quickly and get my knees under it comfortably. I have several hundred pounds of ballast made up of cannon balls as counterweight to offset the weight of the large reinforced canvases!

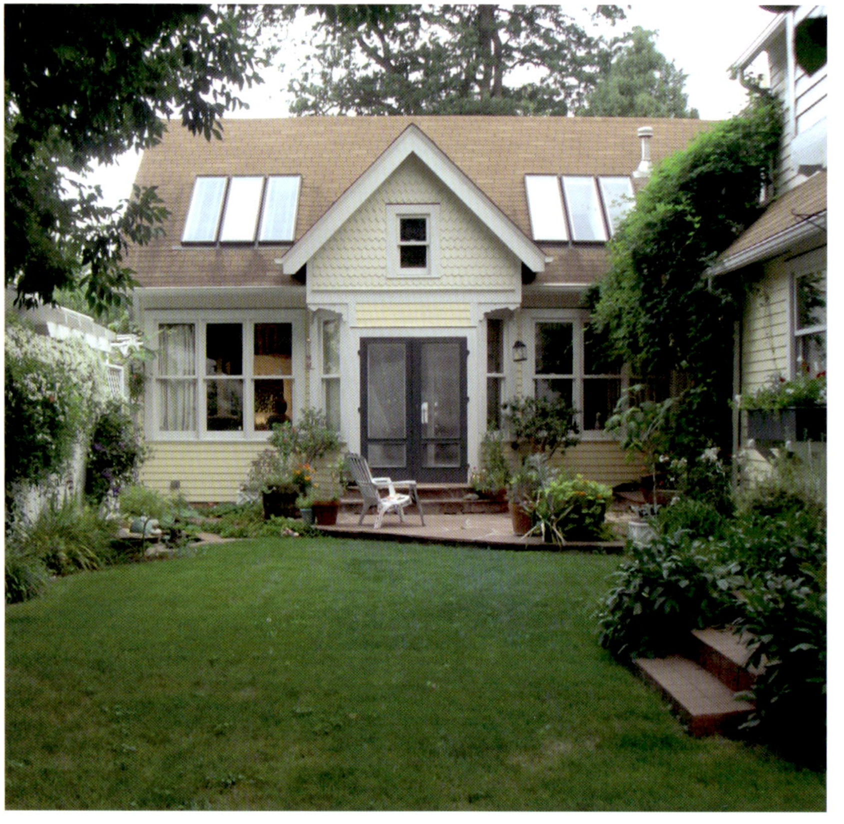

My studio.

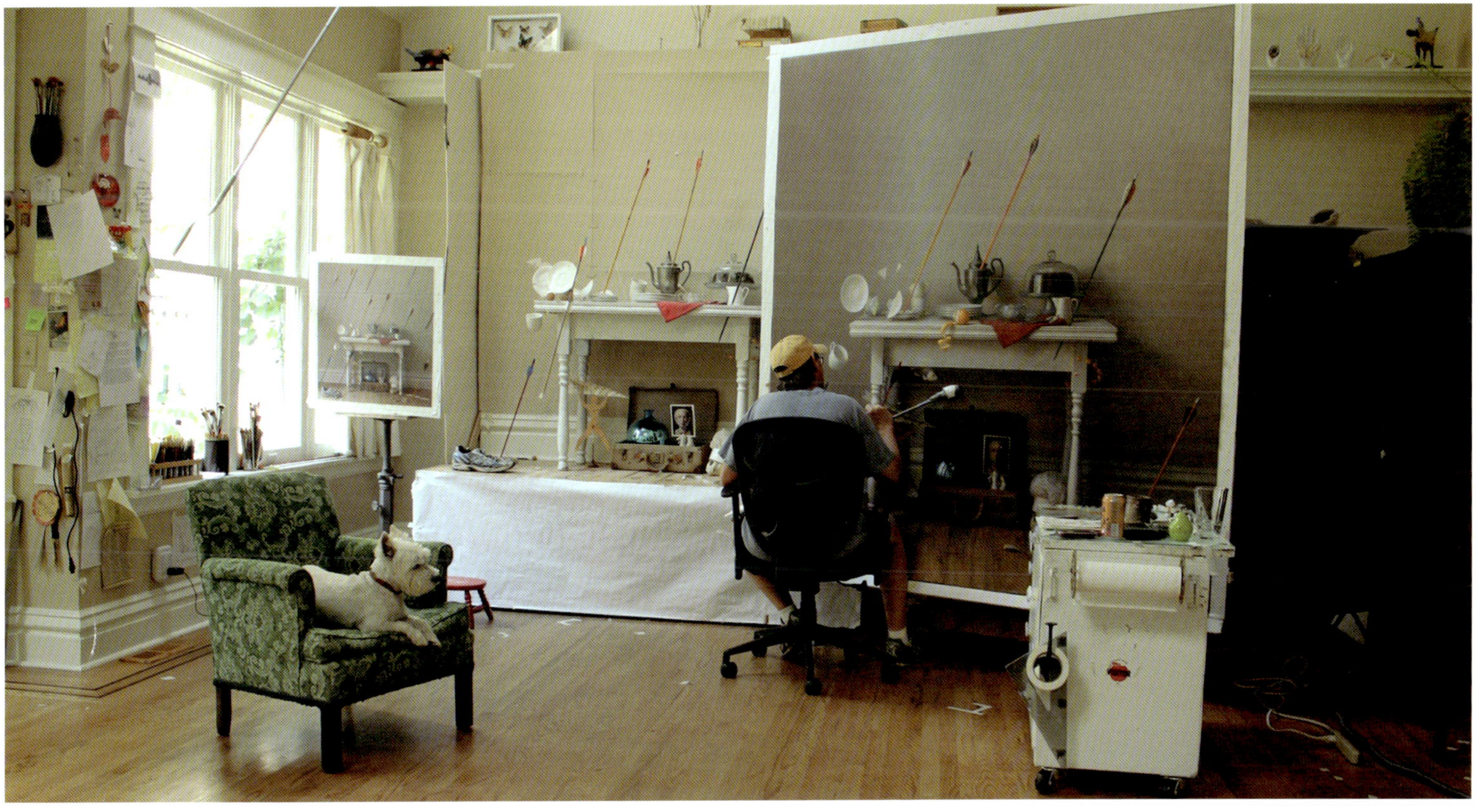

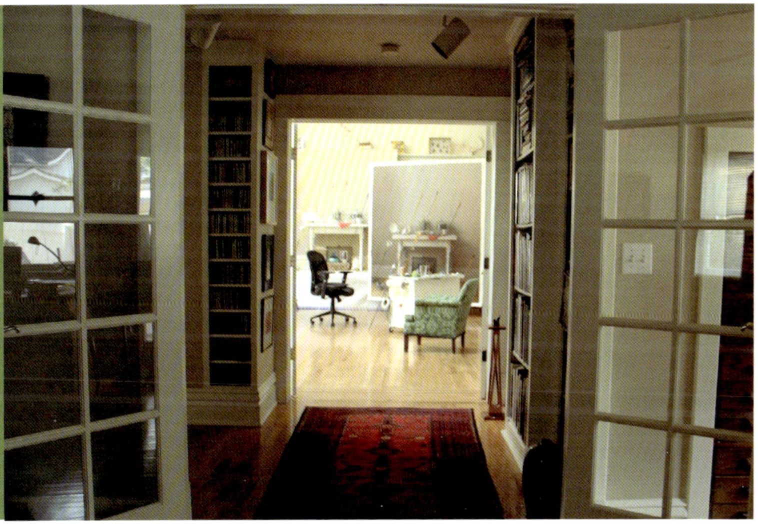

I have a short commute down the hall to my studio every morning. To the right in the hall is my collection of art books and catalogs, which I constantly consult when I work. Courtesy of Robert Jackson

Here, I am working on ***Reign****, a 6 x 7' canvas that took eight months to complete. The small pre-study painting on the left helps me color match for the larger one. My dog Petunia keeps me company.* Courtesy of Robert Jackson.

Martha Hayden

Sharon, Wisconsin

I have two studios. My Wisconsin summer studio is in my home. My family has grown, and I have spread over the whole house and the yard too. I don't have to get dressed and go anywhere. I have a lot of storage (for a lifetime of work), both in the house and in outbuildings. Purchased in 1962, the house was in bad shape, and I have spent much time and energy slowly repairing and restoring. My original upstairs painting space was made from three bedrooms. I removed walls, installed two north-facing skylights, and built over-the-door racks for storage. I love this place, but it isolates me from other artists.

In the winter, it is exciting and stimulating to be in New York City. My loft is in the East Village, and I travel four subway stops to get to it. The space is rough, and I don't feel like I have to fix or do anything; I can just work. It is about 1500 square feet, large enough to make big canvases. It is on the sixth floor, and I have good urban views. I can easily visit museums and galleries, and it is great to have painter friends whose work I care about.

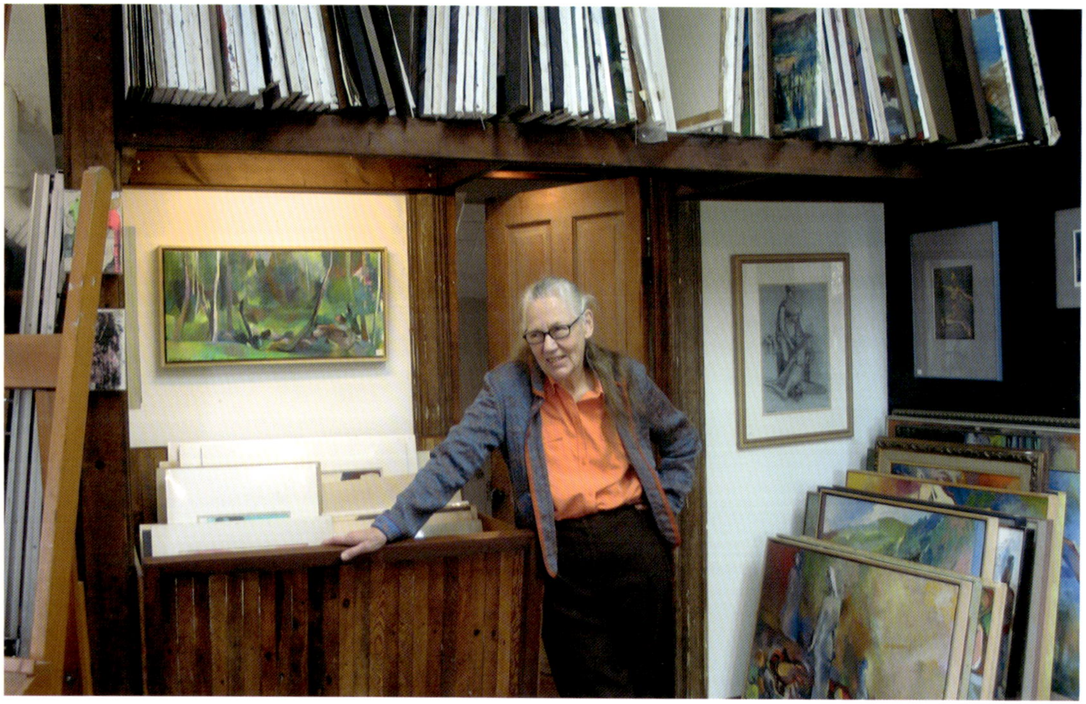

Studio interior with bin for work on paper and overhead rack for canvases. On wall, left, ***The Place****; to the right,* ***Charcoal Figure Study****; on floor,* ***Twin Still Life****.*

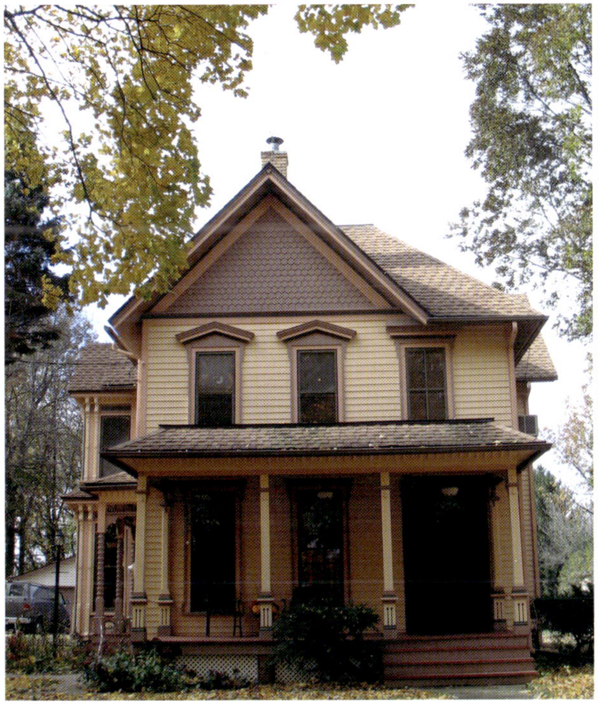

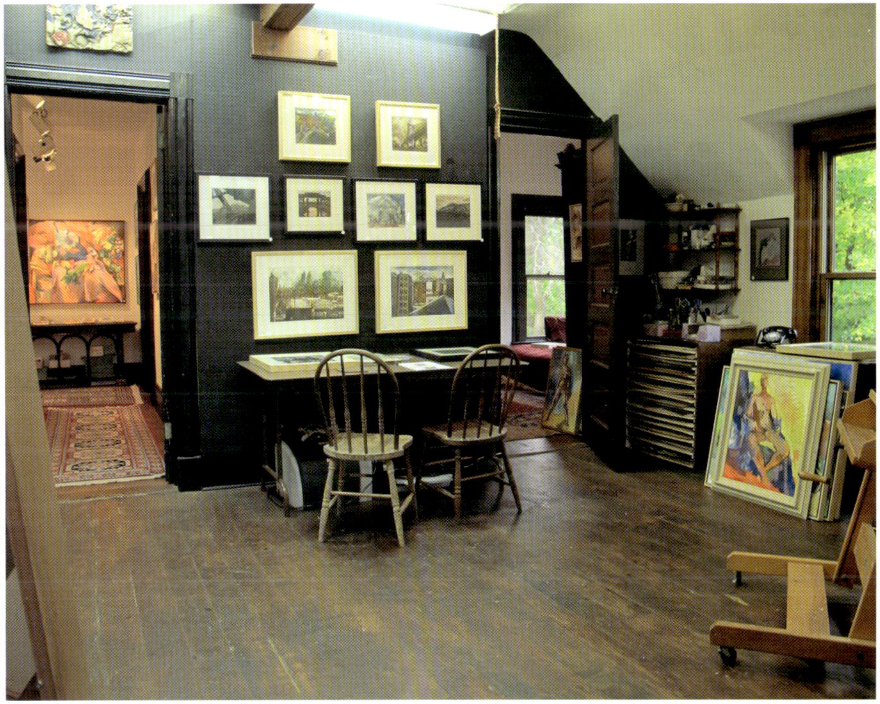

I have extensively restored my Wisconsin studio, which was built about 1870.

My studio worktable. The black wall was for taking slides, but now is a good background for etchings. Courtesy of Heidi Rabe.

I have expanded to fill the whole house. Gallery lights in the hallways illuminate paintings. Left, ***Grief,*** *center,* ***Balance,*** *right,* ***Madonna.***

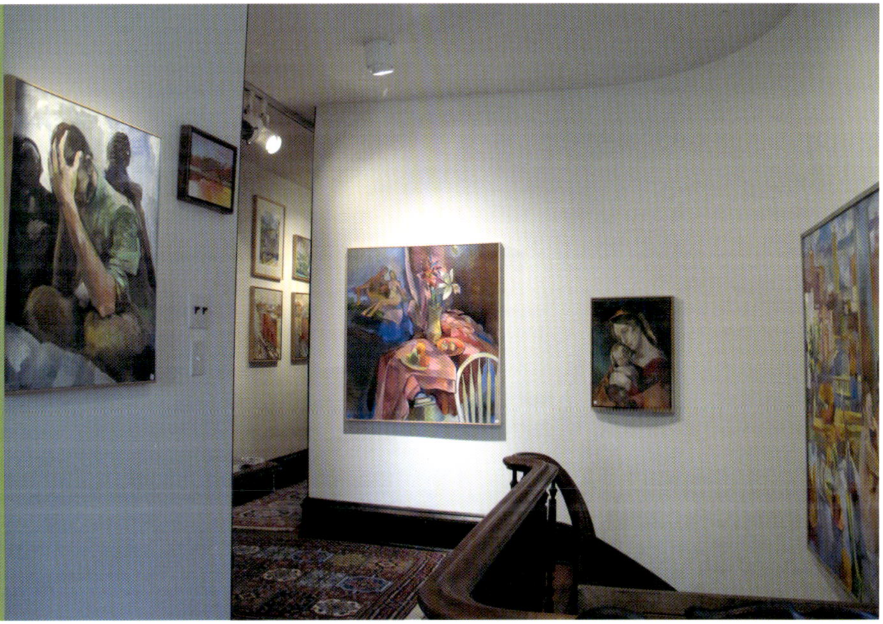

Gayla Hodson

Fishers, Indiana

I work out of my custom-built home—the first home I ever built on my own: it was a new beginning. I had been working from a studio in downtown Indianapolis, but always felt more comfortable working from home. I put in a pool, surrounded by flowers that bloom throughout the spring, summer, and fall, as these are sources of my inspiration.

I knew what I wanted in my studio. First, there needed to be plenty of light! It had to be in the back of my home near my pool, pond, and flowers. For me, my home is a place of refuge and solace. I live in a quiet neighborhood. Sometimes if I am working on larger pieces and weather permits, I paint in my garage, which is equipped with track lighting and windows in my garage door that give plenty of light to paint. It is open and airy; passersby stop to chat, giving me a feeling of connection to my community. I have filled my studio with books, images, and childhood memories that create a feeling of contentment. This is where I connect with my soul and play all day!

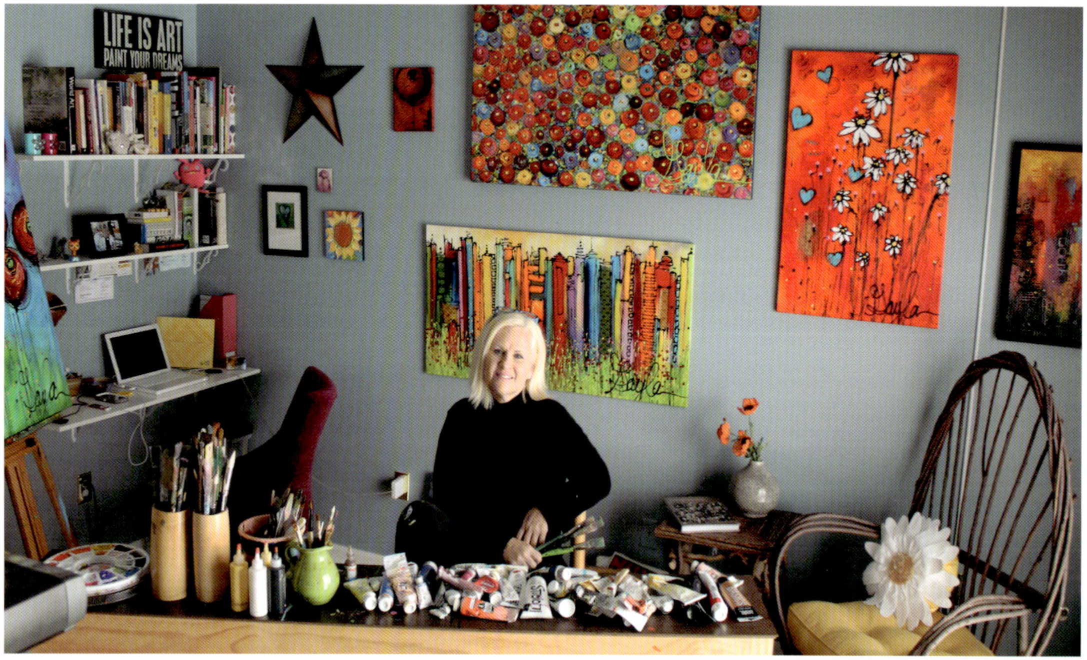

My studio holds a comfy willow chair, my desk with computer and Bose sound system. Bookshelves are filled with biographies of artists I admire and books on techniques. Four art works on the wall are: bottom, ***Infusion of Color****, acrylic on canvas; top,* ***Positive Space****: oil on canvas; center:* ***...not for the faint of heart****, acrylic on canvas; far right:* ***Summer, Winter, Spring and Fall,*** *oil on canvas. The far back wall is filled with newspaper articles and postcards of exhibits.*

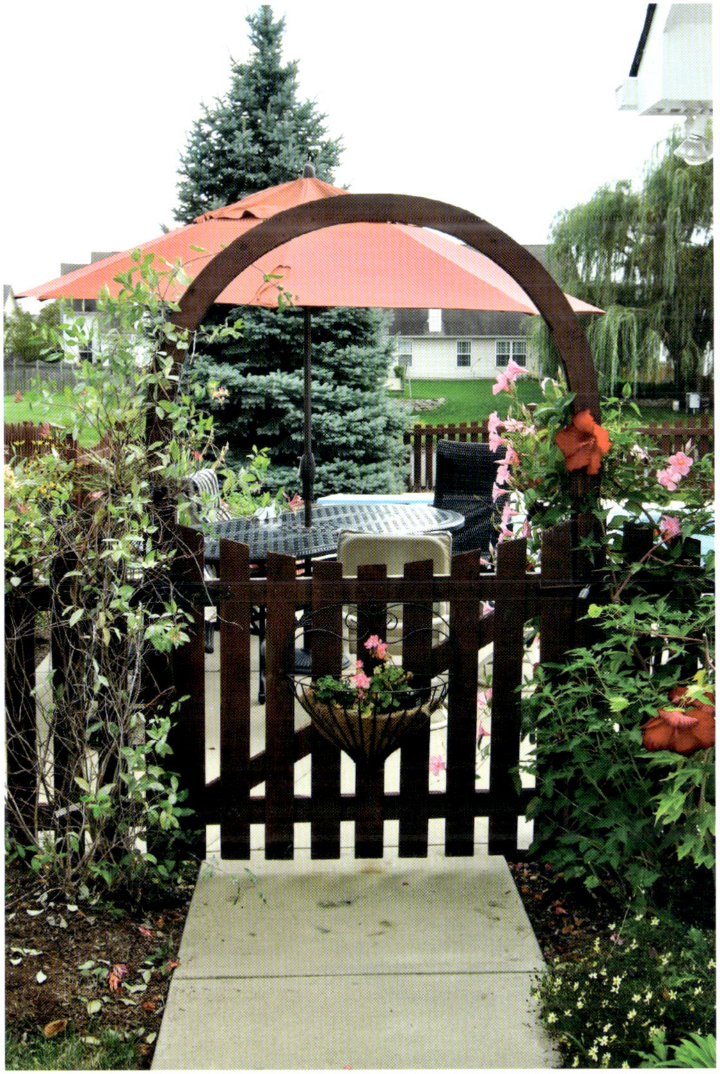

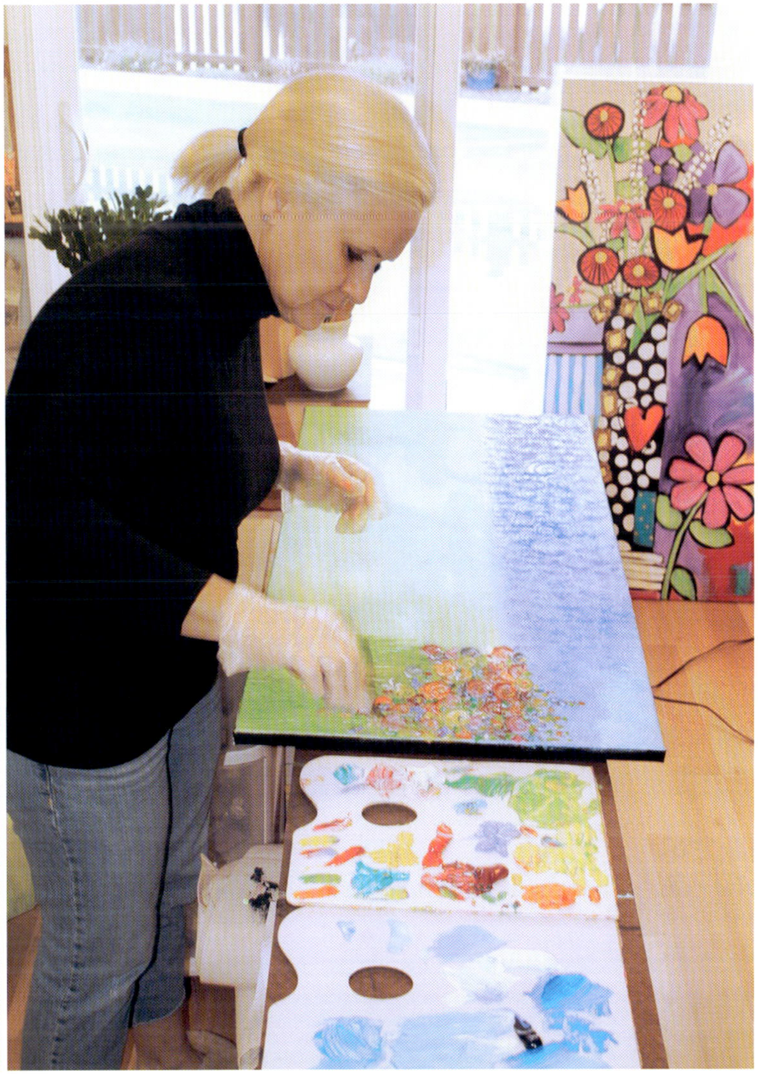

The windows in the garage of my Craftsman-style home provide light to paint. A wooden arbor leads into the back yard to the studio entrance from the back of the house. Courtesy of Daisyhead Photography.

When I work flat, I use a table I had built on wheels so it is easy to move around the studio. In this photo, I am working on an oil painting. Seen through the sliding glass doors, my back yard is a source of inspiration. The painting propped up against the door is titled: ***Cherish Who You Are.*** Courtesy of Daisyhead Photography.

Frank Hyder

Philadelphia, Pennsylvania

In 2001, my family and I were living in the cloud forests of Venezuela during my senior Fulbright research award. Upon our return, I added two stories to our Philadelphia house, allowing my studio to be filled with the air and light I had become accustomed to in the Venezuelan mountains. The soaring ceiling height, huge windows, and open space suit the tropically inspired nature of my work. I kept the space open and covered all the walls with plywood, allowing me to work on every inch of the walls. I attach my paintings and drawings to the wall, never using an easel. I have 8 x 8 feet walls on wheels, which I can push around the room and have ongoing works on both sides of these. I never work on a single piece at a time; I prefer to have as many as ten works in progress.

Much of my work is experimental; so I need time to understand where the work needs to go, rather than knowing what the finish should be.

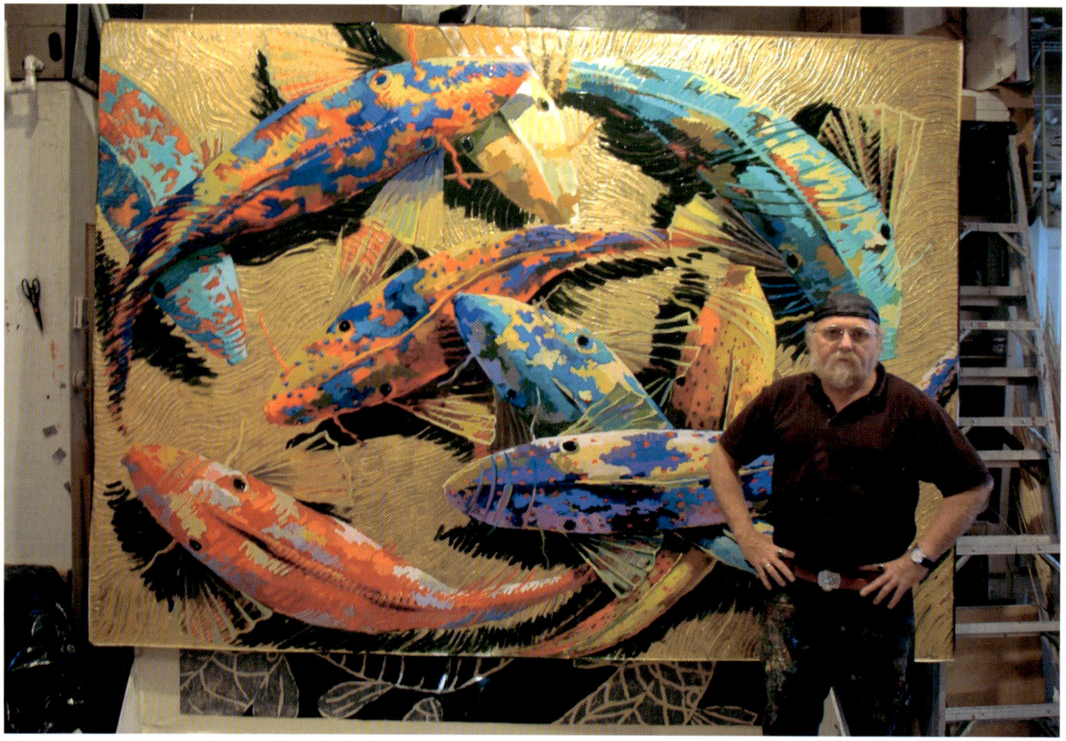

You can see the height of my ceilings here. The painting is ***Golden Circle****, oil on canvas.* Courtesy of Helen Hyder.

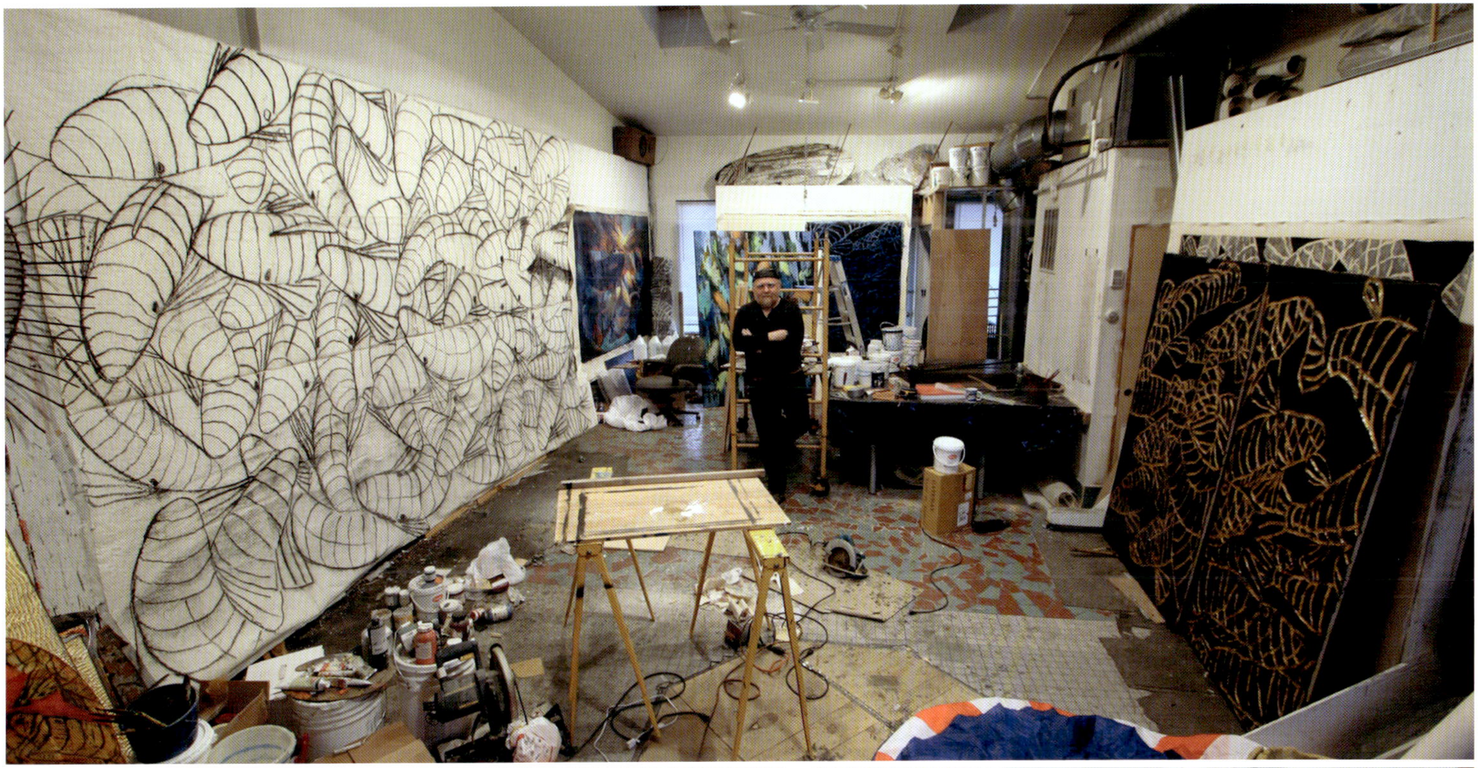

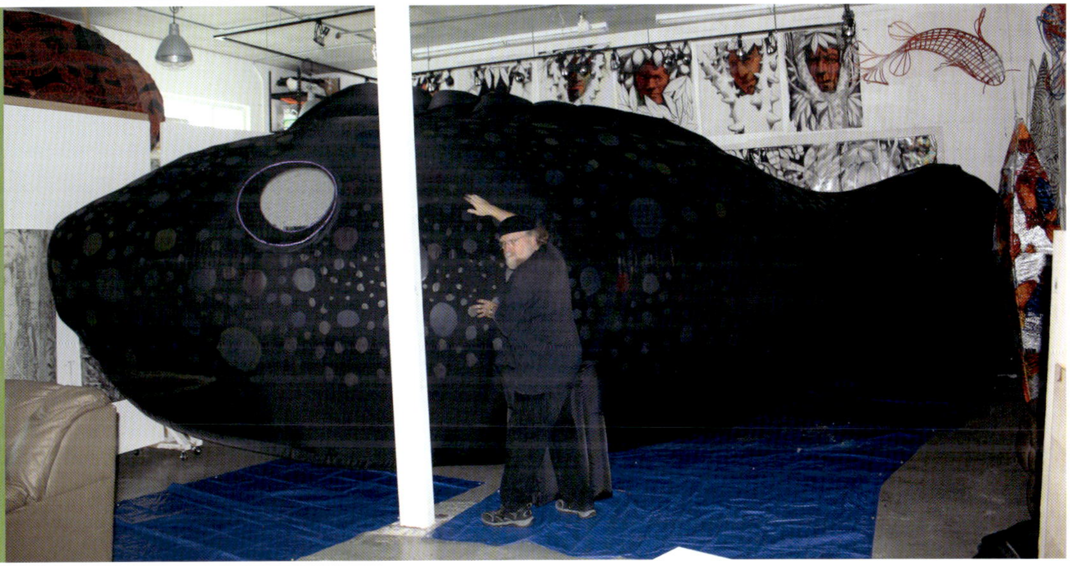

*Studio view with works in progress. On the left is **Gulf Requiem**, and on the right is **Ritmo Negro**. 2009.* Courtesy of John Karczmit.

*I make paintings, sculptures and huge drawings all in the same space but in different areas. The openness of the space allows me to see everything at a glance. Here, I am working on **Jonas' Whale**, a painted inflatable nylon sculpture. 120 x 348". 2012.* Courtesy of Helen Hyder.

Renee Sage

Adelaide, South Australia

I grew up in a suburb of New York City and, even as a child, immersed myself in its art. My parents weren't able to see "artist" as a career path, so I studied psychology and became a special education teacher. In 1972, my life took an unexpected turn with my divorce, remarriage, and move to Australia, where I was teaching and raising four children. When I turned 40, my mother unexpectedly died, and I realized that I should follow my passion to become an artist. I became an art student, studying drawing, painting, and sculpture.

Nature, its beauty, its repetition, its transience, and its unrivalled color relationships and nuances of color, have always affected me. This led me to painting a series of larger-than-life irises, portraits, and women's issues.

When my husband and I were nearing retirement, we decided to add another level to our home—a studio for me, a study for him, and a table for grandchildren to share our passions. My studio sits in the treetops with the rainbow lorikeets, the faraway ocean, the brilliant sunsets, with classical music playing in the background, and inspiration everywhere.

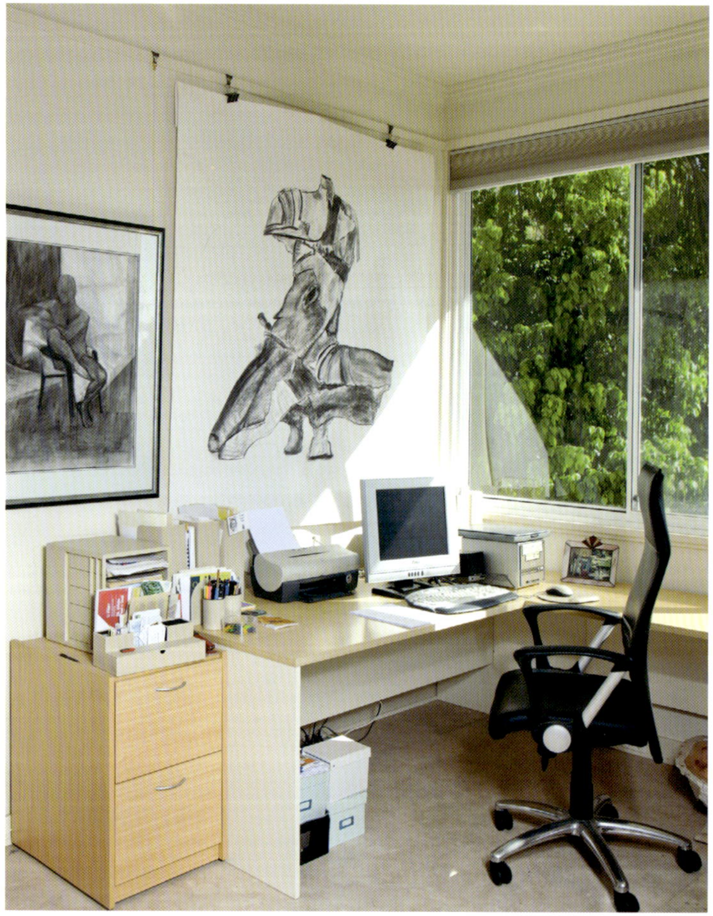

In Australia, the best light comes from the south. The wraparound windows give me views of the city of Adelaide as well as the western sunsets over the sea. My studio contains a computer desk to keep in touch with family and friends and a most useful sink. The two charcoals are Ken *and* Study for Falling Man.

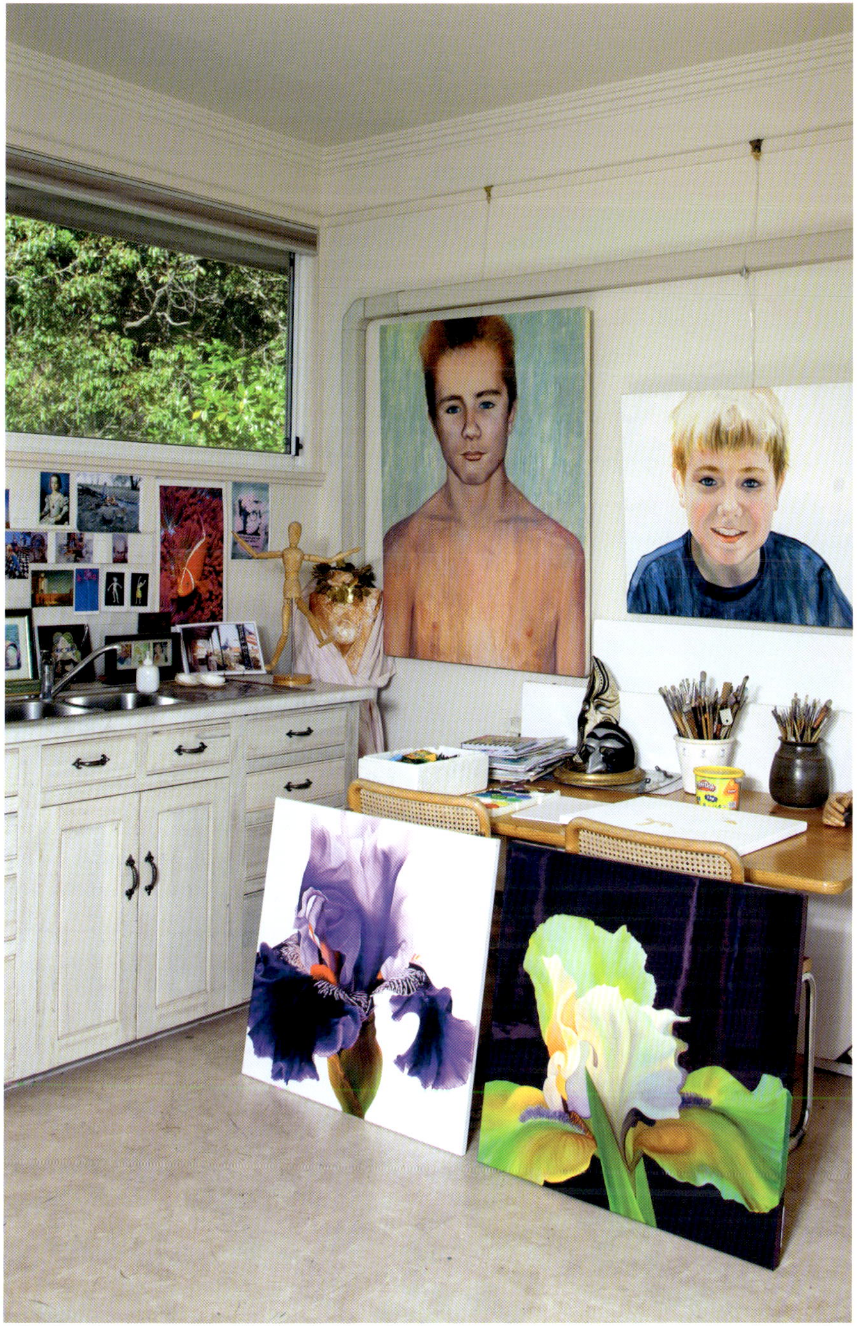

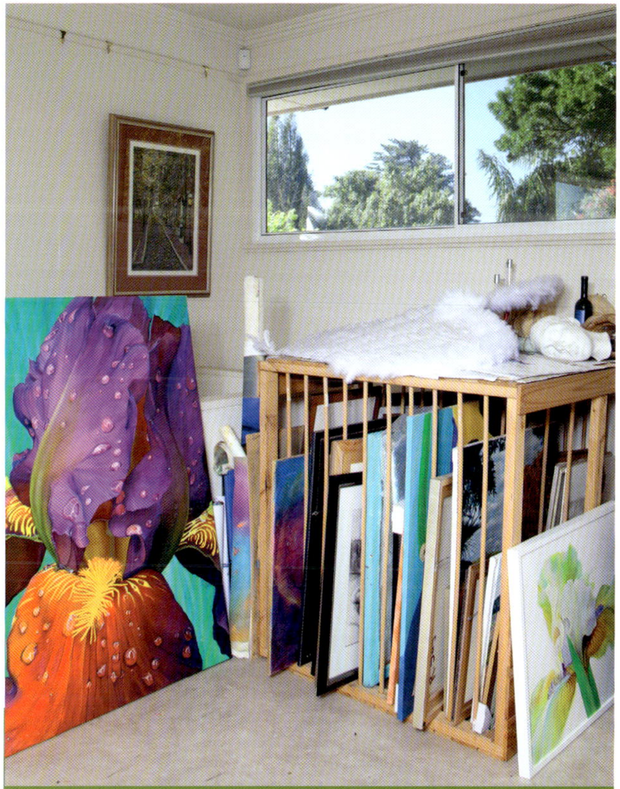

I reserve a table for our five grandchildren, who think it's very special to work in Nana's "real artist's studio." The paintings over the table are my grandson Daniel at different ages.

My family has always supported my art. Our daughter built a bespoke sink and cabinet for me, and my husband built a storage rack.

Stephanie Standish

Terre Haute, Indiana

When my husband and I purchased our beautiful 1915 Craftsman-style home in early 2008, the basement was part of what sealed the deal, at least for me. With three-quarters of the house's footprint as basement space, it seemed like the perfect place for an in-home studio. After spending a few years fixing the space up (painting, updating the electrical/plumbing, and building worktables), it is now a fully functional studio. Two of the basement's four rooms are dedicated to the studio, one for painting and drawing, the other for printing, matting/framing, and storage. The painting and drawing studio, which was originally the house's third bedroom, is my main workspace. Here I compose all of my paintings and drawings as well as all the plates and films for my prints. The printmaking studio is a little bit rougher around the edges with a cement floor and unfinished concrete walls. It's a great space for printing, with a utility sink and lots of lights. We added pegboard to divide the room from the crawl space and use it to hang tools. My husband built my two print studio worktables to help me maximize working and storage space.

Having an in-home studio is ideal for me. As a stay-at-home mother of one, I have the perfect place to duck away and work while my son naps or on the weekends.

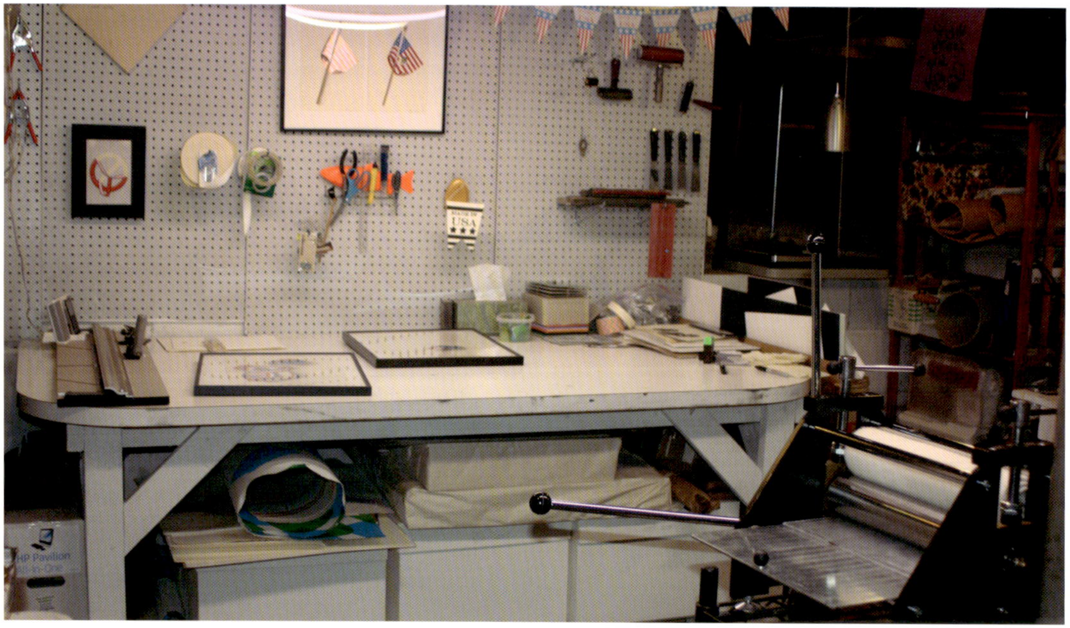

The printmaking studio, directly adjacent to my drawing studio, contains two large worktables, storage shelves, and my small etching press.

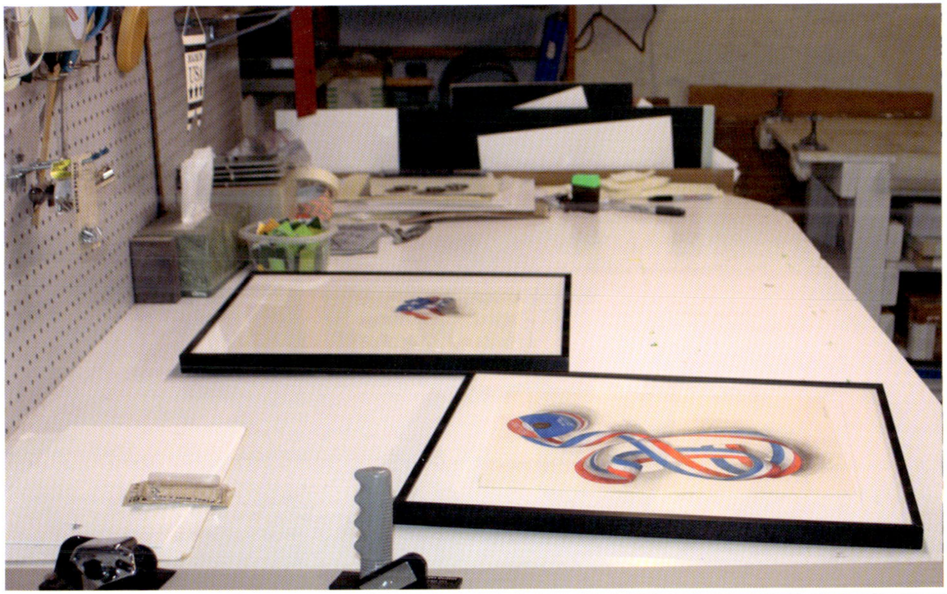

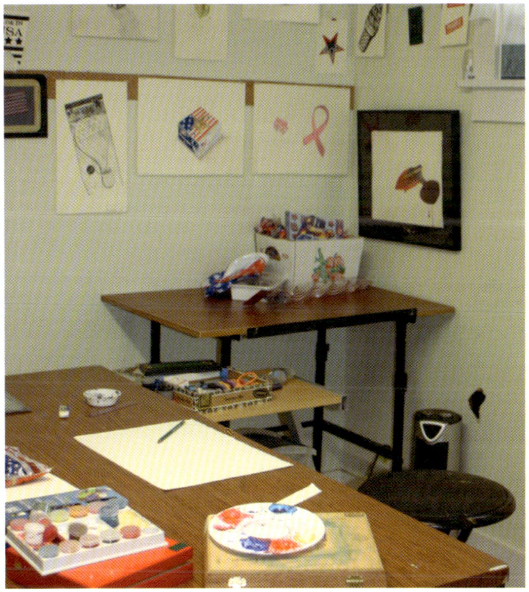

Made from a recycled kitchen countertop, this table serves as my matting/framing table as well as my clean table for printing. The pegboard behind the table is a great place to store tools.

The drawing/painting studio is a converted basement bedroom, which sometimes functions as a guest room. With a view looking out onto our small koi pond, I do all my painting and prep work for printmaking here. My large desk for painting was salvaged from my old workplace. Still life material that I have already painted is displayed in the windowsill.

Using a workbench kit from the hardware store, my husband modified this table to be not only a working surface for printmaking but also storage for paper, artwork, and matted prints.

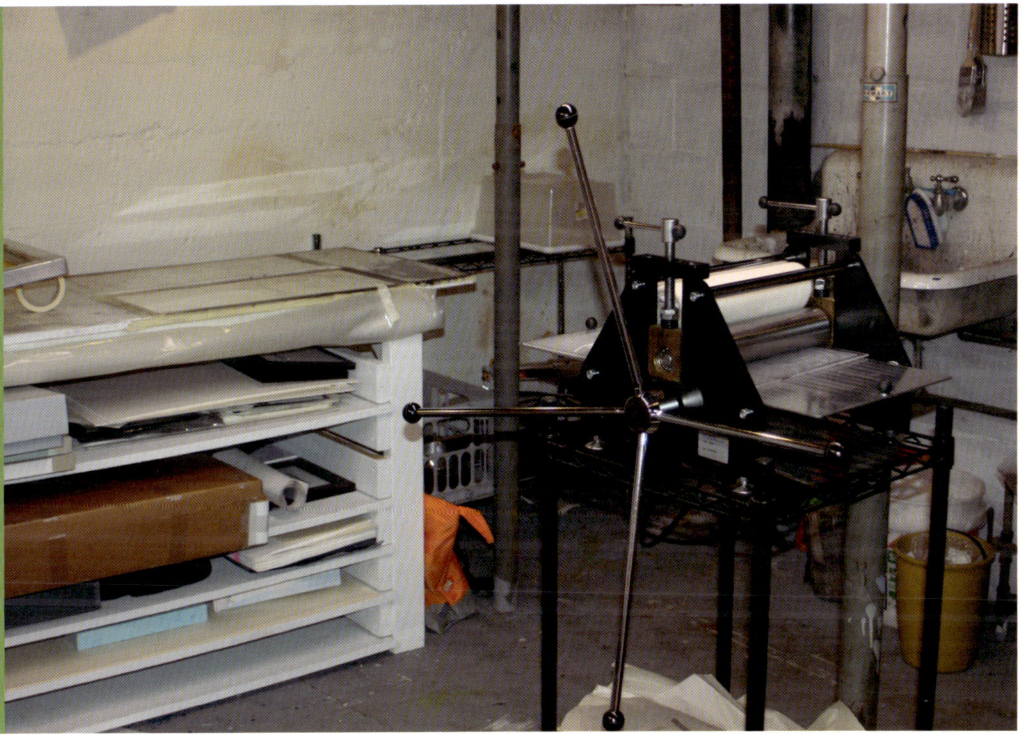

Tracey Tarling

Vancouver, British Columbia, Canada

I live on the side of a forested mountain in Vancouver, British Columbia. My absolute favorite place to be is in my home studio, unfolding the poetics of the natural world through paint. All things in this Pacific coastal environment have a certain narrative of mystery. The mists and soft light conspire to cloak as much as to reveal the essential nature of things. I like to think of my studio as sacred space or maybe a bit of an alchemist's den. I am forever mixing glazes and contemplating color. My studio is filled with recycled yogurt tubs full of messy oil paint tubes of every color: one tub for reds and magentas, one for cerulean and ultra marine blues. I use porcupine quills to unclog the tubes of oil. I love the feel of them in my hand. I can't imagine a studio not being a part of my home. One of the great advantages is to have brush in hand immediately when inspired, even in the middle of the night.

While painting, I often open the French doors and enjoy walking out to the small garden. Drapes diffuse the afternoon light. Photos and scraps of paper are tacked to the white walls. It's a bit of an eclectic mess. A few old cookie tins filled with brushes line the palette tables, which are on wheels. The larger one was built for me and even has a bookshelf where I place resource photos, graphite sticks, or anything that I don't want to lose like my telephone. I like to walk past these new surfaces thinking of all the possibilities they represent.

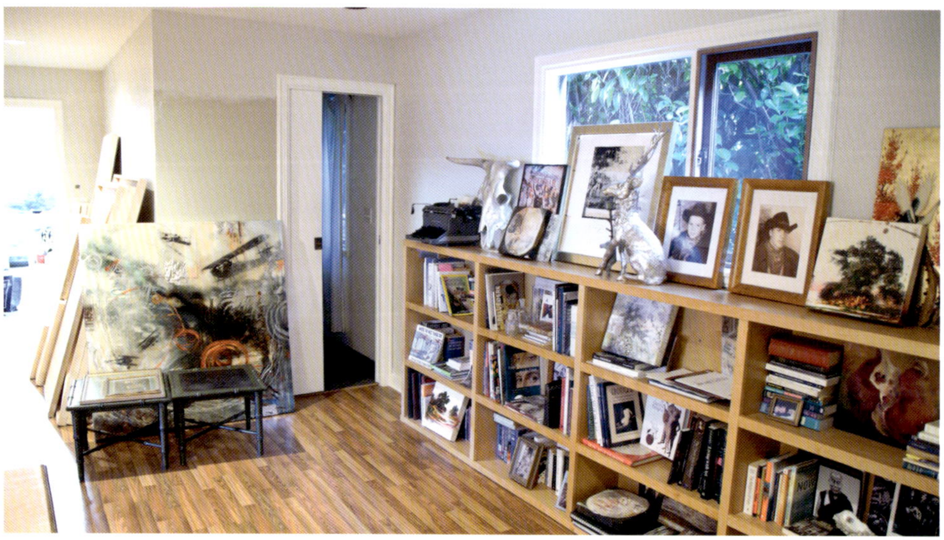

I surround myself in my studio with objects I find beautiful or make me think. All the counters, tables, and even my blue velvet chaise lounge are covered in nests, shells, and driftwood. I have a vertical wooden storage shelf to place wet work. I stack surfaces-in-waiting outside my studio door, spilling into the house. Courtesy of Cori Creed.

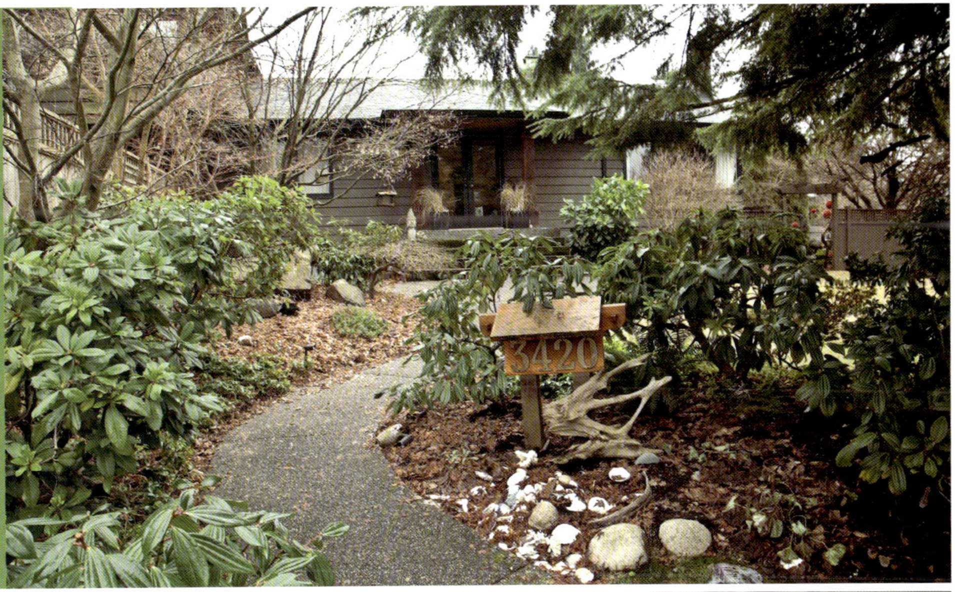

My studio is a converted two-car indoor garage. That's 400 square feet! Courtesy of Cori Creed.

I added a sink, picture widows, and French doors out to the garden. I also added a floor made from mats of recycled tires, the same mats that are usually around skating rinks. I stand when I paint, and it's a lot easier on the feet! Courtesy of Cori Creed.

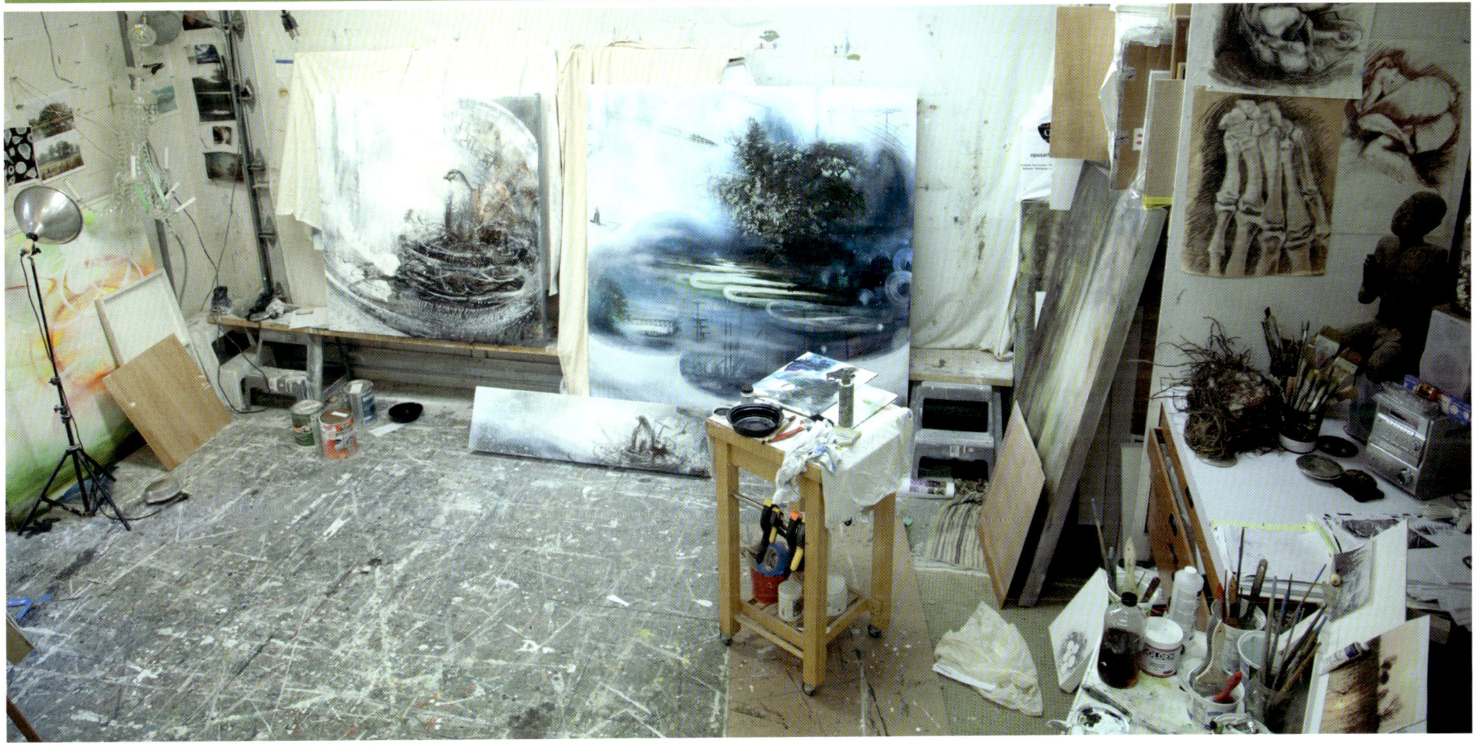

3

Outbuildings

Many artists have either constructed a studio in an outbuilding on their property or renovated a building on the property, such as a barn, garage, or even a chicken coop! This way they can remove the mess and potential noise of a studio from the home.

Kelly Milukas has her encaustic stainless steel table on giant casters in her spacious barn. Courtesy of Marianne Lee.

Judy Youngblood's studio in the evening.

An exterior portal allows natural light to filter into Debra Fritts's studio. Courtesy of Convivial Design, Melinda Hess and Patricia Antelles.

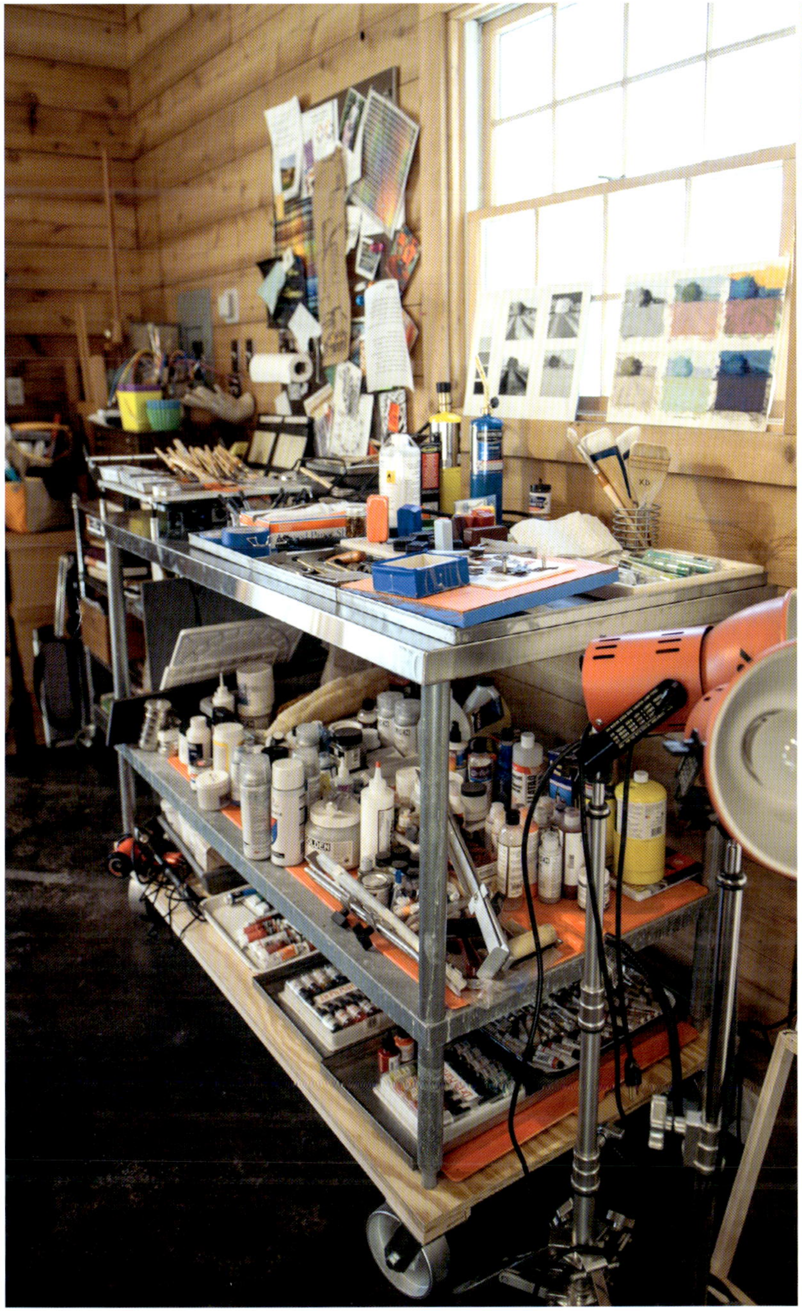

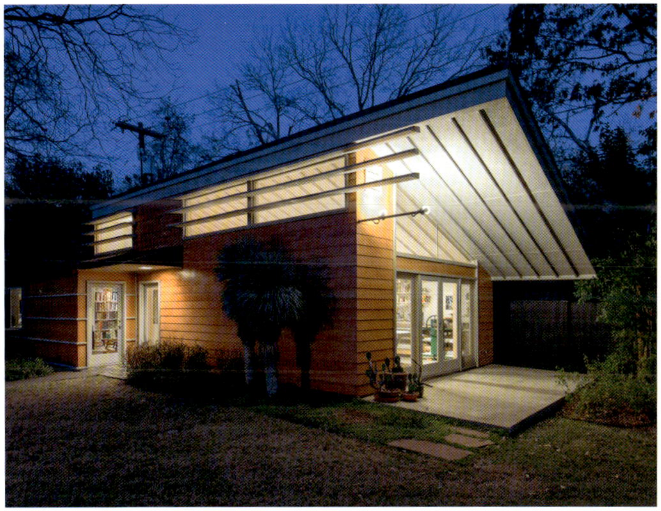

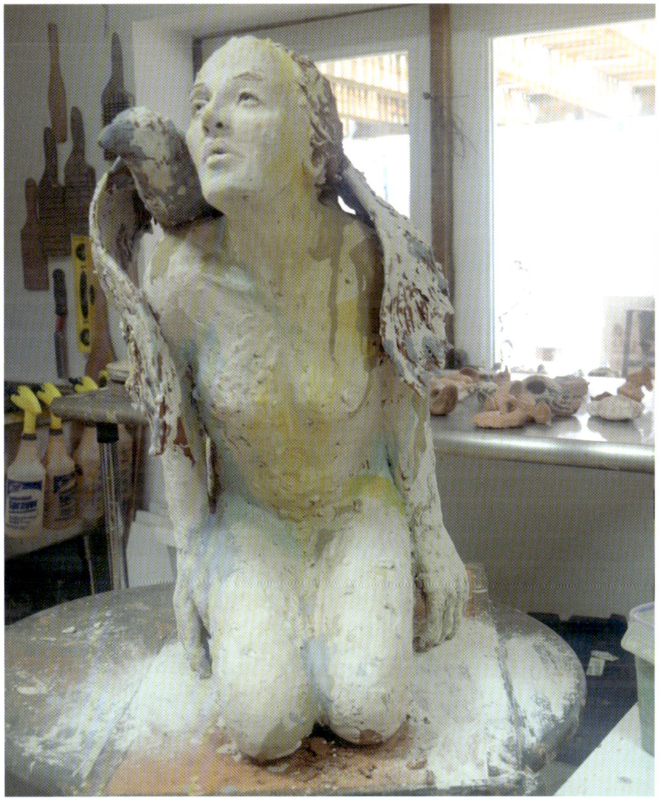

Alan Binstock

Mt. Rainier, Maryland

My studio is permeated with my strong affinity with glass, steel, and resin, and their rich dialogues. A registered architect as well as a sculptor, I designed the studio and contracted it in two phases, doing the mezzanine later. It was built into the existing hill, which creates more mass for keeping the studio warm.

Down the steps, past the winter garden and the stacks of raw materials, stands my 900-square-foot atelier. Heated with a wood stove, capturing lots of natural light, storing too many tools, it serves me well. The 12-foot doors and various cranes support the creation of large, three-dimensional pieces. The mezzanine above the tool room exhibits my smaller pieces and provides a place for fellow geriatric hippies to plug in their electric instruments and jam every month.

Around 6 p.m., I arrive in the studio, which is preheated with a natural gas radiant heater. My sculpting activities are balanced and tempered by a concurrent career as architect at NASA's Goddard Space Flight Center. The continued exposure to near and deep space images, as well as a bit of quantum physics, are powerful influences on my work. All this, balanced with an avid immersion in the teachings of Yoga, allows me to express the nature of the seeker's inner passage while capturing the wonder of the explorer's outward search to find meaning in the universe. All this happens in this second home of mine.

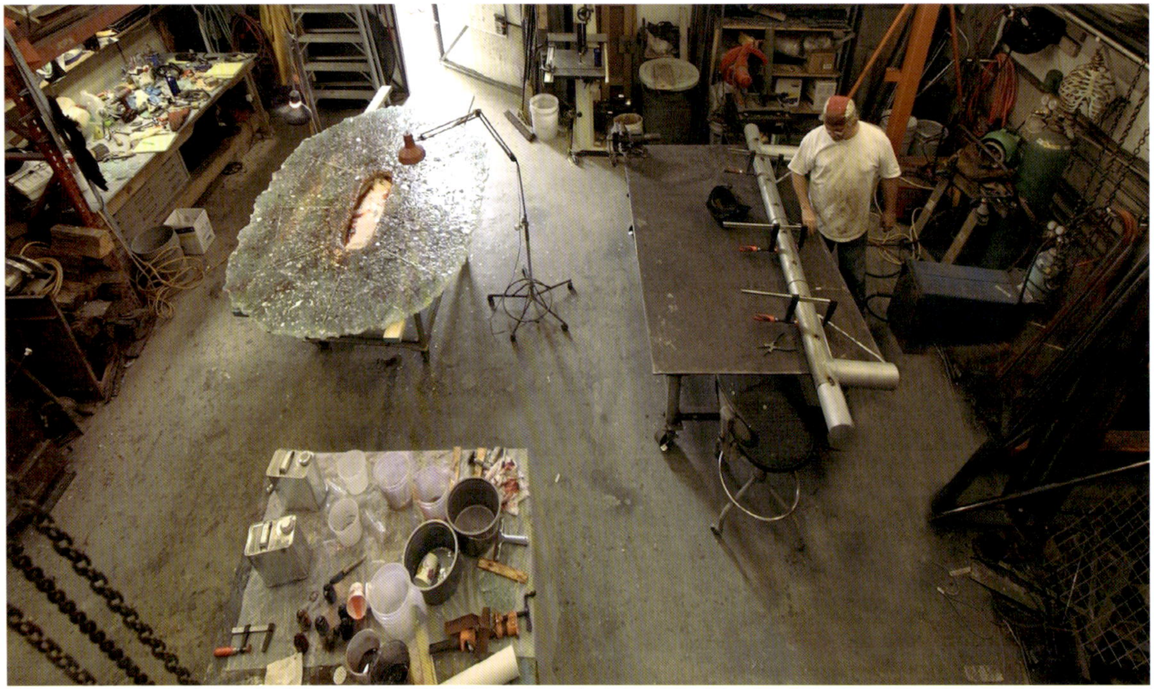

Studio and mezzanine. Courtesy of Carol A. Binstock.

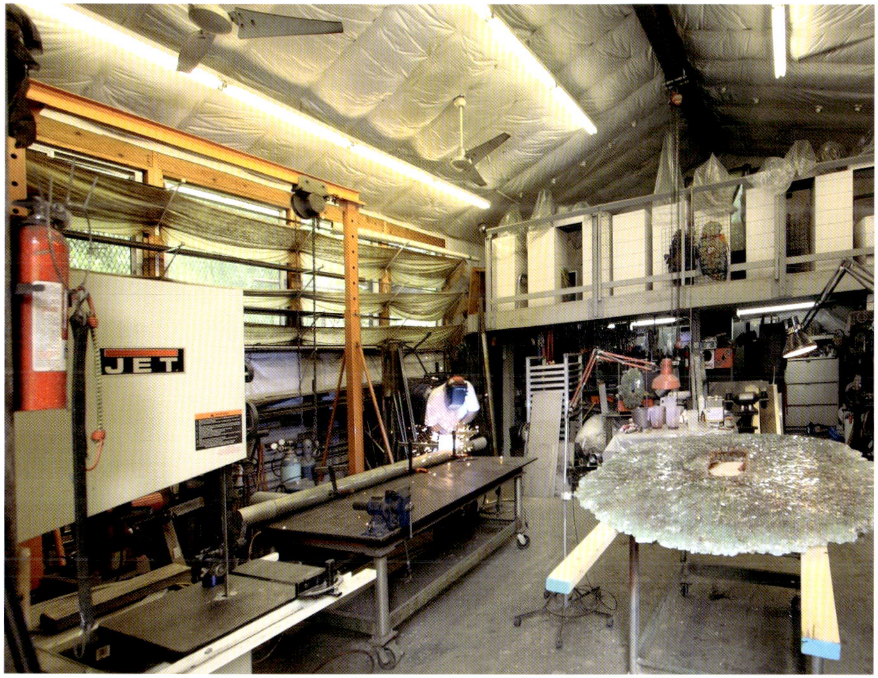

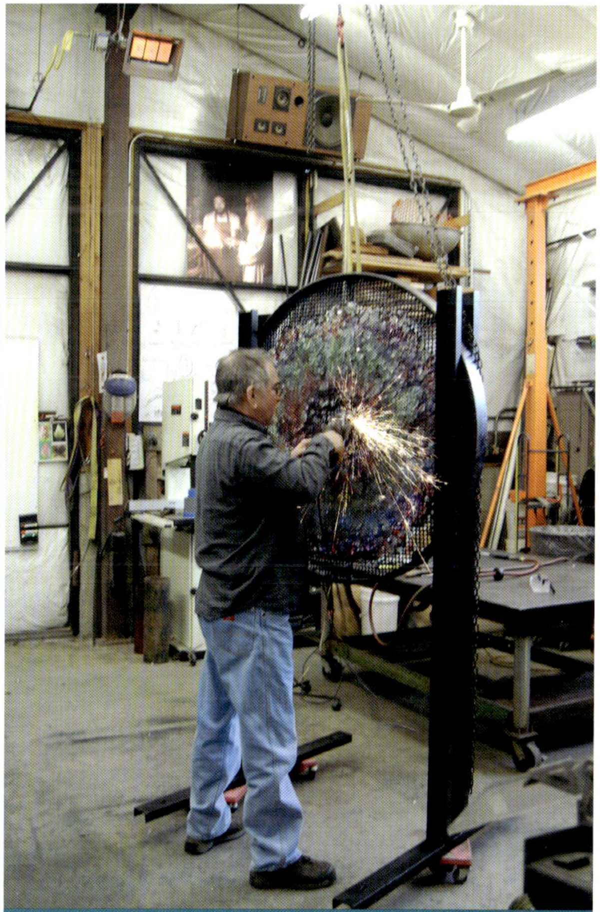

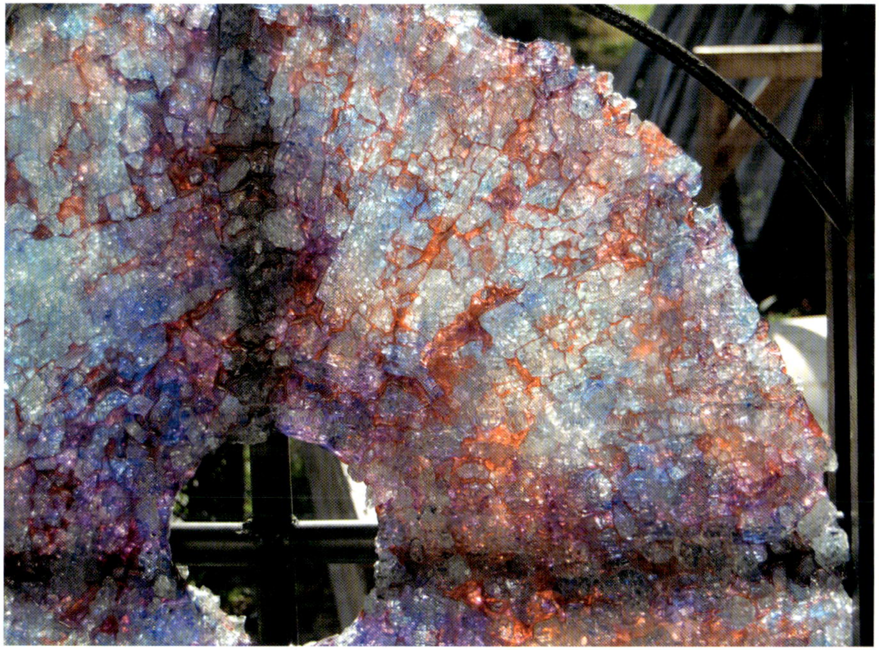

Assembly of second portal. Courtesy of Carol A. Binstock.

Grinding third portal. Courtesy of Carol A. Binstock.

Detail. Courtesy of Carol A. Binstock.

Dimitri Gerakaris

Canaan, New Hampshire

I create artistic environments for people. I began by creating my own artistic environment, which has nourished and informed what I have been doing the past forty plus years.

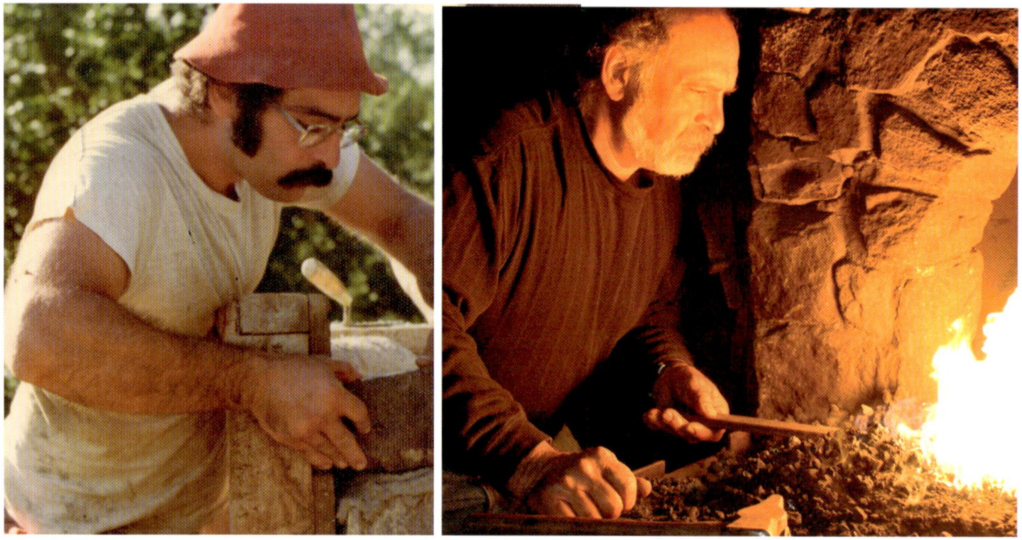

I laid up the stone masonry for my studio forge in 1973 in remote and verdant New Hampshire hill country on the original Appalachian Trail. Granted to the Colonial proprietor by King George III, this land feels very special today. Courtesy of Mary Gerakaris.

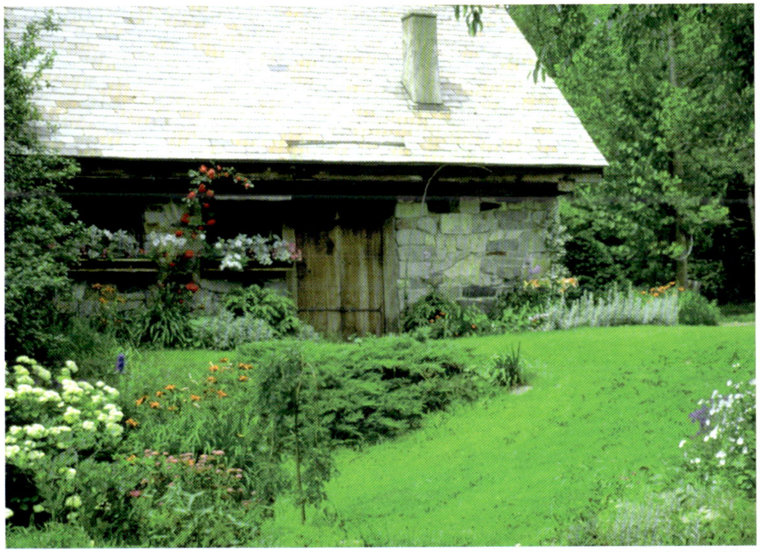

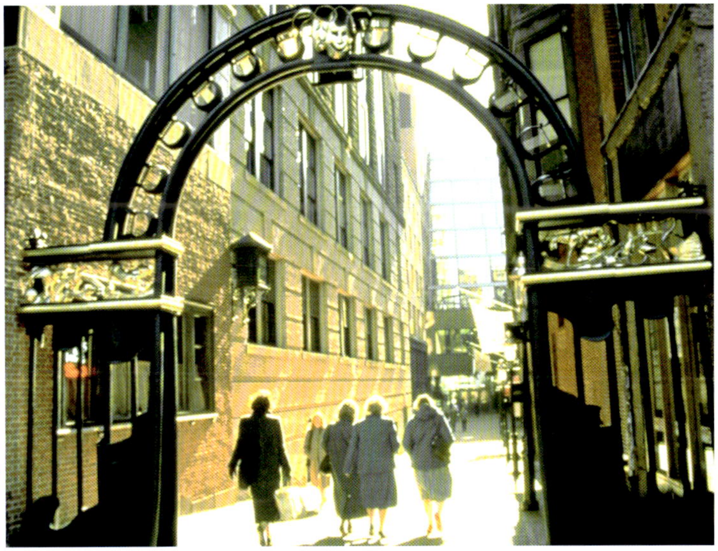

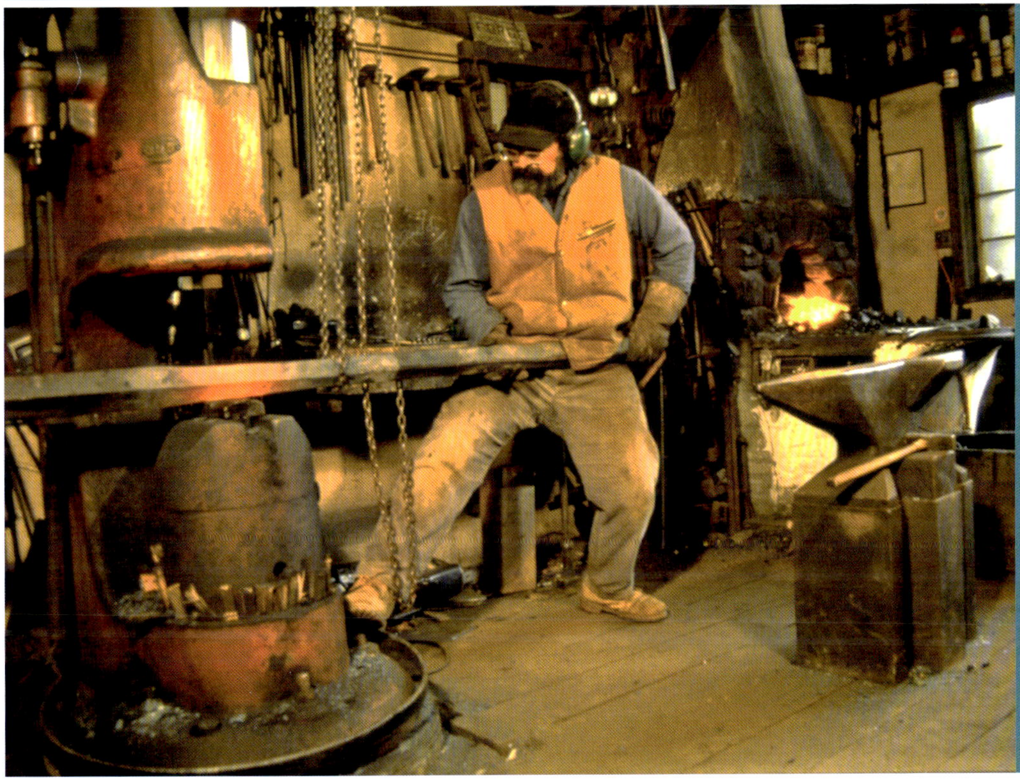

I built the stone building from the ground up, splitting the granite stones with chisels I forged, plastering the walls, slating the roof, doing the landscaping, etc. I feel tremendously grounded and connected to this place where I have been creating artwork all these years—and it's great fun to see visitors react to this most uncommon environment.

Although I also do small works, the high, timbered roof in the studio allows me to tackle architectonic commissions. Here, I am hammering out some of the massive bars that form part of Boston's Boylston Place Gateway, which links Boston Common to the Theater District. Courtesy of Mary Gerakaris.

The final product: ***Boylston Place Gateway****, entrance to Boston Theater District. Galvanized forged steel and bronze. 19 x 27 x 6'. 1988.*

Ken and Julie Girardini

Sykesville, Maryland

Our home and studio are two very different spaces. The studio is dirty, loud, and vibrating with motion six days per week. By contrast, our house is clean, tranquil, and soothing. This yin/yang is a must in our lives.

We designed and built our studio to meet our needs. A large overhead garage door allows us to accept deliveries of large pieces of steel and move artwork in and out easily. Throughout the studio, there are different rooms with different functions and levels of cleanliness. The cutting and grinding room is the dirtiest. The metal is stored in this room, which is where the plasma cutting, grinding, sanding, etc., occur. The welding area is in the main room, where we have a 25-ton press that uses various jigs for pressing metal, a large table saw, two welding tables, and other clean worktables to stage projects that are in production. All of our pieces are sprayed with lacquer in another room, where we have an industrial quality spray booth with filters, so the contaminants can be removed from the air before it is exhausted from the building. We have a "clean" area where finished pieces are stored and packed, ready for shipping or shows. Upstairs in the studio, we have our office and a photo studio, so we can photograph every piece we make. It doubles as a makeshift gallery space during our yearly open-studio show.

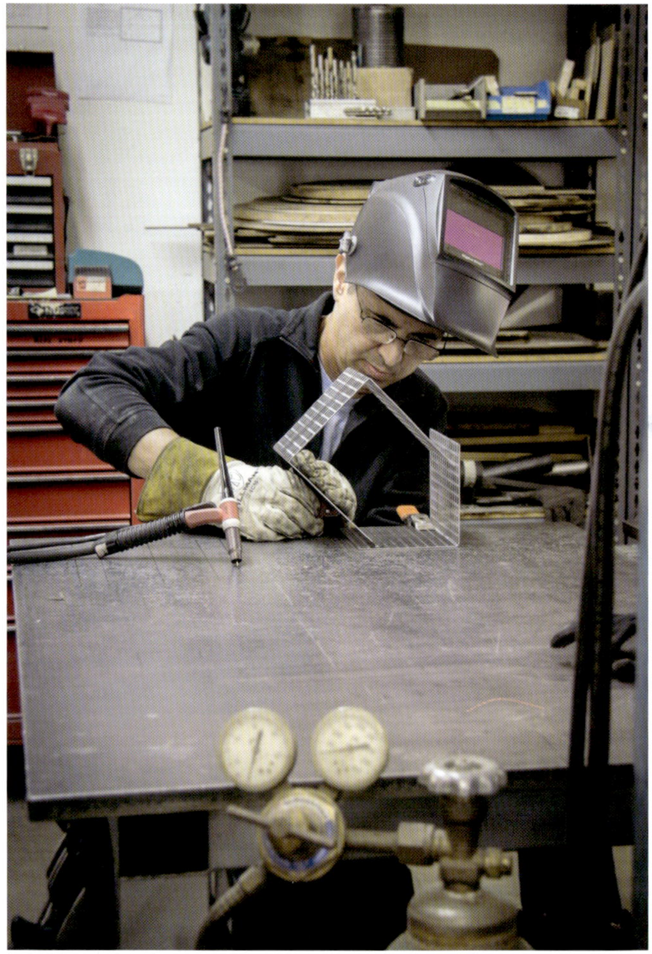

As artists we are hands-on with our materials. Ken is shown welding, and Julie is grinding and letting the sparks fly. Downstairs in the studio, we have our compressors in a clean space to keep the noise out of the main working area. We also have kilns so we can do fusing and slumping of glass and ceramics. We have collected many different pieces of equipment that add to the diversity of what we can do: a potters wheel, sewing machines, cameras, computers, and printers. All of this makes for a true mixed media mecca for making art.

The ever-changing scenes out of our windows inform our work and spirit. Our studio is a walk across the lawn—a deliberate choice we made in an effort to simplify our lives. The outdoor living spaces allow us to see nature and be part of it. The rock garden and terrace with comfortable furniture remind us to take a break.

Our home serves as inspiration for our own work. We keep several of our own pieces and have collected special pieces from other artists so to surround ourselves with beauty.

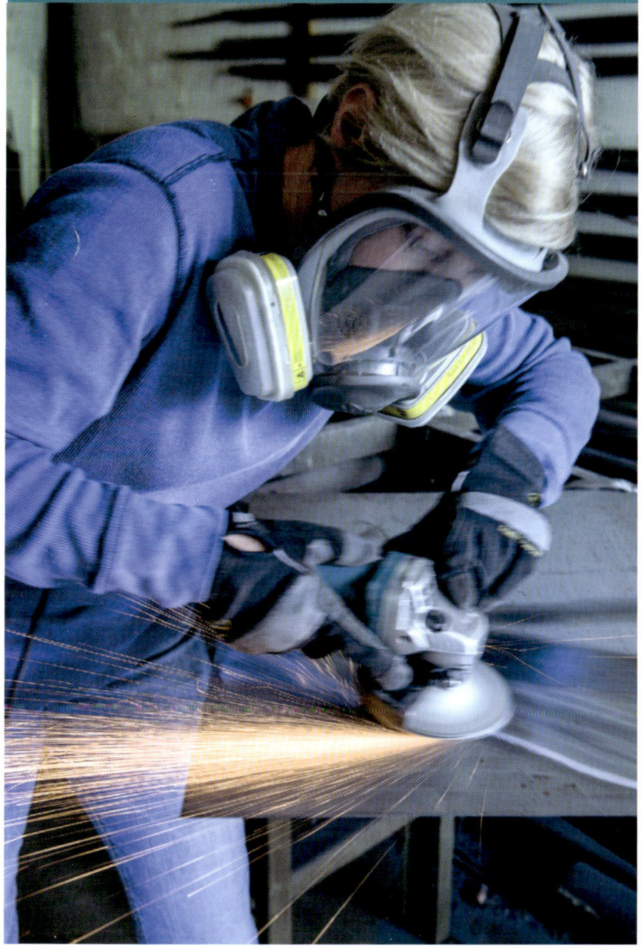

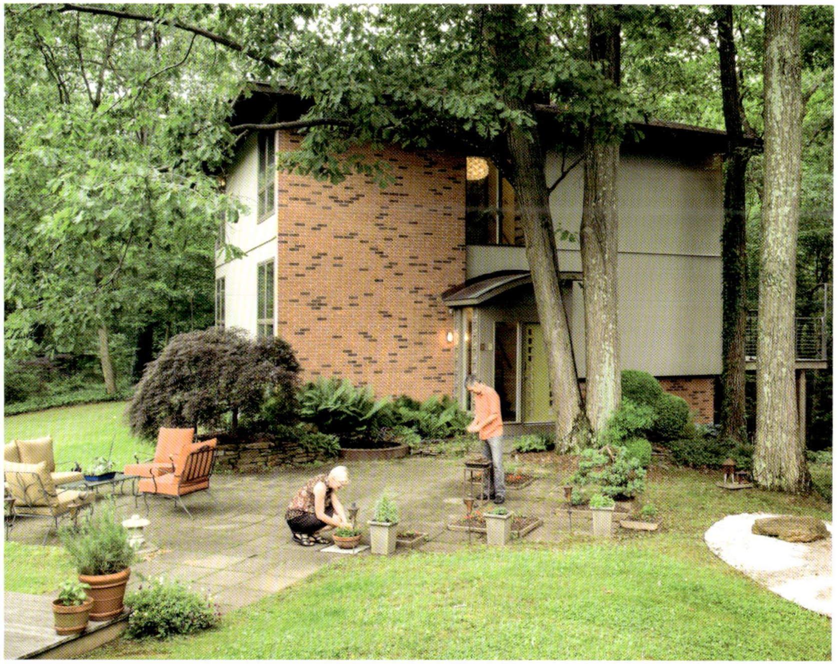

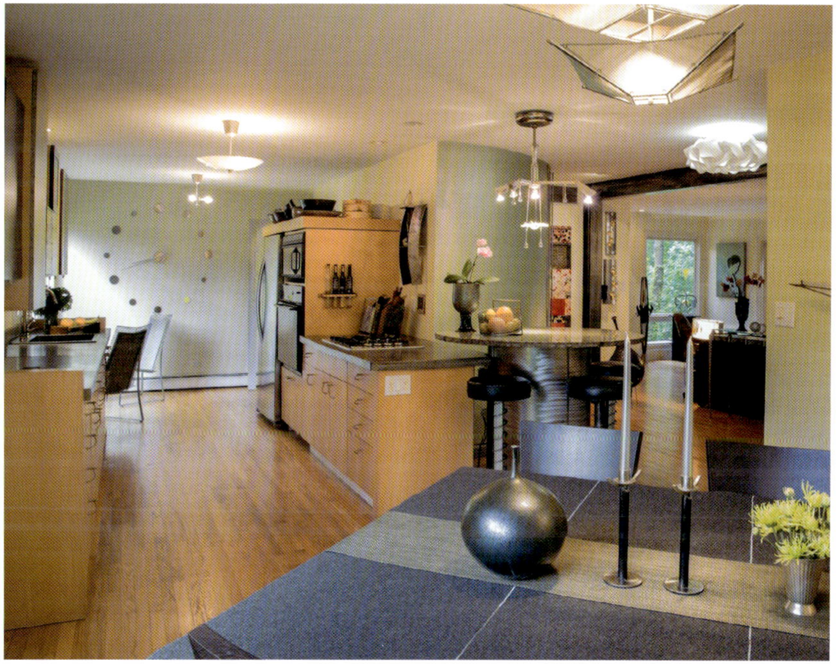

Karen Hackenberg

Port Townsend, Washington

Seattle architects Miller Hull worked with me to design my barn-like studio built a few steps from my home and situated on a secluded bay off of the Strait of Juan de Fuca. The climate in the Pacific Northwest can be overcast, so I made sure to include many windows, allowing any available rays of sunlight to penetrate my creative space.

My current series of *Watershed* paintings are inspired by the ironic incongruity of man-made items of detritus that wash up on the otherwise pristine beach below my studio—plastic PETE water bottles, toy animals, and branded product packages, to name but a few. Collecting this local flotsam, I pose and photograph it in the tidal zone below my studio, and then haul it back, organize, and store it in the studio for reference in my artwork. Painting traditionally with oil and gouache, I lovingly and meticulously craft images of these conventionally "ugly" beach cast-offs, creating a taxonomy of beach trash and a provocative visual juxtaposition of form and idea.

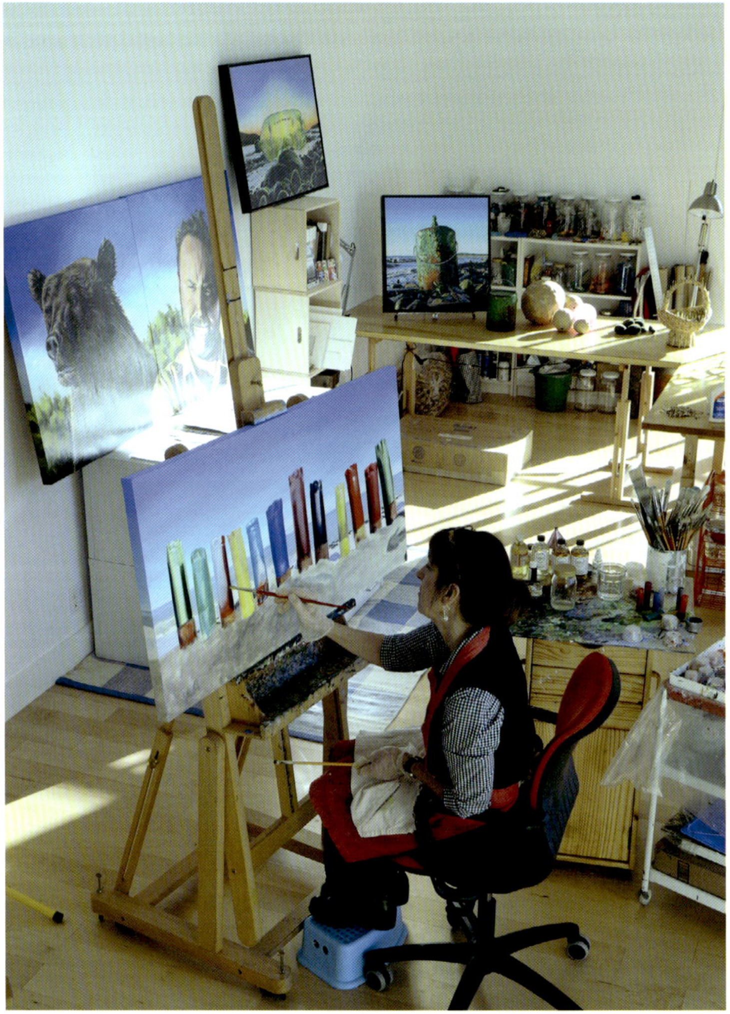

Taking advantage of my large open workspace, the work surfaces roll and are lightweight, enabling flexible arrangements for my painting and sculpture projects. Sorted by kind and color, I store collected beach flotsam in large recycled glass jars.
Courtesy of Charles Kent Wiggins.

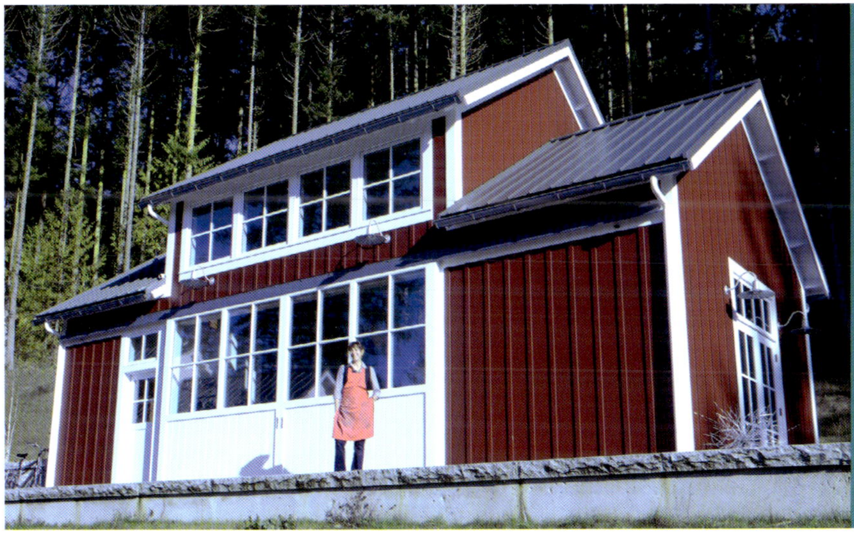

My barnlike studio has large double-doors that slide apart to create a wide opening that overlooks the forest, meadow, frog pond, and saltwater bay below.

The 9-foot tall x 20-foot wide opening in one wall brings the outside inside. When I open the doors on warm days, the forest, meadow, and saltwater bay below become my studio. Courtesy of Charles Kent Wiggins.

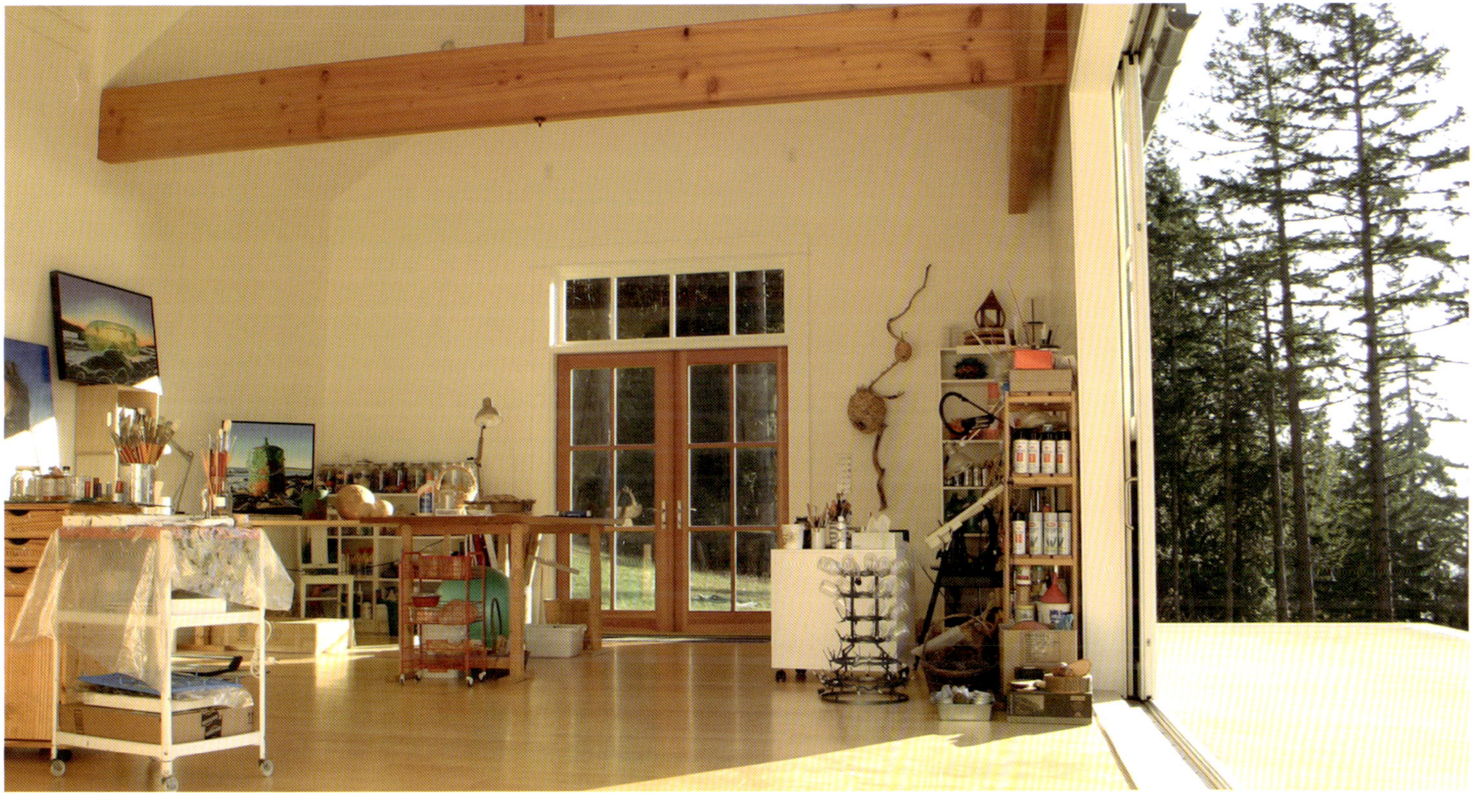

Stephen Hansen

Las Cruces, New Mexico

Long ago, I would live in my studios; then I discovered that I liked living with other people, but I didn't like other people living in my studio. A short commute became necessary. I am now in my third New Mexico studio; I find that each is less "New Mexican" than the one before.

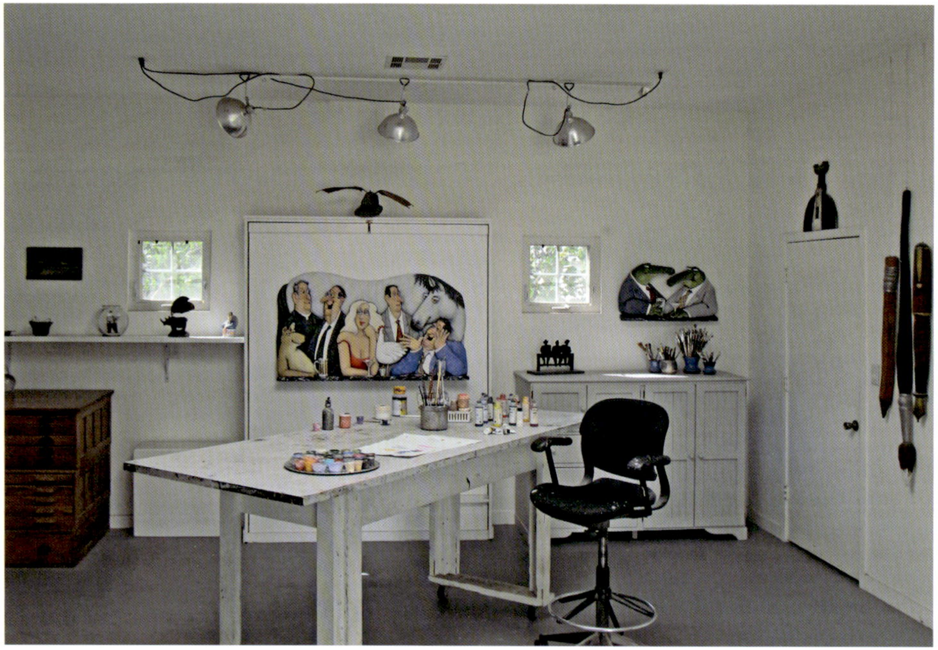

My studios change, but I have been drawing in the same chair for forty years. The paper mache relief, ***A Guy Walks Into A Bar,*** *is in the center; to the right is* ***Litigators*** *made of cast resin. The rest are the wood, steel, and bronze items that gradually fill up whatever space I work in.*

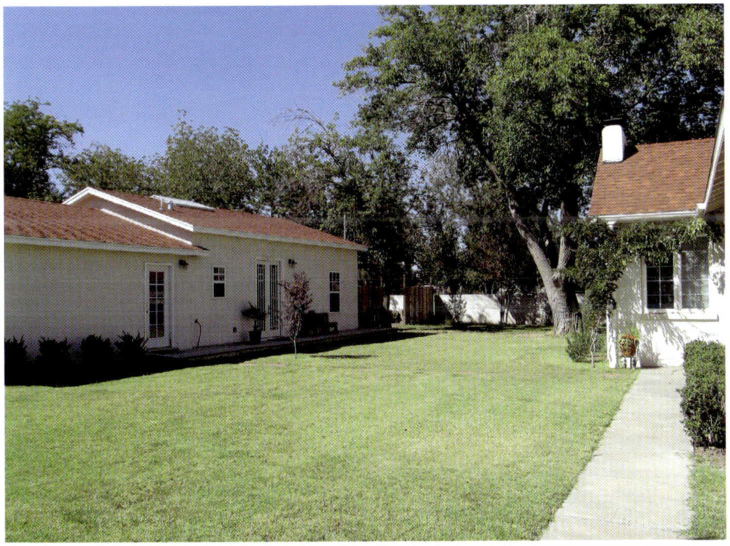

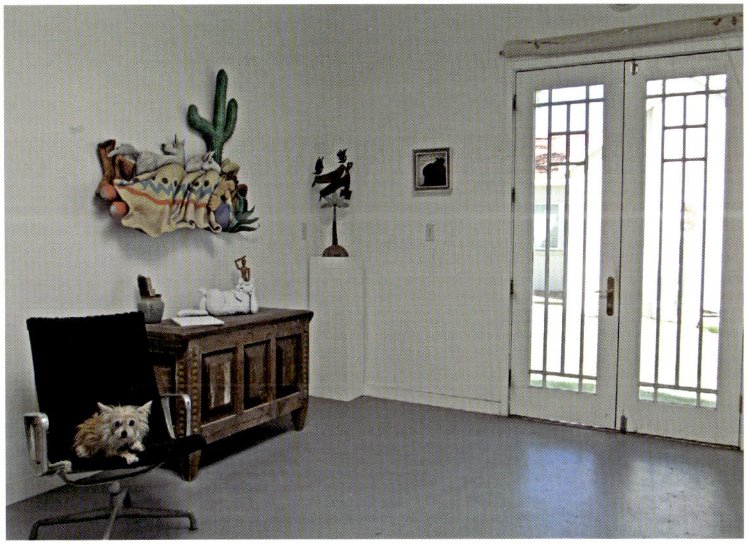

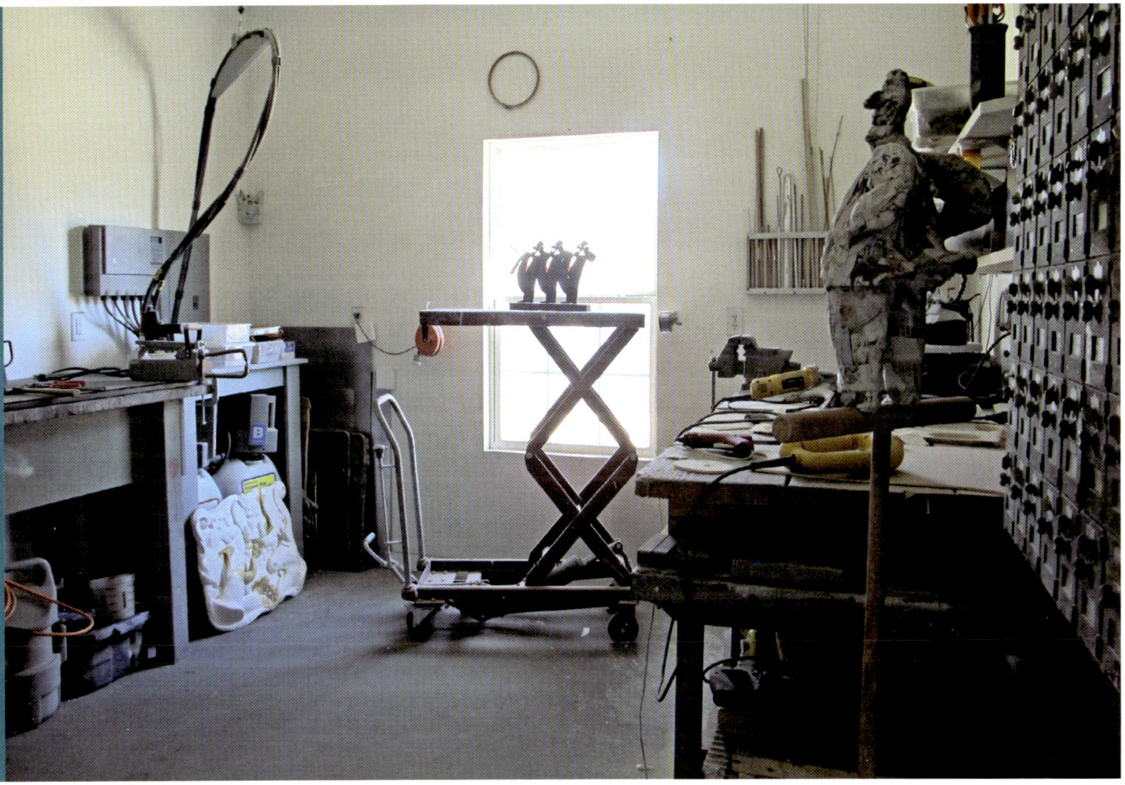

The commute between my house, on the right, to the studio, on the left.

The studio dog.

My sculptures begin and end in the clean part of my studio, but their first transition, from idea to object starts in the dark interior.

Dale Kennington

Dothan, Alabama

My husband and I added the studio, the painting storage, and the guesthouse to the property and renovated our house. My life today is spent in a 15 x 24 x 28-foot studio and a 20 x 16-foot storage room. I get up every morning, pick up a cup of coffee, and walk into the studio. Unless I have an appointment, I spend the day there until the light begins to go. Is it boring? I don't think so. I guess that I'm just used to it.

I paint in the northeast corner of my studio, a place lit with six, 9-foot high, 42-inch wide windows. This much light allows me to paint a little longer each day. Unless I'm in trouble, I usually finish one painting before beginning the next. I have a separate heating/air conditioning unit for the studio, as well as an exhaust fan system (like those used in surgical operating rooms), which runs twenty-four hours a day. The storage room serves as an area for paintings waiting to be varnished or shipped. It also has a separate heating/air conditioning system (to keep it at 65 degrees) and a humidity control unit.

Everything in my studio that can be moved on wheels is on wheels. This means the three easels, the palette table, the large table and various chairs all roll about. Hallelujah!! A different room in a few minutes!

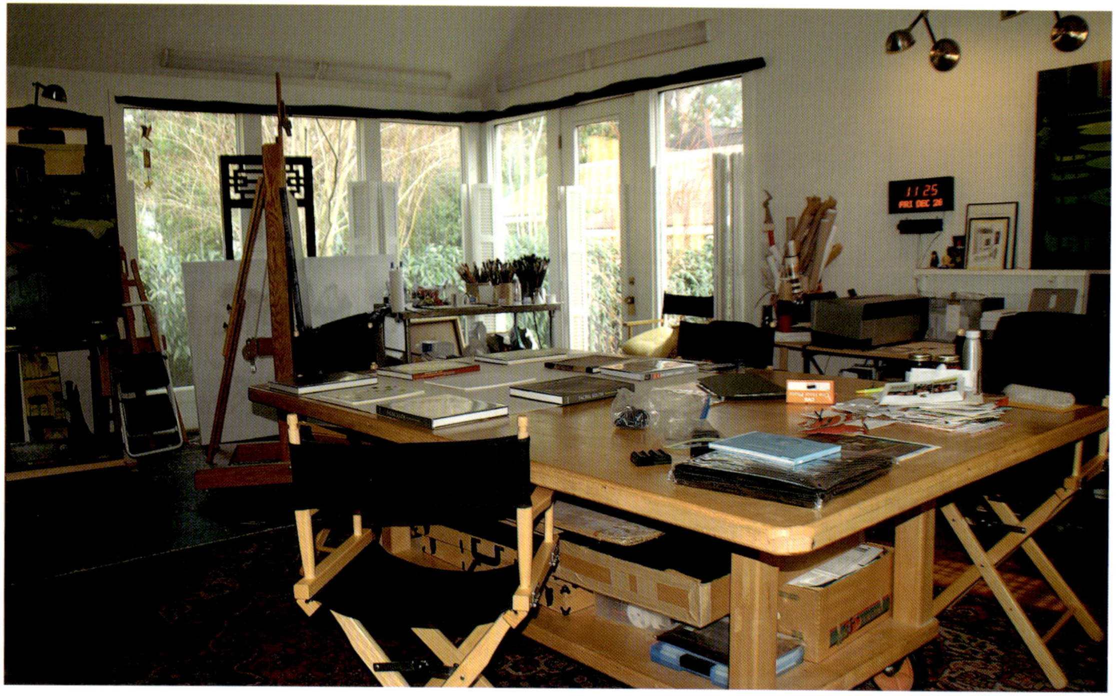

My studio looking north. I especially like the windows and the roll-about table.

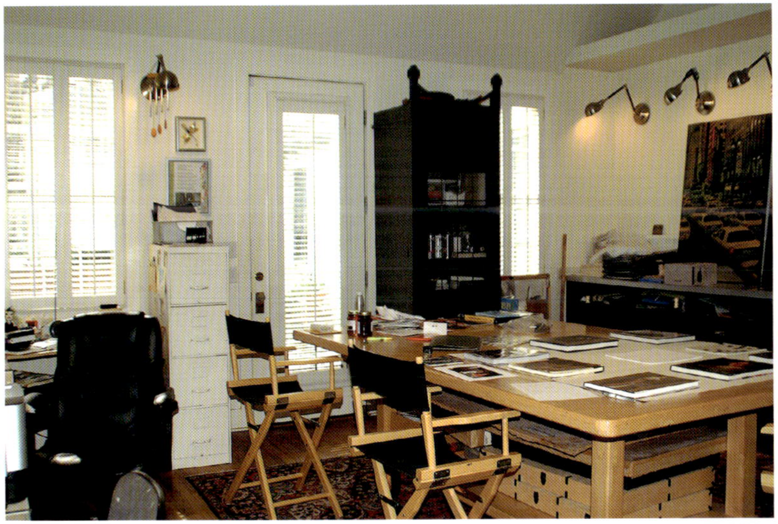

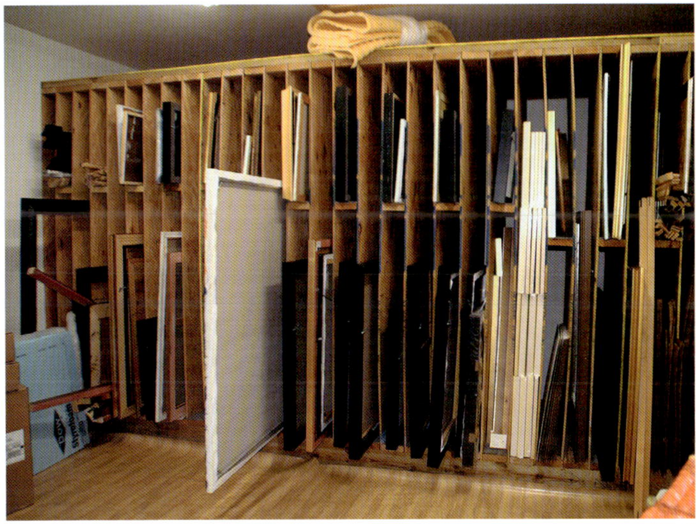

Computer, fax, and three printers are on the left (unseen) in this north view. The window blinds allow me to control the light.

Each slot in my storage shed is 6 inches wide. Every other one is 8 feet tall. The other slots are divided to hold two paintings. I use scraps of carpet glued to the bottom of each slot, so that I can slide things.

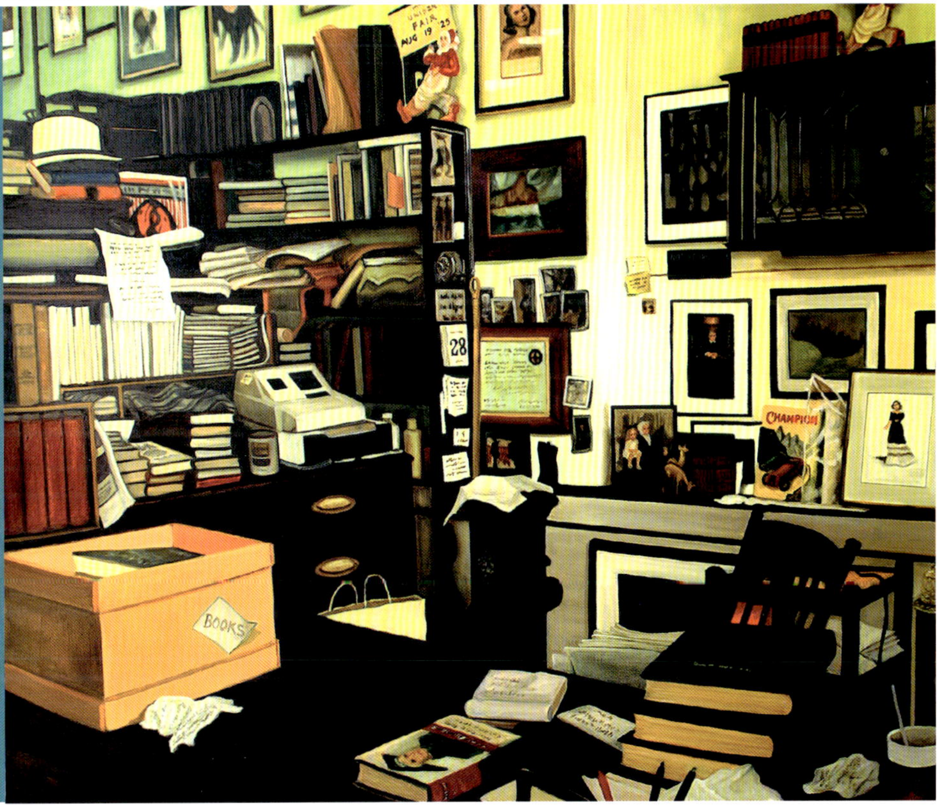

Books and Business.
Oil on canvas. 40 x 30". 2009.
Smithsonian American Art Museum.

Helen Klebesadel

Madison, Wisconsin

We were land rich but space poor. I was on a budget and acted as my own contractor in 2004. I had bought the energy-efficient windows and doors at a factory sale a few years before I figured out how to build a building around them. Working with a friend, I did the architectural drawings and had the specs done to get proper building permits. I hired a Mennonite carpenter to build the 16 x 24-foot studio to my design, using the windows and doors I had acquired. It turned out to be much cheaper to build a stand-alone building than an addition. If it had been attached to the house, I would have had to upgrade all of the wiring in the house. As a stand-alone building, it resulted in a lower tax increase as well. My son and I did all the wiring. It was quite a creative project.

I love my little studio refuge. It's the place I go to create my watercolor paintings. My watercolors run the gamut from careful study to poetic, symbolic, and sometimes political representations of nature and human nature. I enjoy immersing myself in the careful looking that painting from life allows, so my studio is full of objects I love or things I have dragged in to look at for a current work. My subject matter runs toward themes based in women's lives or nature. I sometimes layer metaphoric meaning into the images I create, which are meant to represent larger themes of human interaction.

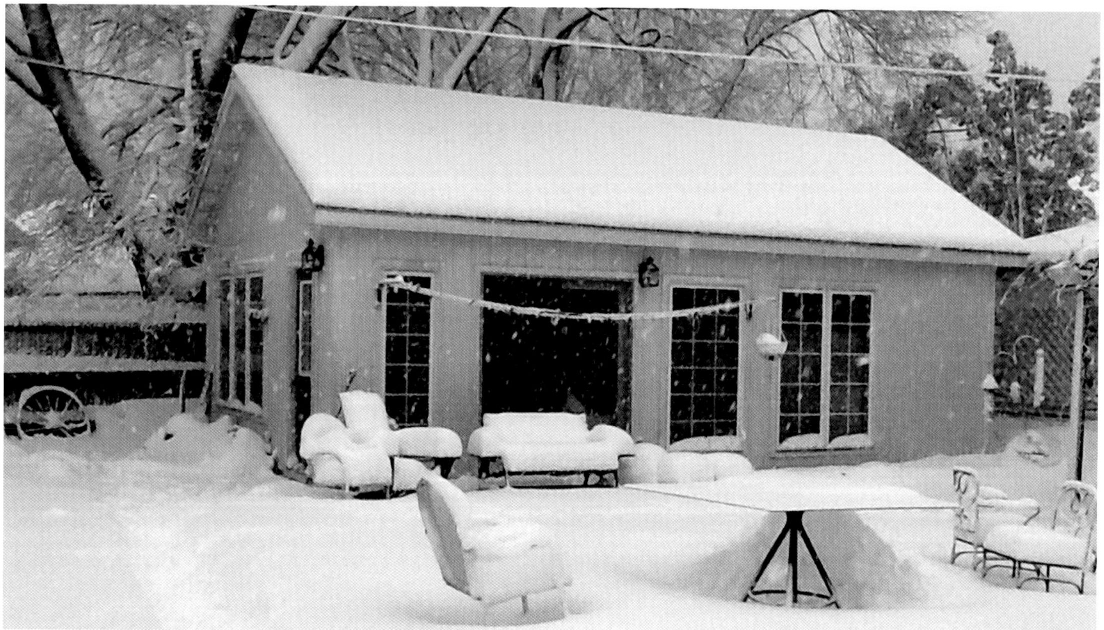

I built my one-room studio with two walls of east and north facing windows and two solid walls so I would have places to mount the work and excellent light. The ceiling fans and windows allow for good ventilation and cool breezes. The Wisconsin winter is a little daunting, but the cabin is well insulated. I keep a shovel handy. Courtesy of Andy Manis Photo.

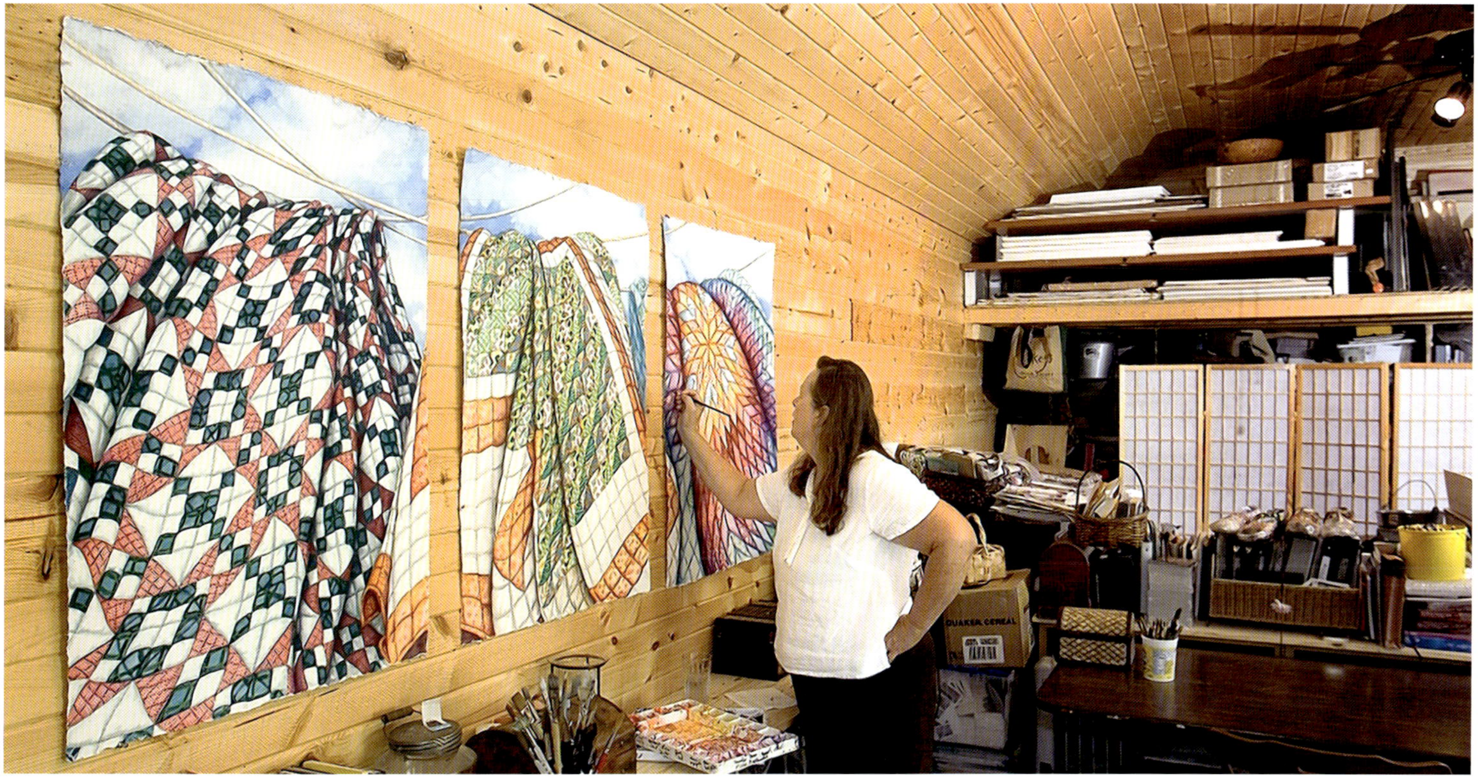

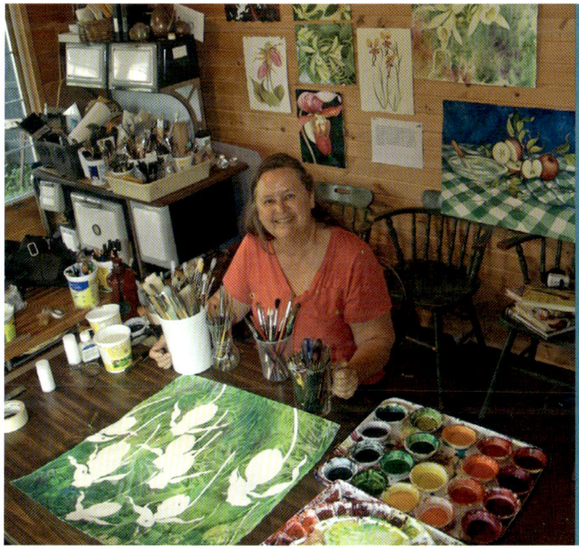

I usually work on flat tables and pin the works in progress to the wood paneling, where I can look at them and think about them. I'll often work on the details of the paintings while they are pinned to the wall. Courtesy of Lori Ushman, Madison, WI.

For large works, it's important to be able to put them up and get back far enough to see how they will look from a distance and if there are finishing touches needed. I built the studio with two walls of windows and two solid walls so I would have places to mount the work and excellent light. Courtesy of Andy Manis Photo.

Kevin Lyles

Gallipolis, Ohio

When we first moved to the southeast Ohio, land was inexpensive, but the right house was not. So, my wife and I bought land to build our home. Not having much experience with construction, but having sufficient carpentry skills to get by, I first built my 1200 square-foot studio. It was my plan to buy materials for our home and store them in the studio.

As a sculptor, my forte is using a variety of materials and techniques: welding, casting in glass and metal, working in clay, carving, and fabricating. In the studio, I have a large and open central bay, a 20-foot hoist, and two double-story side bays. One bay is for materials and the other houses all my tools and machinery. The wide doors look out upon a valley and pond. A year later, I built my house, just fifty yards up the hill.

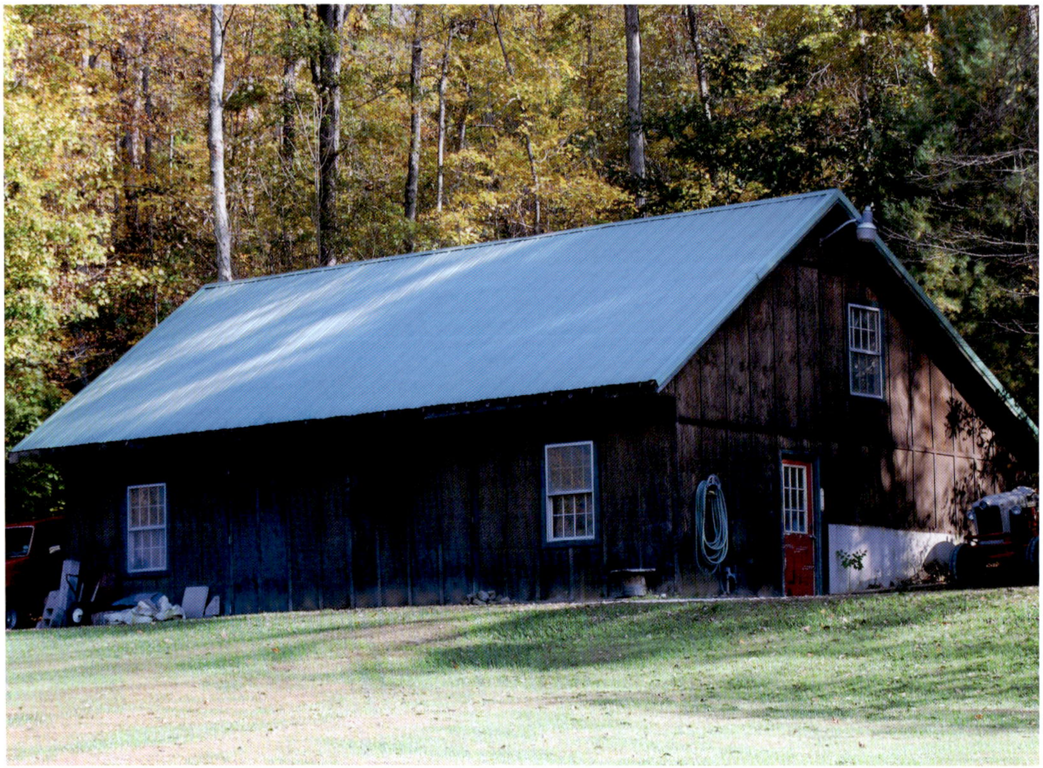

My studio is a 32 x 40-foot banked pole barn with two stories, a metal roof, and exterior plywood siding.

Here is an interior view of the studio showing the large open central bay. Two of my indoor works, ***Stacked Column*** *and* ***Chaos,*** *can be seen sitting on the floor.*

This side bay of the studio is where I create most of my work from the tools and machinery I have collected. Sitting on the table saw is my ***Farmland Forest*** *maquette.*

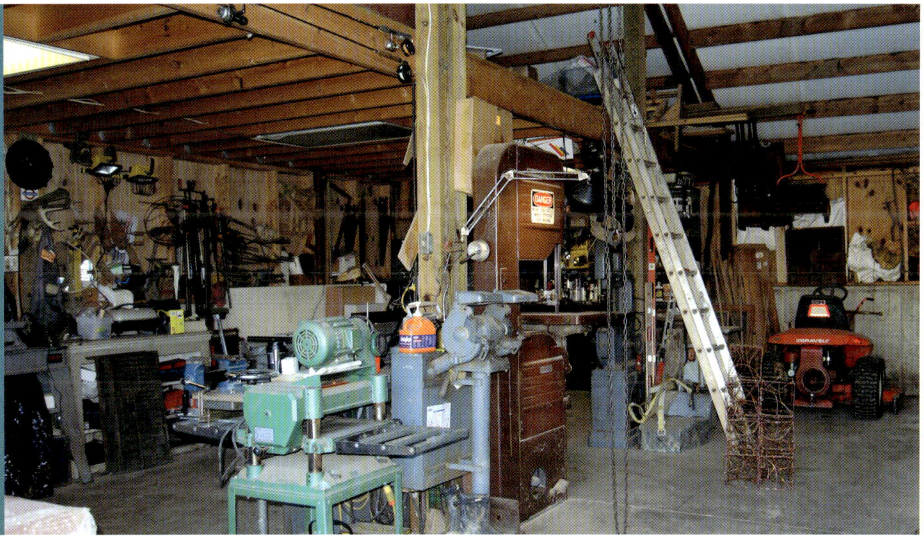

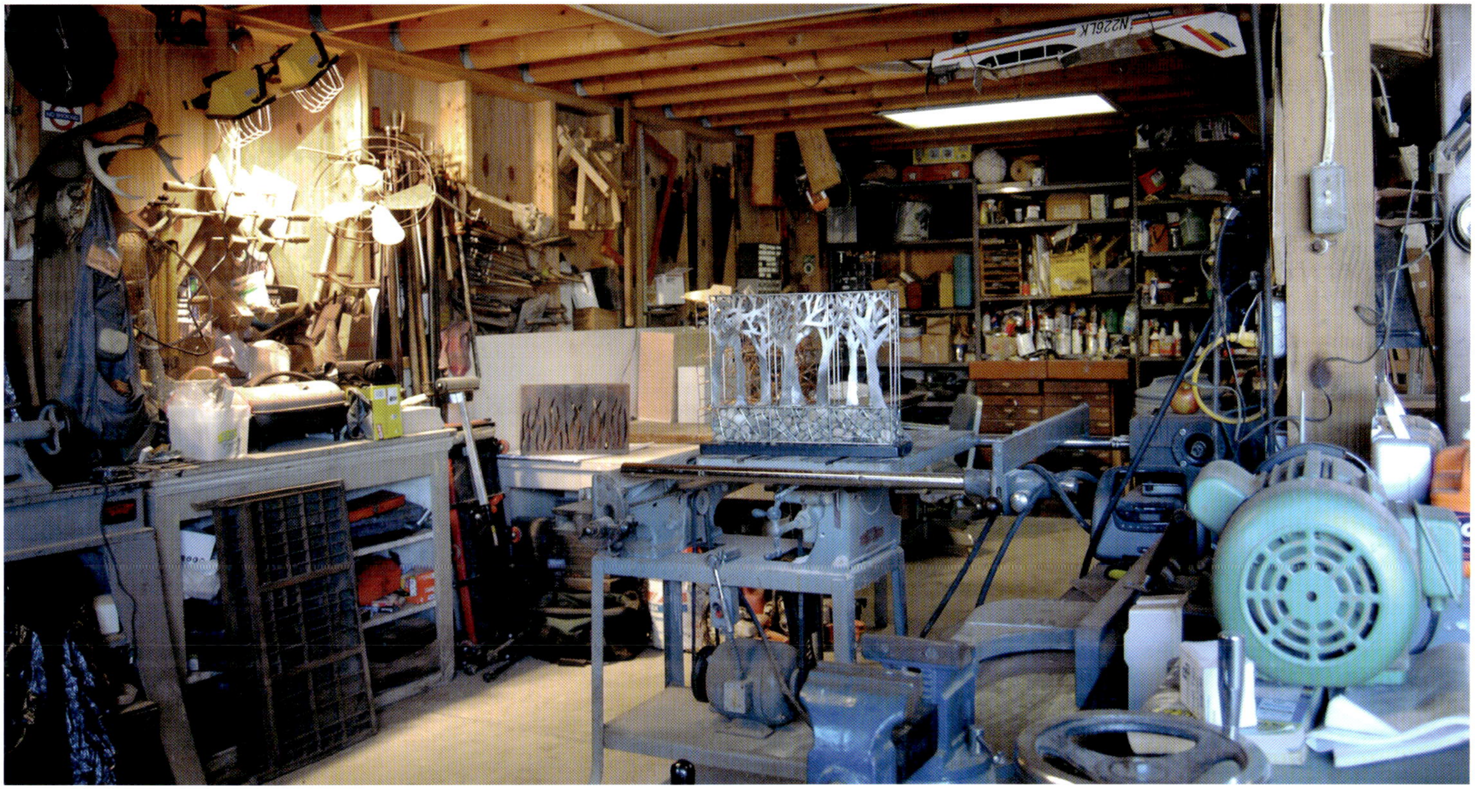

Elizabeth Miller McCue

Yardley, Pennsylvania

As a child I remember assembling models of ships and airplanes, gluing all the pieces together, and then painting them. I guess I was always a builder, bringing parts together to make a whole.

My studio is "my space"— and it is my space, and my space alone—to work predominantly on to-scale maquettes/models for projects, commissions, and editions of designs. I have ample supplies of balsa and basswood and the essential glue gun. The space is intimate and quiet, full of light, with six skylights and Palladian-style windows facing east and west, and absolutely no computers. I love experiencing the light above me, moving from morning to afternoon to evening, observing changes in the weather, and catching sight of the occasional bird flying or leaf floating by.

I prefer to work on the floor when I'm laying out the design for a site-specific project, or on the walls for a relief piece. If awarded a commission, I move to the industrial space of a foundry or fabrication shop where I can work on a large scale with assistants and lifting and welding equipment. When finished at the foundry or shop, the sculpture is then returned to my studio where I complete its patination. I maintain an outbuilding for storage of working materials.

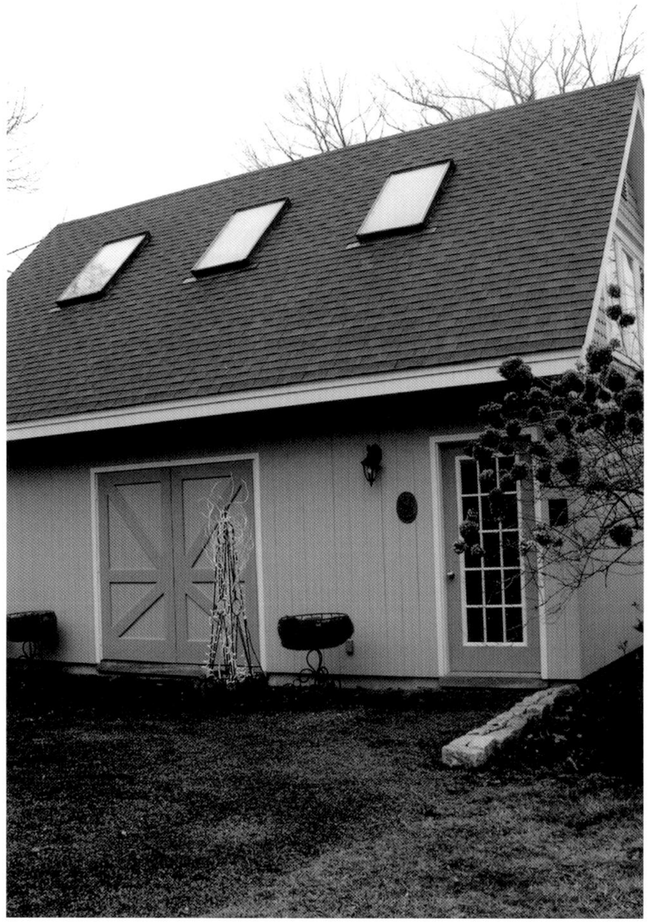

My studio is ready for visitors to celebrate the season and view new projects underway.

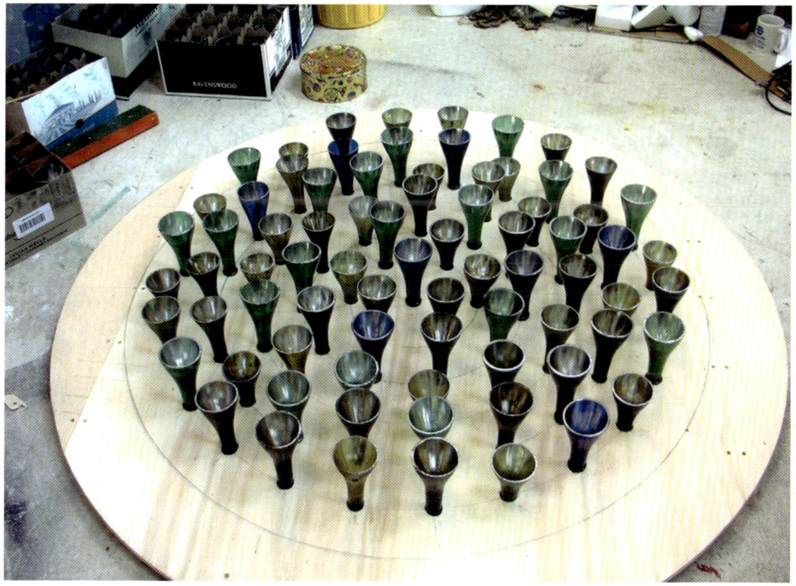

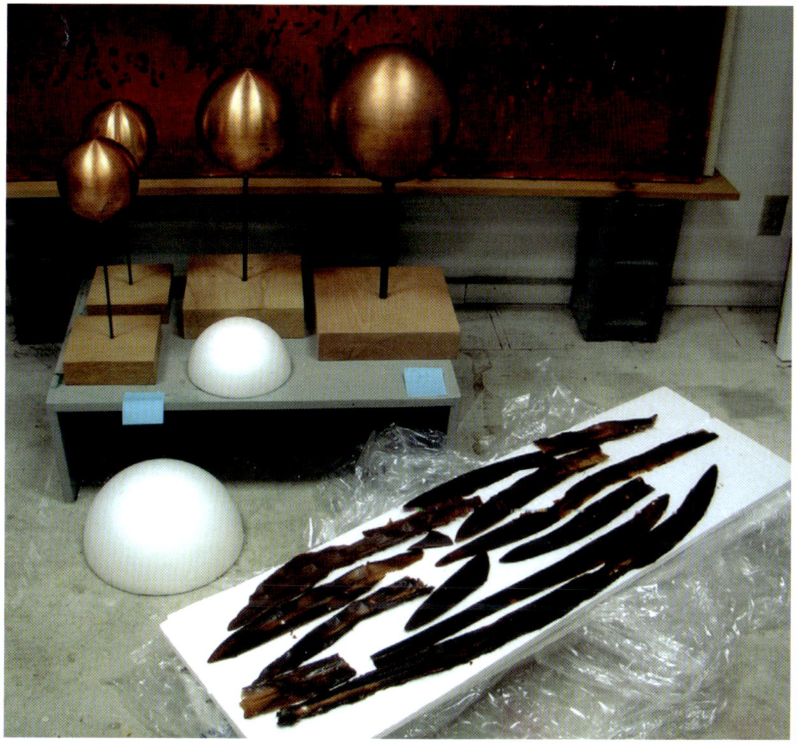

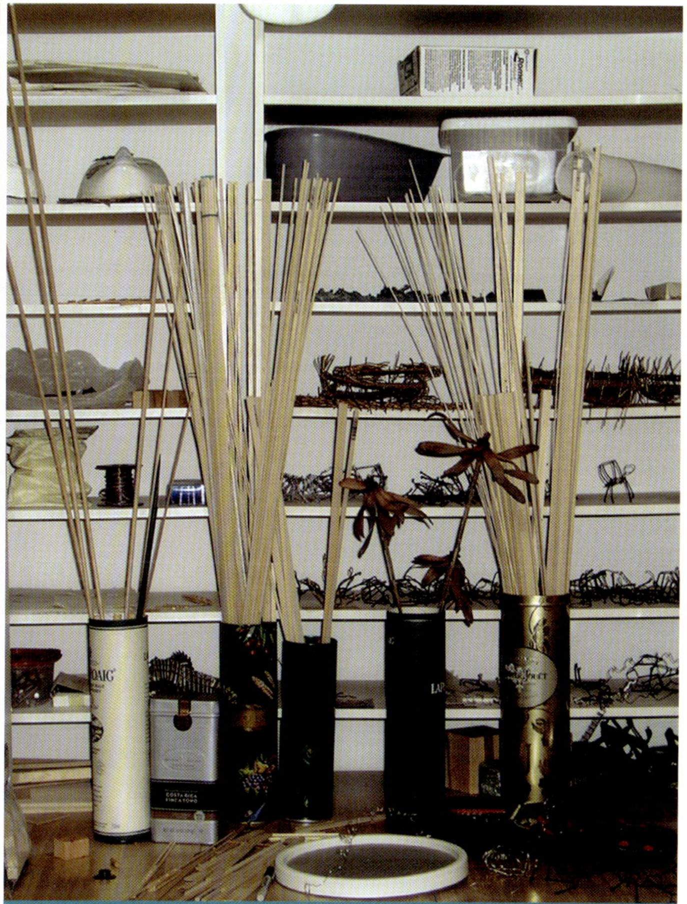

*My spacious and level concrete studio floor serves as the perfect drafting and layout table for **Oasis.***

A full array of balsa and basswood of varying dimensions, cutting tools, and the essential glue gun provide the tools for the making of maquettes for projects and commissions.

***Life Unfolding**. Preparation of editions. Bronze spheres and wax leaves ready for lost wax casting prior to shaping and bending to conform to the styrofoam pattern.*

Kelly Milukas

Tiverton, Rhode Island

My Bow House Studio is part do-it yourself, part pro-converted barn. It is located at the end of a gravel road behind our country home. The journey down the winding road passes by a 25-acre animal farm, river marshlands, and a light-filled forest. The serene setting is the perfect backdrop for creative work. The studio's cedar panels and high vaulted ceilings give me room to think big and make art that is my signature style: "A deconstruction of common structure with big color and bold shape."

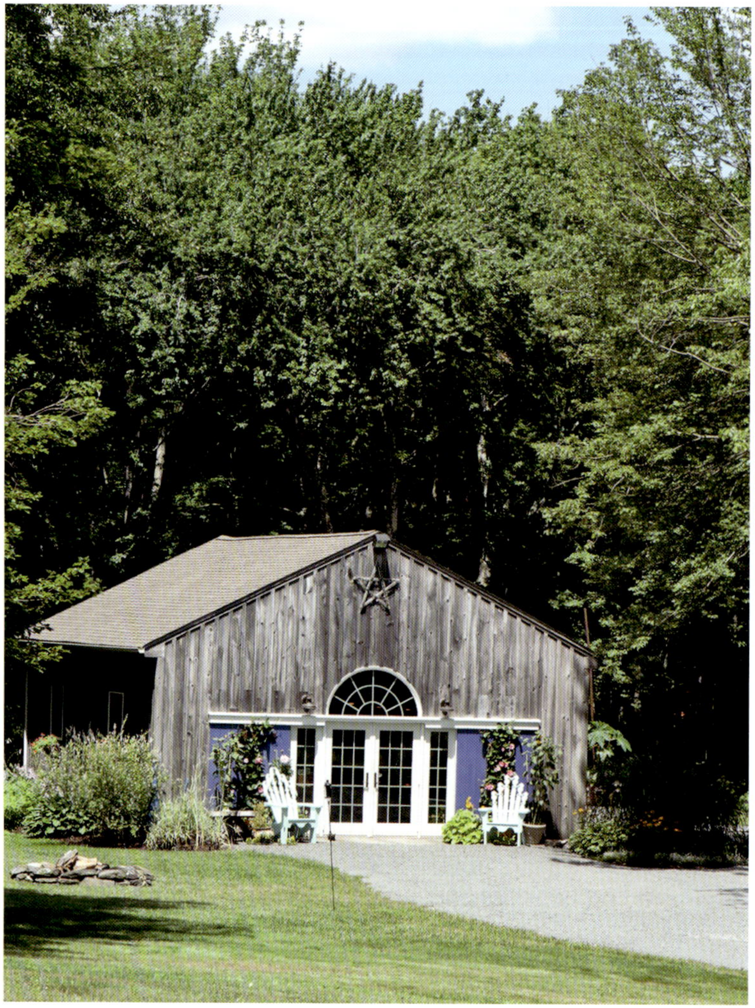

My studio is an outbuilding at the back of our eight acres. Courtesy of Marianne Lee.

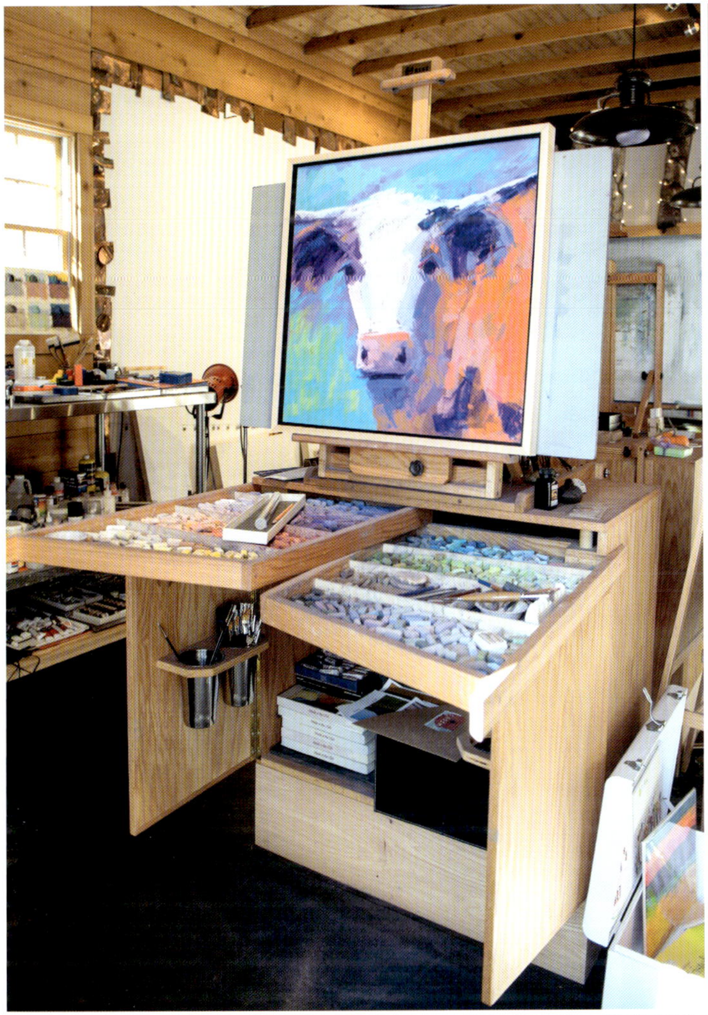

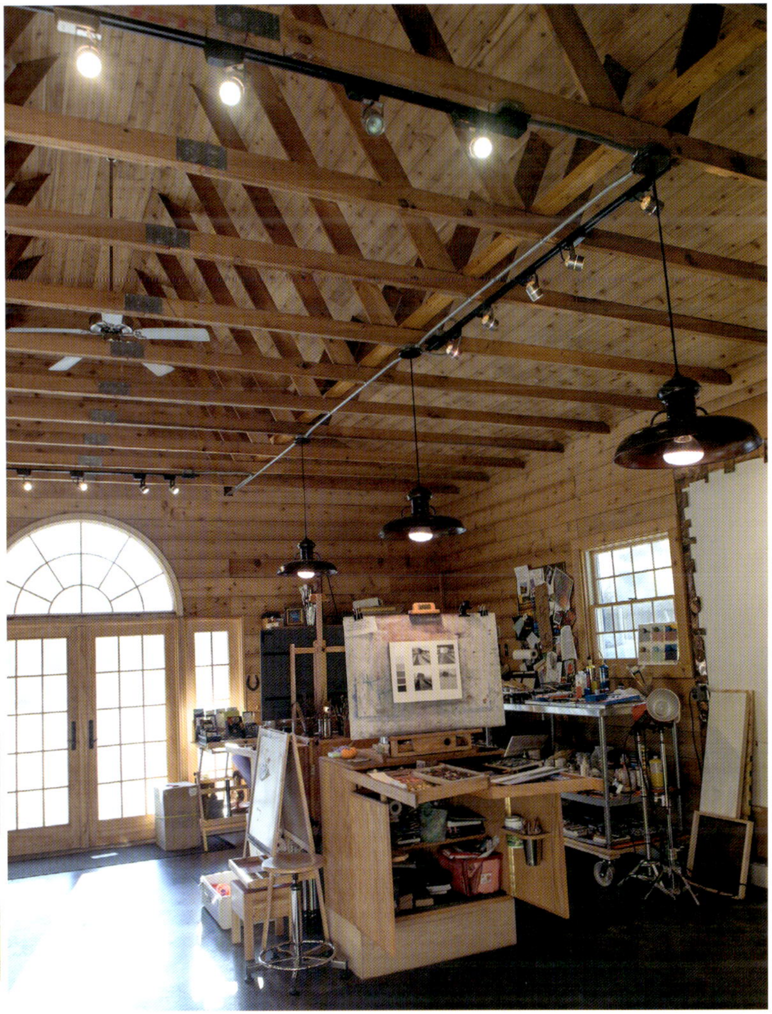

My pastel easels host over 2000 pigment sticks. On the easel is ***Quiet Confidence****. Pastel. 2012.* Courtesy of Marianne Lee.

A pastelist's dream! These desks were originally designed for world famous pastelist Urania Christy Tarbet. I have two of them—one for a friend and one for me. Courtesy of Marianne Lee.

Kenneth G. Ryden

Yorktown, Indiana

My country studios are an inspiring place to live and work. The main structure is perched on a high bank overlooking a wide fast-flowing creek. My wife, Lynn, and I often sit on one of the three levels of deck facing the ravine to watch deer meandering through the woods or a great blue heron fishing. Our land provides a great home for our menagerie of animals and a place to enjoy riding our horses.

The studio interiors feature high ceilings, natural pine, and open spaces. The great room is illuminated by ample sunshine filtering through large windows that overlook the creek at the bottom of a ravine. Track lighting highlights the gallery area. A large designing and clay modeling area comprises almost half of the structure. With a 16-foot ceiling and a large door opening to the outside, the space can accommodate many creative options. It is easy to move works-in-progress outside to study the effects of natural light. The spacious rooms also serve as galleries to display pedestal works and large clay modelings. A secondary studio houses a complete bronze casting foundry with space for welding and finishing bronze castings. With a little help from friends and neighbors, we make a celebration out of every bronze pour!

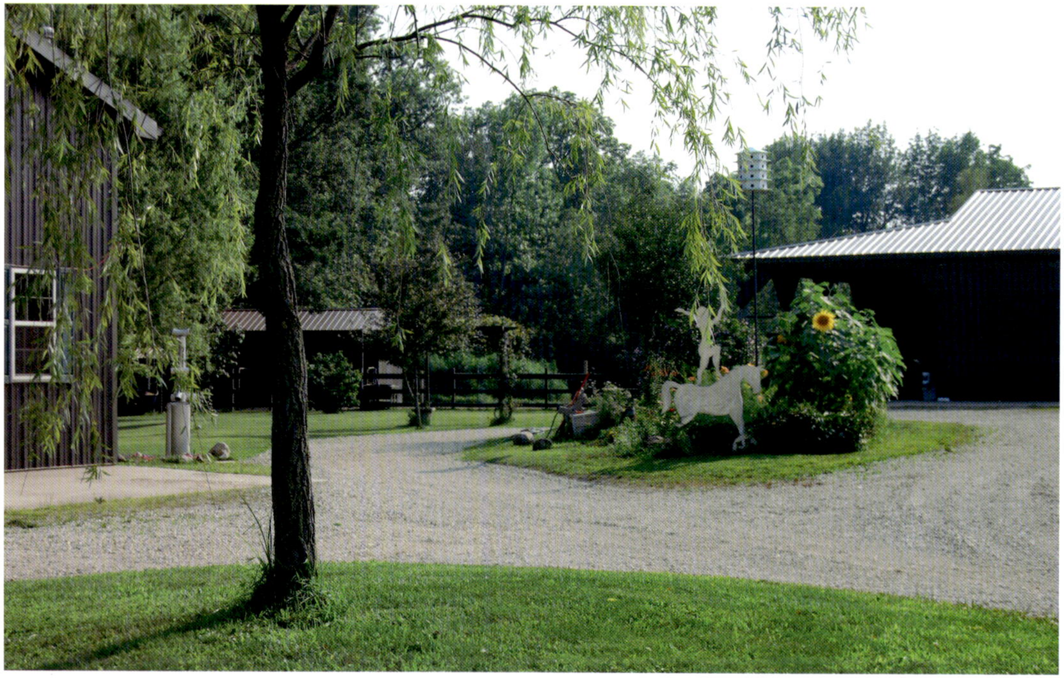

My studio with aluminum sculptures on grounds.

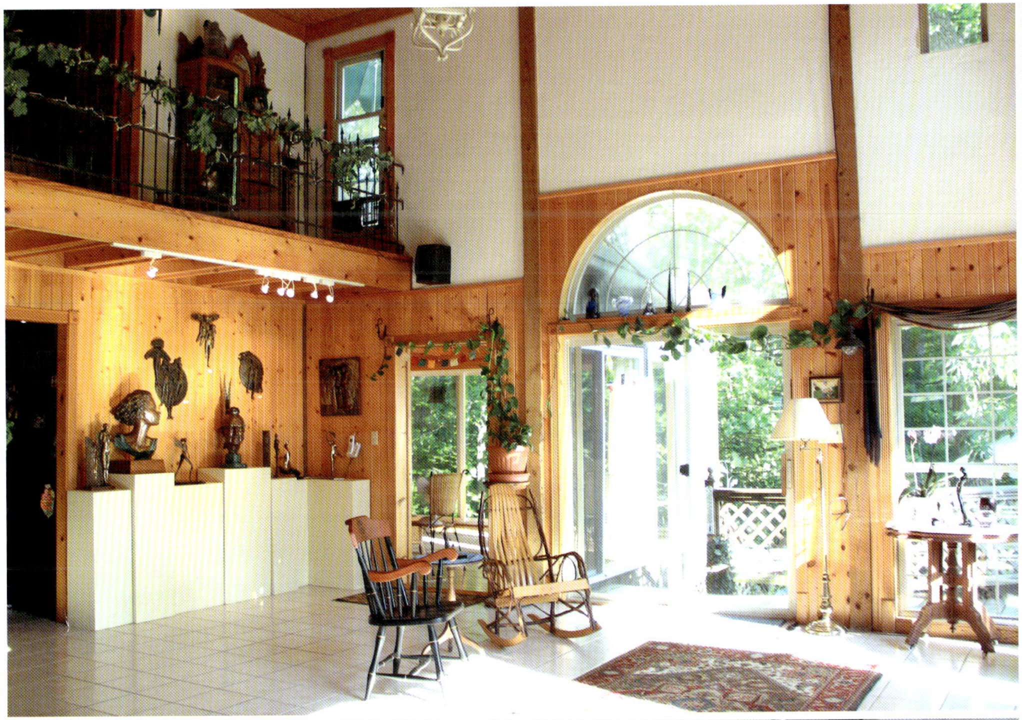

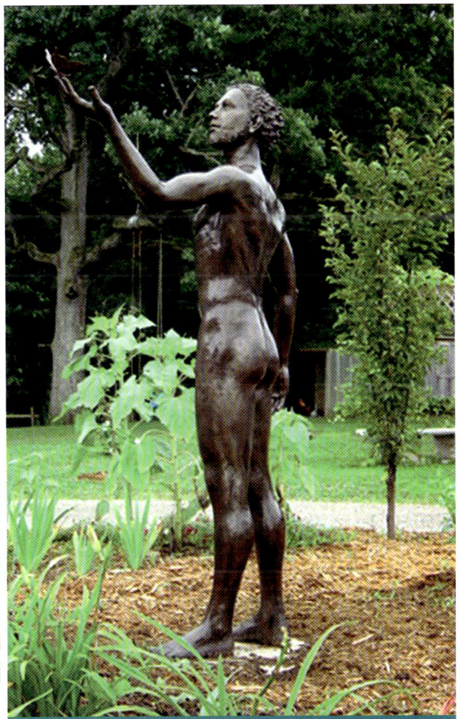

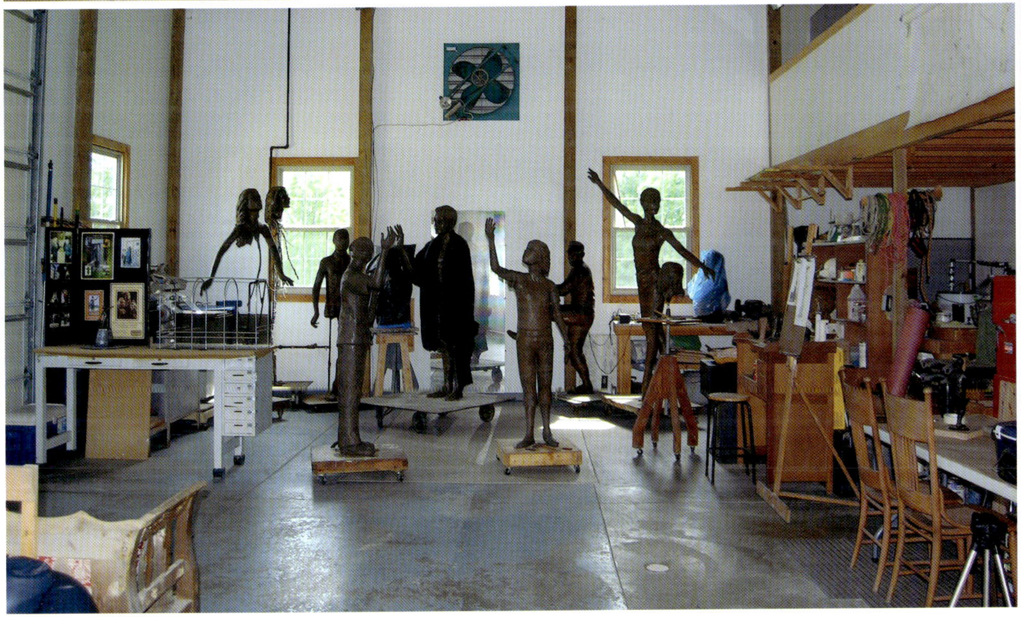

Studio great room with numerous bronze and glass sculptures.

Studio workroom with clay modelings used for my bronze sculptures.

My ***Garment of Life*** displayed in the studio garden.

Melinda Stickney-Gibson

Mt. Tremper, New York

I grew up in the Midwest, surrounded by hundreds and hundreds of uninterrupted acres of corn and soybeans, with the beautifully accidental tree or creek bed for graphic "punch." There was also the intimate relationship with the seasons: the subtle changes of the landscape, color, and light from one season to the next. Then I had that sensitivity that all artists seem to be born with, the need to make the mark and "see" the internal and external worlds as almost inseparable and interchangeable.

I now live in the Catskill Mountains of New York, about an hour-and-a-half from New York City. The innate, intimate relationship with the natural world that I felt growing up has not changed, only deepened. I lived and painted in New York City for many years, while also keeping a studio up in the mountains, and only when I was in the mountain studio did everything feel balanced and possible. So, ten years ago I bought some land and basically recreated my city loft, in the woods! The place is surrounded by state land on a dead end road. The forms of nature, the mass and shapes of rocks, the stands of trees in winter, all linear and graphic, the color and activeness of a stream after a storm, and the dense explosions of color in the fall, absolutely inform my work.

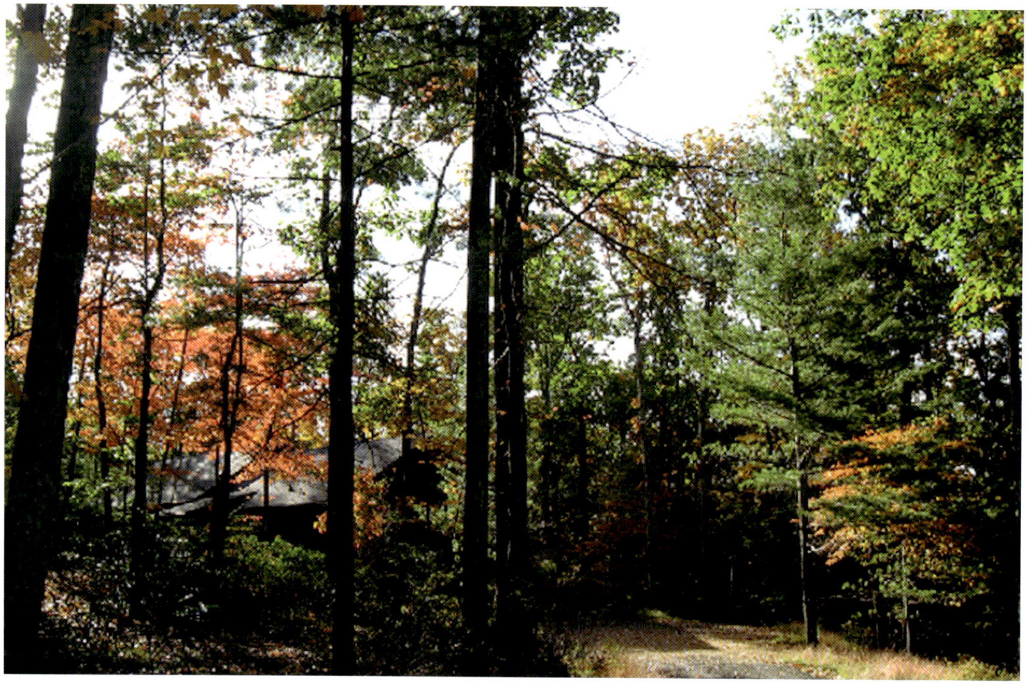

My house and studio in the mountains.

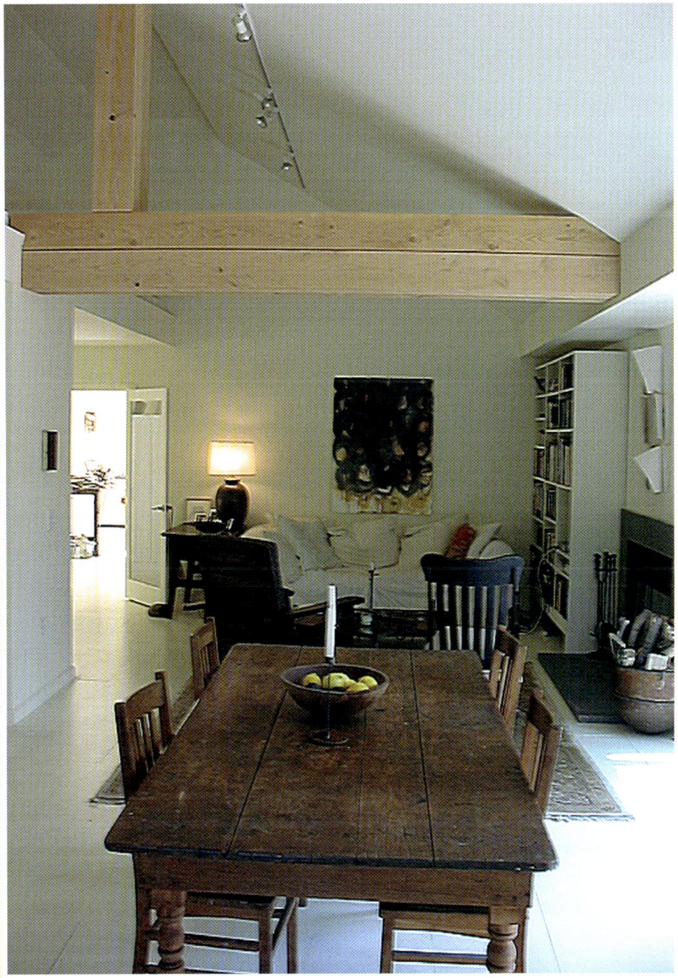

My living area, looking into the studio at the rear. The painting is **Wish Holes.**

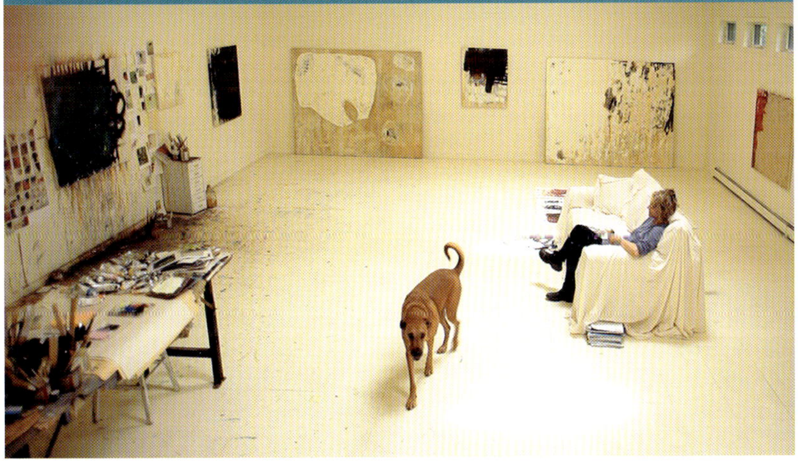

I am an "abstract" painter, whose "model" is completely real, and never, ever static. I decided to have lots of wall space for my work, as I work on a dozen or more paintings at once, moving from one to another. Skylights let in a lot of natural light, and French doors let me step out into nature. Vickers + Beechler Photography.

Judy Youngblood

Dallas, Texas

My studio is a separate building across the backyard from our mid-century modern house. In addition to my workspace (22 x 30-foot), the building includes a storage area, office, bathroom, and covered porch. To have as much natural light as possible while keeping out the hot Texas sun, there are specially designed fins on the west-facing clerestory windows and a covered porch that shades the southern windows.

I work on paper making paintings, relief prints, intaglio prints, and mixed media pieces so my studio is designed for making both paintings and prints. It contains a large intaglio and relief press, a utility sink, an etching hot plate, a glass-topped counter, and a place to dry and flatten paper. Especially helpful are two large rolling tables that I use constantly. All the walls in the workspace have a pin-able surface, so that I can easily display works in progress, ideas under consideration, as well as a variety of objects of potential creative interest. The storeroom provides display for framed works of art, flat files for paper storage, and adjustable vertical storage for framed pieces. I keep big supplies (rolls of paper, bubble wrap, and photo lights) on top of the vertical storage. In addition, my separate office supports my digital work and houses my art.

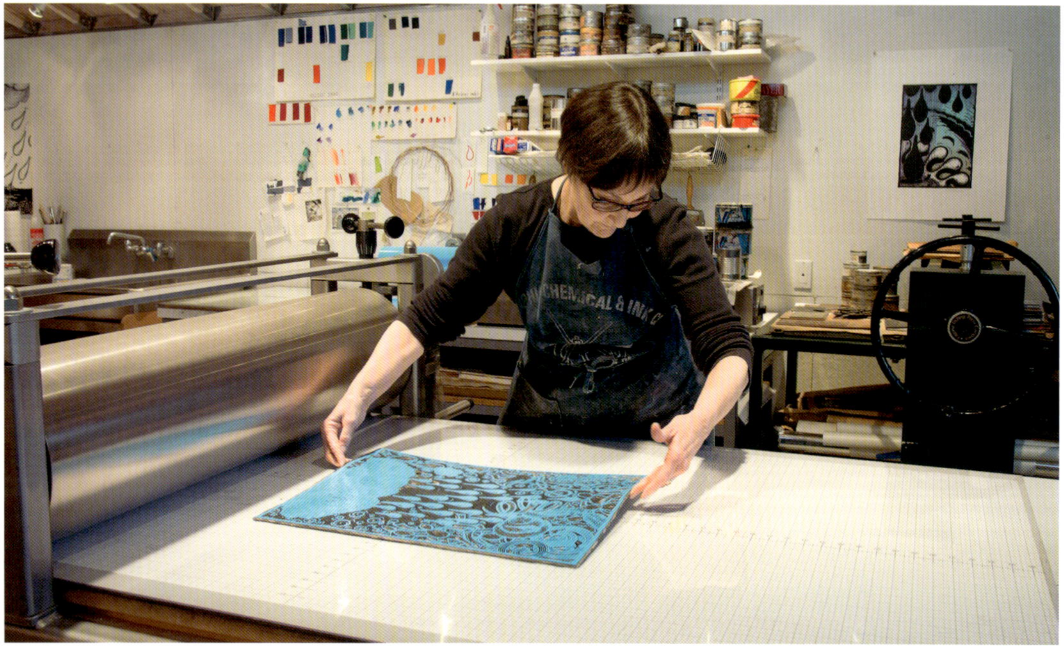

In my studio, I am laying an inked linoleum block on the press for printing. My relief print, ***Splish****, 2010, is in the background.* Courtesy of Peter Poulides.

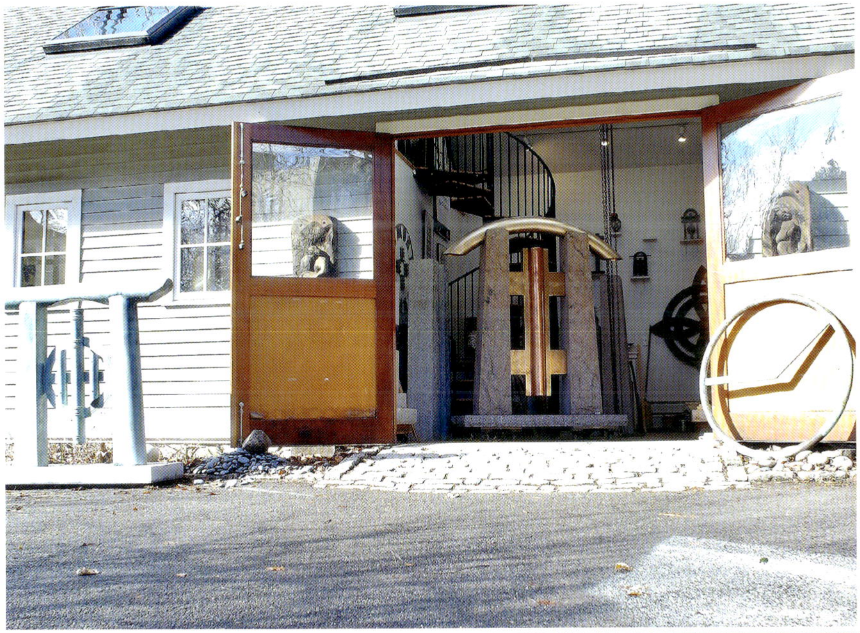

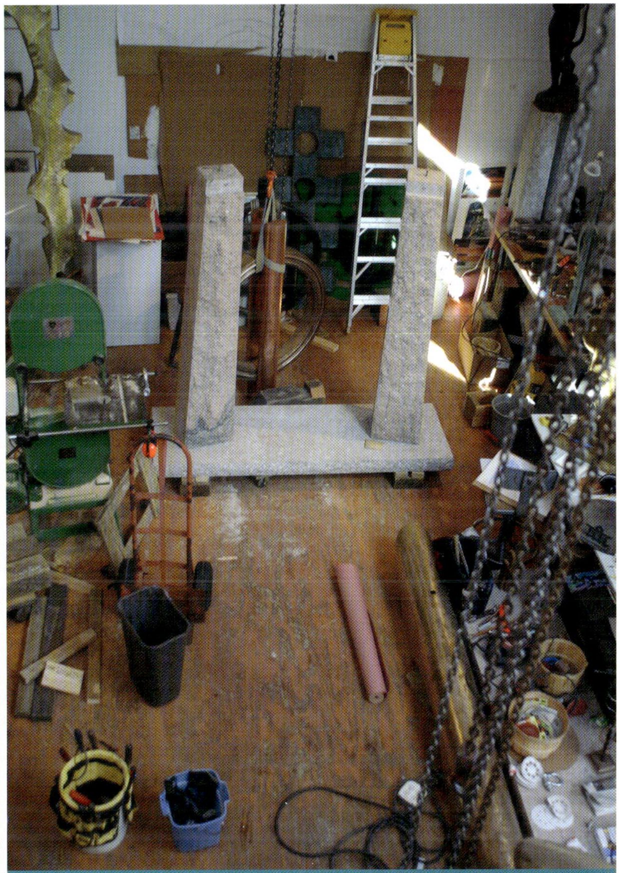

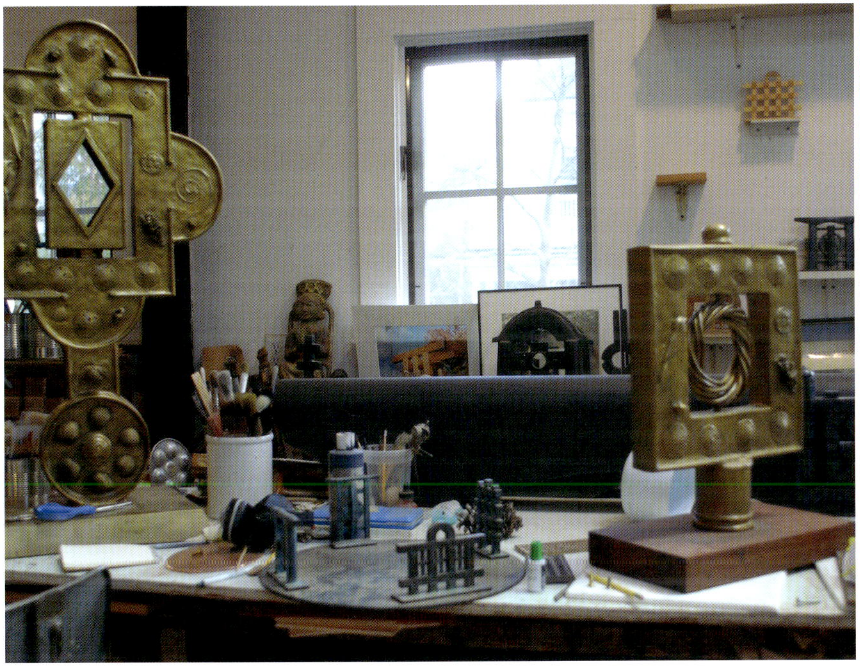

There are occasions when the studio space gets emptied, and my sculptures go out into the world; I am finally done with them. That is when I like to have a big dinner with at least twenty-five sculptors at a long plank table, eating and making raucous noise under my slings and chain falls. The history of art is the history of artists who share tools and strategies. It's the history of noisy artists.

Of the high shine golden bronze pieces on my bench, ***Byzantium*** *is on the left and* ***Green Hope Coil*** *on the right. The blue-green* ***Jerusalem Gates*** *is at the center.*

Debra Fritts

Abiquiu, New Mexico

As a child, I loved playing in the mud—always had dirt under my fingernails. Today, I continue to allow the earth to feed me information for my art and for daily living. My expression is basic, yet it intrigues me to continue this exploration in clay and with the figure. Working intuitively from pounds of wet clay, I find that forms appear and stories develop. The search continues until I reach to the core: the spiritual level of the sculpture. Then the work can speak.

I am exploring new territory in the West while embracing my Southern heritage. The open space and the quiet in Abiquiu, New Mexico, have proven to be very powerful and important in my personal life and to my art. I am surrounded with information from the land, the light, the history, and the air. The mystery of this area has pulled me into a new awareness.

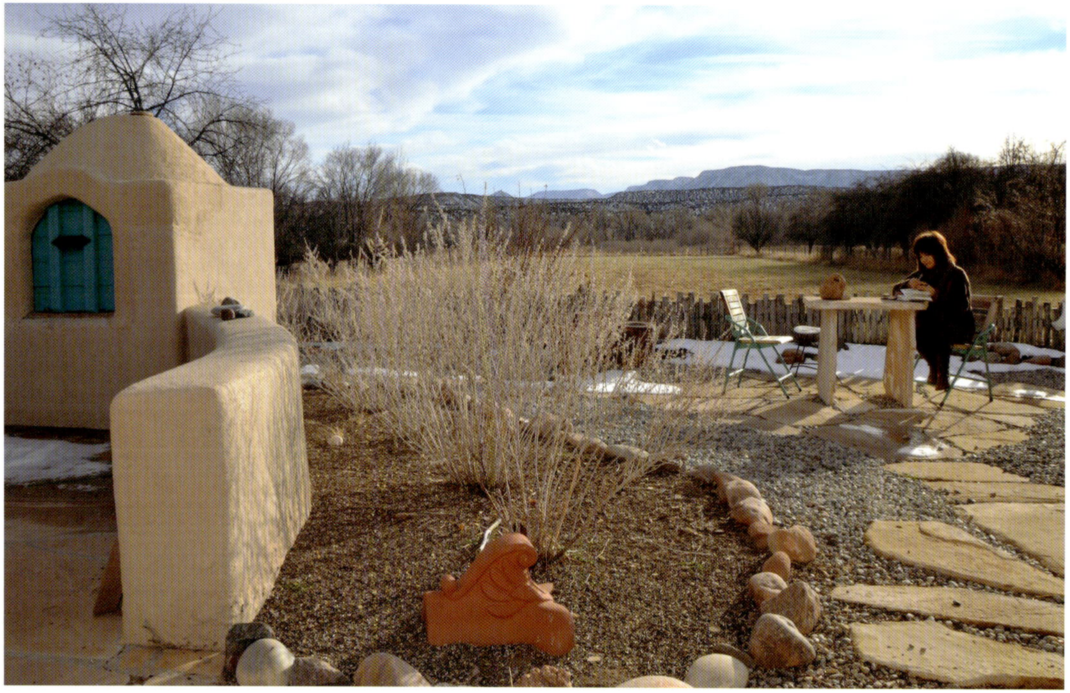

Rock walls built by a local stonemason from Mexico separate the studio and home. My personal peace is found by honoring this land—so rich with history and symbolism. Courtesy of Convivial Design, Melinda Hess and Patricia Antelles.

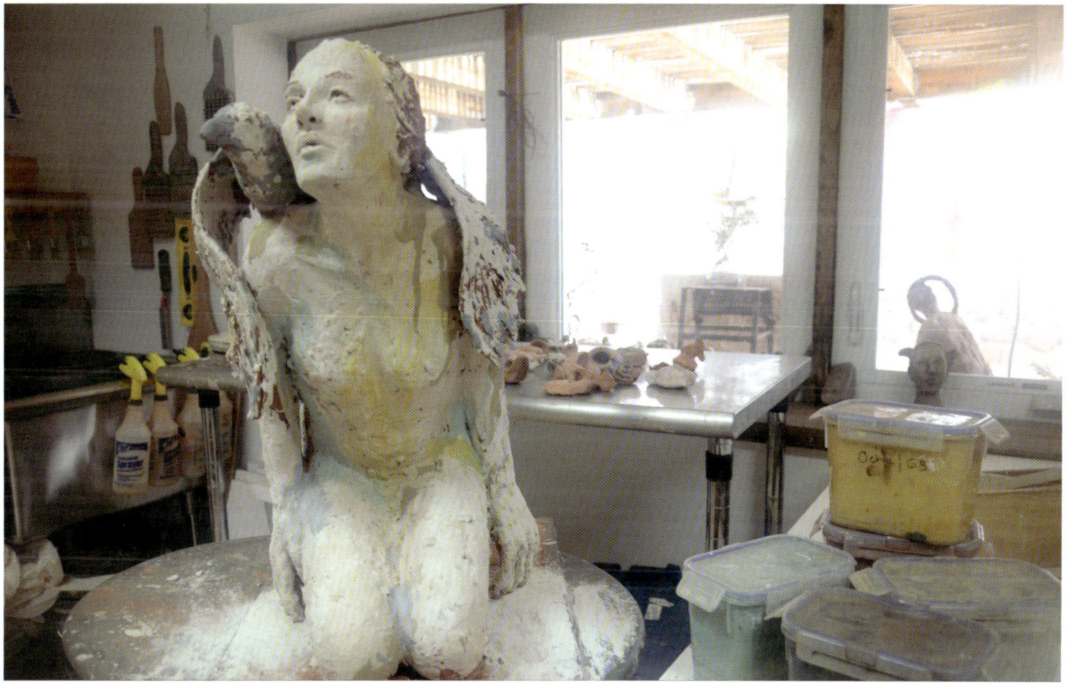

Interior shot of the studio showing the exterior portal. Allowing the natural light to filter into the studio is a plus when working with the surface of my sculptures. On this piece, oxide stains are being applied. Courtesy of Convivial Design, Melinda Hess and Patricia Antelles.

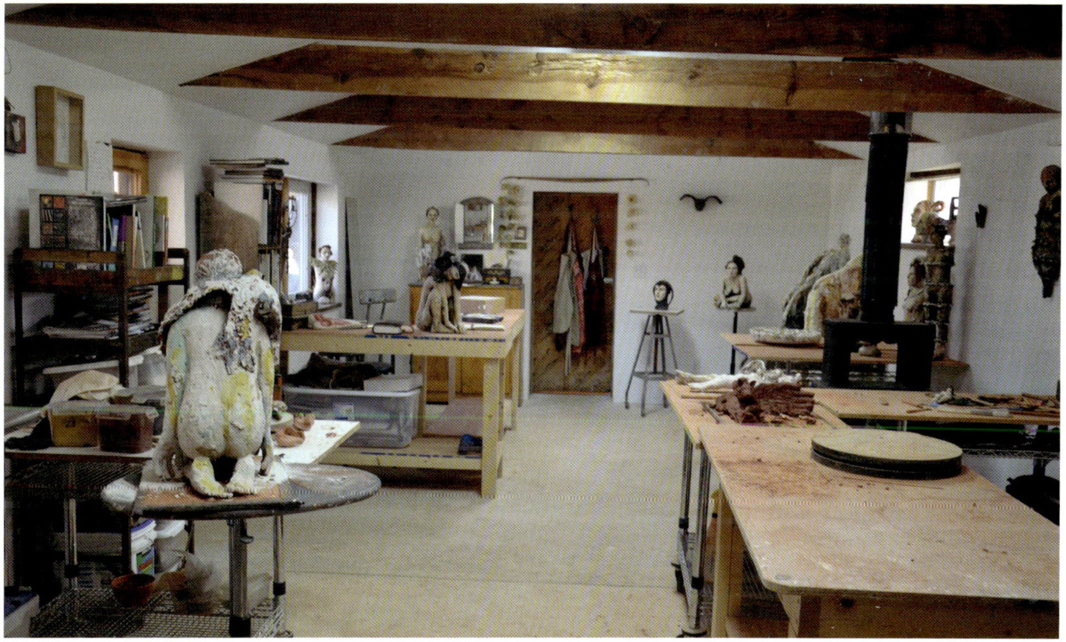

My husband, Frank, and I were told the WPA gave money to the local farmers in the Chama River Valley in the late 1950s to raise chickens, and this 1300 square-foot cinder block building was one of the few chicken coops still existing. We tried to keep as much of the old wood—the rafters, the interior doors and window sills—and added a concrete slab for the floor, insulation and the interior walls, stucco over the cinder blocks on the exterior, and glass windows. A wood stove heats the building. The former chicken coop is now our studio and near our adobe house. Courtesy of Convivial Design, Melinda Hess and Patricia Antelles.

Nancy Gaucher-Thomas, NWS

East Greenwich, Rhode Island

Built in 1743, the "Potter House" is a 1½-story, gable-roofed cottage with a mid-Victorian exterior. The Gaucher-Thomas studio, originally the carriage house, was renovated and transformed in 2003 into what is now my home away from home: my quiet space of uninterrupted time where I am free to think, dream, and experiment, where I escape to find peace and solace from the world outside.

Inspiration finds its way in many forms. Reference books and imagery help to inspire and challenge my way of thinking, motivating, and pushing in various directions. I am continually fascinated and inspired by the landscape of the face.

My studio is arranged in a way that best suits the process of which I am accustomed to working, with easel and materials readily at hand. Still-life objects that have been painted time and time again find a special spot on a shelf that spans a studio wall; studio lamps are within reach and used when a special effect is called for. A carpeted model platform also serves as staging for still-life arrangements and gallery area during the annual open studio tour.

Music is essential during the time I spend in my studio and helps to set the mood.

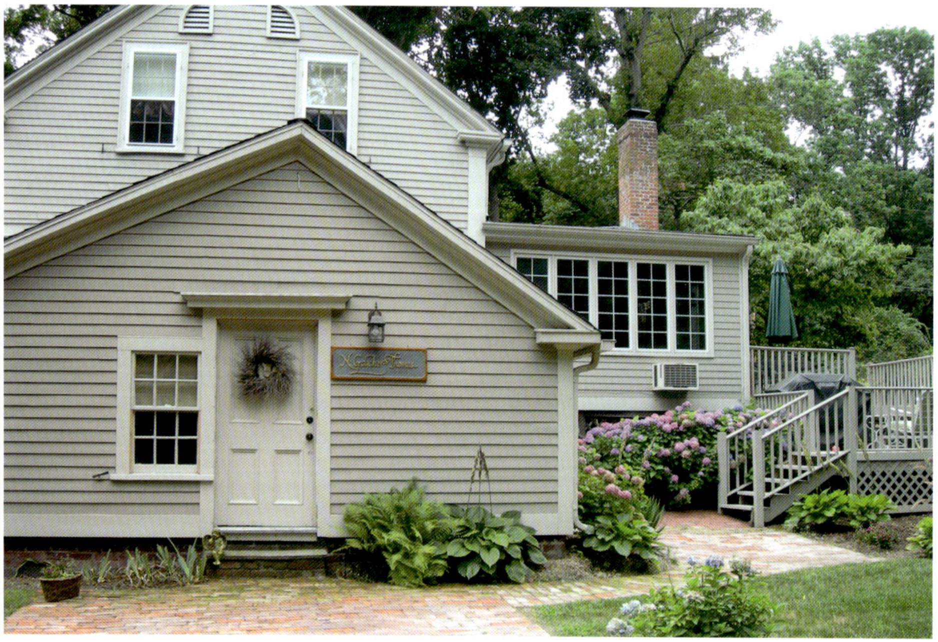

Exterior entrance to the Gaucher-Thomas Studio

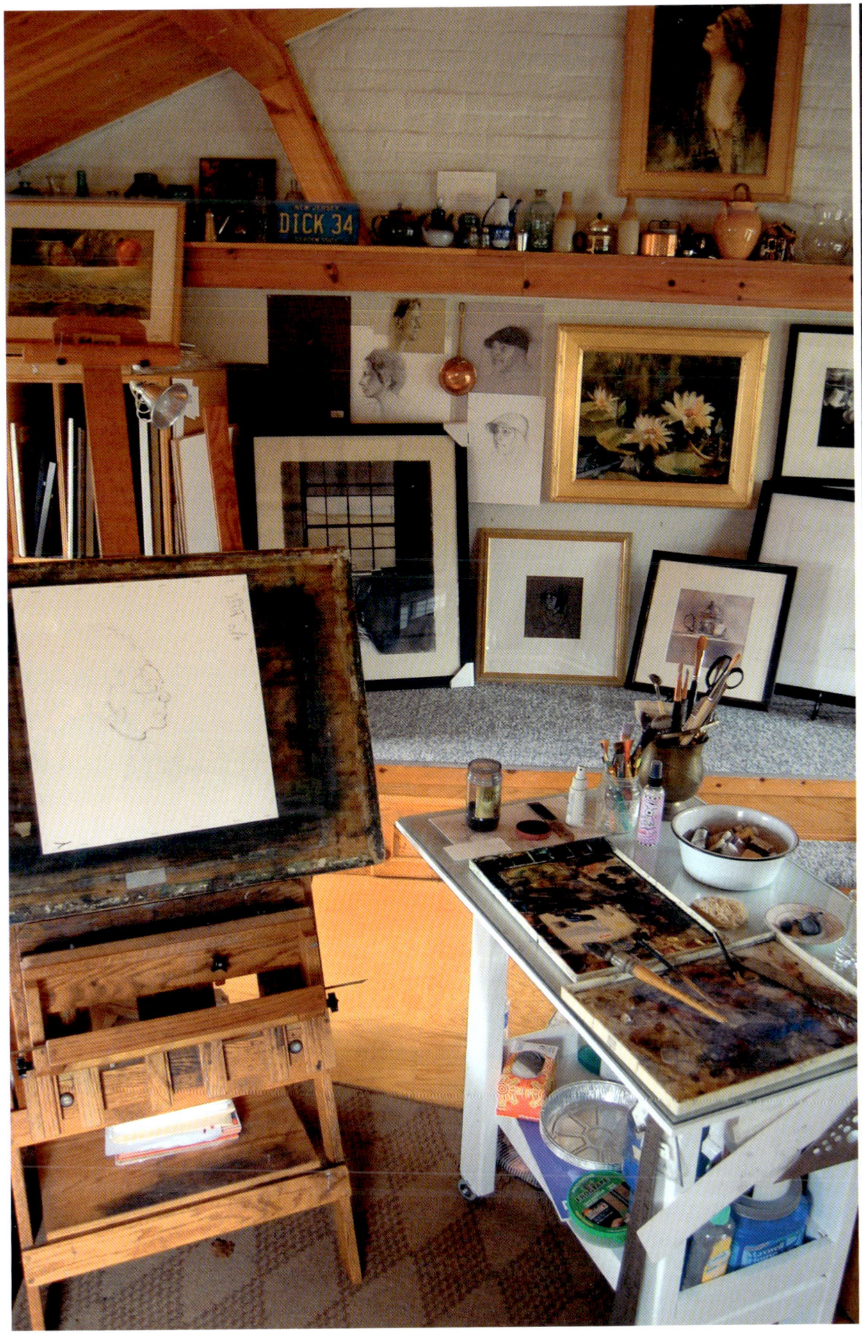

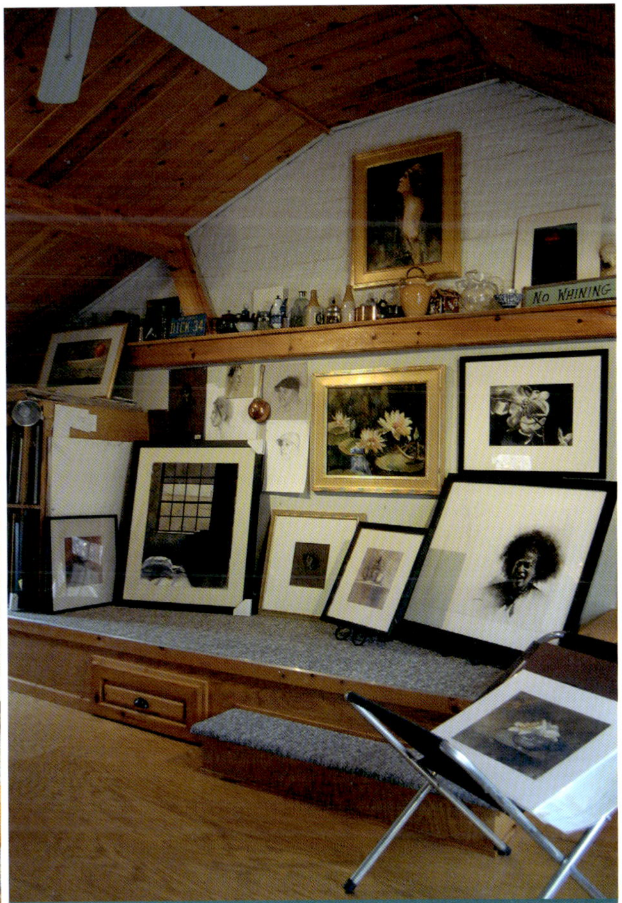

Easel and workstation. Courtesy of Courtney L. Cutler.

Model platform and storage area with overhead ceiling fan, recessed lighting and tongue and groove ceiling. My work shown left to right: ***Montgomery Street****, watercolor;* ***Young Girl Wearing Cap****, charcoal/white chalk,* ***Lotus Reflections****, watercolor;* ***Descending*** *and* ***Bianca VII****, charcoal on Mylar.* Courtesy of Courtney L. Cutler.

Gale Jamieson

York, Pennsylvania

My studio is located in a hollow on a small farm in southern York County, Pennsylvania. I have resided here for over 30 years, and the 200+year-old log house and barn reflect my nature and my work. Being in relationship with this land and its structures has been a big part of my life and a strong influence on my work.

My studio is in the upper part of the bank barn, which has evolved from a simple open space to three workspaces, with a large loft used for storage. The first section is where the majority of the work occurs. The middle section is primarily a woodworking shop; the third area is a quiet comfortable space, which is intended for an office and cleaner work, such as drawing, research, writing, and contemplation.

My process-oriented sculpture draws inspiration from the natural world, as well as from our culture. Often, the material and place are the source. A strong component of my work is related to the concept of impermanence and our relationship to the natural world. This gentle land has offered me countless opportunities to observe the unfolding of nature, its cycles, and the way that time leaves physical traces and imbues a resonance of memories.

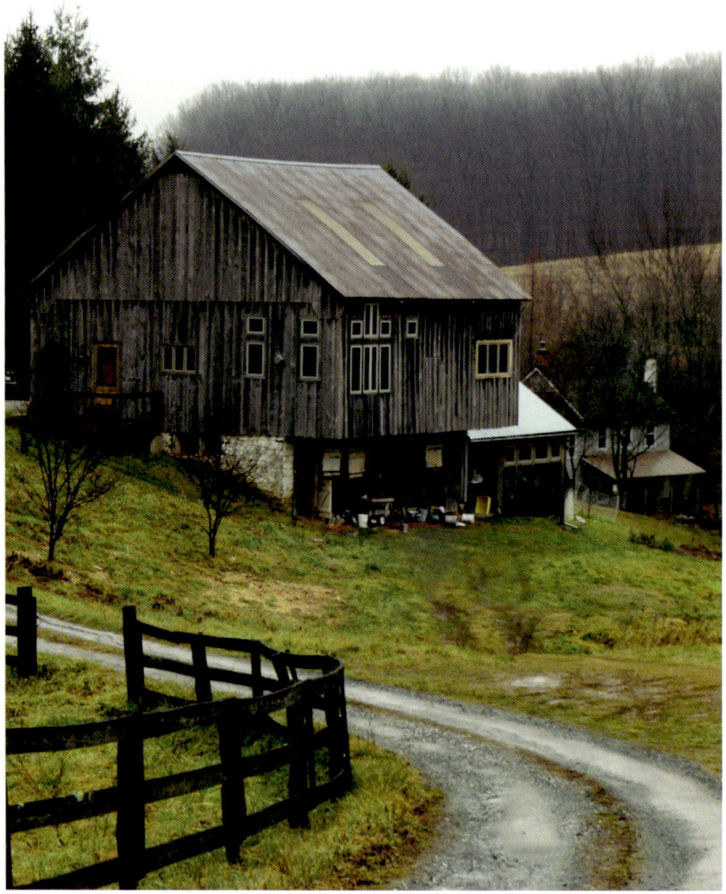

Homestead. My studio is in the upper part of the barn.

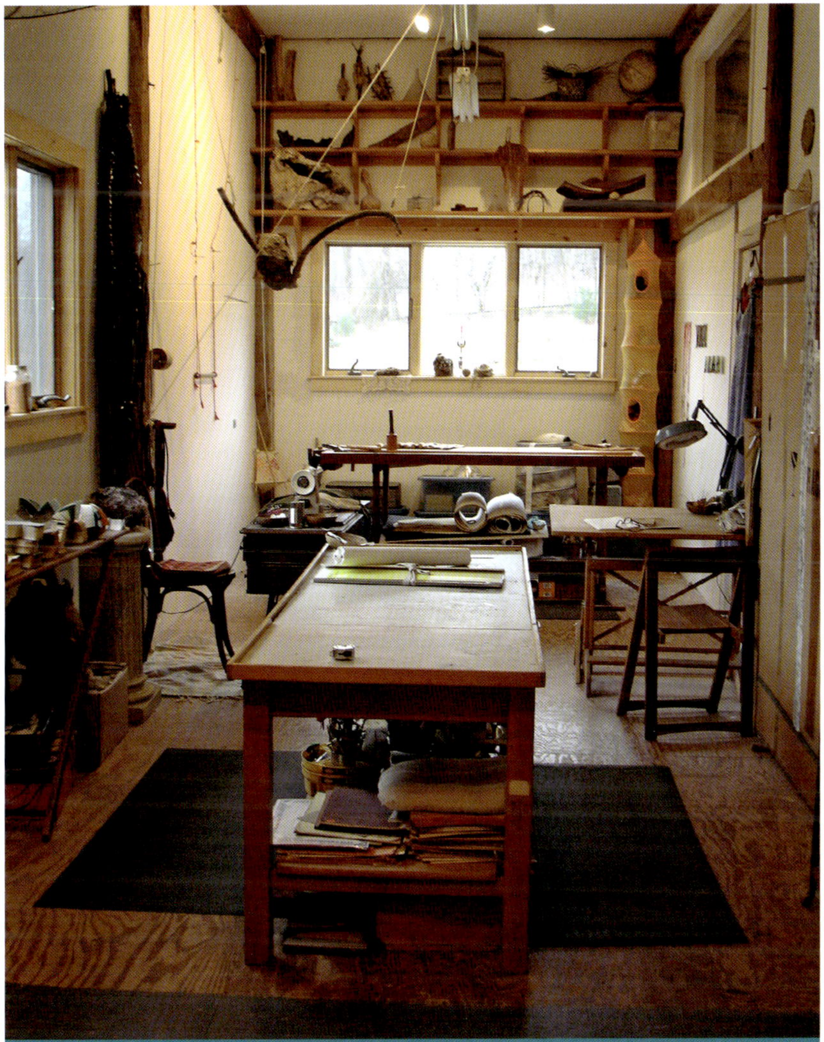

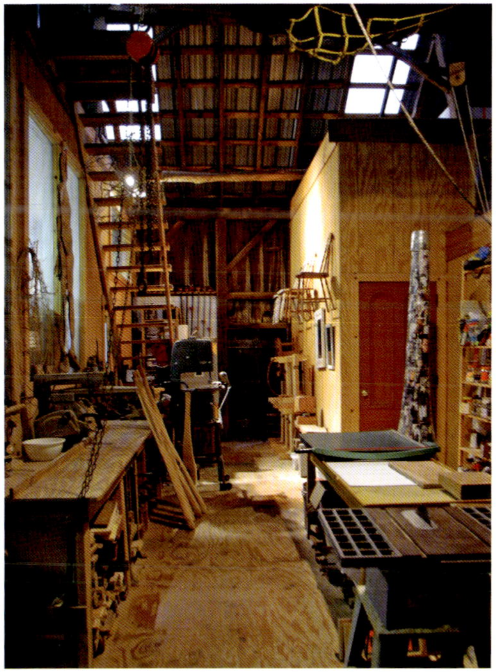

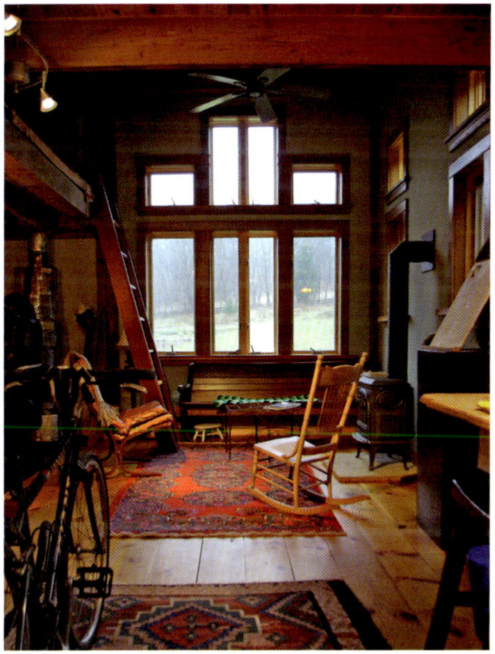

My main working area overlooks the farm meadow and hollow.

The central open area is the woodworking shop.

The third section of the barn is an area used for quieter work, drawing and as an office. It provides a peaceful place to contemplate.

Margie McDonald

Port Townsend, Washington

My studio is an aluminum trailer from the 1950s. It is 40 feet long and 8 feet wide, with lots of windows, which is very important for a full-time artist in the Pacific Northwest—given our many grey days. My husband, Alan Katz, a shipwright, and I gutted the interior and paneled the walls in mahogany. We lived in "the hallway" for five years until 2012, when we moved it to another location on our property, and it officially became my studio.

Along one wall is an 18-foot counter at three different heights. A large collection of hand tools, including many styles of pliers, is in easy reach. A home-built wood shelf holds many spools of wire. Other shelves hold hundreds of jars containing objects like crab claws and recycled bronze boat screws. At one end of the studio there are two comfortable chairs with a wood stove and an area where I like to work on the floor.

I find being surrounded by art and potential art inspiring; sometimes accidental juxtaposition can be the starting point. I use simple hand tools and mostly recycled metal to create biomorphic sculptures that evolve through fabrication rather than a preconceived plan.

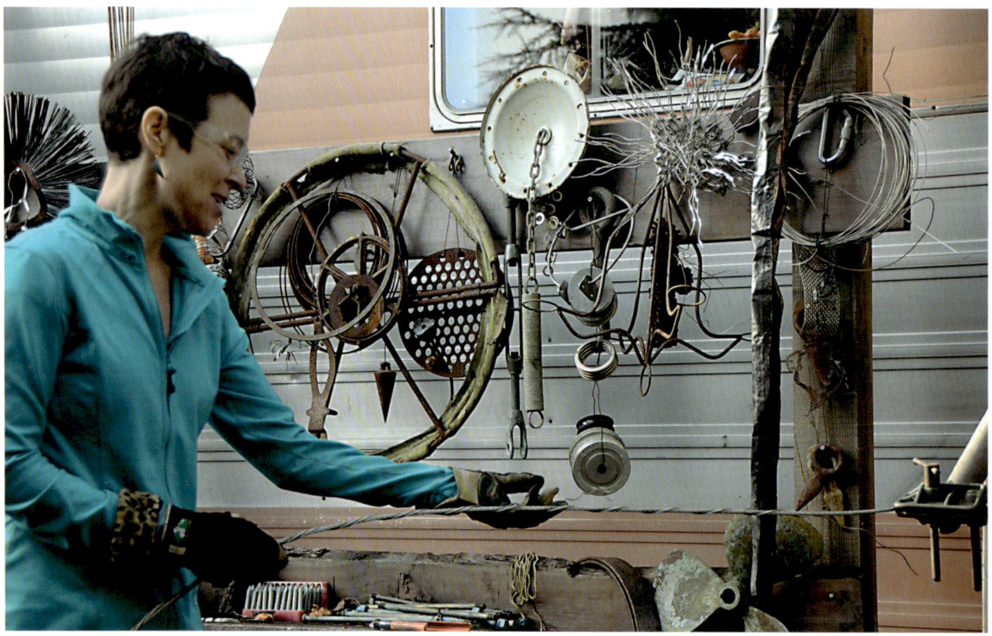

I work outside as weather allows. Large wood planks add stability to the roof frame and are placed at a convenient height with a workbench below. Courtesy of Charles Kent Wiggins.

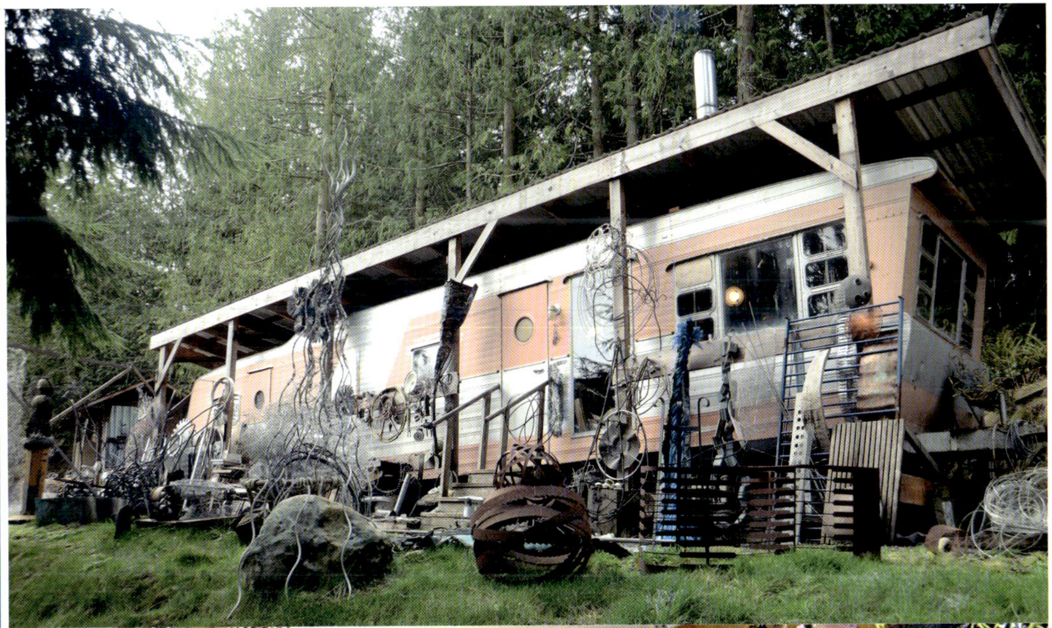

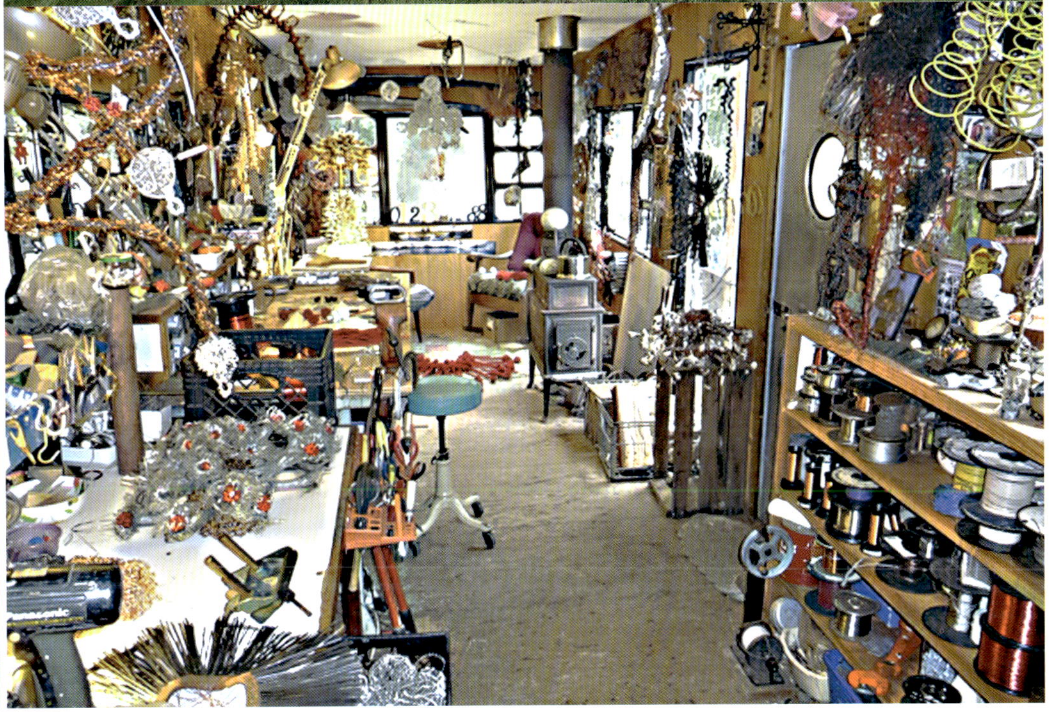

Raw material, considered potential art, surrounds my 1950s trailer studio. Tall cedars dominate the background. Courtesy of Charles Kent Wiggins.

The walls are covered with sculpture in varying stages of development. The long bench on one side holds a couple of vises and many hand tools. Courtesy of Charles Kent Wiggins.

Carol Oldenburg

York, Pennsylvania

I love to paint. I love the action of painting and the challenges of problem solving that come with each creation. I love the variety of subjects placed before me via commission or my own curiosity. And I love making something beautiful that can touch the sensibilities of others.

In turn, my 1920s bungalow home and converted garage studio extend that creativity. The home is a nest that rejuvenates the spirit; the yard and gardens are places to work and be inspired; and the studio is a practical space in which the outer and inner worlds come alive through painting.

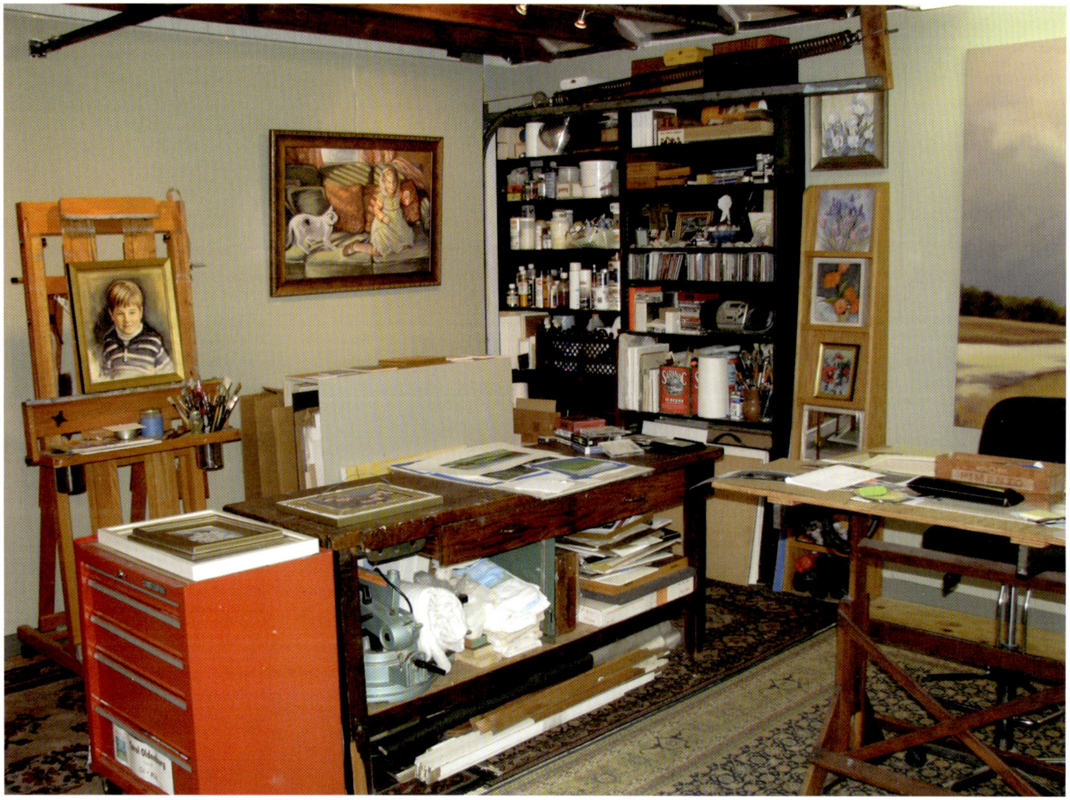

A lit display wall has been built across the garage door. Supplies are stored on the shelves and in the Craftsman tool chest. An old carpenter's bench serves as storage and a framing table.

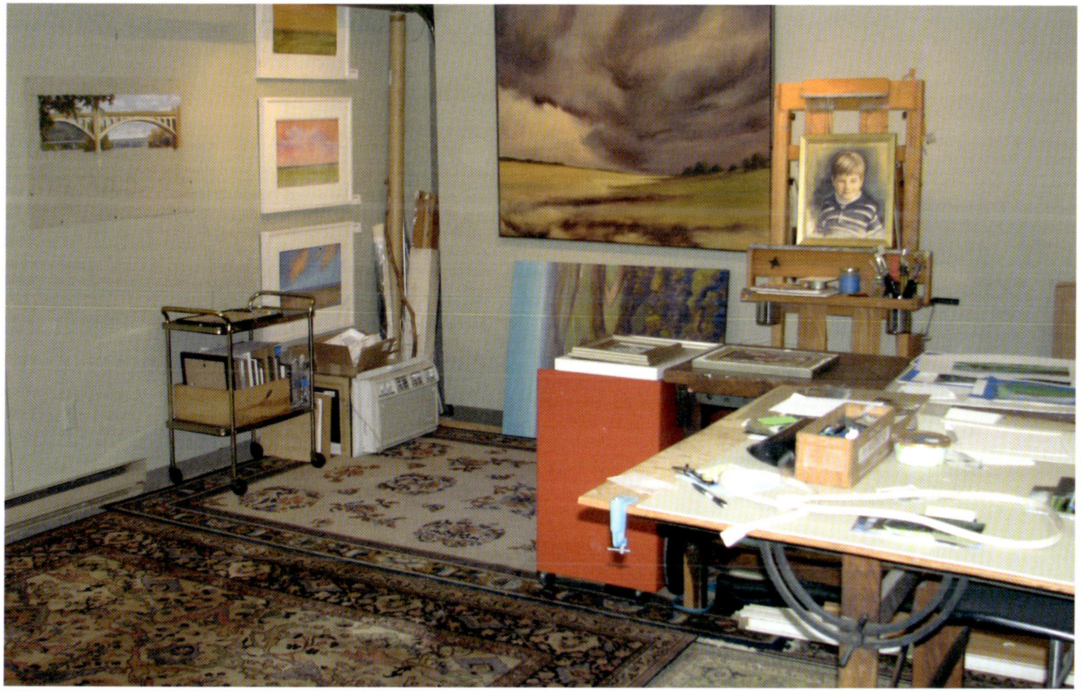

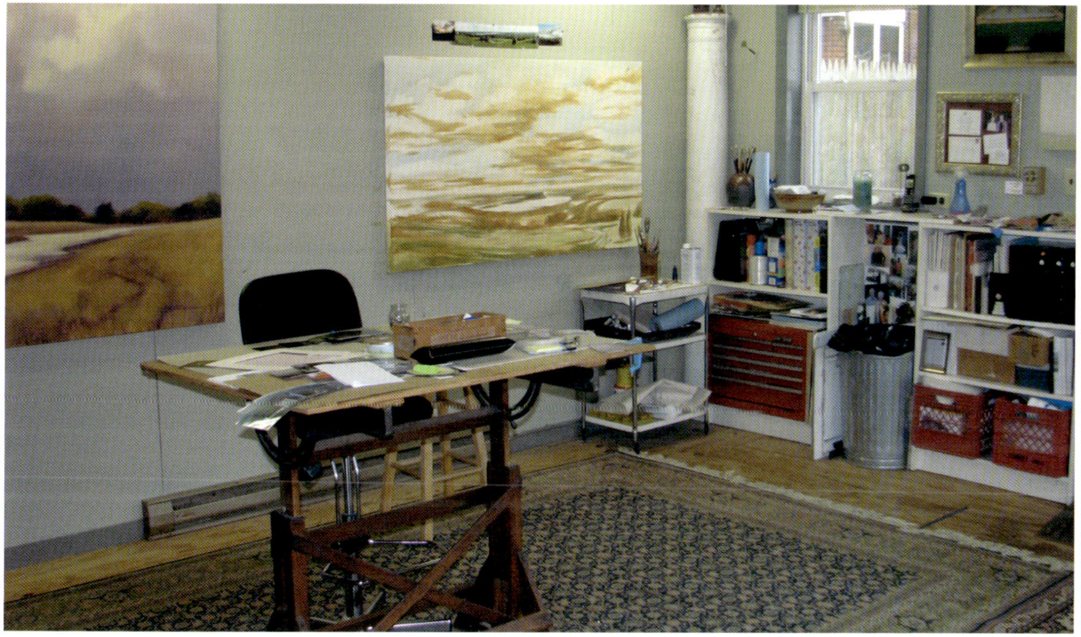

The back left wall of the studio is used for display and also to work on pastels. Teacarts are handy for moving between workstations when multiple projects are going on.

The wall behind my drafting table is used for painting large landscapes. I utilize both artificial and natural light throughout the studio and a HEPA air purifier to keep air quality high.

I love to work in this room in the mornings. It has phenomenal lighting and great cross ventilation. This room, which adjoins a small but full kitchen, functions as a dining/conference/gathering area.

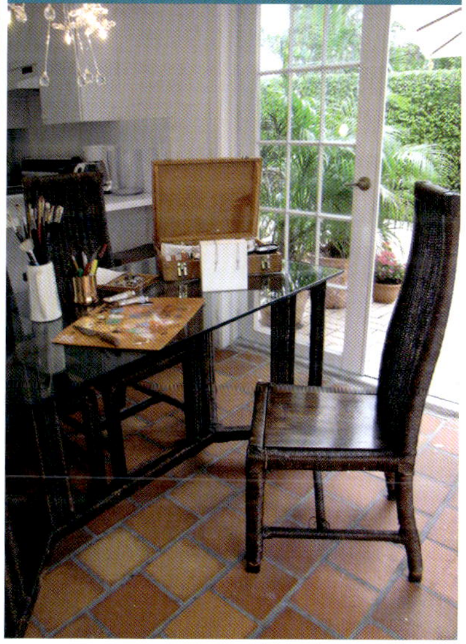

Tere Pastoriza

Miami, Florida

My studio sits just about 50 feet from the back door of my house. It is an eighty-six-year-old structure, originally built as a carriage house. Although it may have housed a Model-T at one time, it now houses ideas, art works, and an occasional guest.

It is workshop, laboratory, storage, and gallery. It is a gathering place for friends, where many lively discussions have taken place over the years, ranging from the hilariously infantile to the profoundly sublime. My studio can be a blissful refuge from chaos, and sometimes it is chaos itself. It is where I draw, paint, read, and listen to music and to myself. It is a living, breathing thing that always reflects who I am at the moment.

For practical reasons, I find it very convenient to have a studio just steps from my house. For one, I can work in my pajamas if I want to. More than once, I've awakened in the middle of the night with an idea that I just must put into effect immediately, and so I do. It is also very easy to work right into the night. I feel very fortunate to have this particular space to call my own.

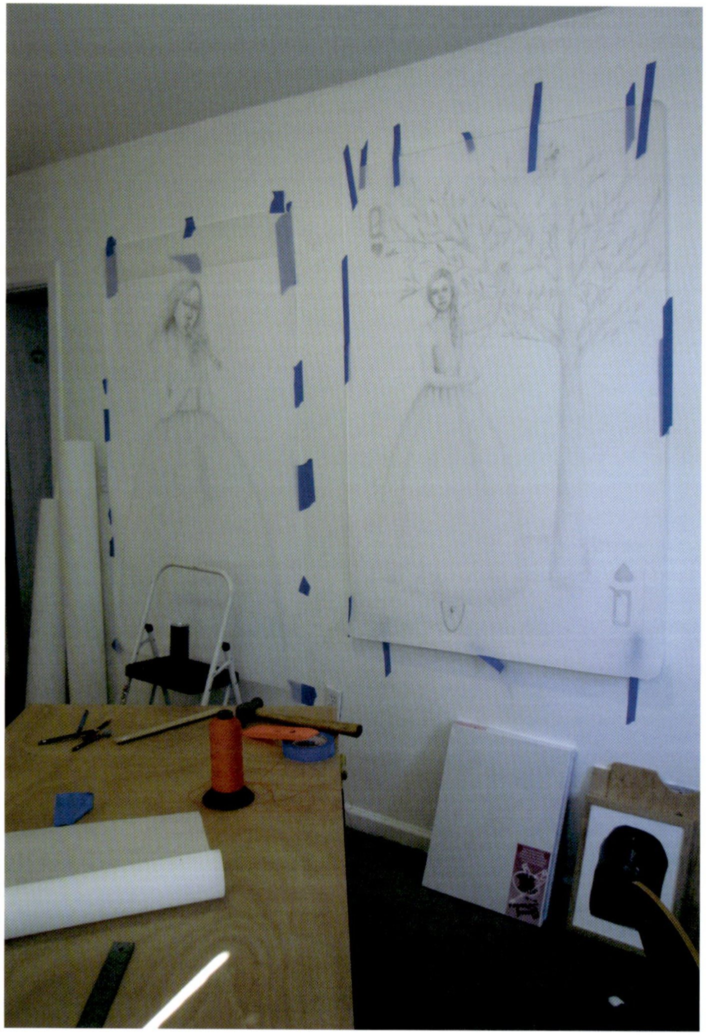

This wall is set up with large drawings, which are in different stages of completion. I am using two different types of paper here: Yupo, a Japanese paper, serves as a beautiful background for the delicate and translucent Mylar. Painter's blue tape secures these drawings to the wall.

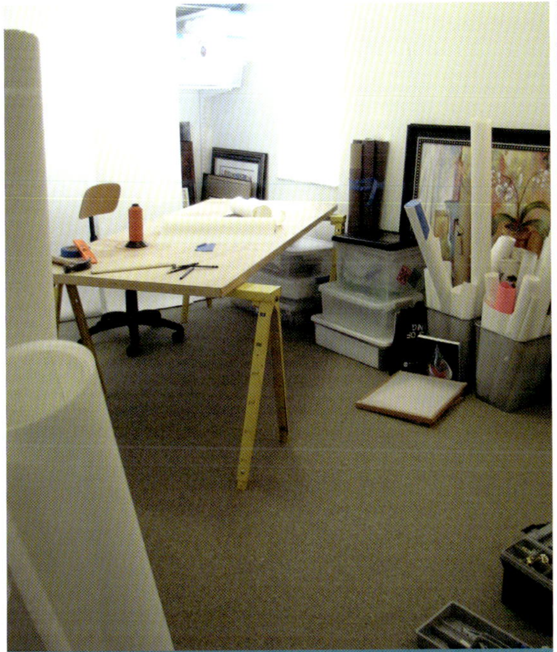

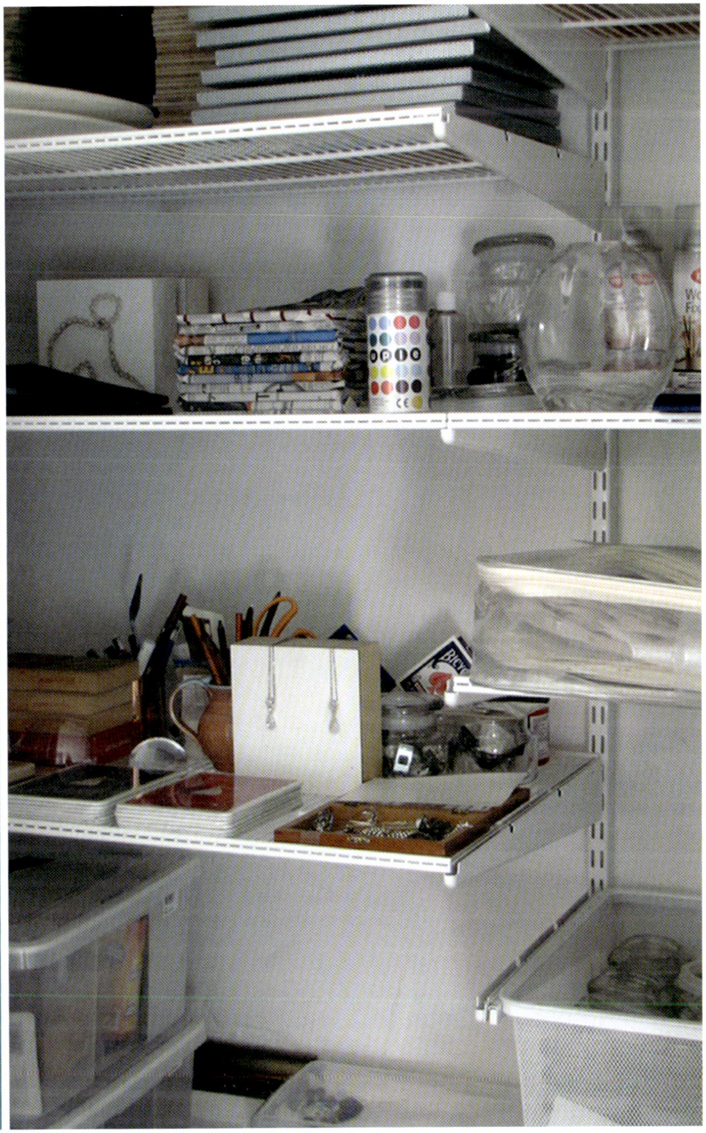

This is the part of my studio where I do most of my work and keep the materials that I use most frequently. This room never looks quite the same. The collapsible, makeshift table is a door and two construction sawhorses.

This is one of four storage closets in the carriage house. Here, I store art supplies, inspirational materials, and small works. It is almost always more organized than the room that surrounds it—the studio!

Florence Putterman

Sarasota, Florida

I examine the world through my painting. My work usually springs from an actual experience visually recalled. It can also be a sort of reverie, bringing back many recurring memories from earlier works involving the non-verbal symbols of man and animals and their interrelationships. When I am painting, I allow the canvas to tell me what to do. I start the painting by applying thin washes of paint, overlapping each one; as the paint mingles, images emerge, and the painting starts to take shape.

I have two racks on either side of my room in which I place the paintings as I work on them. This gives me an opportunity to study them as I am working on some other project, talking on the telephone, or exercising. The front room is mainly for producing; the backroom is for storage and framing.

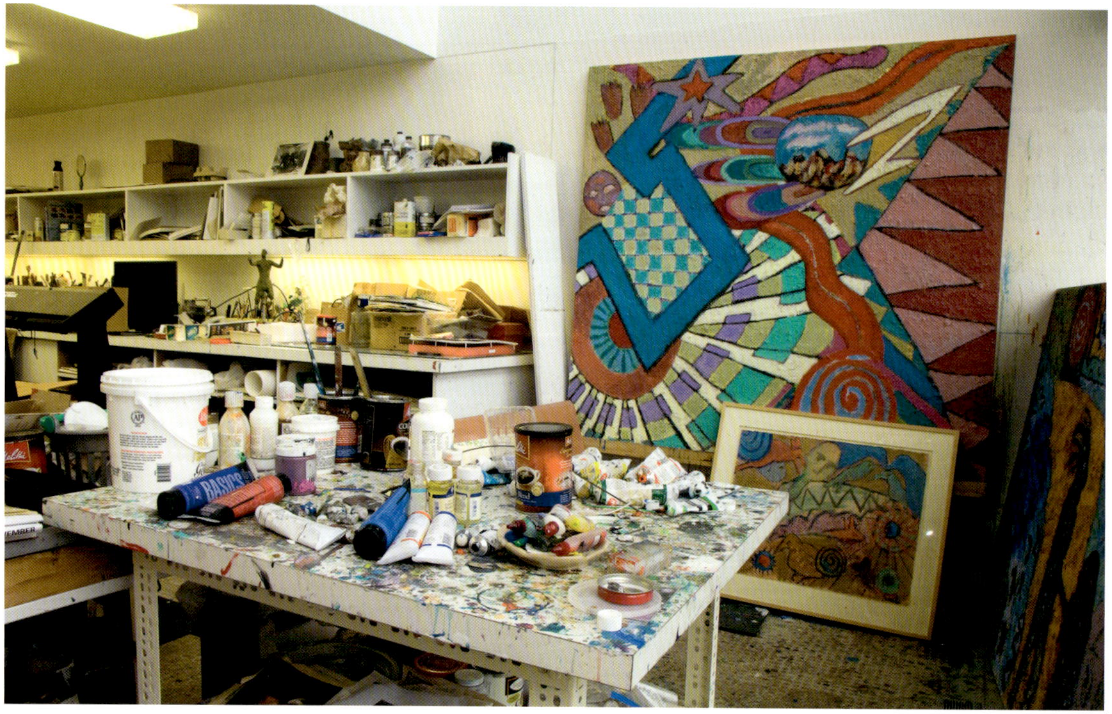

I have many shelves and storage areas so the studio remains quite open for me to work in without tripping over paintings. My shelves can handle many framed works, and there are shelves for storing paper and canvases that are not stretched. My husband helps with the framing and shipping work, and he has his area to work in. Courtesy of Kerry Shirk, The Picture Place, Shamokin Dam, PA.

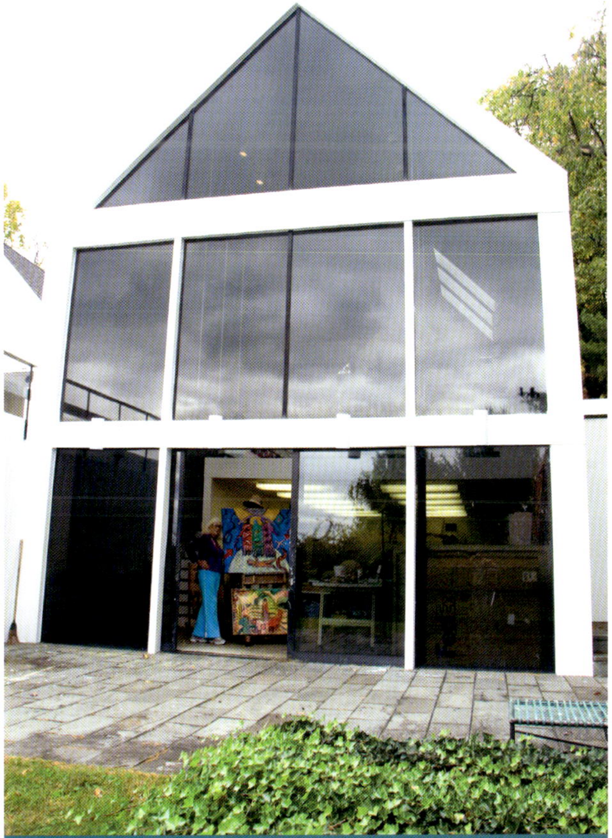

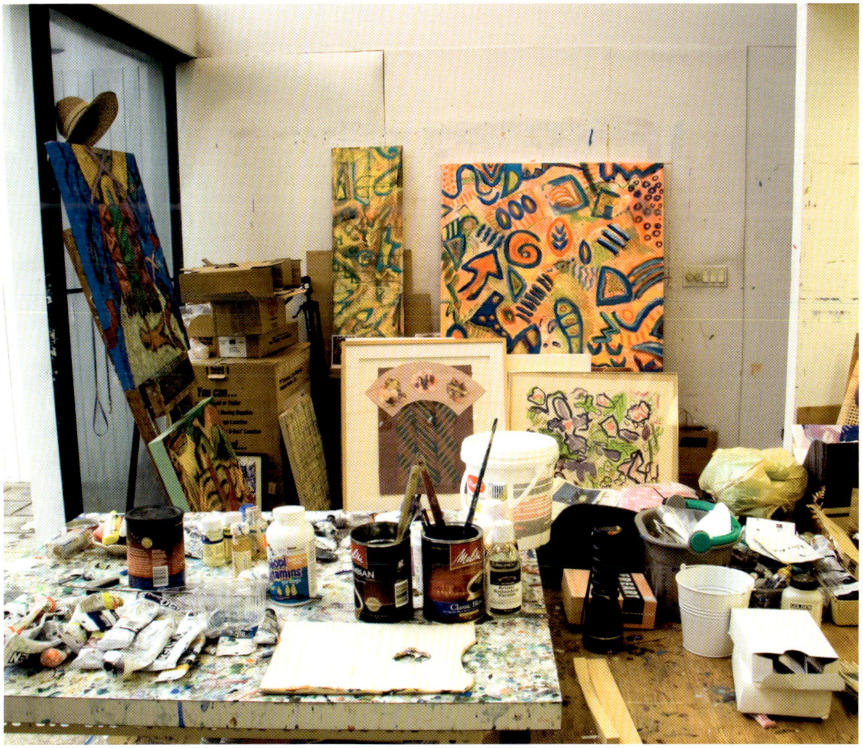

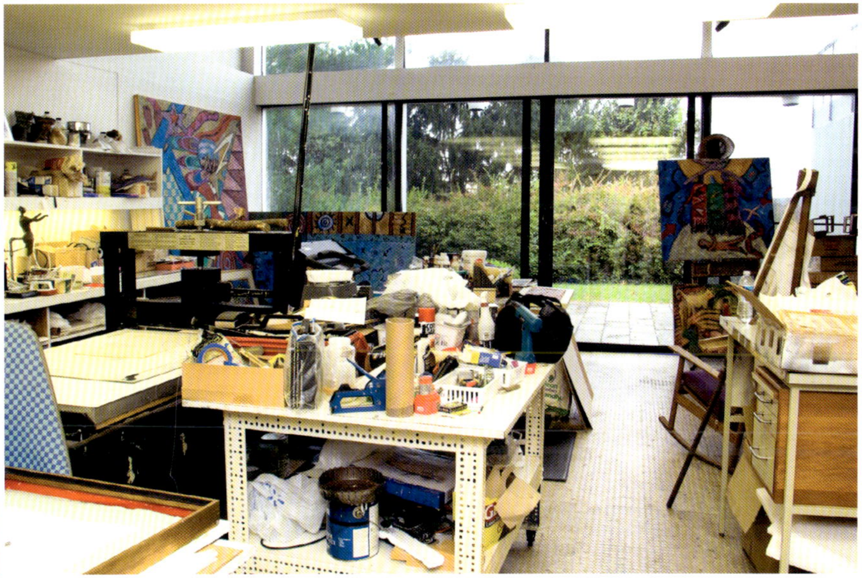

The front room is mainly for producing; the back room is for storage and framing. I have several areas in both rooms with drawers to store the many prints I have produced over the years. Even though there may be much going on, it is easy to find everything as the layout is well organized.

Amanda Richardson

Cornwall, England

In designing my studio, I wanted a welcoming space that I would always be glad to enter, both light and versatile with generous storage. My studio is surrounded by a large garden, and I consider this to be part of my working process, providing much of the inspiration for my art. The setting is a wooded valley near the Lands End, the most westerly point of England. The magnificent granite cliffs and windswept moorland of this area are also important to my art.

My primary medium is fabric collage, and my work varies greatly in scale. The studio has two floors, so furniture and fabrics can be moved upstairs releasing a space 20 x 30 feet for big commissions. Both floors have skylights as I love to work in bright spaces.

I am fascinated by different ways of creating art, always fine-tuning the techniques I use and juggling the space to accommodate these disciplines, particularly the many techniques used in dying and patterning fabrics. I thrive on abundance and surround myself with a rich array of hand-dyed fabrics that form the palette for my art and allow me to express the excitement I feel in the natural world.

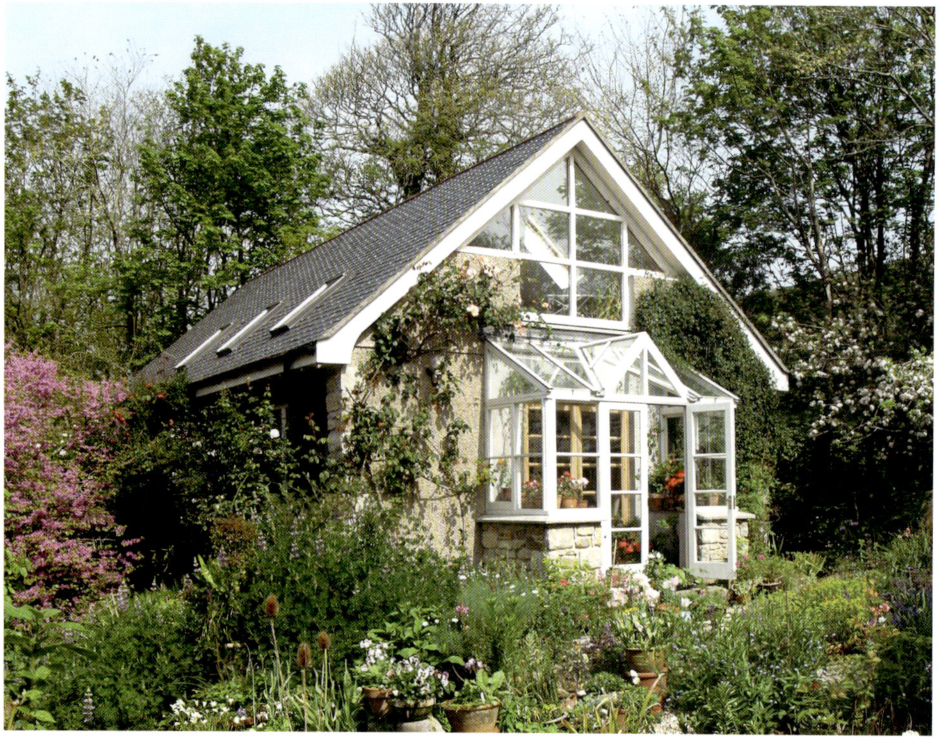

The studio is set in two-and-a-half acres of gardens, which I consider to be an integral part of my artistic process.

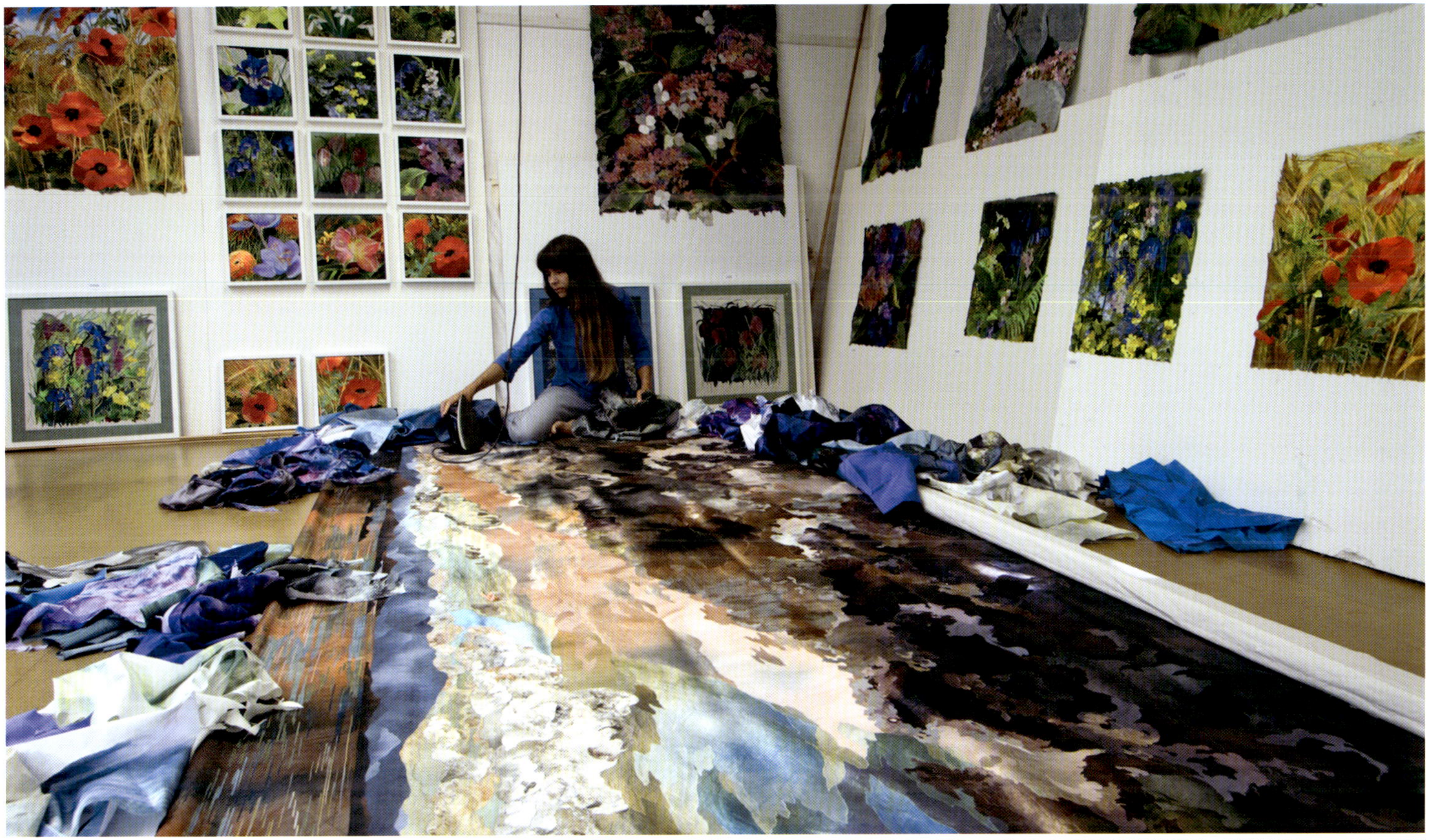

Before beginning a collage, I hand-dye all the fabrics I intend to use. With large commissions, I work on the floor with the fabrics I have prepared all around me. As people often visit the studio, I am also surrounded by artwork on the walls. These include **Barley Field with Poppies** and **Hydrangea Aspera**. Courtesy of Vivien Howse.

I use iron-on adhesives so an iron and pair of scissors are my most frequently used tools, seen here while working on **Strawberry Tree Feast**.

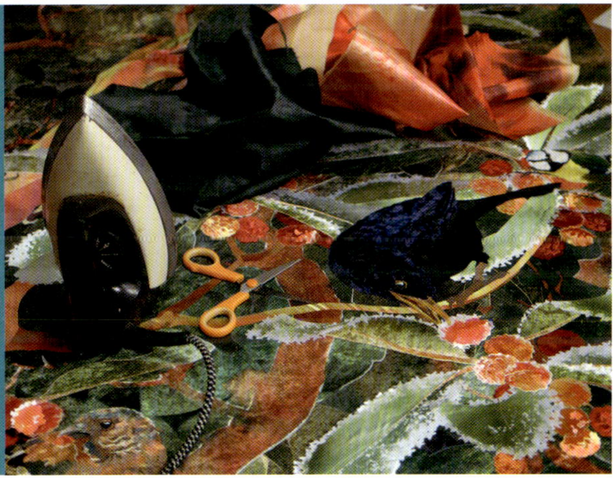

Ebeth Scott-Sinclair

Chapel Hill, North Carolina

The property where I live and work is steeped in history and natural beauty. Our house (a converted grist mill built in 1878), a stacked stone dam and mill race (c. 1790), and several other structures are located along a creek, in the woods, and in the fields. My studio used to be an unfinished storage attic on the third floor of an outbuilding that housed chickens at one time. Seeing the space as a diamond in the rough, my husband renovated it for use as an art studio.

I resonate with the simplicity of my studio with its hardwood floors and white walls. It is a long and narrow space with windows at each end. Stairs divide the room into two sections forming work and sitting areas. It is unpretentious, open, and not overly organized. There are pockets of creative clutter. My work is a visual exploration of stories, emotions, and the possibilities that we don't readily see. Where I work is an integral part of that creative process. My studio supports and inspires me to be adventurous, vulnerable, and authentic in my art.

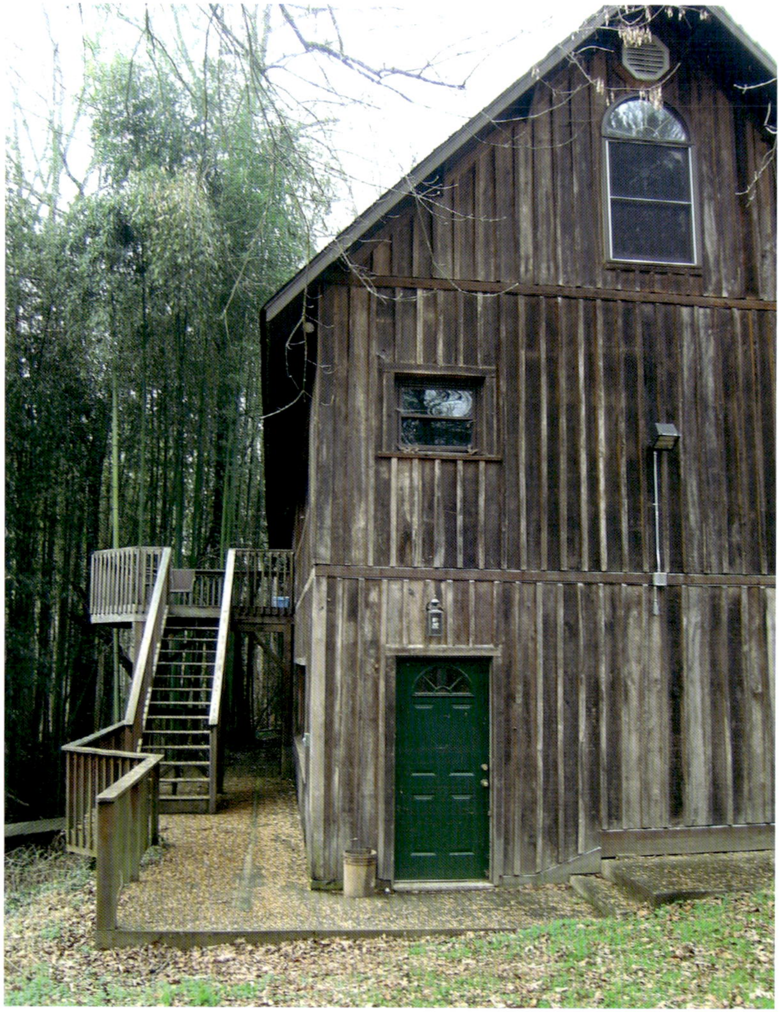

The arched window on the third floor is at one end of my studio, which runs the length of the building.

My painting station. Paints, brushes, and palette knives are stored in drawers and shelves in a roll-a-way cart. Bins, inherited from my stepdaughter's dorm room, hold clippings, sketches on scrap paper, charcoal, and rags. I use folding tables for work counters.

My "idea" station. Ideas for color, texture, and composition for my paintings and collaged pieces often originate here. I store reproduction vintage fabric swatches, decorative paper, blank canvases, wood boards, and a variety of drawing paper on open metal shelves.

The sitting area. In the background are **Play a Volta** and **Lady Triumphant**, both acrylics on canvas.

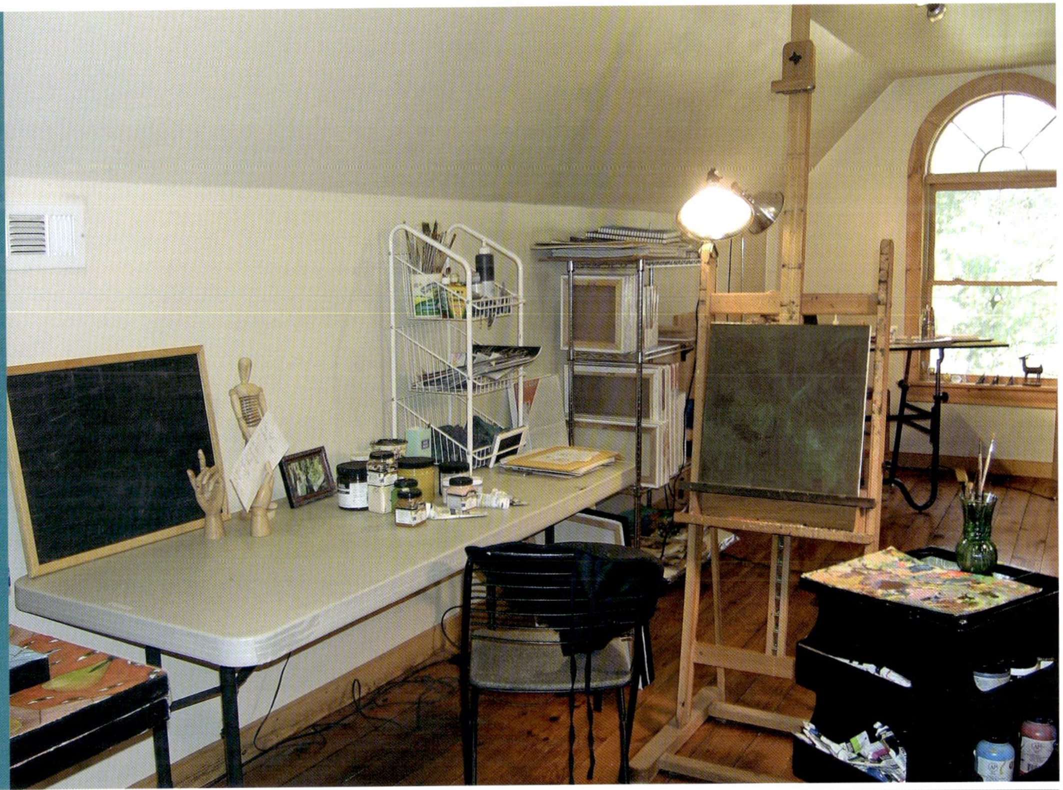

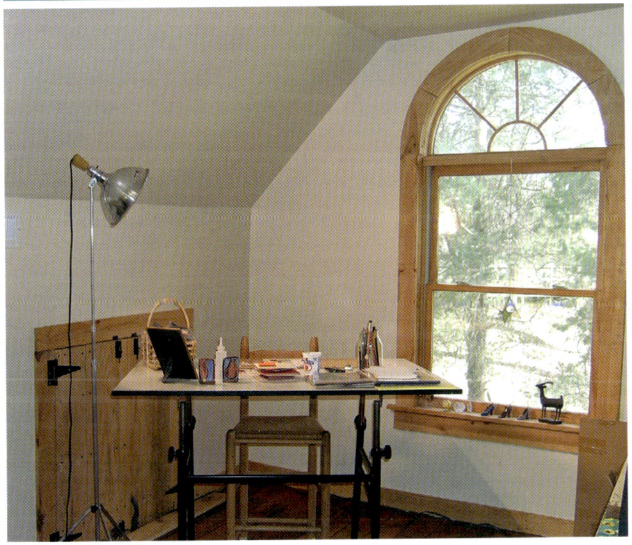

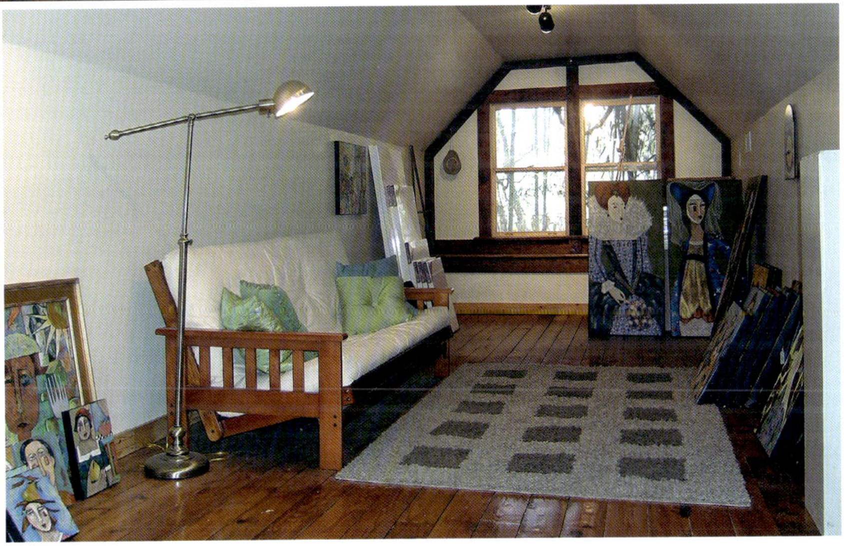

Graceann Warn

Ann Arbor, Michigan

In 1985 my husband Geoff and I found a one-room schoolhouse for sale. Built in 1836, this structure, with its huge paned windows and 12-foot high ceilings, had irresistible charm and unlimited potential. It has been a constant work in progress, as we create living spaces while respecting its integrity. In 1997, we built a large addition, which includes my studio on two floors. On the first floor I have my woodshop; on the second floor is my painting studio, with windows on three sides.

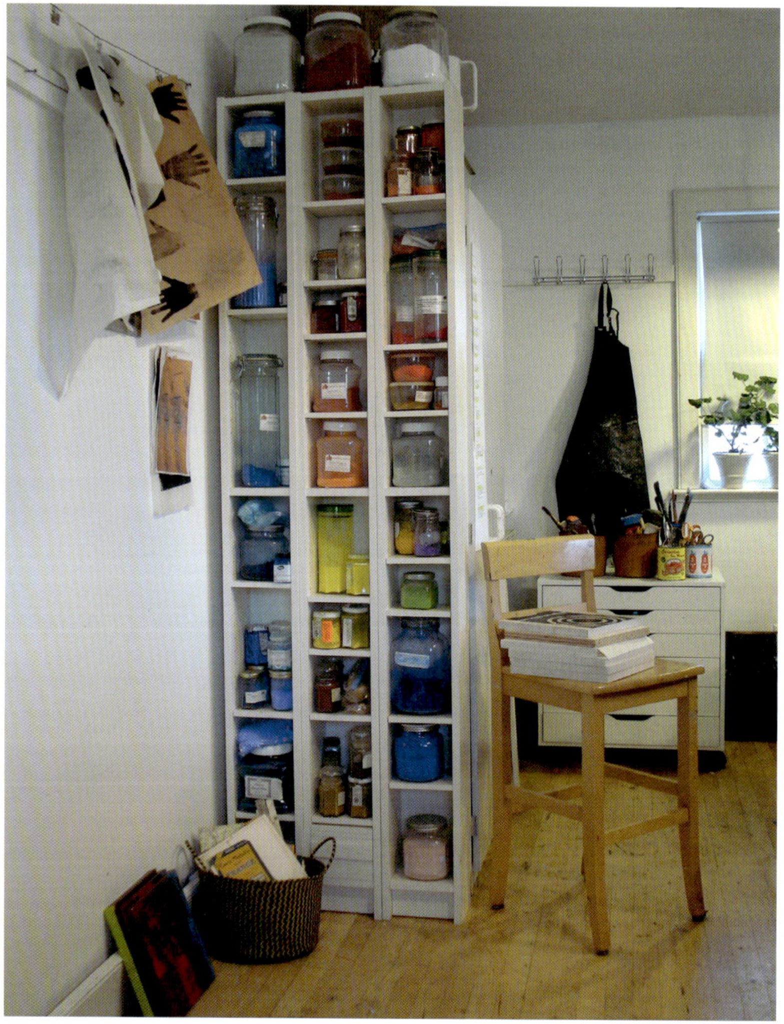

My pigment tower in the painting studio. These dry pigments are used in the encaustic paint I make.

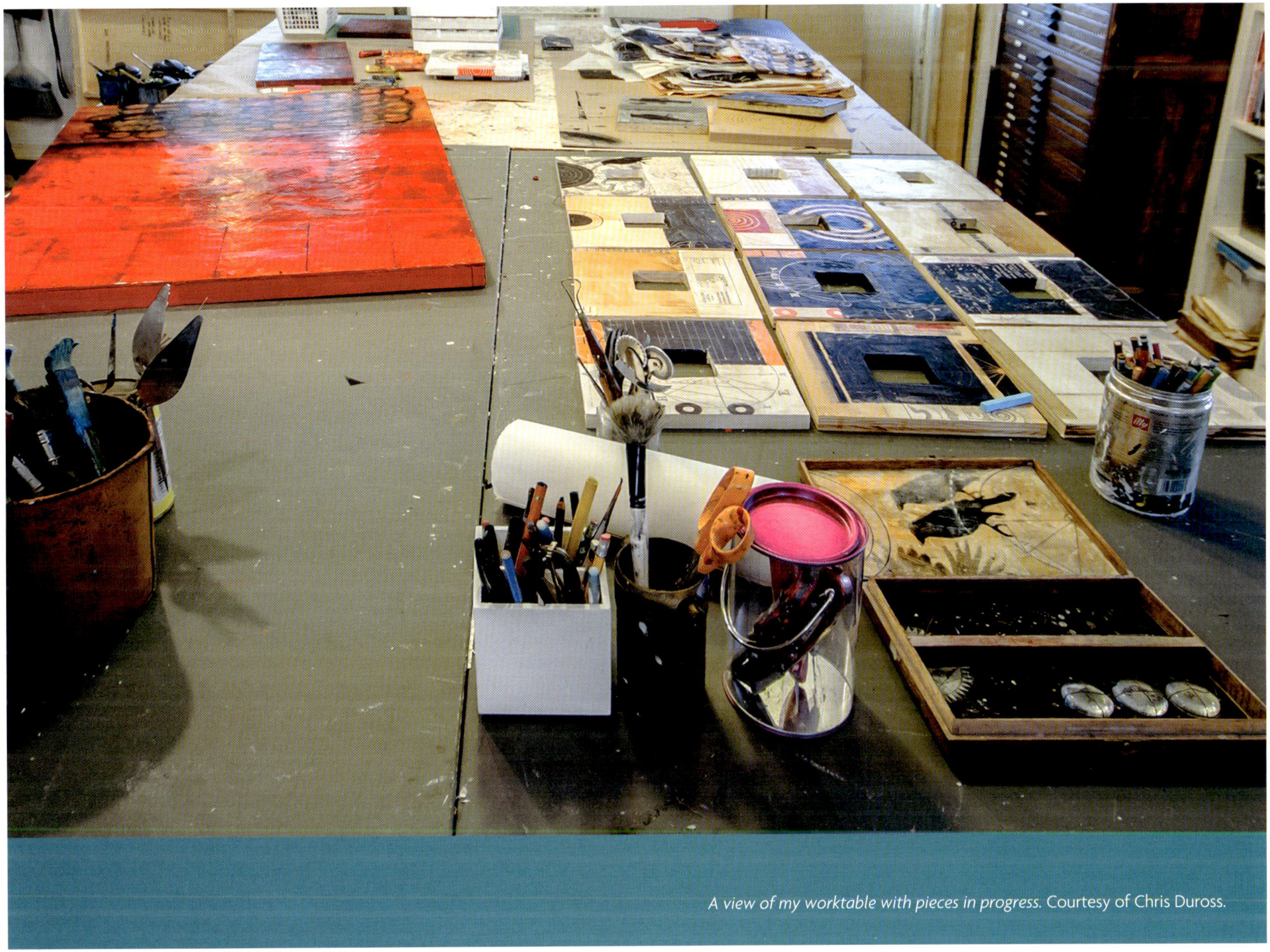

A view of my worktable with pieces in progress. Courtesy of Chris Duross.

George Fellner

East Haddam, Connecticut

My studio environment inherently enhances my fine art photography, involving the exploration of "Imaginary Realms." It is an open, flexible space that allows me to free myself from outside distractions, with optimal natural lighting, ambient/electronic music, and expansive views of the Connecticut River valley. Upon setting up for a photo shoot, I allow myself to become fully immersed within a mode of clarity and multisensory awareness. I basically embark upon a journey involving the macro photography of stones and crystals.

As I gaze through the lens, I search for compositions that are formed by patterns, colors, textures, contrast, and tonal gradations. Simultaneously, I open my senses and allow my mind to contemplate messages from history, mythology, multi-cultures, geology, biology, and astronomy. These themes offer multiple points of departure, and my mind is stimulated to visualize a myriad of possibilities. The voyage of discovery evolves, as hidden memories and inner dreams occasionally filter through. A stone may trigger the recollection of an old dream from my childhood. As I become truly immersed within the image potentialities, ancient and future fantasies, as well as planetary- and cosmic-scapes, traversing space, time, and dimension are often conceived. Ultimately, my studio provides the perfect spatial context for creating new realities through my fine art photography of abstract expressions.

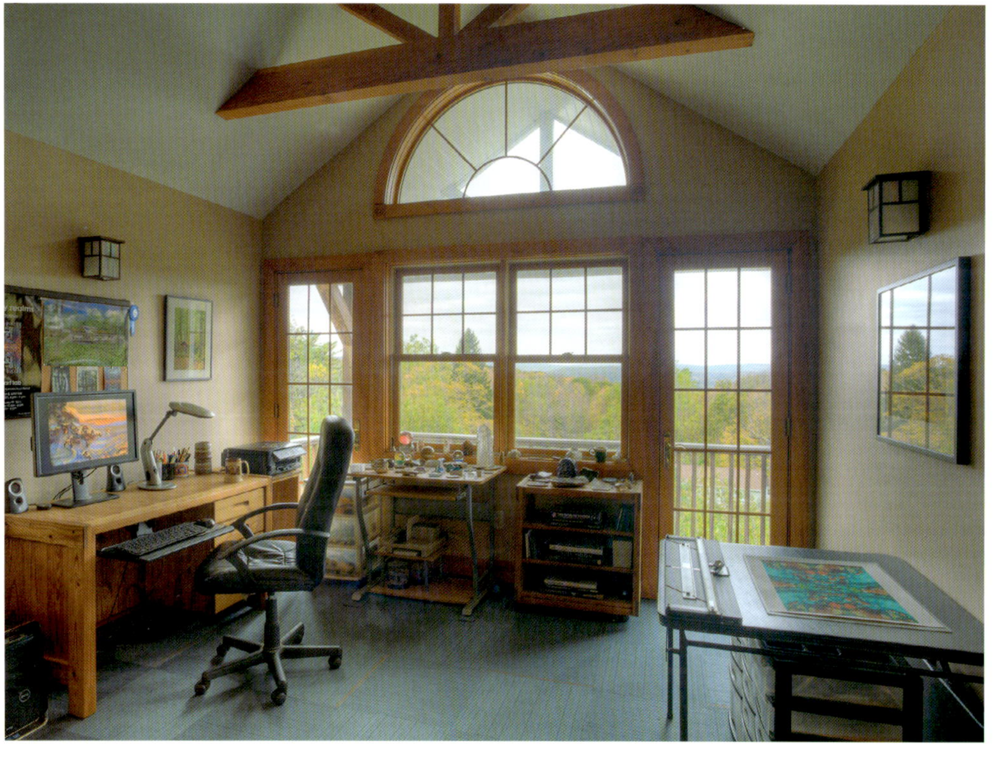

As an architect, I designed my house and studio to be fully integrated with the site context and to celebrate the views of the Connecticut River valley. This space allows for an optimal setting for writing and photo editing, fed by inspirations from the natural landscape.

My spacious studio has ample wall space for exhibiting my images, as well as for storing my library of books on mythology, history, sciences, architecture, and photography. There are also old cameras, crystals, rockets, and dinosaurs sharing the shelves. The seating area allows for socializing, reading, writing, sketching, planning, and dreaming. It is a place for challenging my imagination and for creating concepts.

Pele Awakens on Kilauea. *Digital pigmented ink archival print. 20 x 13". 2013.*

My photo shoot setup has a Canon digital SLR camera and 100mm macro lens on a tripod and two Softboxes with CFL lights. I typically prop my source stones and crystals upon the curved acrylic base, covered with black fabric, for proper placement and orientation. The Epson printer allows me to print up to 17 x 22" prints in-house.

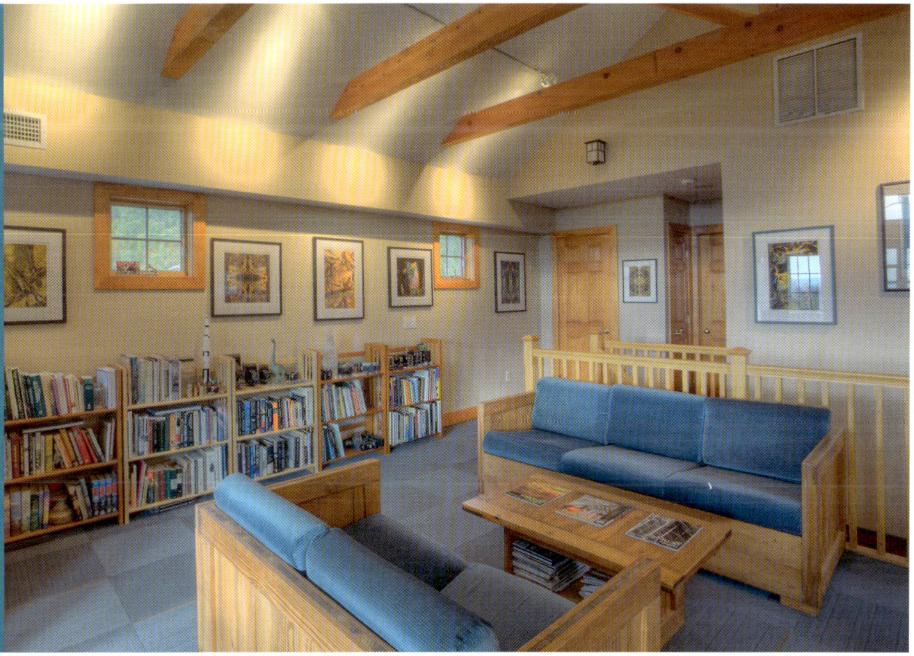

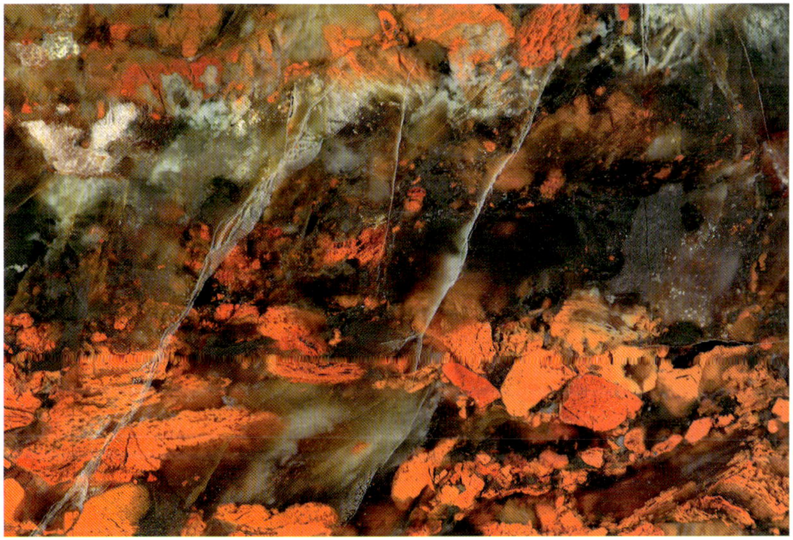

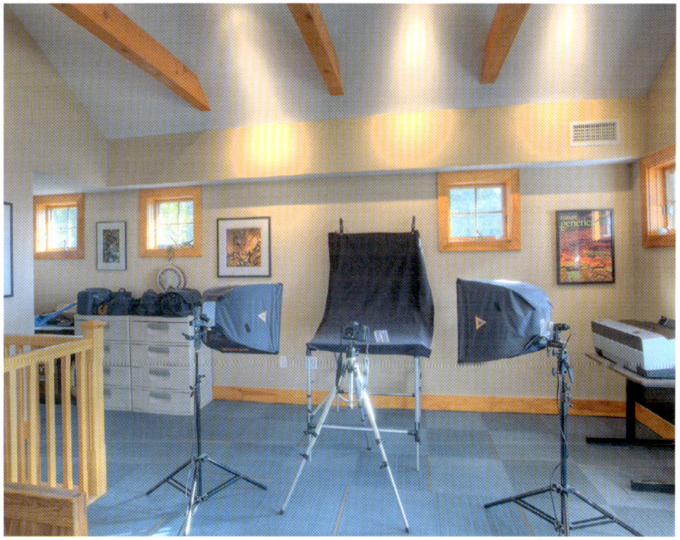

4

Rental Space

Renting space is an age-old tradition. Some artists rent spaces with other artists in former manufacturing spaces, while others may just rent individual space. Light is always the deciding factor.

Kathleen Westkaemper keeps her paintsticks in an old melamine cafeteria tray.

The studio of Karen Hibbs is in an old factory complex, offering lots of natural light and ample room to work.

A northern exposure and a skylight provide natural light in Nina Weiss's studio.

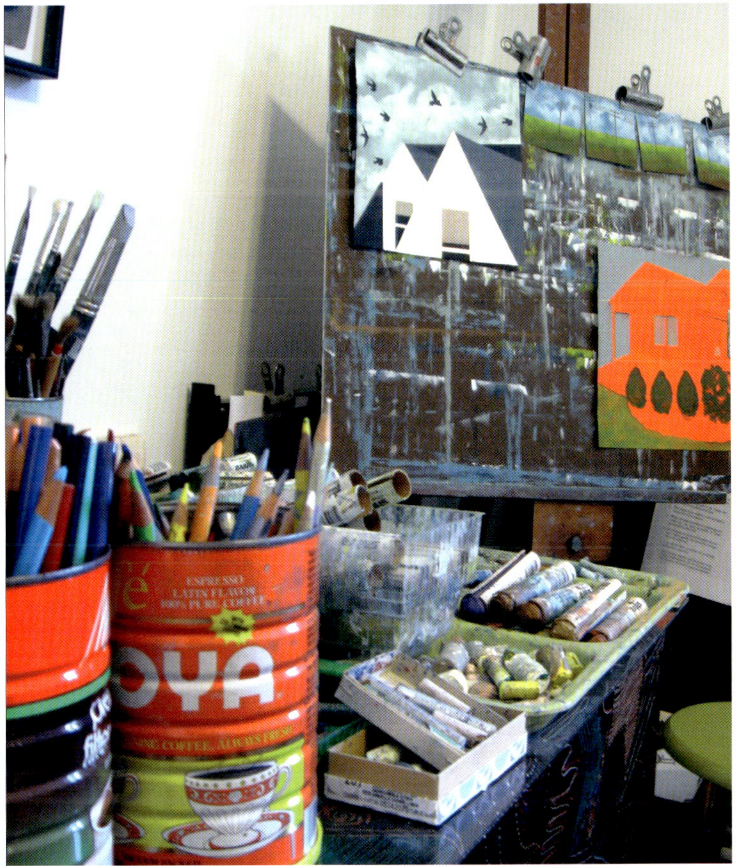

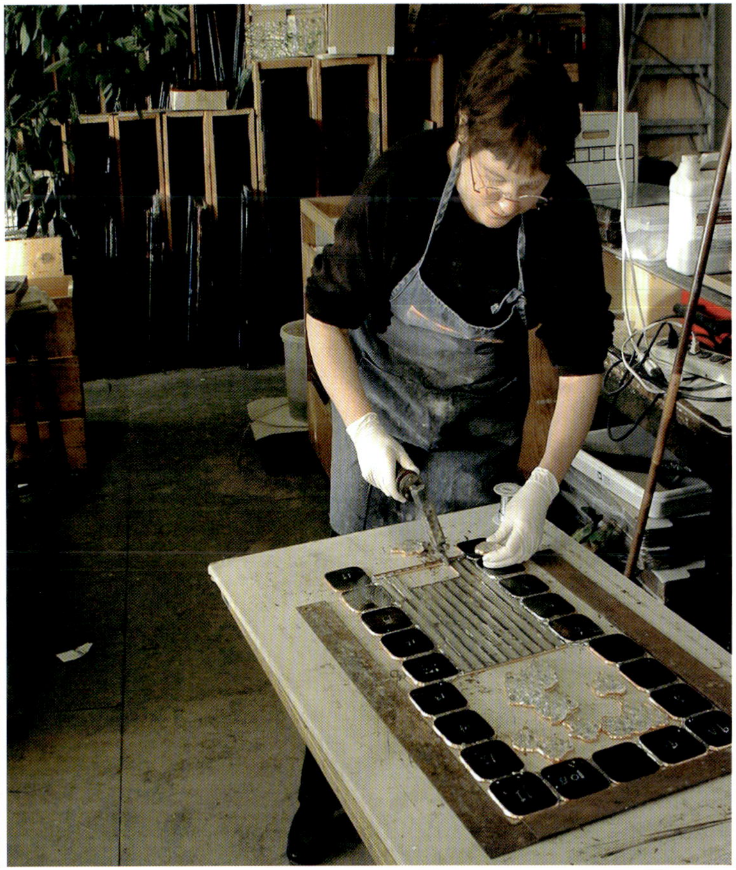

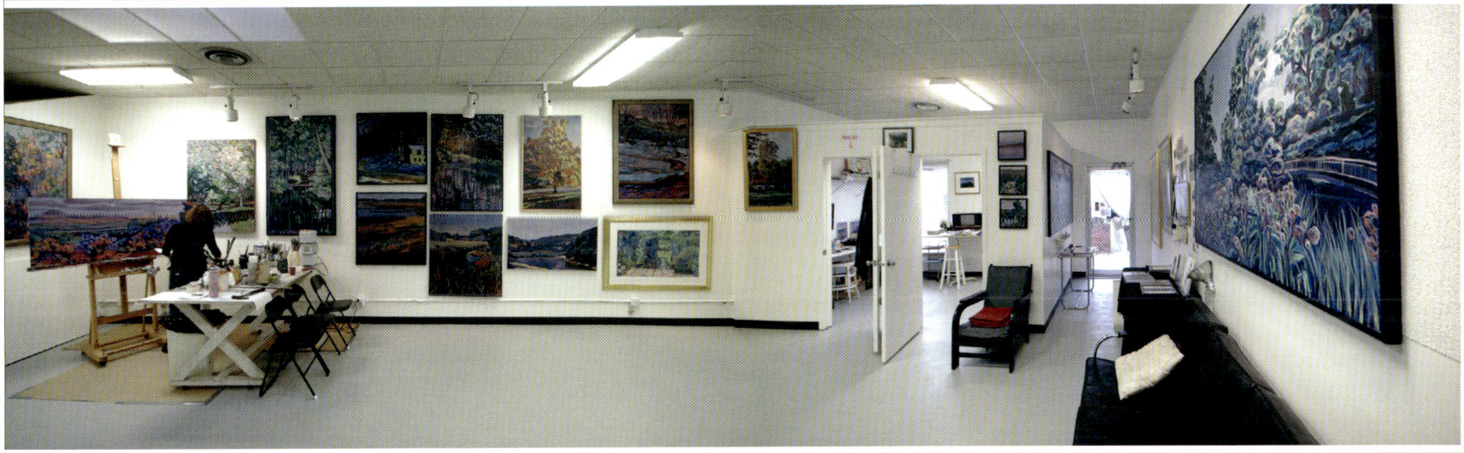

Stephanie Barenz

Milwaukee, Wisconsin

My studio is located in the Third Ward in Milwaukee, Wisconsin. I am part of a group of creatives called Plaid Tuba, which was the brainchild of nationally renowned artist Reginald Baylor. In the 3800 square-foot space, there are artists, graphic designers, a production company, a fine art printer, a studio manager, a writer, a lawyer who specializes in creative law, and a musician.

I love my space because it operates as an open studio. The public is welcome to come and visit the Plaid Tuba headquarters whenever they like. I get to see many people on a daily basis. Some artists may find this overwhelming; I find it inspiring. I have never really liked working by myself and have always done my best work when I have been part of a community. Since we are located in the Third Ward of Milwaukee, we are in close proximity to many other artists, galleries, and design firms. My day is spent painting, meeting with clients, marketing my work, and visiting other creatives in the neighborhood.

I work on a large, 4 x 8-foot table, and my space is used for building and prepping panels as well as painting. When the city of Milwaukee has Gallery Nights or our building, which houses many other galleries and artists, has events, my studio turns into a gallery.

I have worked in many studios, including a printing studio in Italy, a small apartment in China, a printmaker's collaborative in Chicago, and graduate studios at Washington University in St. Louis. Plaid Tuba is my favorite space to date. I am very blessed to be able to work in this environment and I hope to for years to come.

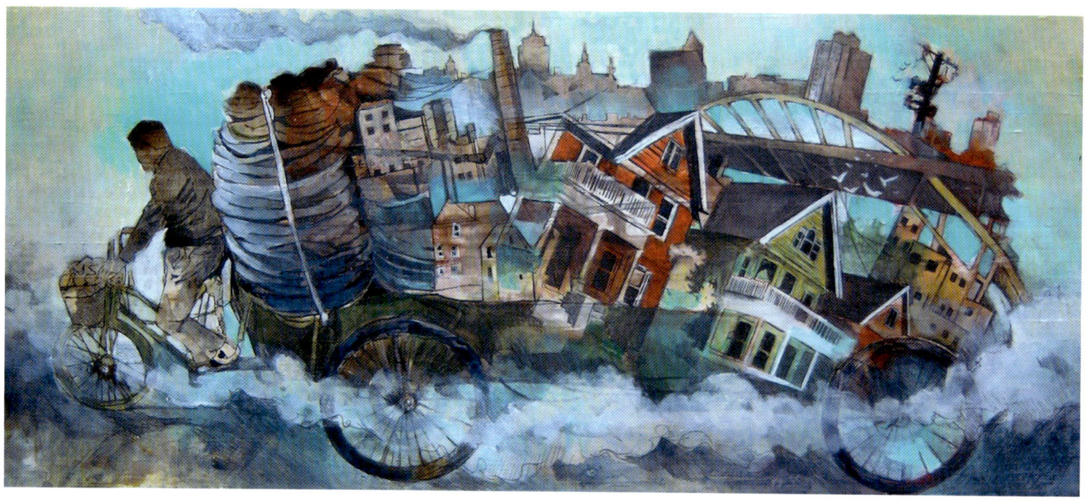

Bicycle to MKE. *Mixed media on panel.*

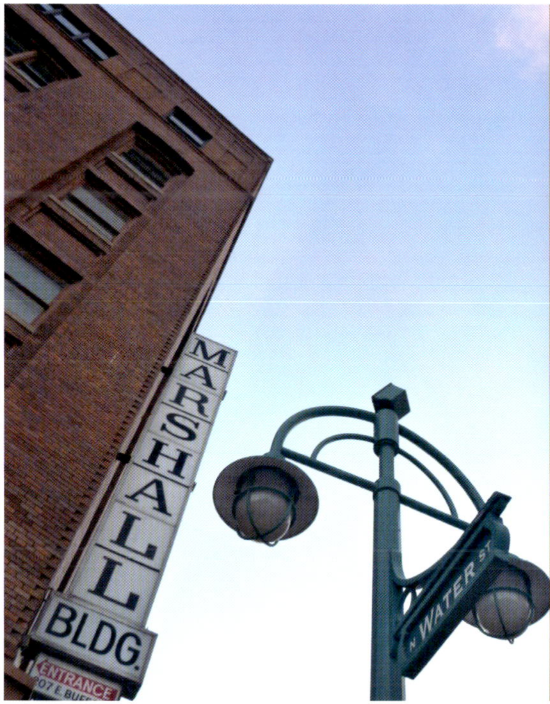

My studio is located on the sixth floor of the Marshall Building in Milwaukee, Wisconsin. It is located on Water Street, a popular place for people to hang out, so I am in a prime location for traffic.

I have shelving to hold all of my supplies. I like to work on my paintings on the table instead of an easel. The studio walls only go up half way, which encourages an open studio policy.

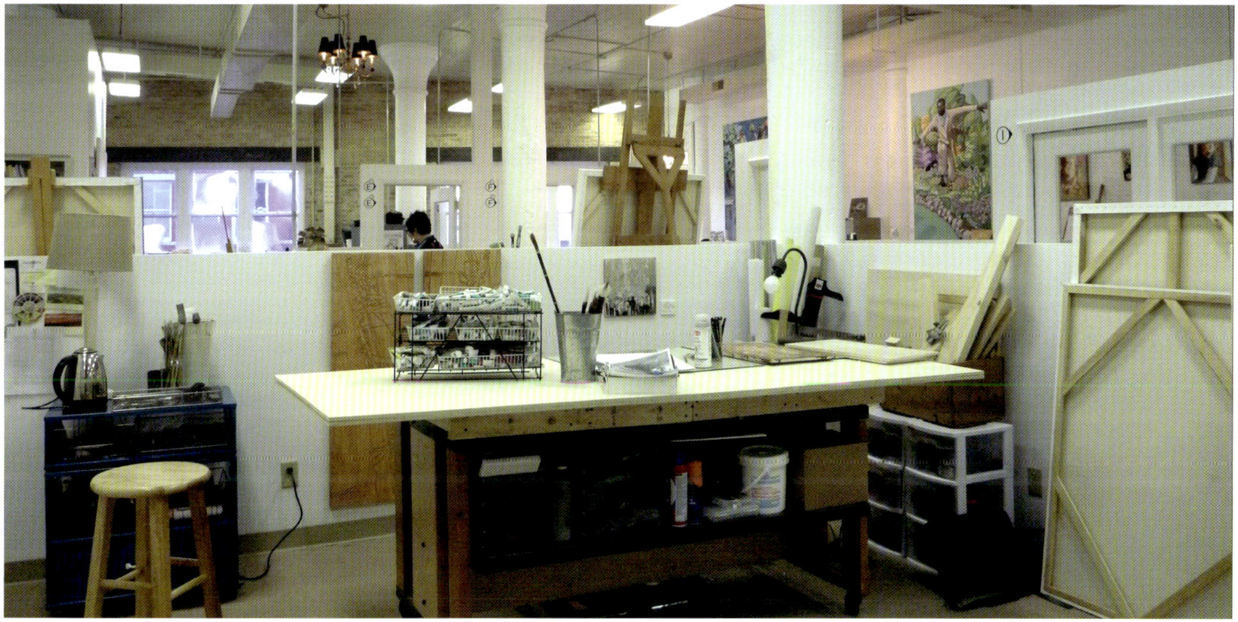

Leila Daw

New Haven, Connecticut

My studio is in an historic, nineteenth-century, industrial factory building, buried deep in the bowels of a more recent facade. The antiquity of the building suits my mindset—while working, I often think of myself as an Age-of-Discovery explorer/mapmaker. I work on many things simultaneously, so I need a lot of space for all my works in progress, plus all my collections. My work references mapping, and it grows out of both imagined and real connections to the Earth. I collect all kinds of stuff, pieces of the world, which might relate to locations or conditions I create. The physicality of the materials I use is important; often the work develops out of these collected materials, which lie all over my tabletops and sometimes the floor. Most of the time, my work is large, because the world is large. I also make tiny panels I call Map Icons; these require just as much room while in progress as the large work does. Mercifully, my studio is 1600 square feet and has 14-foot ceilings.

I've built walls on wheels that I can roll around to reconfigure the space depending on my projects. I have a couple of armchairs and little tables to make cozy corners, which migrate, depending on the walls.

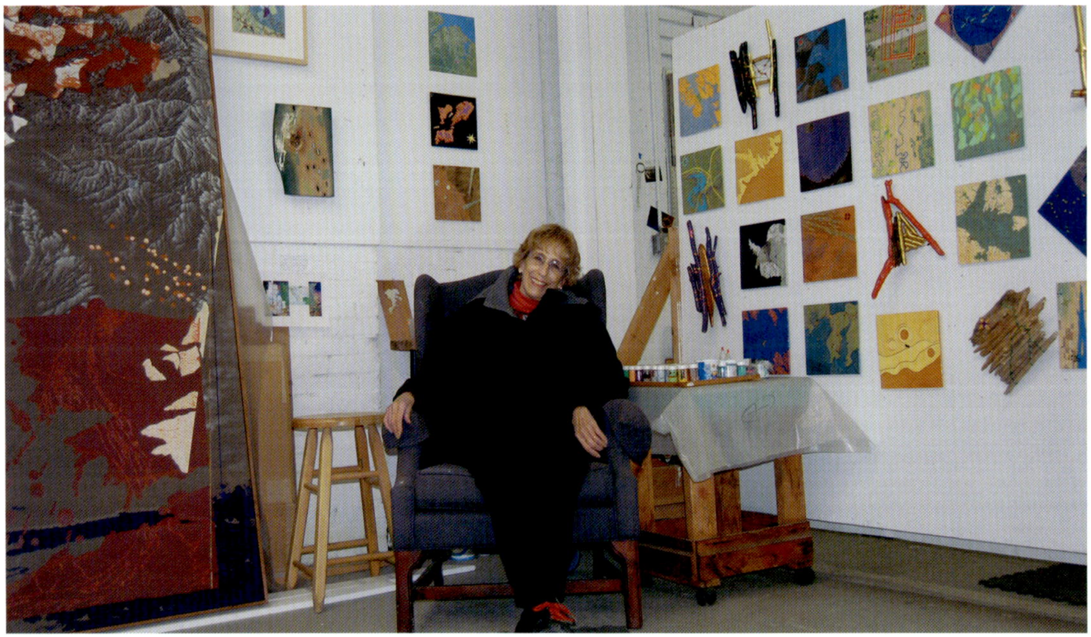

The studio heat is on an old steam loop, and heat comes on twice a day. When I get too cold to work efficiently, I snuggle into one of my armchairs in a corner to warm up. On the left is the edge of ***Doesn't Stand A Chance****, and behind me and to the right are some of the Map Icons.*

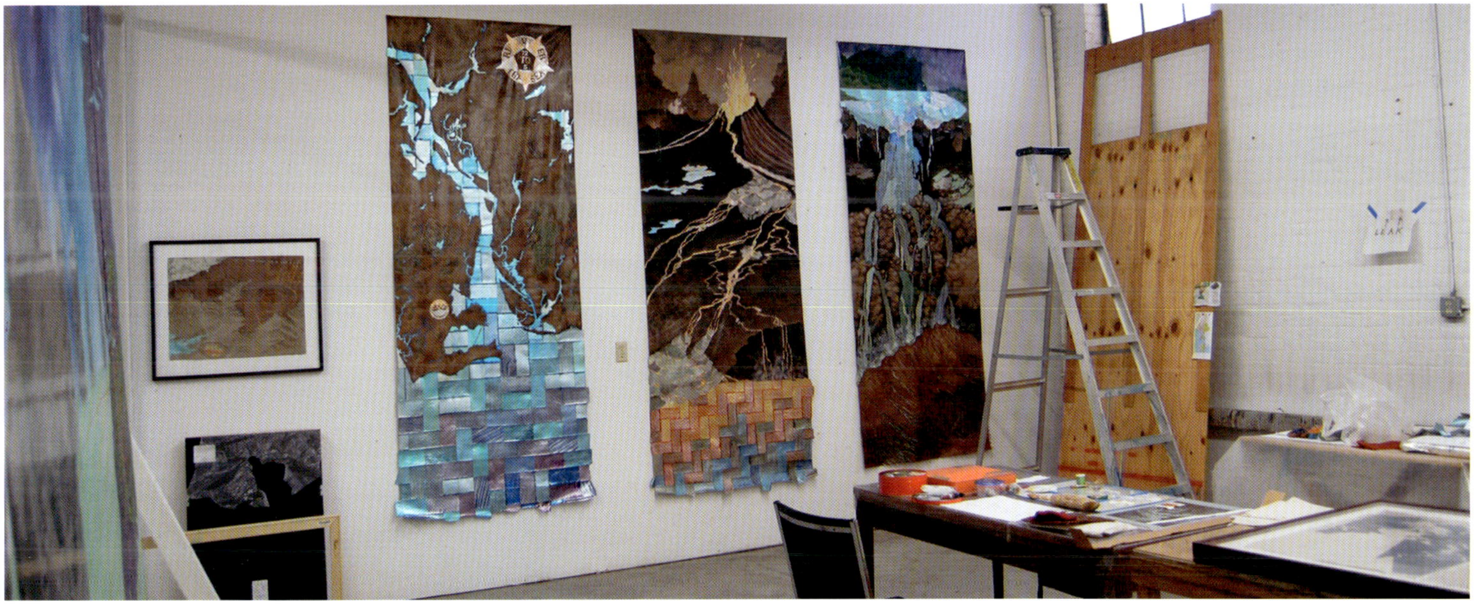

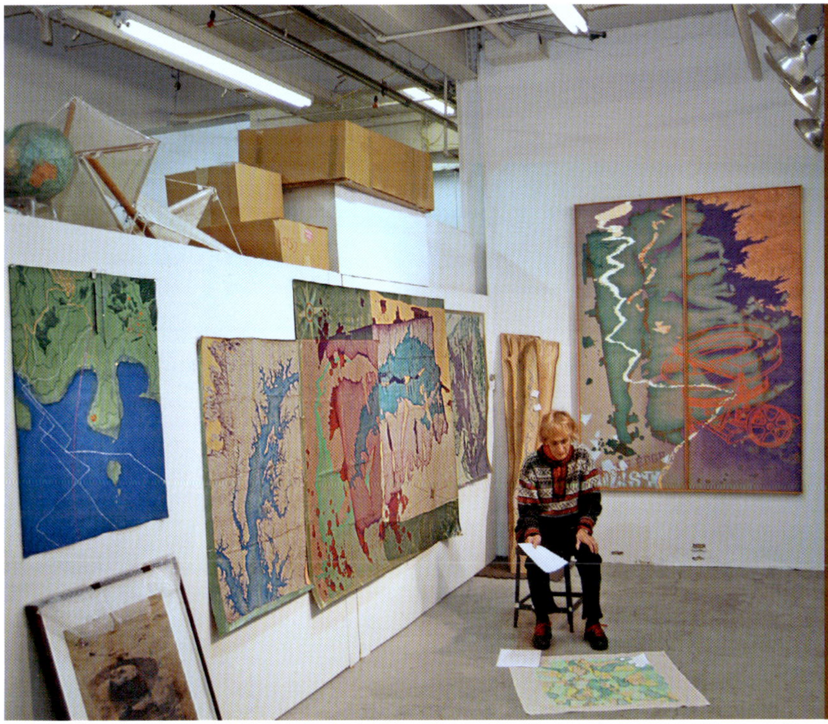

I tend to work on the floor or on tabletops. The plywood structure (behind the ladder) is a device I made for lifting tall work so I can see how it will look hanging. It's easier to attach the work to this and raise and lower it than to climb up and down the ladder.

I like the openness of space above me. The light is a strange mixture; a few high frosted windows along one wall, old fluorescents, and some supplementary clamp-ons on top of the rolling walls, to prevent dark shadows. The low wall on the left is the back of my plywood shelves.

Karen Hibbs

New Haven, Connecticut

My studio is located in an old factory complex now known as "Erector Square," formerly the A. C. Gilbert Co., famous for the Erector sets and educational toys they produced and the source of much of the gear that was close to my heart as a child. So, it was something of a homecoming for me to have landed here, some 27 years ago. It is a large place with enormous windows that supply lots of natural light, which is great for color selection (if a bit frisky in the winter), and room for the surprisingly vast amount of stuff and equipment I use in the making of each piece. This place has become a second home to me and an important source of working space for the greater New Haven artist community, as well as for many small businesses, from architects to yoga studios.

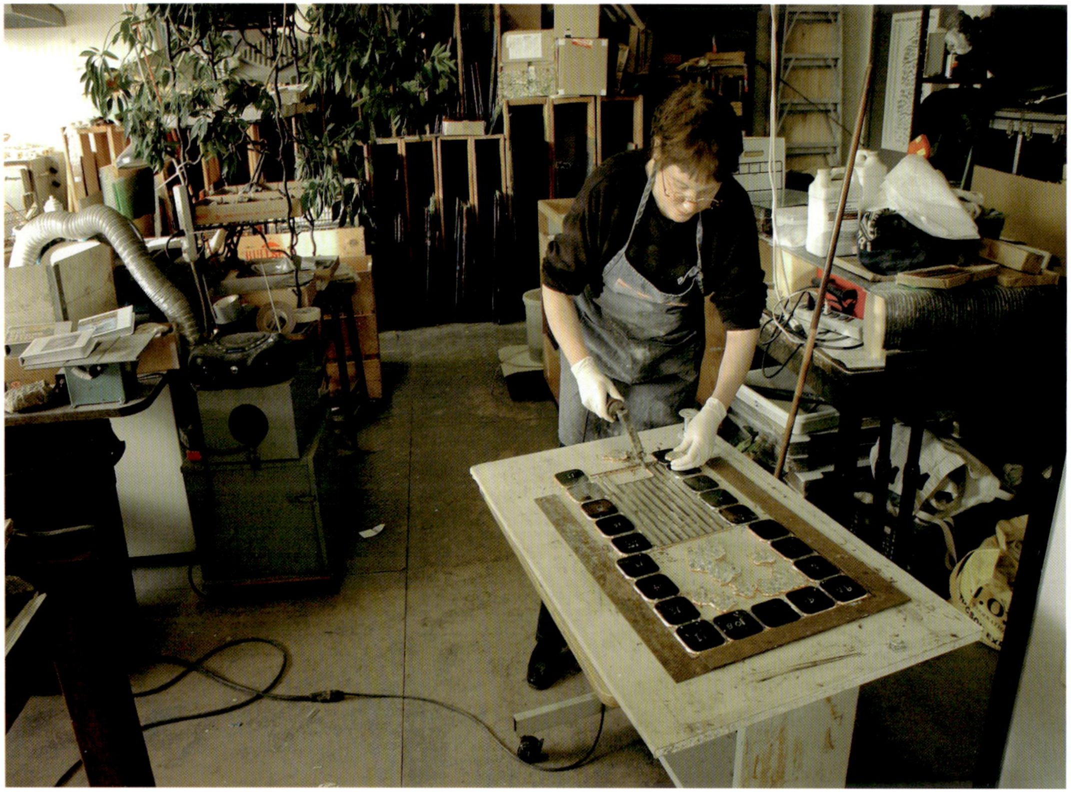

The truth is, I have, and use, so much stuff for each piece that my place is always in some degree of dishevelment.... as am I.

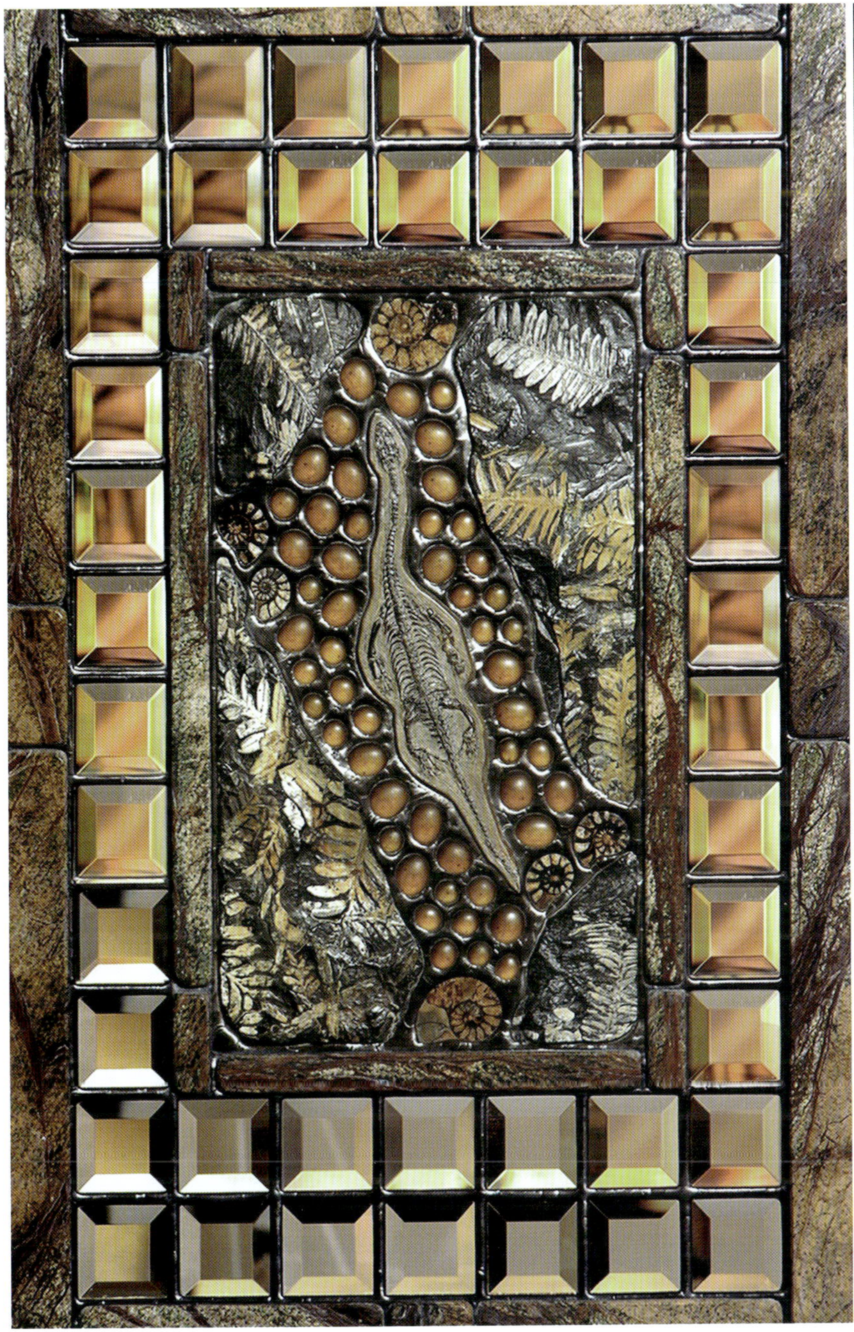

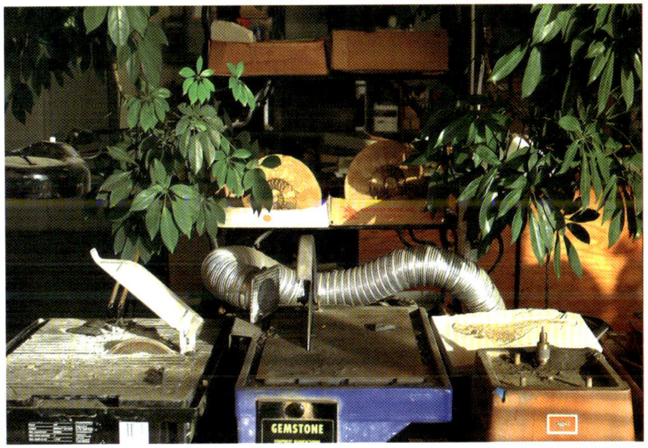

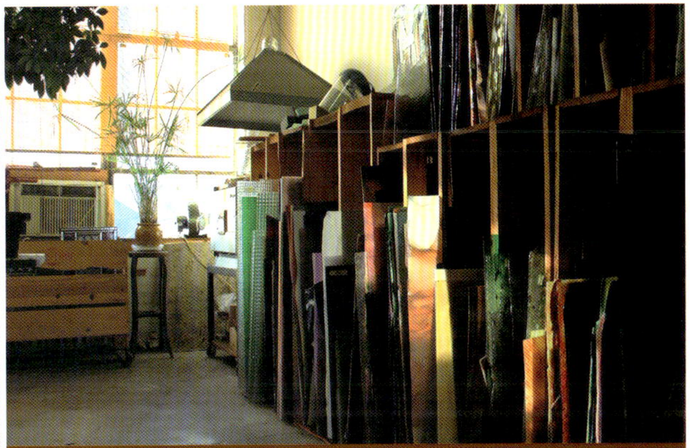

Past Life. Fossils, marble, glass, metals. 18 x 28."

Much of my palette is glass, and I keep it in sight, along with many fossils, minerals, my glass castings and the like, because if I see it I will use it while composing. .

Anne Marchand

Washington, D.C.

I am very much a city creature. I love being able to walk and clear my mind during the creative process. My studio is in the center of a thriving neighborhood filled with artists, restaurants, and businesses. It takes minutes to pick up a tool at the hardware store or grab a cup of tea. I am on the first floor of a turn-of–the-century Victorian townhouse. I have a large painting room where I lay out canvases, pour layers, and manipulate materials to create an interesting surface. The high ceilings allow air and space for creative thought in this process-based work.

This flexible space doubles as a presentation area for visiting clients and consultants. Everything I need, from music to books to paints, is within easy reach and allows me to paint without interruption. I use a system of metal hooks to hang canvases on the wall where I can step back and make decisions on the direction a painting will take. Built-in storage holds much of my inventory. Two floor-to-ceiling windows flood this space with sunlight in the mornings. Open windows provide natural ventilation. I can leave the painting room to read and conduct business in my front office while the work is drying and then go back to the painting whenever the muse calls.

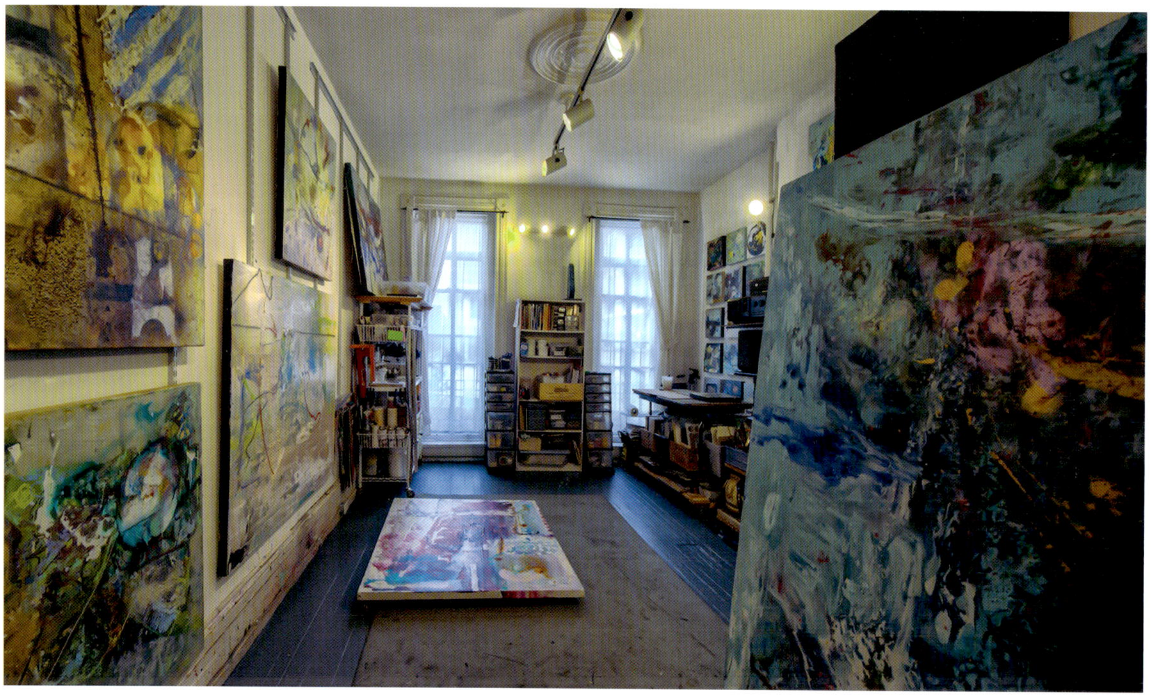

My studio has large windows for light. On the walls are my acrylic and mixed media paintings: ***Core*** *(UL),* ***Meter****, 2011, and* ***Motion*** *(R). 2013.* Courtesy of William Stewart Photography.

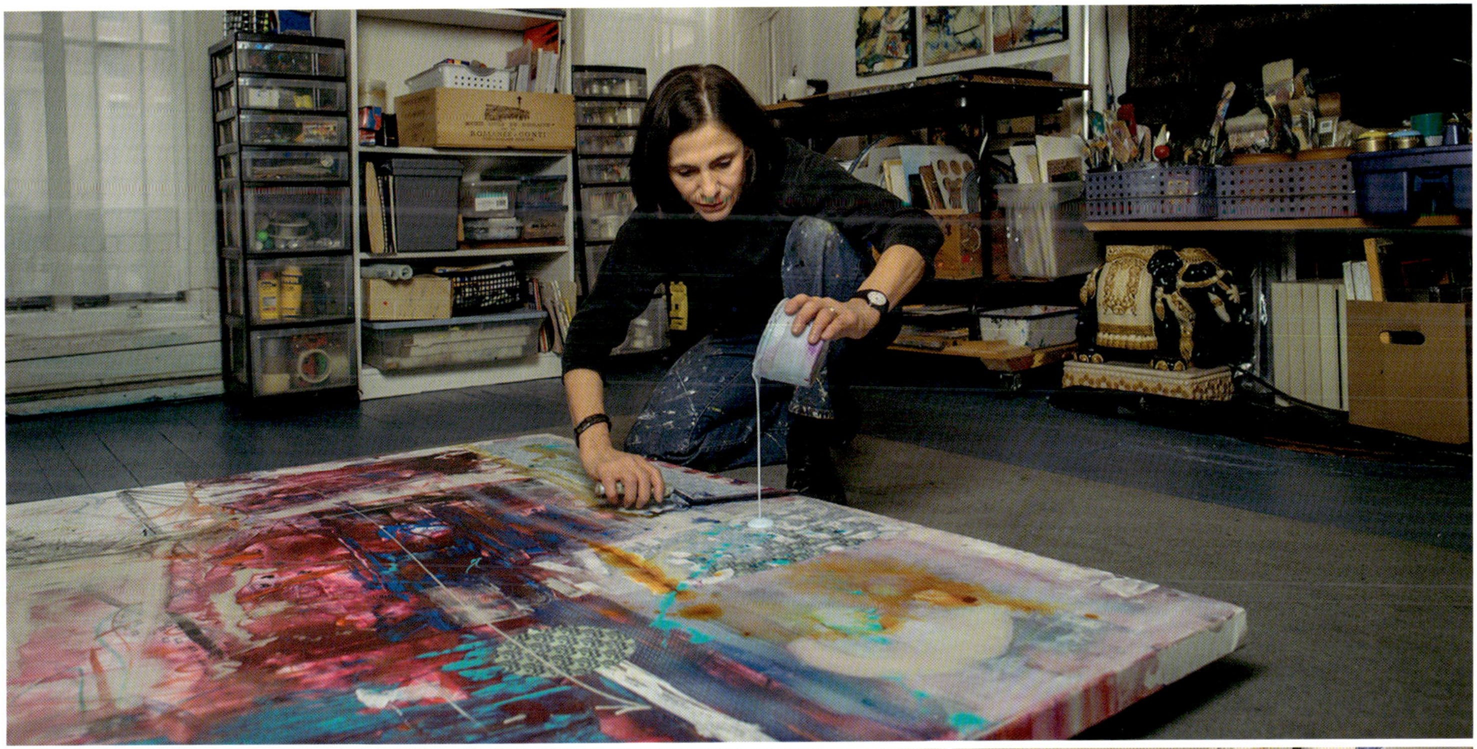

I paint canvases on the studio floor. My materials are stored in bookcases and bins from the local supply store. Ceramic elephants secure a shelf for brushes. On the wall and floor are paintings in progress. The spacious room assists working in a large scale. On the floor is my work in progress. On the wall is ***Adrift*** *(UL). Acrylic. 2011. Courtesy of William Stewart Photography.*

My paintings hang on a metal wall system. I store paint on a rolling metal shelf with a built-in work surface. A wooden crate, rolling cart, and a built-in storage unit hold supplies and inventory. On the floor is a work in progress. Courtesy of William Stewart Photography.

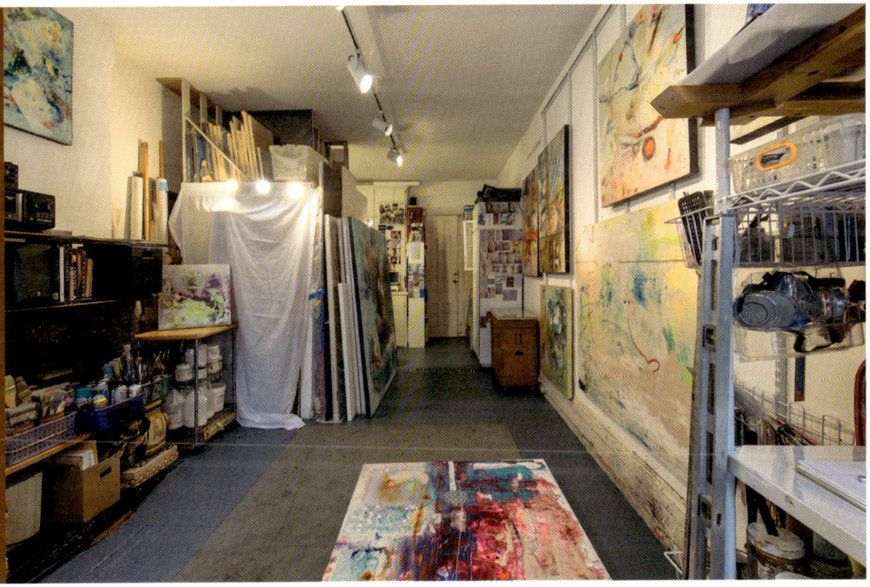

Kate Pond

Burlington, Vermont

The word *studio* implies a calm and peaceful place. But, instead of a studio, let's call my large industrial space a *workshop*. Here, I am squeezed between another sculptor and an overhead crane business. There is a lot of activity in our space, and fabricating sculpture is noisy and seldom delicate. I love immersing myself in the mess of it all. With the crane set up close by, I can build large sculptures. And I have the company of a feisty young sculptor on my other side.

Sometimes, for materials, I look for aged, rusted steel with a beautiful patina. I use a plasma steel cutting machine to form it into shapes; to secure the piece, I use my trusted oxy-acetylene welding torch.

When making a large public sculpture, I weld together a small maquette; then a local fabrication shop welds the full-sized sculpture. With a more complex sculpture, I meet with an engineer from Colorado, and we fabricate it together in Denver. Corten steel is my favorite material. My signature cut is a slightly jagged edge with an inviting texture of physicality.

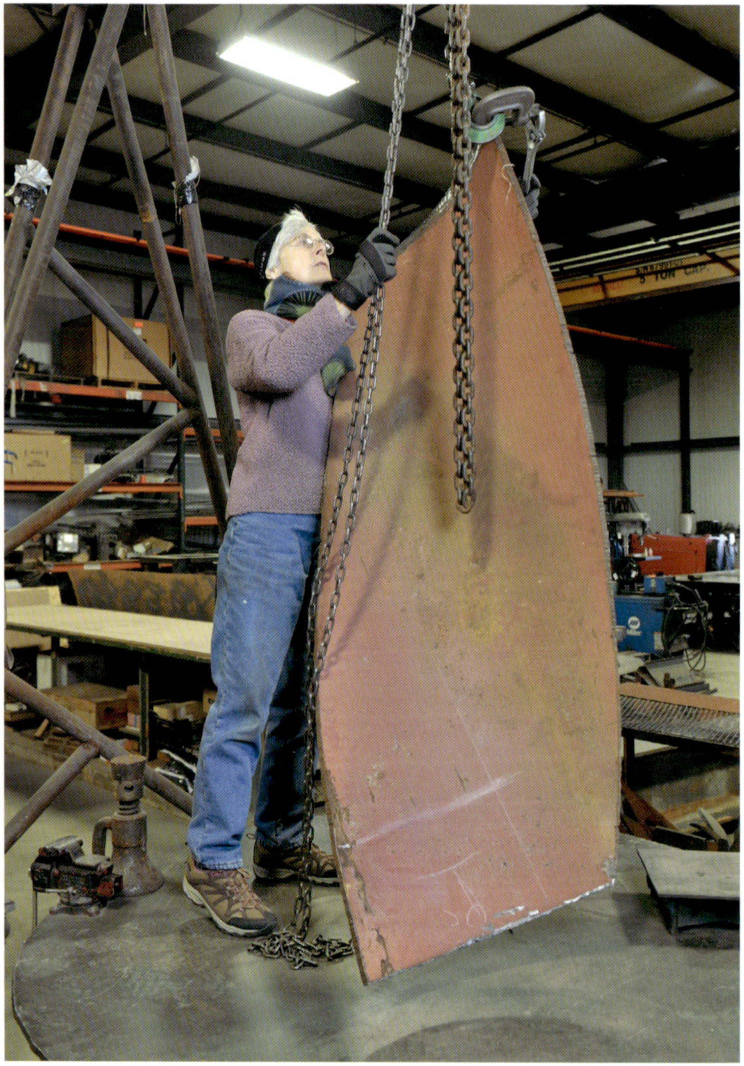

It is easy to move a heavy shape of steel into position with a chain fall and my gantry. Courtesy of Brad Pettengill.

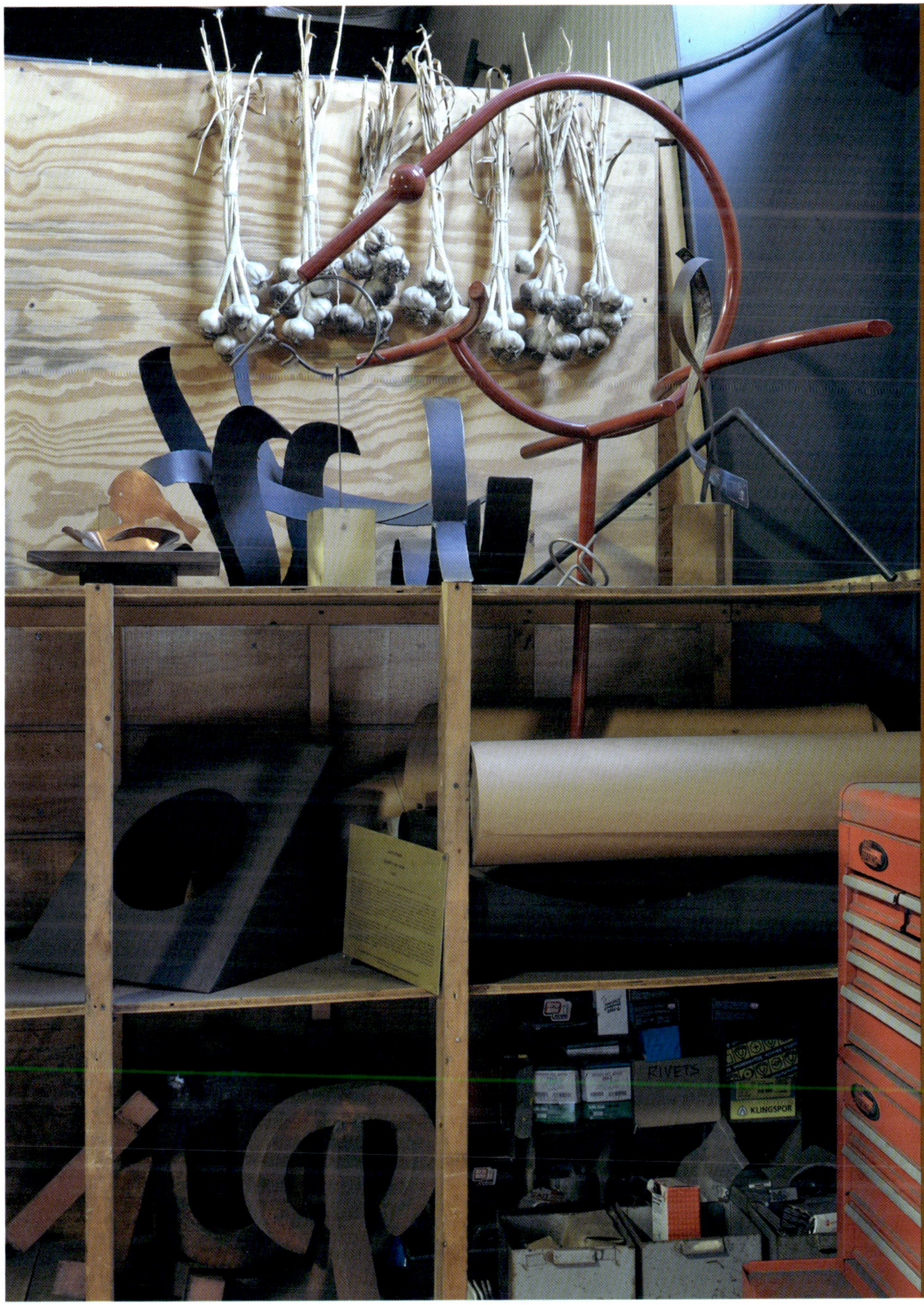

The rusted steel maquette in the left center shelf is ***Sunfix****, a small version of the U.S. Port of Entry piece in Highgate Springs, Vermont.* Courtesy of Brad Pettengill.

Barbara Purchia

Bedford, Massachusetts

After I retired from high tech in 2008, I found myself with the opportunity to explore my artistic side for the first time in many years., Feeling adventurous, I decided to try the stained glass studio in my little town. My interest in nature and natural resources helped influence my passion for working with bright, vibrant colors and experimenting with sliced agates, bevels, rondels, and open spaces to produce one-of-a-kind abstract creations as well as more traditional pieces. Unwilling to give up my newfound artistic outlet, I teamed up with six other women who shared my enthusiasm. We pooled our resources and opened the first stained glass cooperative in Bedford, Massachusetts.

We are renting space in the historic Bedford Railroad Station, which was built circa 1874. Our needs included a lot of open space and a sink for rinsing our pieces. The Depot building was perfect, with a wooden cathedral ceiling, lots of windows, and wooden beams for hanging our works. The studio has provided me with a creative channel to grow and learn more about the glass medium. It has also created a close-knit supportive community of stained glass artisans who admire, respect, inspire, and learn from one another's work.

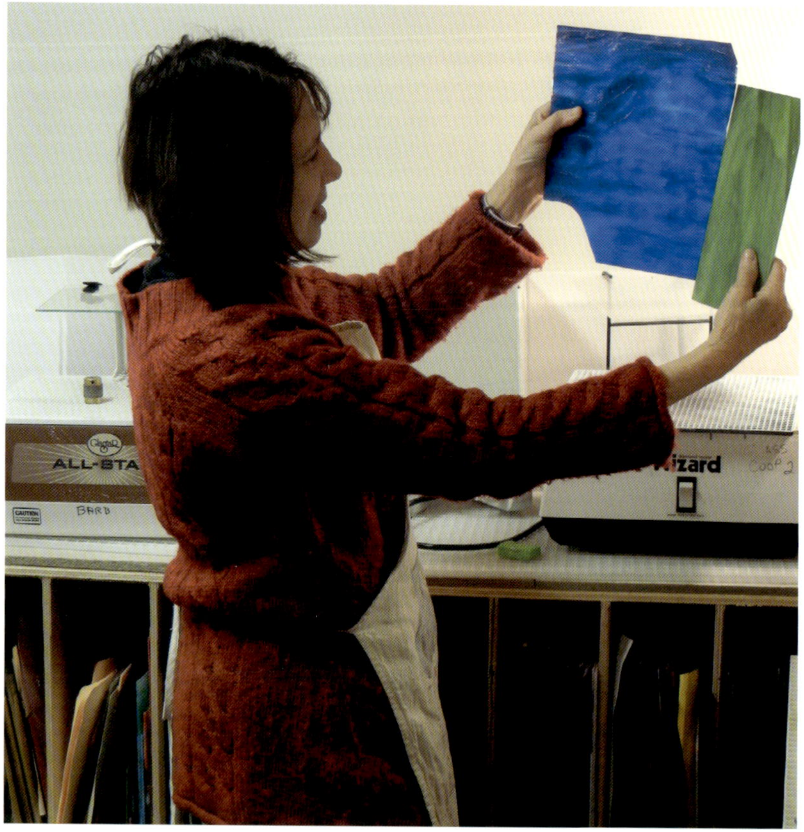

The custom-made worktables give us sufficient room to take our pieces from start to finish. They also have ample storage underneath with two shelves—which we have totally filled! Each full member has one side of the worktable and one shelf of storage. We can accommodate up to four people per table. Courtesy of Paul Purchia.

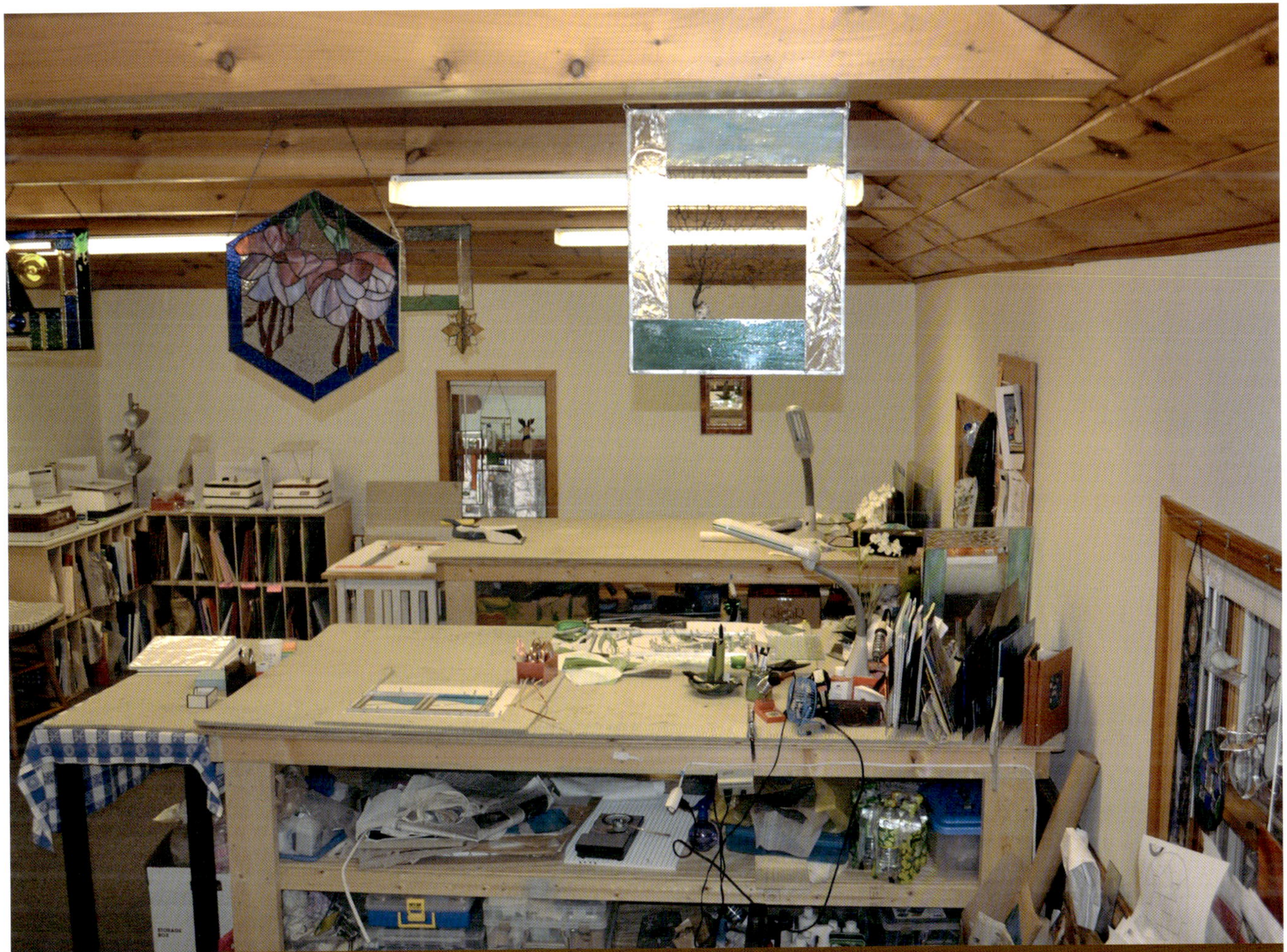

We opened our studio in June 2010. We have approximately 523 square feet of space on the second floor. We have three worktables, two grinder stations, a light table, and two glass storage shelves, which we also use as grinder stations. The cathedral ceilings add character and warmth Hanging from the wooden beams is **Sunrise Water** on the left, **Fuchsias** on the right, and **Yankee Division** in the background.

Mario Quilles

Santa Fe, New Mexico

I work both from my home and in a shared studio in an artist's complex, where I enjoy the company of other ceramists.

After studying ceramics in Los Angeles, I was on my way east, when I stopped in Santa Fe, to say hello to an old friend. The light and sunsets amazed me. I found a house with a kiln and 220 volt service. The place was surrounded by greenery and cactus, which gave me a starting point for my work. Although cactus is green in tone, the flowers are extremely colorful and influenced me. My work reflects the southwestern environment.

The textural surfaces of my pieces are achieved by working from the inside with tools I've made from tree roots. My finishes are low fired, either raku or electric cone 0-6. The glazes are commercial glazes or engobes. Many of the pieces have shapes of undersea vegetation, combined with cactus textures. Glazes are sprayed on at low pressure to create visual movement.

My sculpture reflects the past and present, and my new work looks into what might be the future. Santa Fe has a vibrant art community that I am glad to be part of.

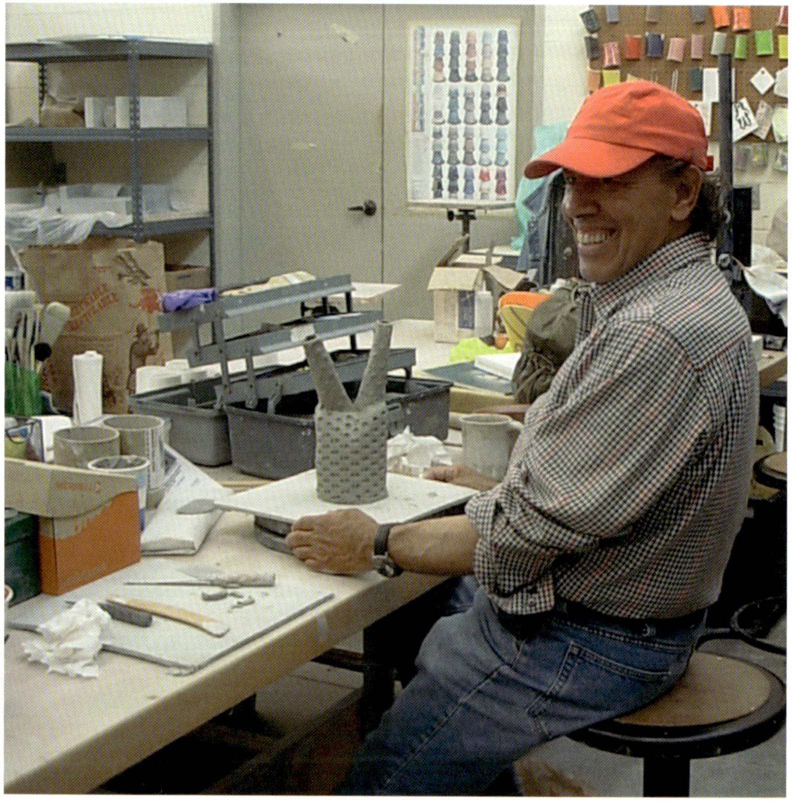

My worktable gets crowded. Courtesy of Ellen Koment.

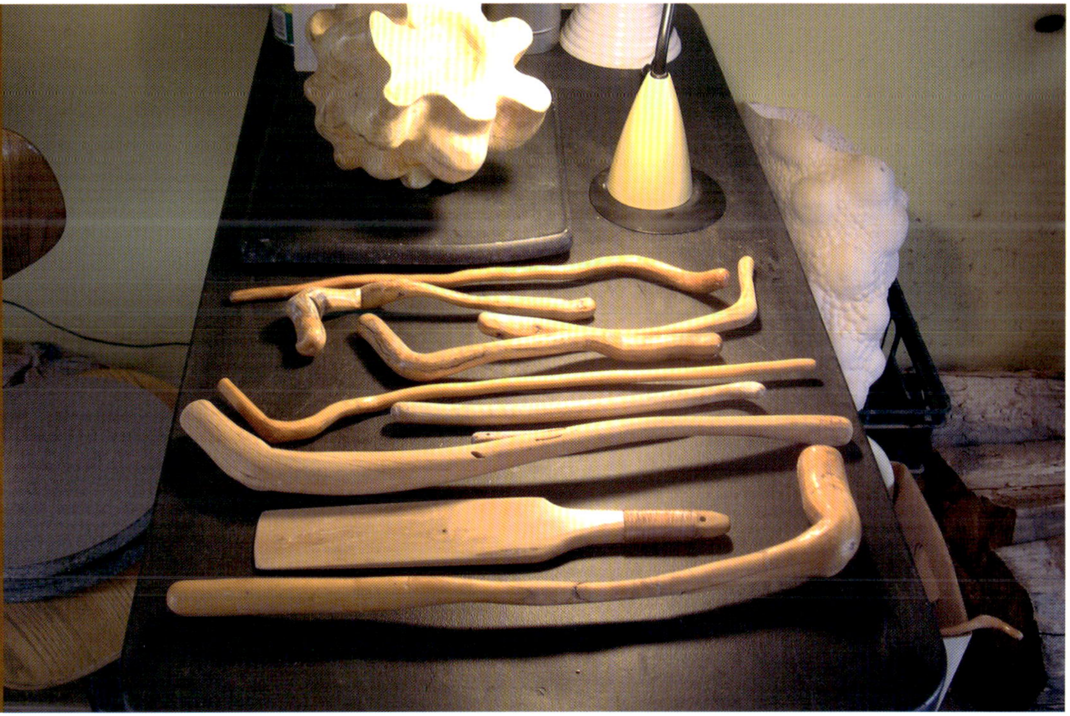

Tools made from roots of fallen junipers. Courtesy of Ellen Koment.

An accumulation of pieces. Courtesy of Ellen Koment.

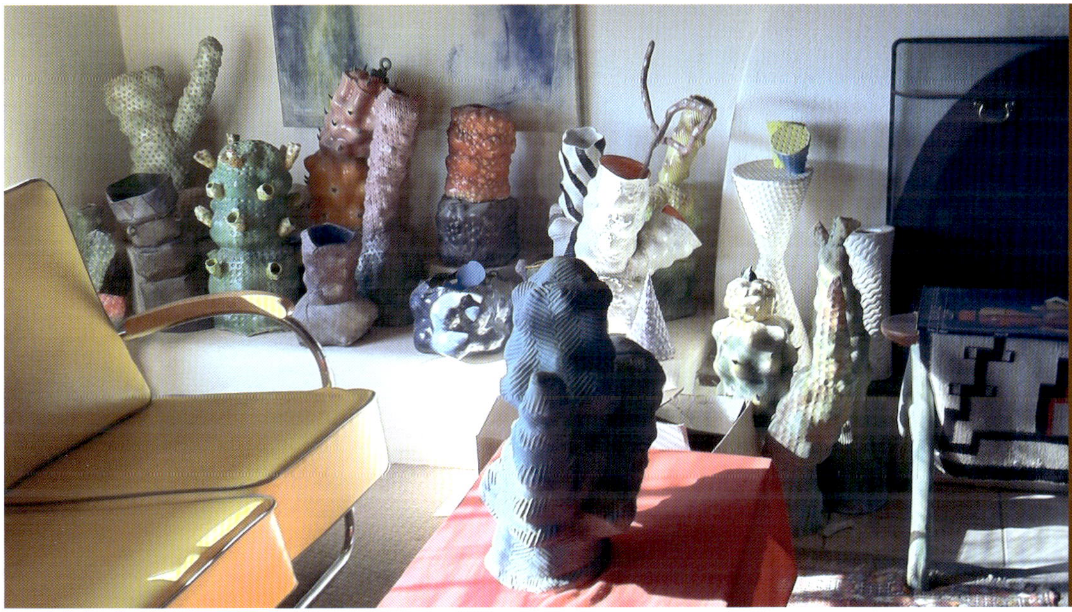

Ellen Rolli

Boston, Massachusetts

I have maintained my studio in the SoWa Arts district in the South End of Boston, since 2005. The building, at 450 Harrison Avenue, houses over 60 artists and hosts First Friday Open Studios monthly and Weekend Open Studios twice a year. With a combination workspace, gallery, and a venue to teach a monthly workshop, it is ideal. I paint most days, commuting there five or six days a week. I often start the day by enjoying contemplative time in my sitting area. I enjoy a cup of coffee while thinking about a work in progress or considering beginning a new painting. I have been painting non-objectively for several years now, and a large format suits the style of work I create. Thus, my canvas sizes include 36 x 48", 48 x 48", 36 x 60", etc. My work area is set up between my two large studio easels. One may store a large completed piece, the other a painting I am working on.

Other paintings hang on my "gallery wall" for visitors to see. I am so fortunate to be in studio space that inspires me to create a place where the public can see my work and where I can share my process with others. I am also grateful that my studio is housed in a building filled with many other fellow artists, who can offer a very special camaraderie!

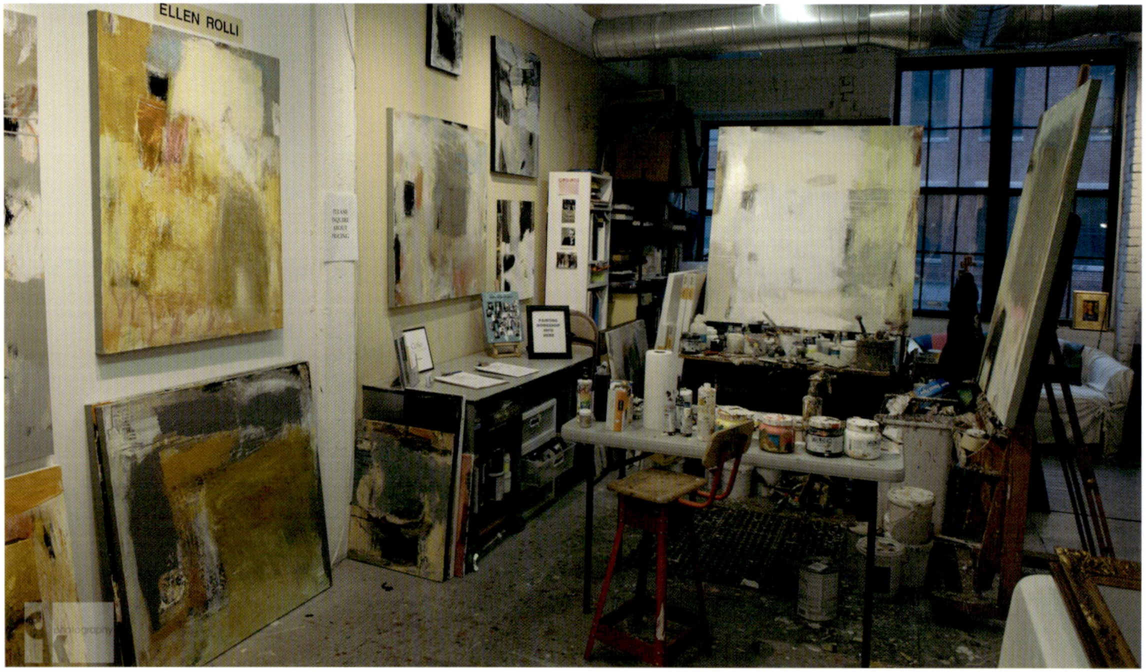

My second floor studio with its three large windows is less than 700 square feet. When entering into my studio, my gallery wall is on the left where I showcase recent works, and my workspace is straight ahead. The large square painting on easel is ***Soft Balance*** *(mixed media 48 x 48").* Courtesy of Debby Krim.

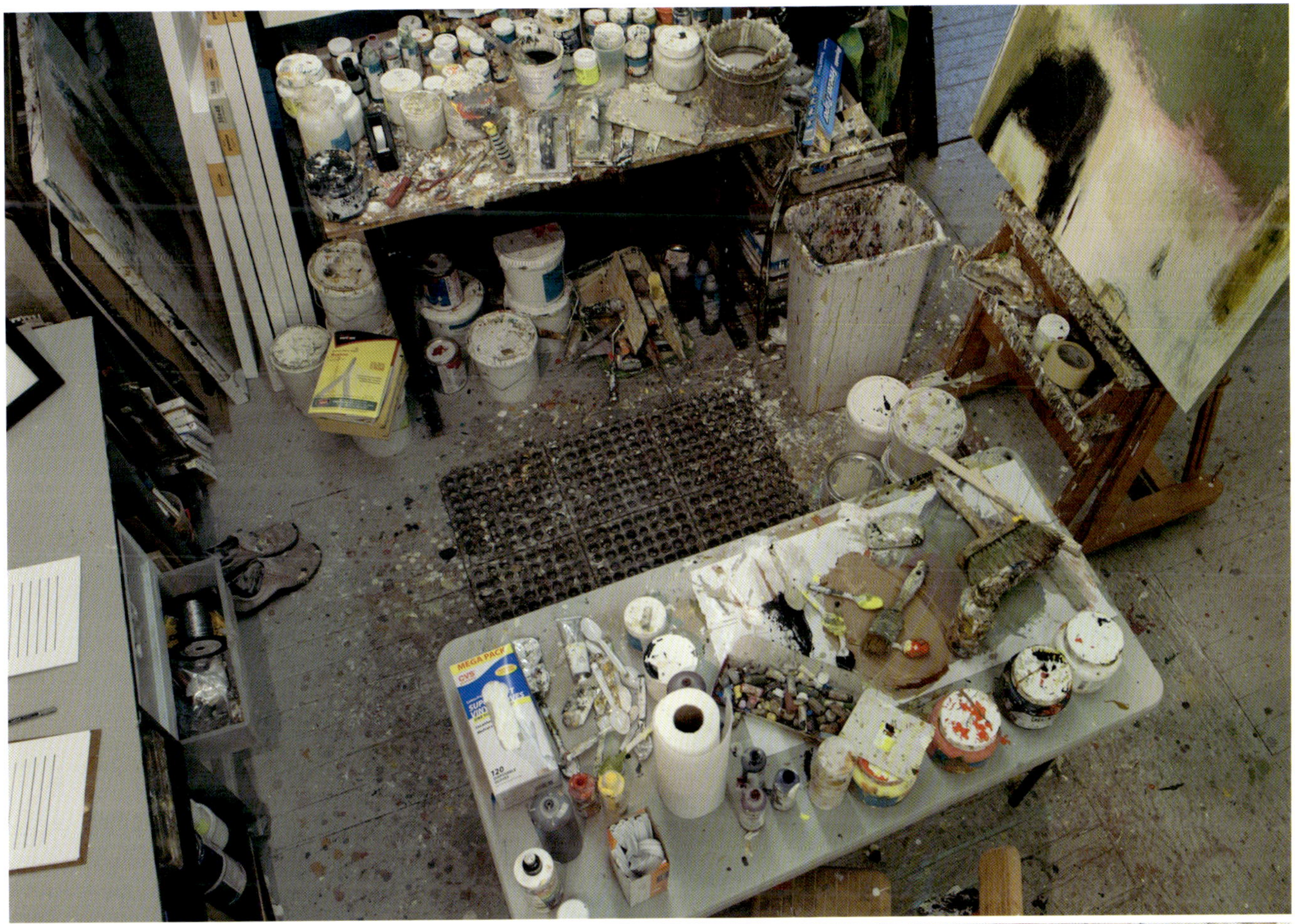

This aerial view captures my work area. I go back and forth between the two work surfaces, with everything I need close at hand. I stack my new canvases nearby. On the easel is **Italia #2** (mixed media, 36 x 48"). Courtesy of Debby Krim.

This table surface serves as display space and a "sign up" area for my workshops. Storage for miscellaneous supplies is below. The drawers in the middle house hanging/wiring tools. To the right of those drawers are my painting shoes, which I change into before the paint starts flying! Courtesy of Debby Krim.

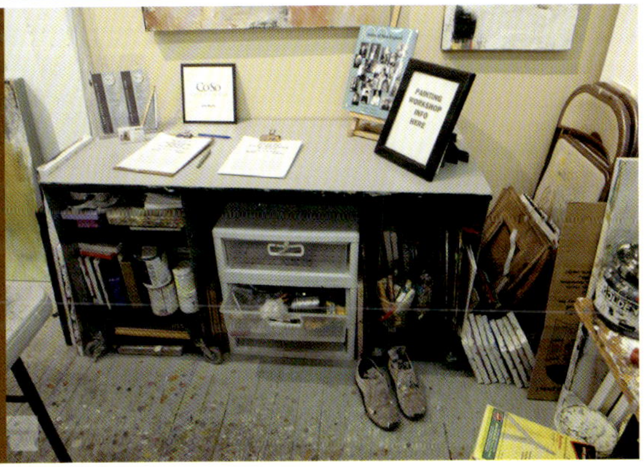

Greg Spitzer

Medford, Massachusetts

I have been working at Hillside Sculpture Studio (HSS), in Medford, for four years. The original building was converted into a studio and gallery space that is now a large ,two-story, open room with exposed wooden beams. The glass roof panels and large wood-framed windows provide ambient light throughout the year. The banks of industrial lamps and spotlights over my work area augment the natural light. During our annual receptions, the offices and hallways function as a gallery.

My work area allows me to store raw stone and has room for my tools and worktables. Because of my focus on stone carving, I made several alterations after moving in—specifically a portable dust collector, industrial fan, and filters. These changes minimize my impact on studio mates, while I cut and grind stone. Since my training in Italy, however, my dependence on power tools that create dust has diminished significantly.

HSS is an amazing space that is equipped with an array of wood and metal shop tools necessary for creating all types of 3-D art. With this equipment, as well as the in-floor foundry, I have learned more about welding, mold making, and metal casting. Although I have rented space in only two artist studios, I can't imagine finding a shop that is better equipped and I consider myself very fortunate.

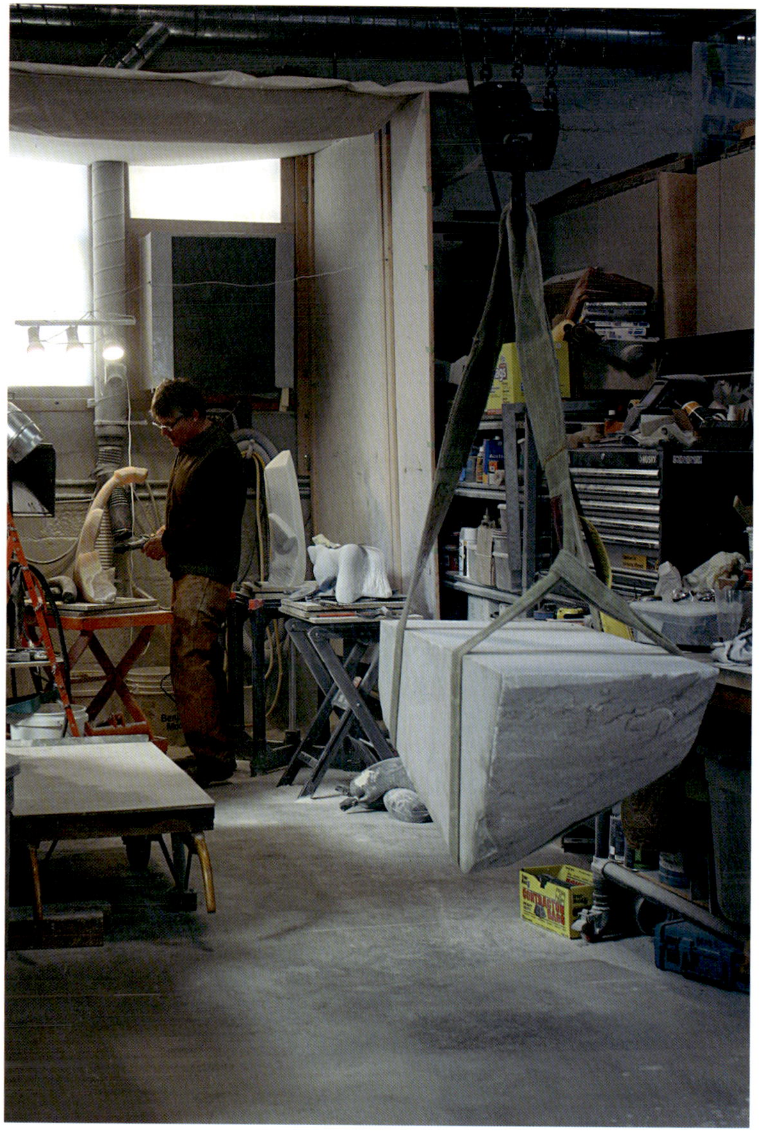

A large block of Carrera marble hangs from the crane in my workspace. A few works in progress can be seen below the large window.

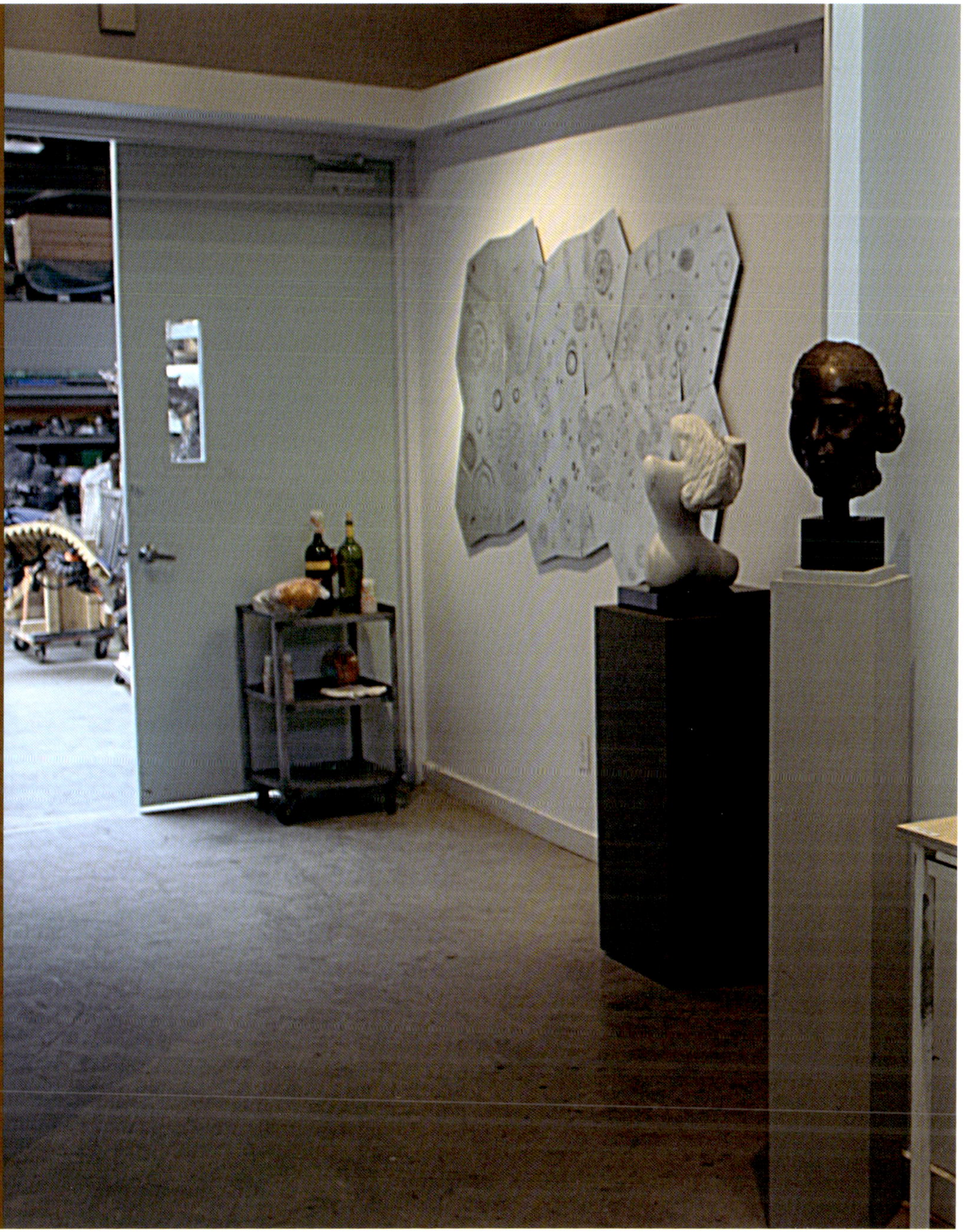

*The hallway leading to the studio workspaces. The sculpture on the far right is my **Athene**; on the gray pedestal is **Woman Combing Her Hair***

Pringle Teetor

Creedmore, North Carolina

Our studio is a cement block and metal roof outbuilding. We built the equipment ourselves. The building originally held the kilns for one of the owners many years ago.

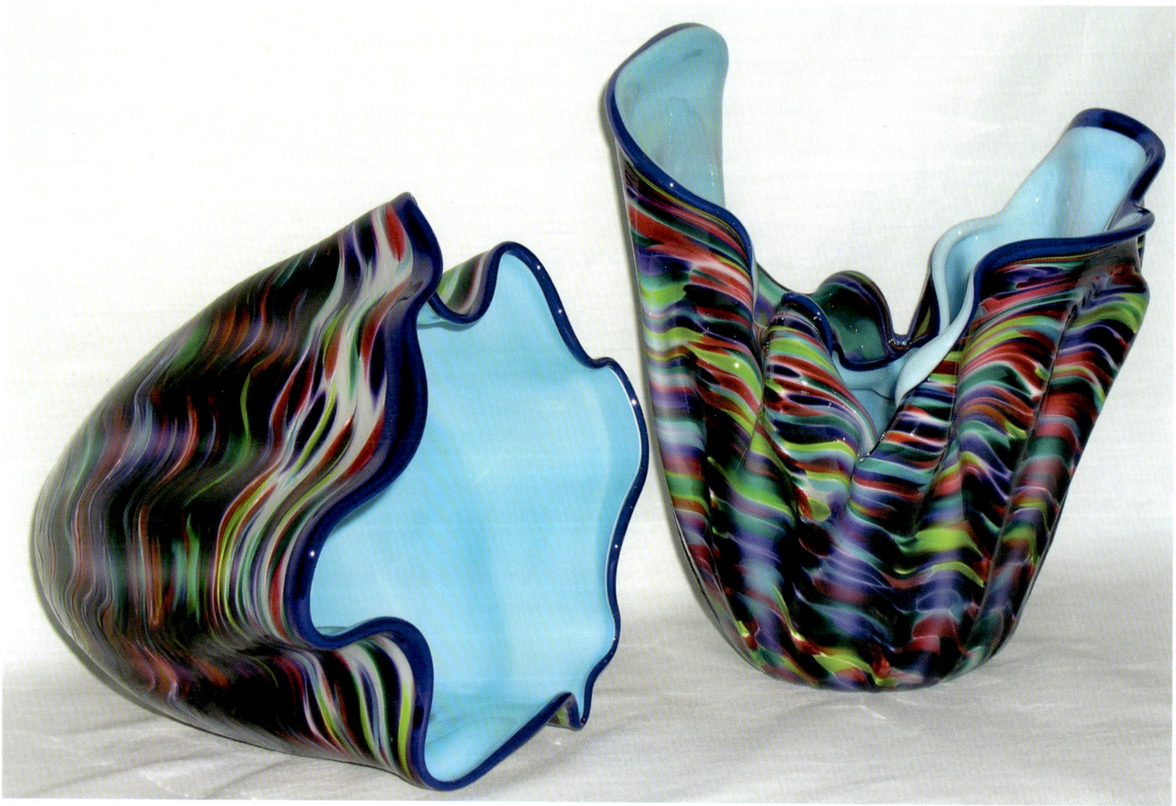

Aegean Dreams. *Blown glass. 2012.*

Our studio.

In one corner of our studio stands an electric furnace we built from a kit. It stays at 2100 degrees holding up to 150 pounds of molten glass from the time we turn it on in the fall until we shut it down for the summer. Clear molten glass is rolled in the scoops full of frit (small bits of colored glass) to color the piece.

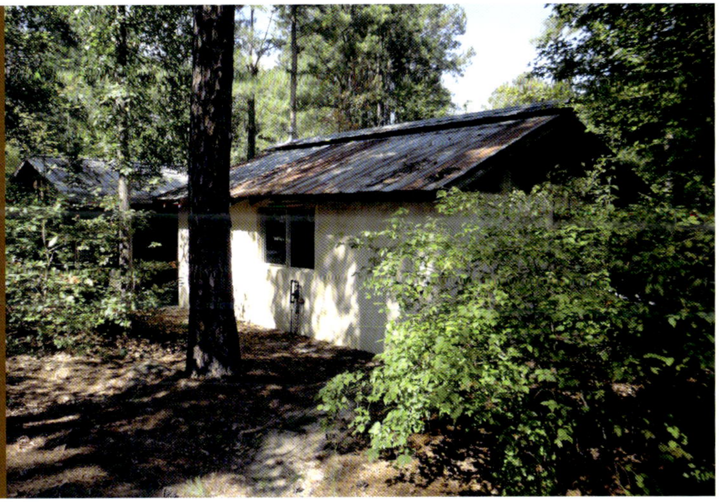

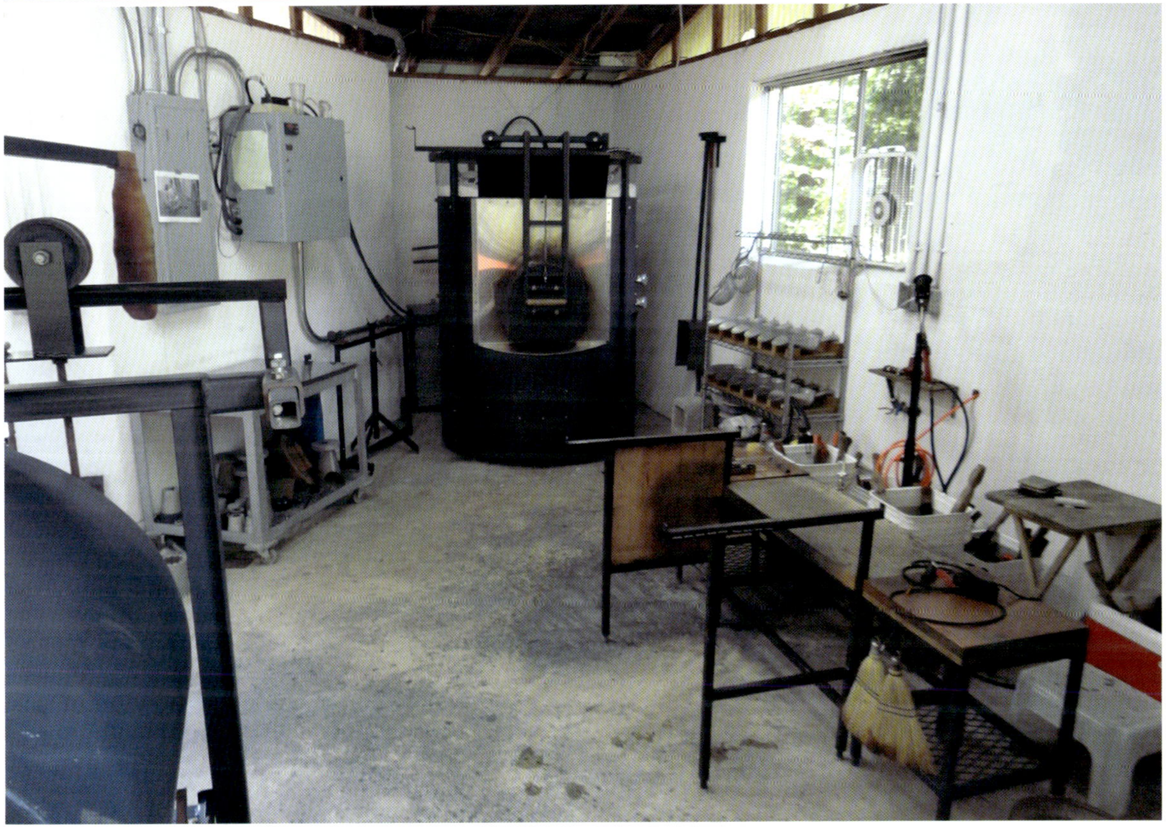

Nina Weiss

Highland Park, Illinois

After many years working in a home studio, I am thrilled to be in my new space: big, white, clean, and full of light! The studio has room to utilize as a gallery and work and teaching spaces. Openings, classes, studio tours, and client and consultant visits are a welcome part of my studio practice. The courtyard building is home to other artists' studios, encouraging a community for open houses, openings, and sharing the important tools of our trade....like coffee, staple guns, and drills.

I like being able to display finished paintings and works in progress and now have plenty of wall space. All the studio furniture is on wheels to allow for different working configurations, leaving floor space for stretching and preparing large canvases. My easel is placed under the overhead skylight. This full-spectrum lighting is important in the development of the layers of color and optical mixtures in my paintings.

The work goes beyond traditional ideas of a green landscape. My landscape paintings draw the viewer into a heightened vision of gesture and hue, depicting nature with colors that are intense, lush, and dramatic. I tease out the complex colors of nature, creating layers of contrast, line, and form. The big new studio allows me to explode these explorations into larger paintings and inspires my continual creation.

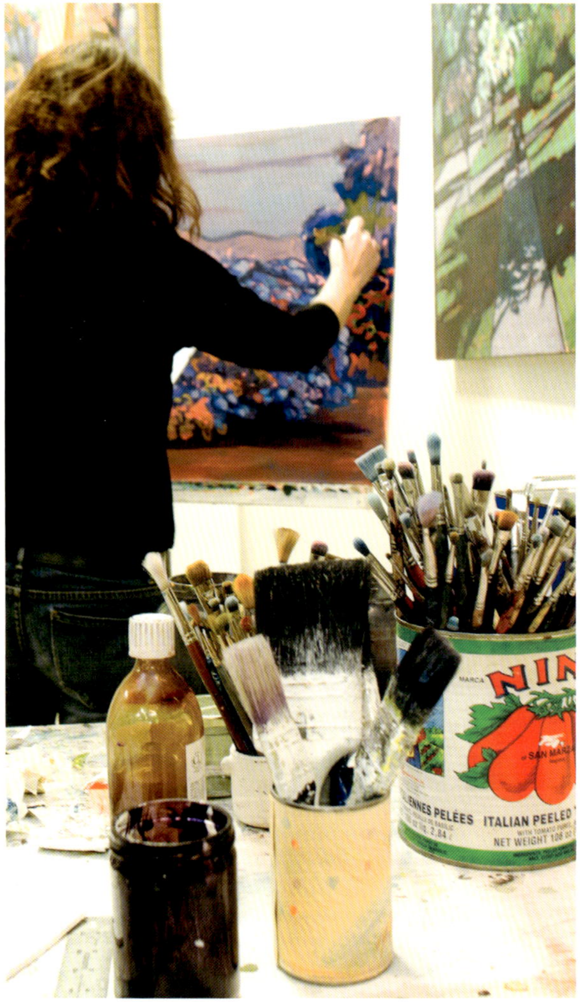

My worktable and easel are under the skylight with everything I need in reach. My palette is a piece of glass backed with white foam core; it rests on a wooden pedestal on wheels so I can move it around for large canvases. Courtesy of Evan Kane.

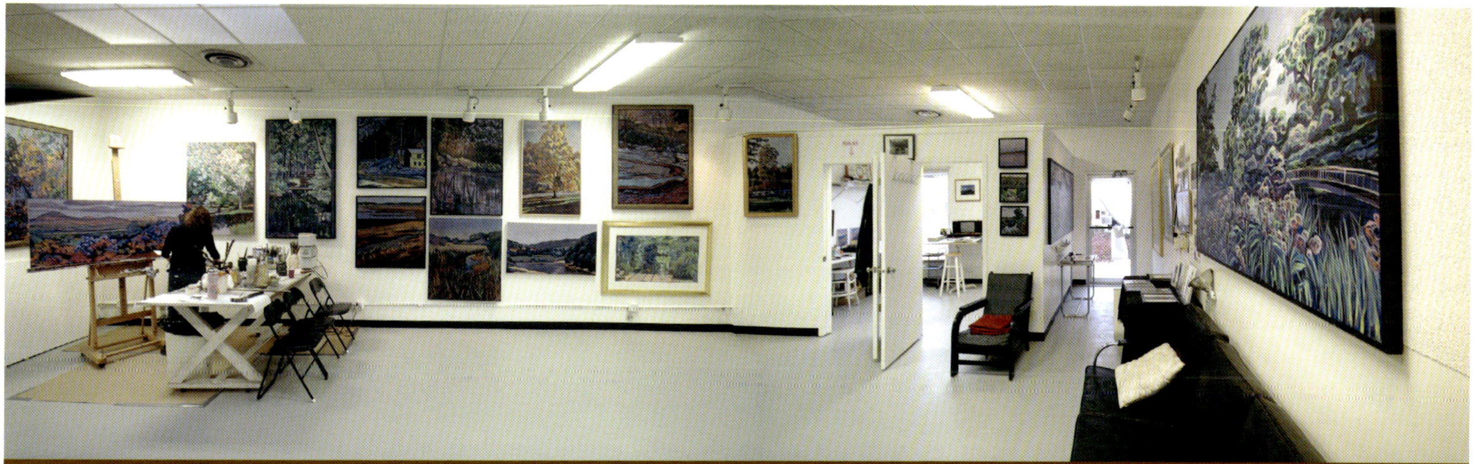

My large workspace has northern light and a skylight with additional windows facing a courtyard. A separate light-filled office also has a drawing table and more storage. Courtesy of Evan Kane.

John McConnell

Winchester, Massachusetts

My studio—and my architecture office, too—is located in a grand old mansion, Sanborn House, built high on a hill in 1908, by the son of the founder of Chase & Sanborn Coffee Co. Lavish living led to bankruptcy, and the house passed to another family, then to a community of nuns who ran an adjacent school for girls, and finally to the Town of Winchester. The town has now leased the property to the Historical Society for restoration as its headquarters and to serve as a cultural center for the town. The former bedrooms on the second floor have been leased to a couple of architects, a laboratory equipment sales firm, and me, a fine-art painter.

The space is quiet and the dramatic view to the center of our picturesque New England town center—yes, complete with white steeple—is always inspirational. From my French doors, I witness every sort of weather and condition of light. An L-shaped space, my studio provides a corner for my computer desk and some art books, as well as industrial shelving for paintings in various stages of completion. Closets and shelving behind a folding door give me much more storage. The rest of the room is for my easel and tamboured, although it, too, has become filled with paintings awaiting either finishing or delivery to galleries. Here is the one place where I can completely lose myself concentrating on making a painting, which is, after all, the point.

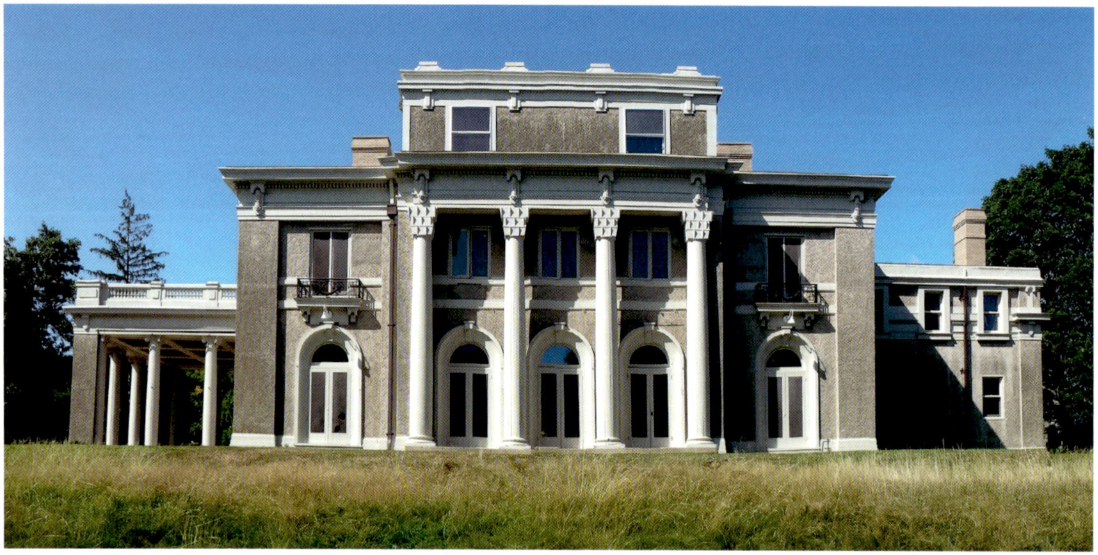

A downhill view of the east facade of Sanborn House. My space is behind the window and the French door on the second floor, just to the right of the center window.

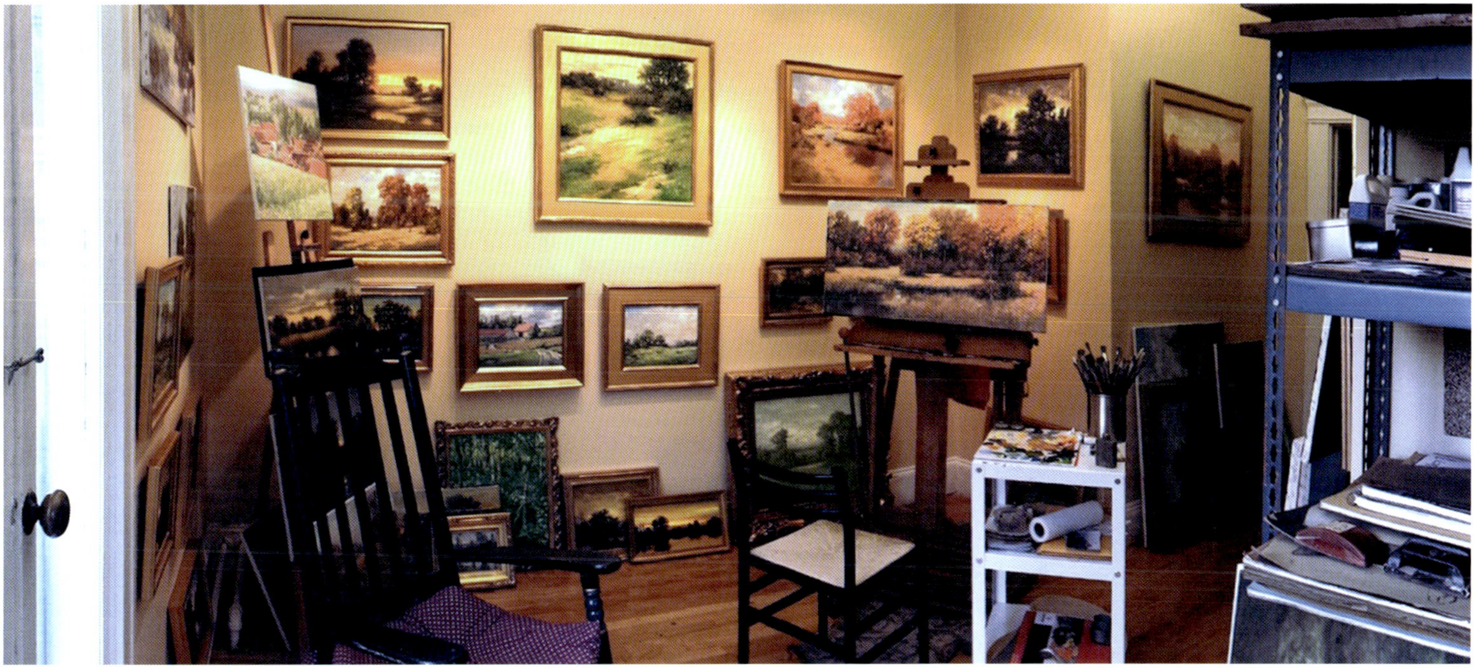

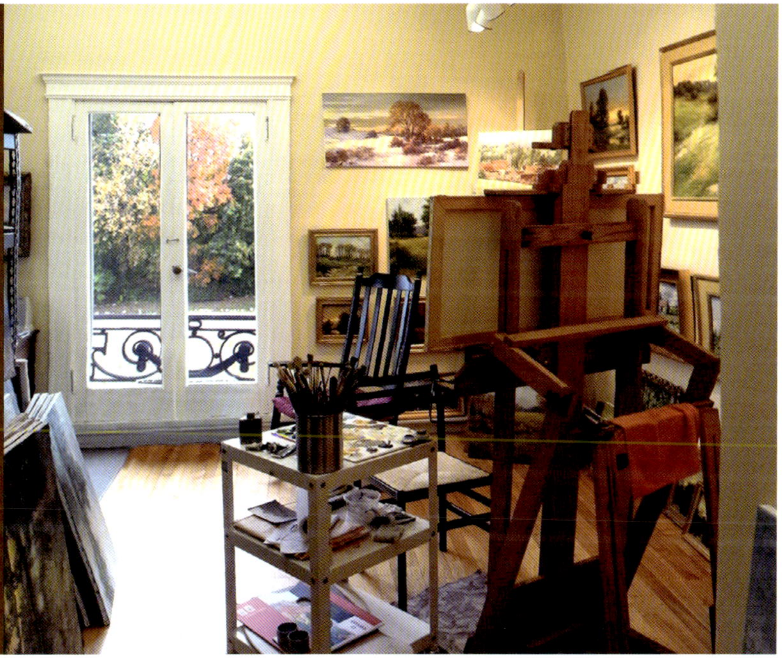

Northeast light from the French doors to the left falls beautifully on the main work easel in the center of the room. The walls are lighted to form the principal display area for more-or-less finished paintings. On the easel: ***Theme and Variations; Bolton, Massachusetts****, and on the wall just above it,* ***Housatonic Valley****.*

French doors open onto an ornamental iron railing and an expansive view to the town center in the valley below. On the wall to the right of the doors: ***Sunset after Early Snow****.*

Cheryl Holz

Aurora, Illinois

My studio is located in the downtown heart of a midwestern river city. Once the site of a building that housed a movie theatre-turned-office building, I've converted a former rabbit warren of insurance cubicles into a wonderfully functional studio space. I look out onto the Fox River, a constant source of inspiration. I have my own space (locked door), but there are other studios on the same/second floor, each with a separate space, as well as a private investigator and writer/professor.

As a mixed media artist, I compulsively and continually add tools and techniques to my arsenal. I need a place where I can build in wood; sculpt in concrete and other modeling materials; press, preserve, and store botanical and geological specimens; do online research; create and print silkscreens; store and adhere a multitude of collage materials—and then, finally, I get to PAINT! Each task has its own allotted area. And, of course, there also needs to be space for the practical: finished works and the mountain of bubble wrap for packing and shipping.

I collect bins and containers of all sizes, and everything has a home; although in the midst of a creative burst, all hell breaks loose and chaos ensues! In the down times, theoretically, I can return everything to its bin, shelf, or drawer. I love my space; the ideal studio: a safe haven where I can let down my guard, crank up the tunes, and follow my muse without worrying about the stains I am leaving on the floor, wall, ceiling...or dogs!

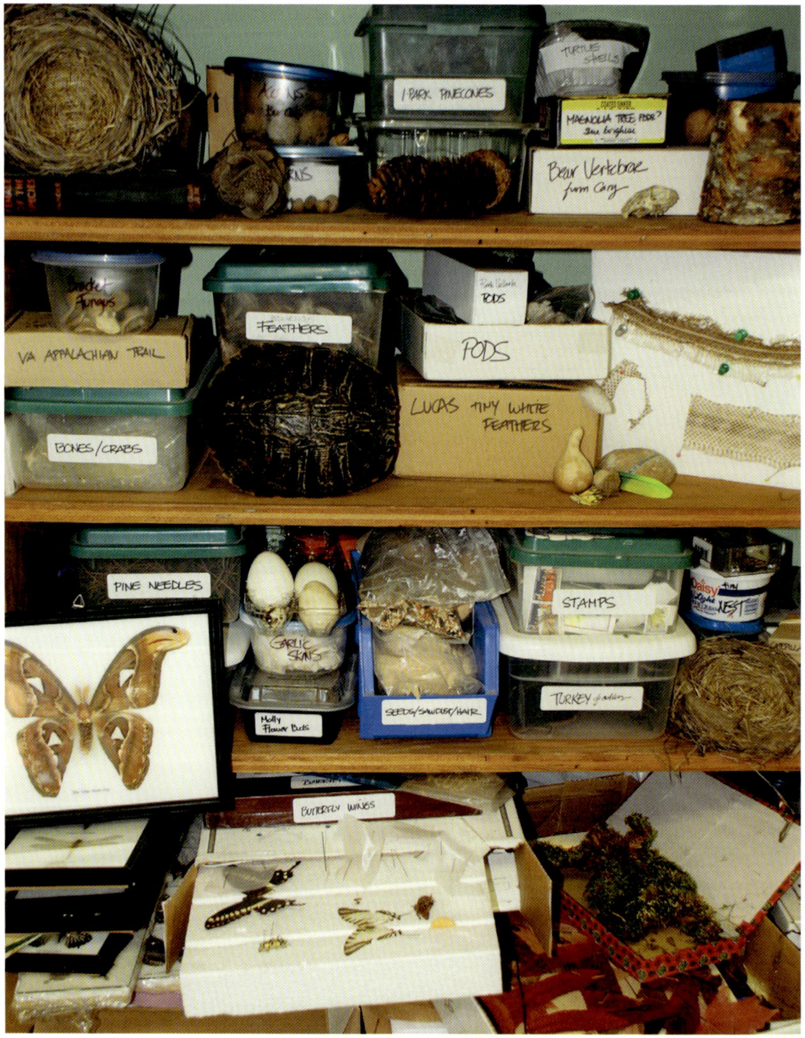

I try to contain the results of years of collecting in a wall shelf that once held insurance forms. I record any information that I have on specimens I've collected. Everything, from snakeskins to boxes of pressed leaves, sorted by color fills the shelves to overflowing.

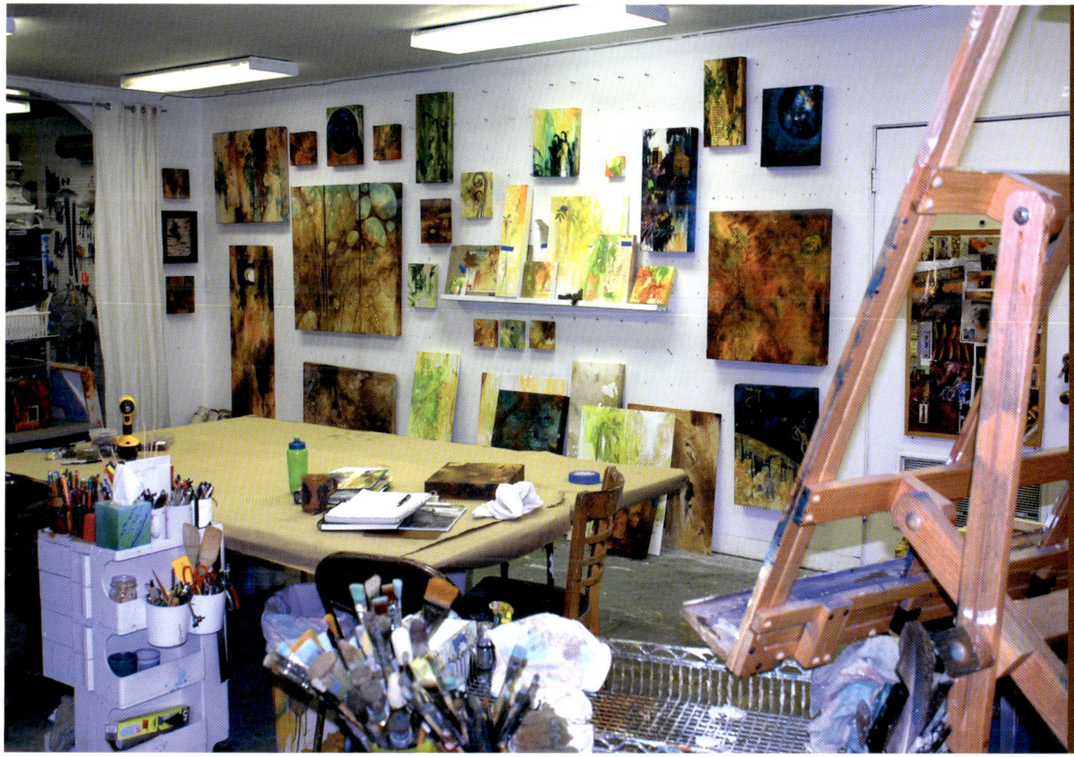

Typically, my hanging wall is composed of finished and unfinished pieces. An oversized easel can accommodate heavy low relief work, and a rolling paint cart can travel to wherever I need it.

Any new additions to the studio must be on wheels! My taboret can follow me to wherever I sit and plan out my next piece. Bear, my furry assistant/security guard, usually monopolizes the couch. Courtesy of Victor Von Ehr Photography.

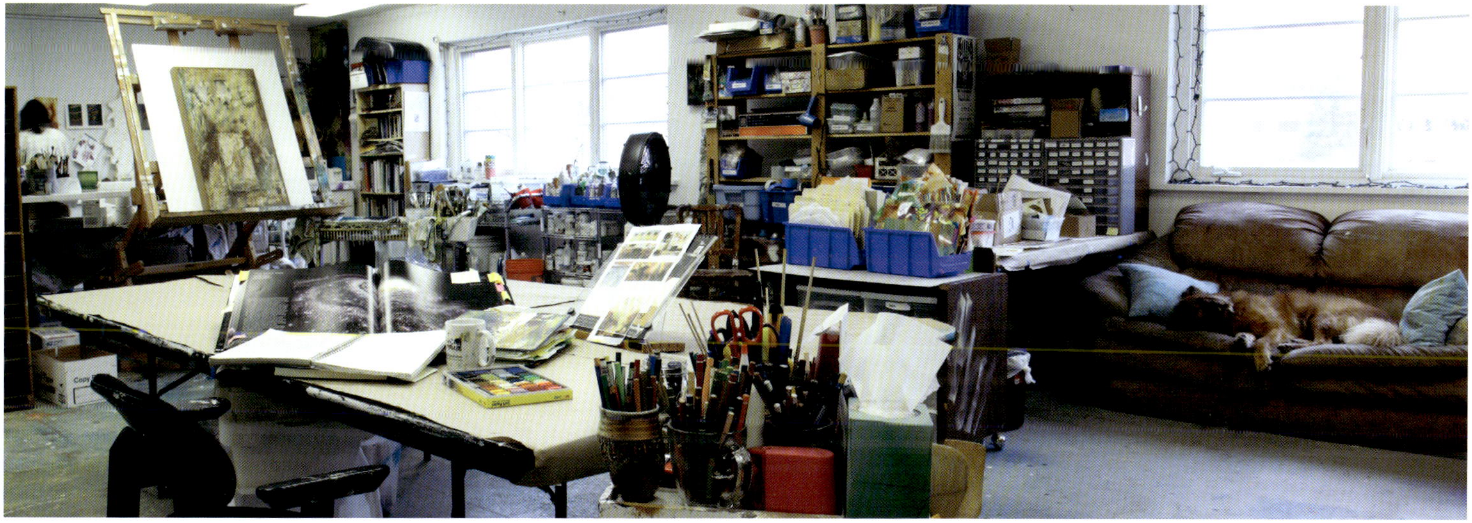

Tjelda vander Meijden

Brookside, New Jersey

The studio that I rent is an outbuilding, attached to a bay garage area, nestled behind a historic 1722 farmhouse on Pitney Farm, in Mendham, New Jersey. My late friend and renowned artist Duncan Pitney built this vaulted studio with one window, "so not to be distracted by the outside world." The skylight provides north, indirect, cool light where values and contrasts are consistent, providing an ideal atmosphere to paint from life.

Plein air paintings and conceptual images are realized in my studio, a place of refuge, solitude, and contemplation. The studio is an intricate part of my identity and inseparable in the development of my art-making as a plein-air painter and master printmaker.

Metaphorically, my work explores the transient nature of our time on earth—an ever-changing place of refuge and peril—and the quest for immortality inherent in the human spirit. The isolation that my skylight studio space provides challenges me to grapple with the many complexities of this emerging reality.

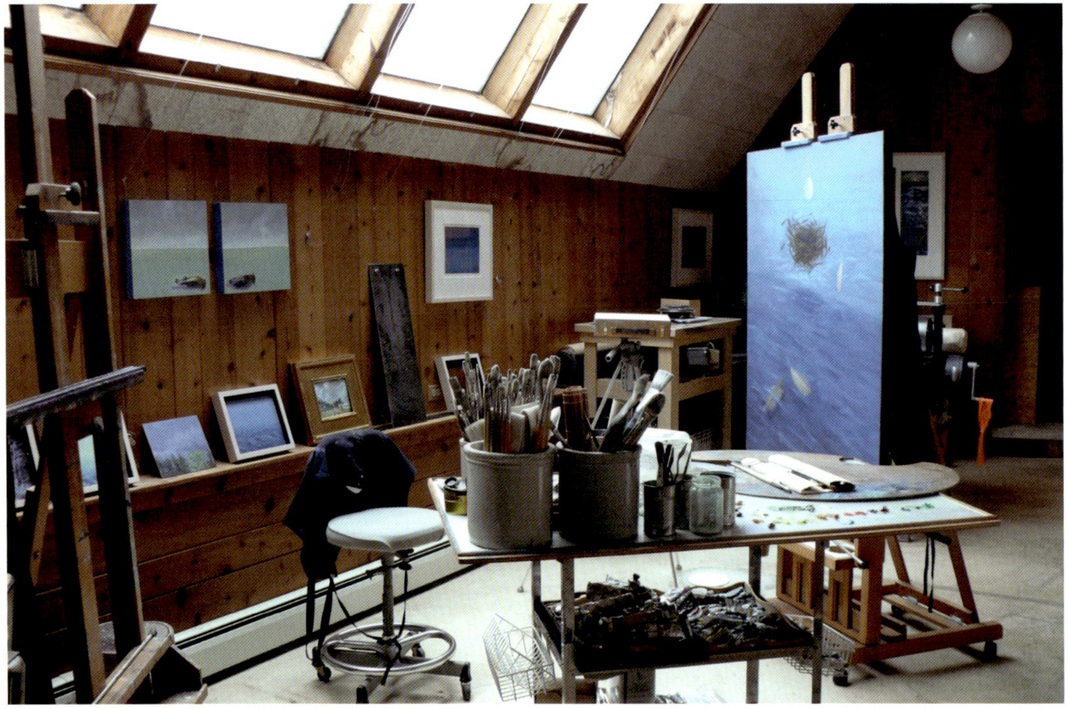

The 30 x 18-foot studio is divided between painting and printmaking. The furniture is retrofitted with wheels to move about as needed for printmaking sessions. Photo courtesy of Gail Mooney copyright 2013.

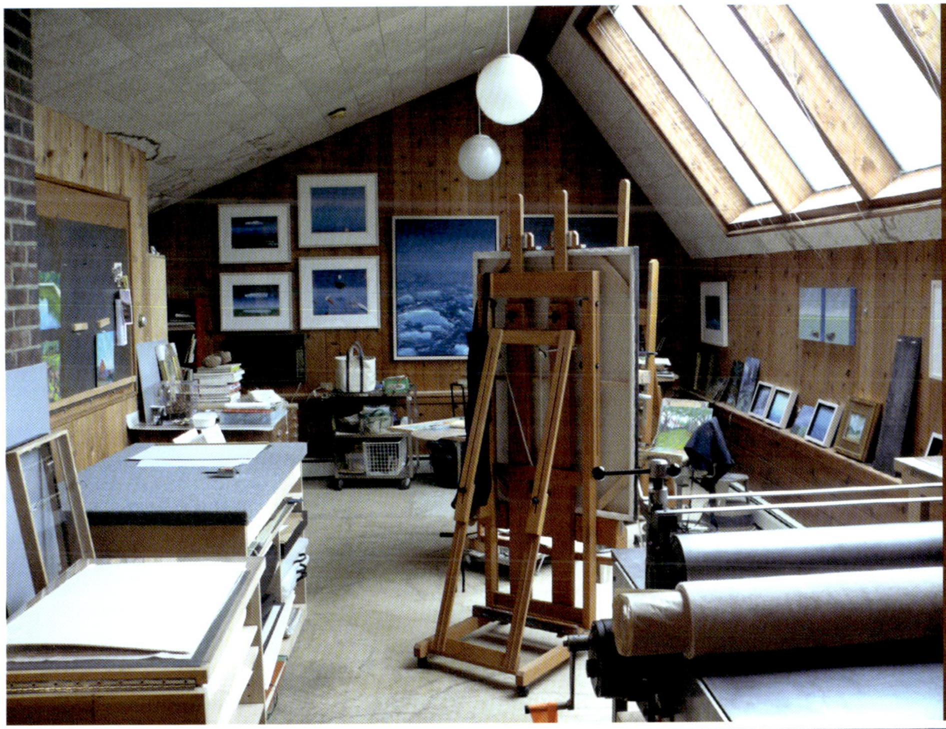

View of the painting studio with Best Classic Santa Fe II Easel. An 8-inch wood rail runs the perimeter of three walls to display my works of art. Photo courtesy of Gail Mooney copyright 2013.

View of the printmaking area includes a Martech Etching press, a custom cabinet (right) designed for storing paper, blotters, and etching blankets with a drop leaf extension used for "wet packs" when printing. The inking area is designed with SoLux track light that provides daylight spectrum for color balance when mixing inks for printmaking. Photo courtesy of Gail Mooney copyright 2013.

Works in progress are displayed on an 8 x 4-foot sheet of steel using rare earth magnet pushpins to hold heavy papers and painted panels. The grey, rug-top cabinet stores portfolio cases and is used for framing. Flat files (right) house prints and paper for printmaking. Photo courtesy of Gail Mooney, copyright 2013.

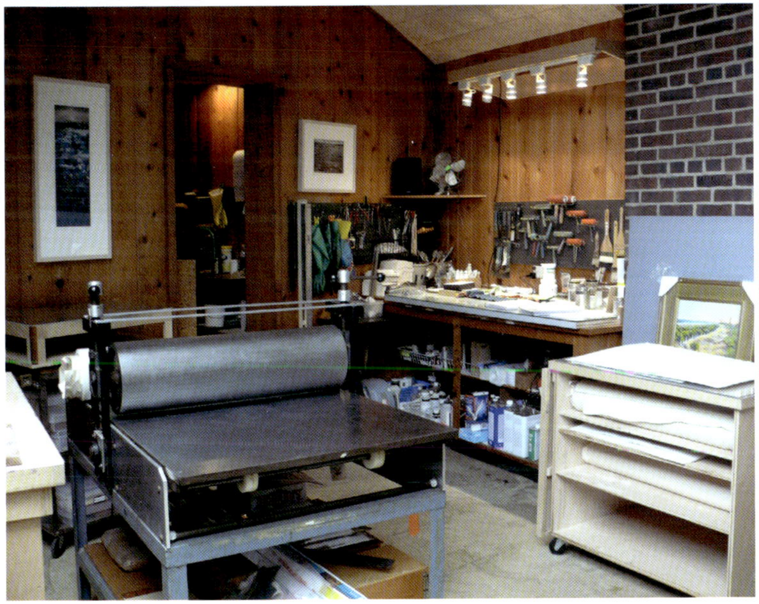

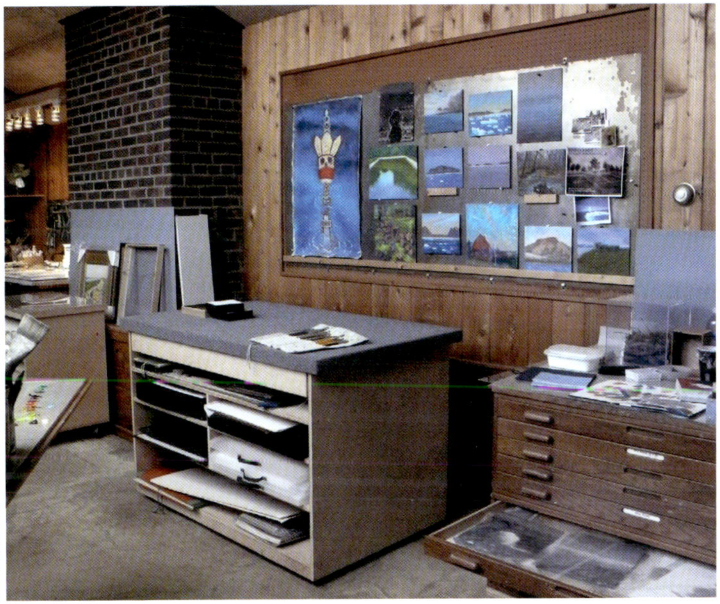

Kathleen Westkaemper

Richmond, Virginia

My studio is on the second floor of a charming Italianate building constructed in 1928 situated in the Museum District of Richmond, Virginia. I am grateful to have this studio/living space where I can work at any hour however brief the available time. Here I surround myself with images, books, CDs, and other inspiring objects. The windows overlook historic magnolia and crepe myrtle-lined Richmond streets, and I have amazing sky views.

My work is primarily prints and paint stick drawings on paper. I've worked in this studio for over ten years. I use the wrought iron balcony for sanding woodblock supports for my drawings and prints. At night, the bathroom becomes a darkroom, where I prepare cyanotypes or solar etching plates that I develop using a light box.

In the studio, I have an etching press, an easel, and a drawing table. Containers of paint sticks, oil pastels and pencils are adjacent to the easel. Drawings in various stages are clamped to boards. Under the tables and supply-filled carts are racks for paper, etching plates, prints, and drawings. Tucked in between table and racks are much used paper and mat cutters. All available space is utilized, making routine cleaning and reorganization a constant creative necessity.

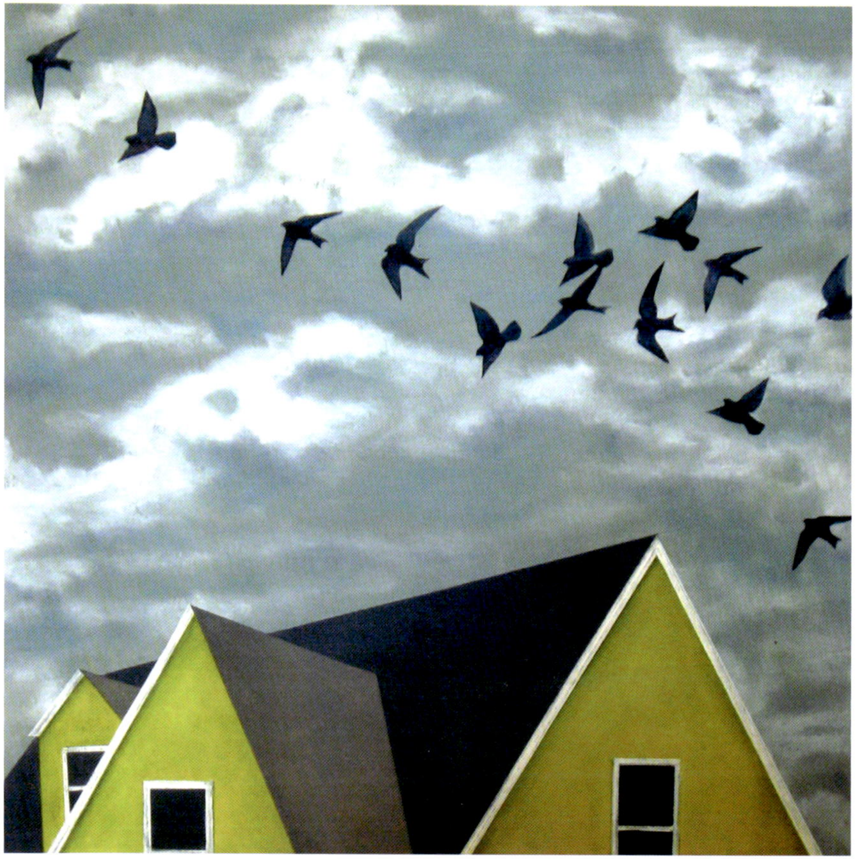

Passing Blackbirds*. Paint stick and graphite on gessoed paper. 22 x 22". 2012.*

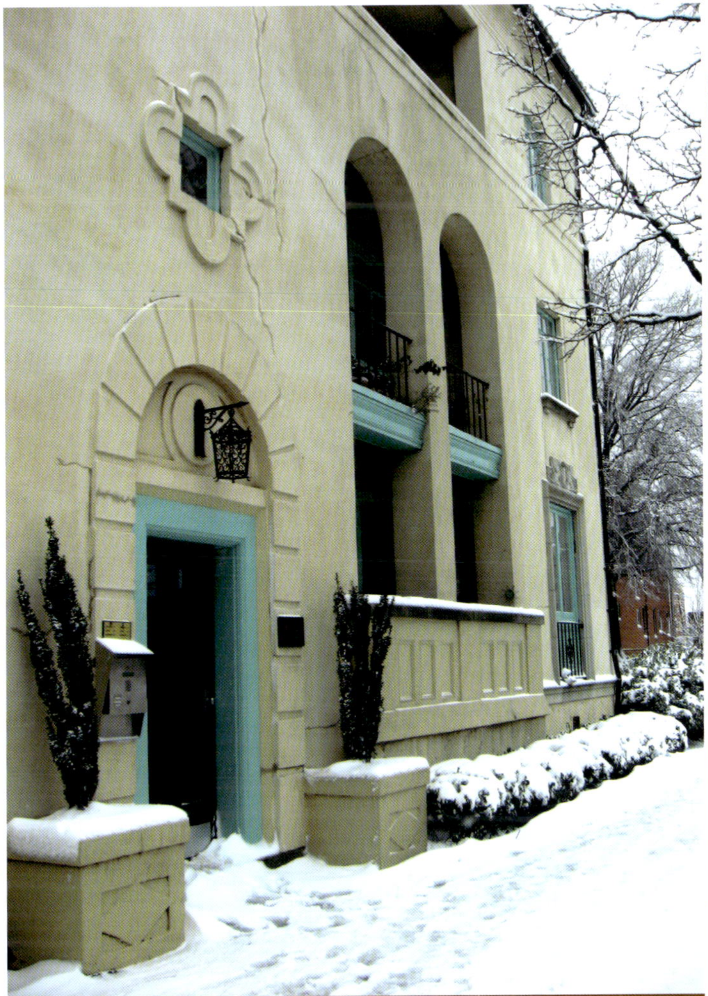

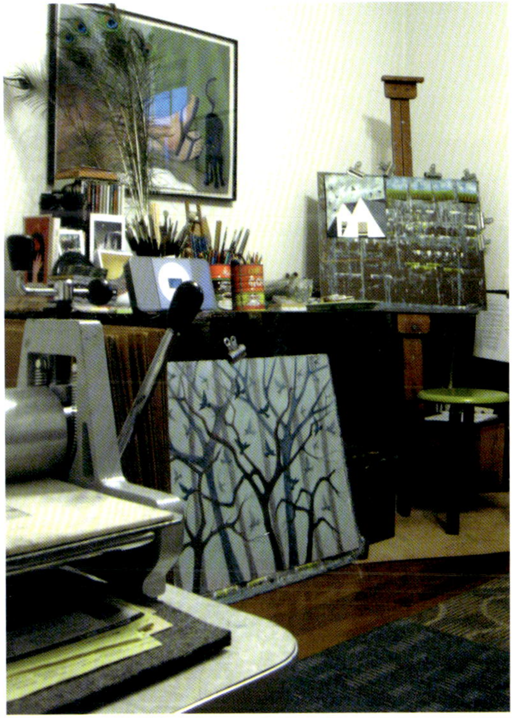

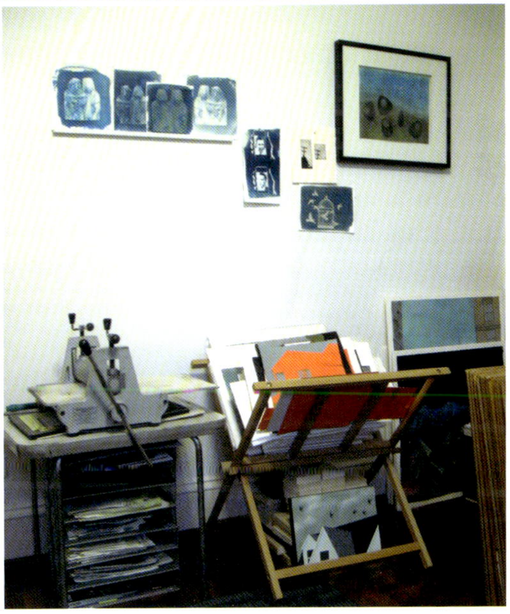

I'm on the second floor of this building in the Museum District of Richmond, Virginia.

The easel is next to a table covered with drawing supplies held in various recycled containers. Hidden under the table are flat racks that store paper, drawings, and prints.

The etching press is on a small retro kitchen table.

5

Studios in Other Places

Then there are studios in academe, whether in high school or at the university level, and studios that artists carry on their backs.

Agamemnon Otero. My workspace with glass mixing pallets for my Circle of Life painting.

Paula A. Allen's Pass A Grille, Florida, studio has a wonderful outdoor courtyard surrounded with bamboo, flowers, and the nearby Gulf. Courtesy of Dylan Marvin.

The Helmet Project, *a work in progress in Gary Chapman's studo.* Courtesy of jerrysiegel.com.

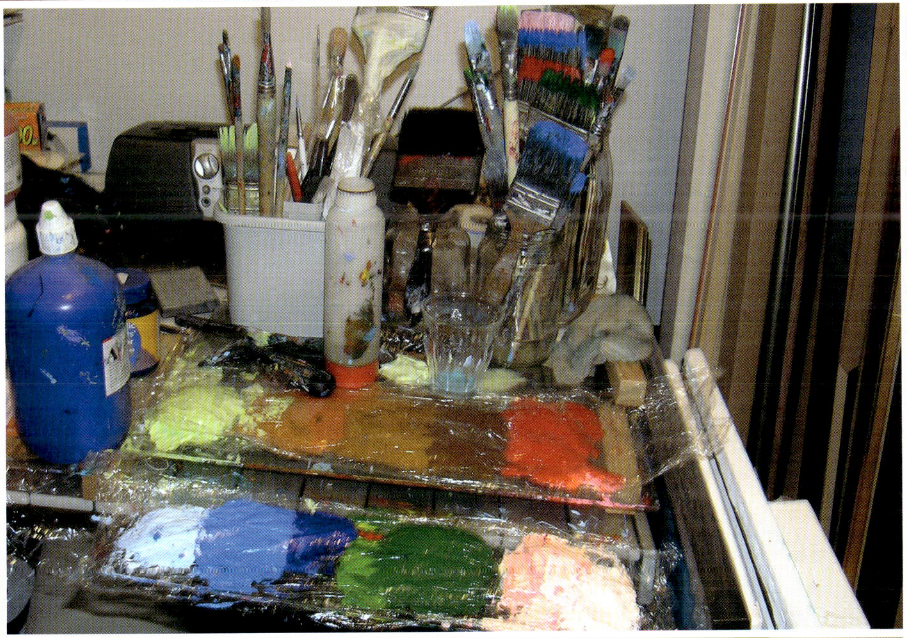

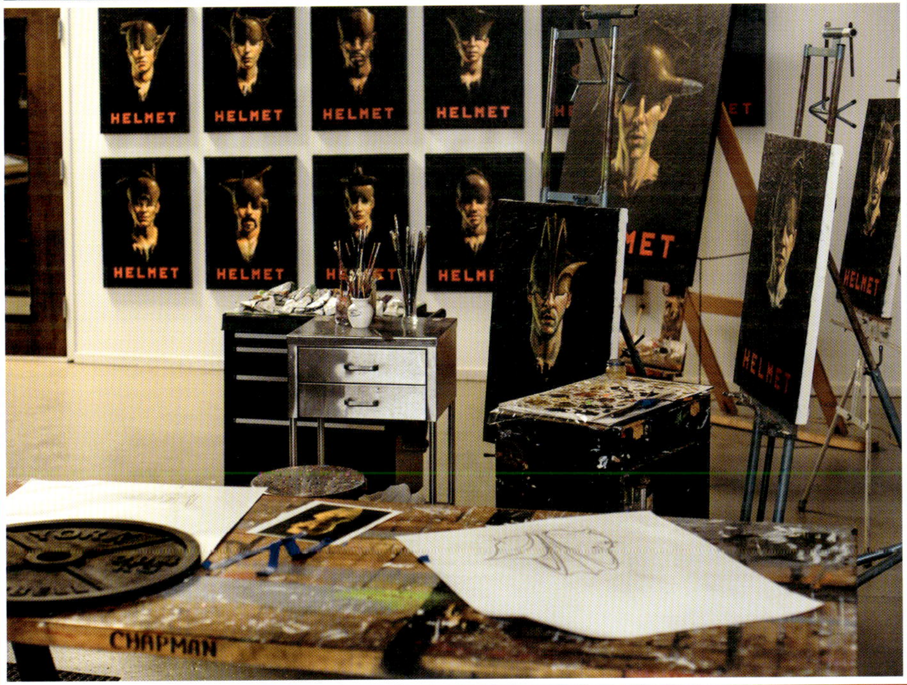
HELMET
CHAPMAN

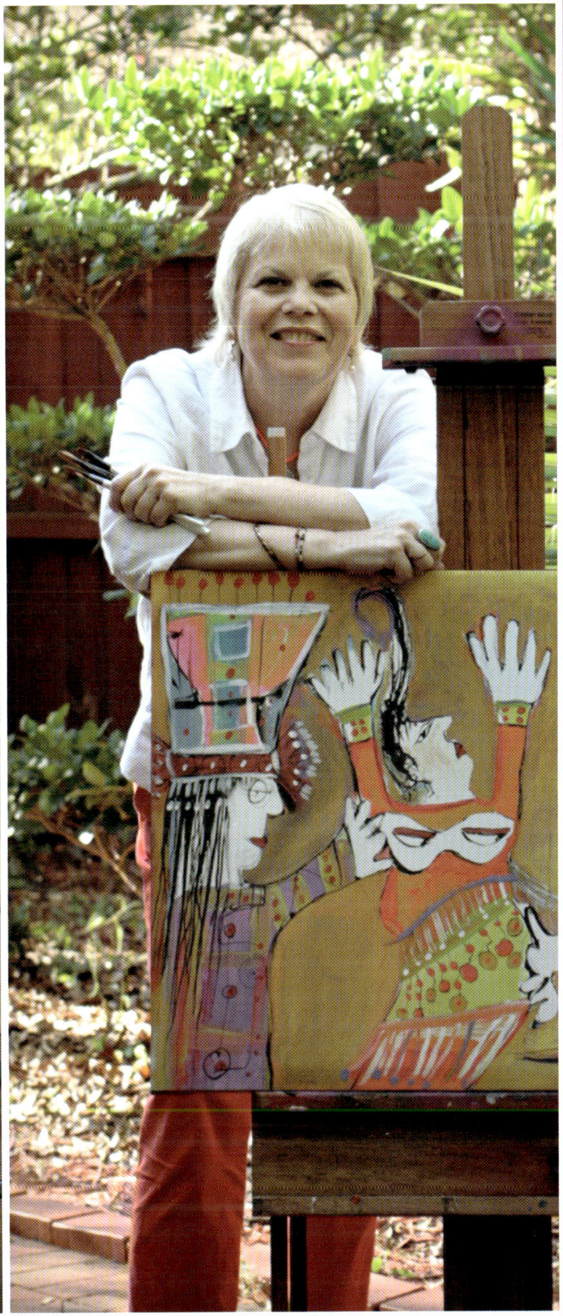

Gary Chapman

Birmingham, Alabama

My studio is a sanctuary. I am very fortunate that the University of Alabama at Birmingham recognizes and supports its faculty's creative/research in this way. My English bulldog, Pickles, loves the studio as well, and accompanies me almost every day. At just over 1,200 square feet, I have a large space, which I have divided up into various workstations. With more than half dedicated to painting, the rest is divided into a workshop, lounge/drafting/drawing area, and a gallery space. With 16-foot ceilings, the studio maintains an open feel as it flows naturally from space to space. The studio receives natural light from a 5 x 12-foot skylight and a long bank of windows, up high on the south wall. Daylight-balanced fluorescents help to complete the overall ambience. A 13-foot wide garage door allows me to easily pull a truck into the studio for loading, away from the elements, and accommodates my motorcycle as an additional perk!

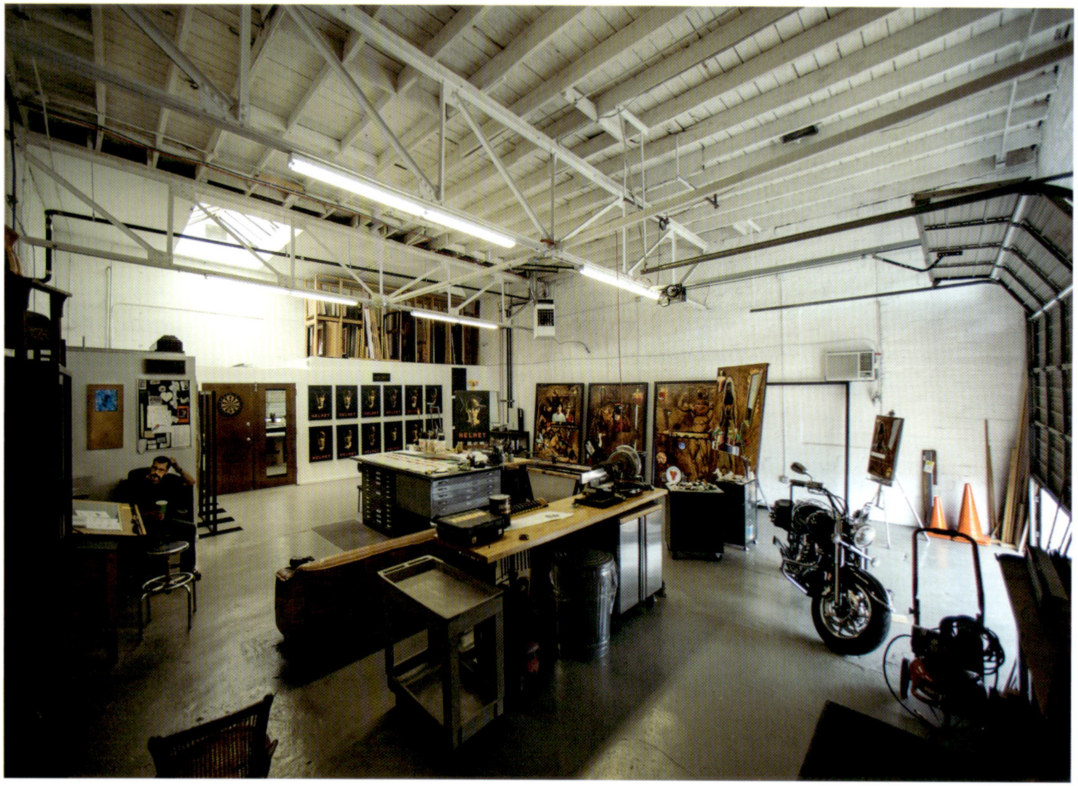

Overview of the studio. Courtesy of jerrysiegel.com.

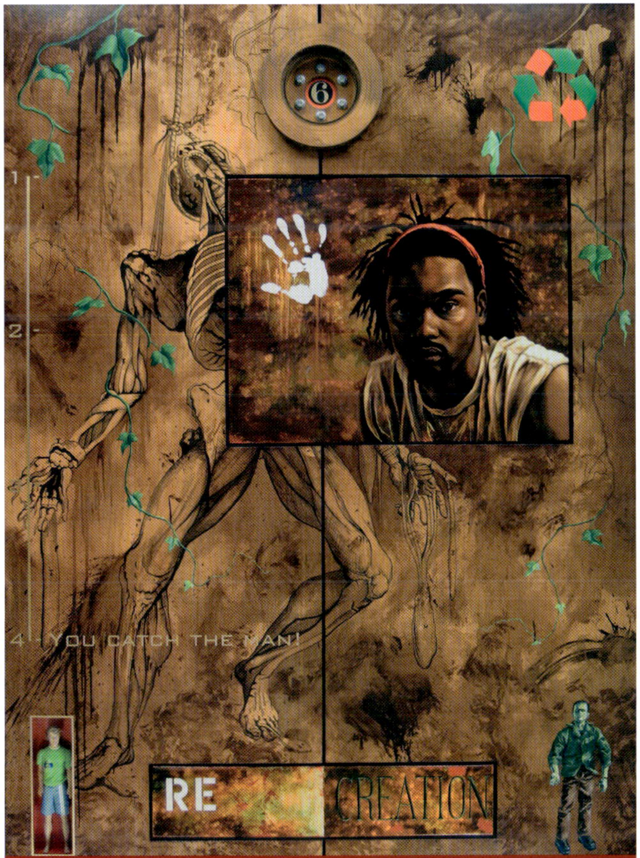

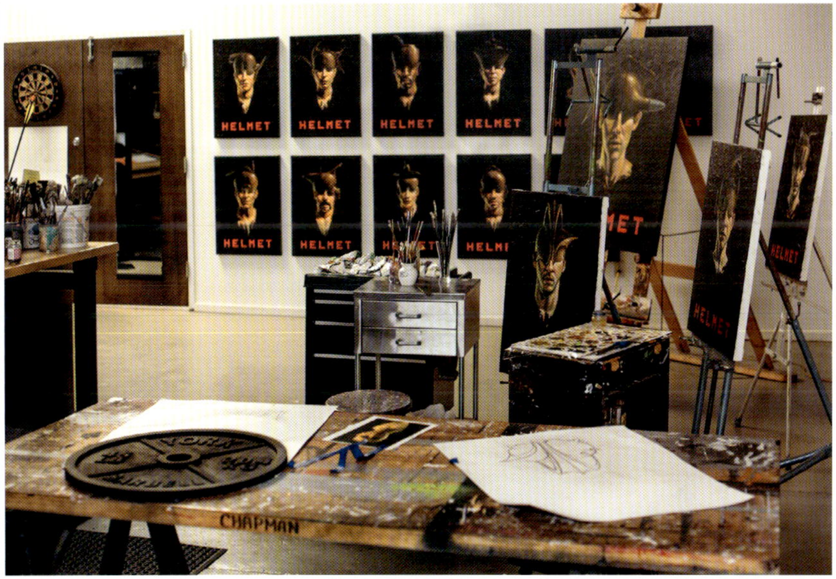

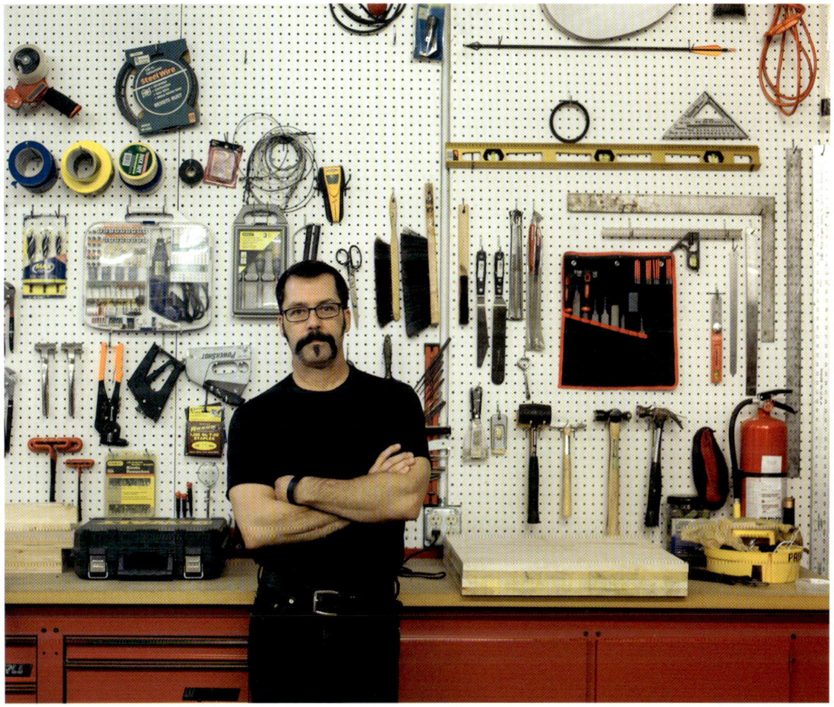

Re Creation. *Oil and gold leaf on canvas, inserted into wooden panels with mixed media and found objects. 84 x 64". 2008.*

*The **Helmet** Project*. Courtesy of jerrysiegel.com.

The tool wall. Courtesy of jerrysiegel.com.

Bill Reid

Racine, Wisconsin

For over thirty years, my studio has been tucked in the corner of an elementary school art room, among the clamor of kids at The Prairie School in Racine, Wisconsin. As the school's resident artist, I am on display for everyone to study—a living diorama of a real, full-time artist at work. It is a wonderfully symbiotic relationship.

Our home is surrounded by nature, both real and in steel. A dolphin hooked up to a BBQ rotisserie bops up and down to welcome guests. In the back yard, a horse fearlessly jumps through a tree, a cardinal rides a narwhal, and a 6-foot tall butterfly carries an anvil through the wildflowers. I am an equal animal opportunist (EAO). Inside our home, many of the animals are working fixtures. *The Garden of Earthly Beelights* is a four-poster, flamingo head bed. *Northern Light,* a northern pike fish with three light bulbs in its belly, illuminates the kitchen table. Still, we eat dinner by the light of the *Octopus Candelabra.*

Our two-car garage houses five art cars: three pedal cars—an anteater, a catfish, and a manta ray; the *Holey Roller,* a woodpecker built from a utility vehicle; and my most ambitious work to date, the *Bee Bomb,* a highway-legal convertible built off the chassis of a Ford Escort.

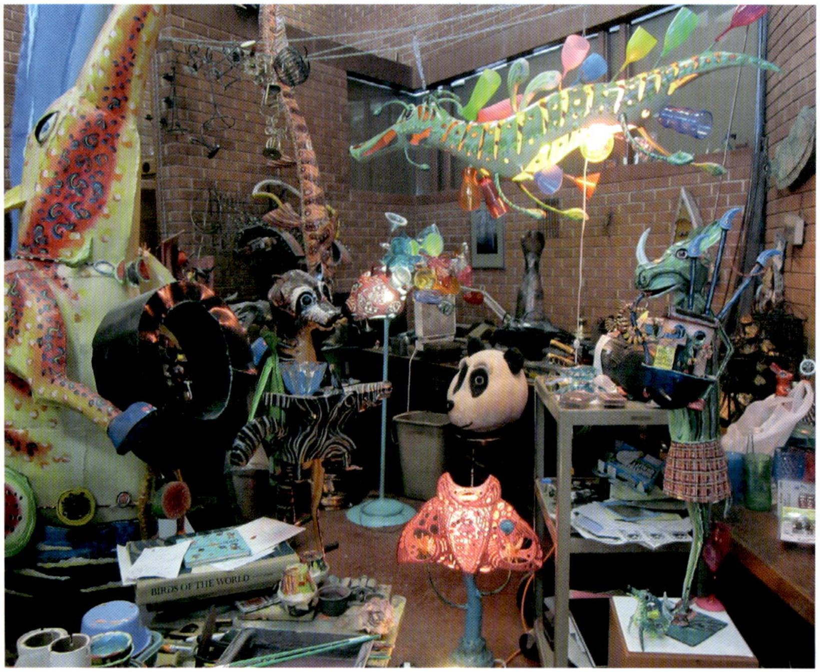

My studio at The Prairie School in Racine, Wisconsin.

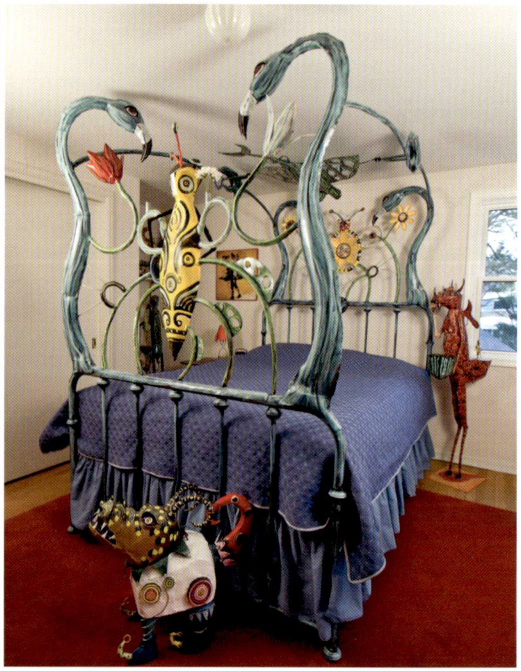

Faithful beasts in the ***Garden of Earthly Beelights****.*

A Piece-a-Bill Kingdom.

Northern Light *lurking in the kitchen.*

Reflections of home life.

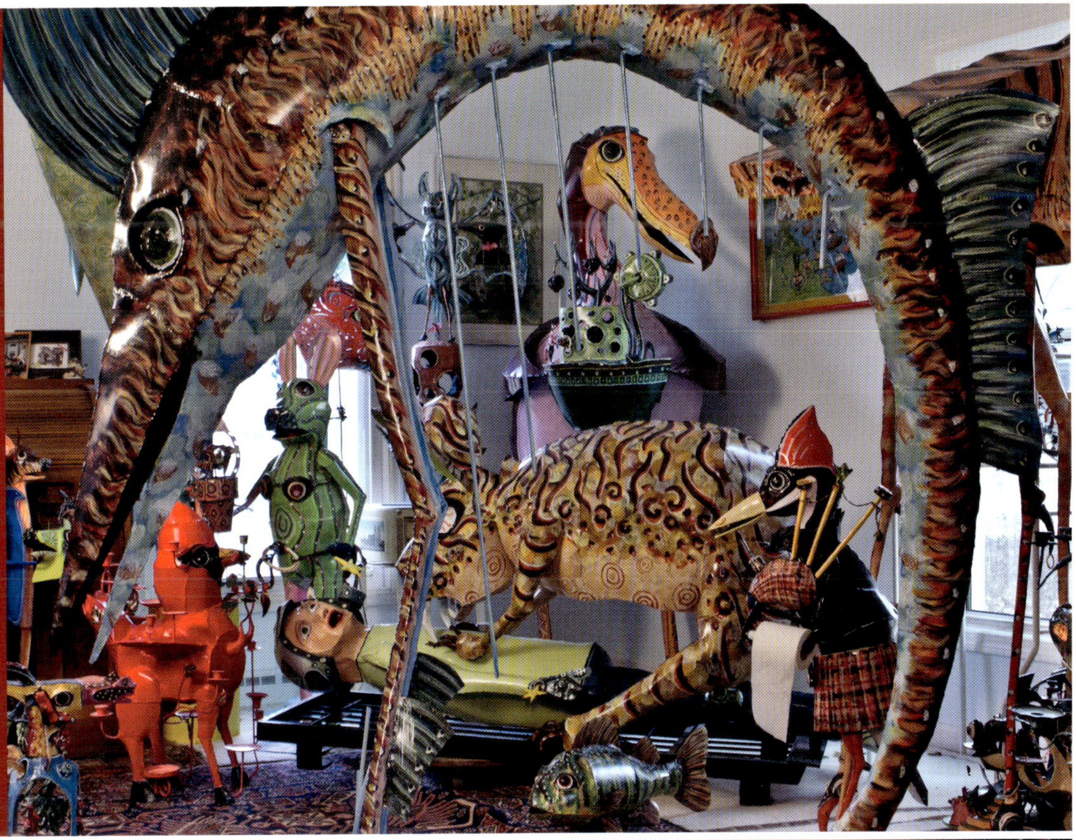

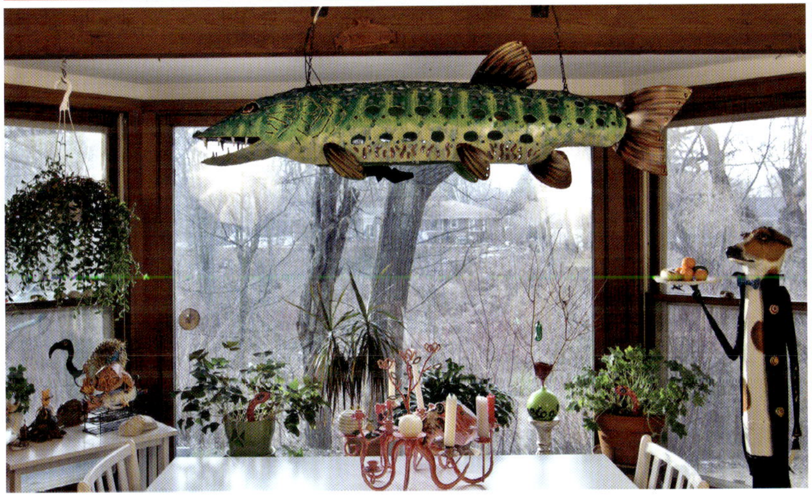

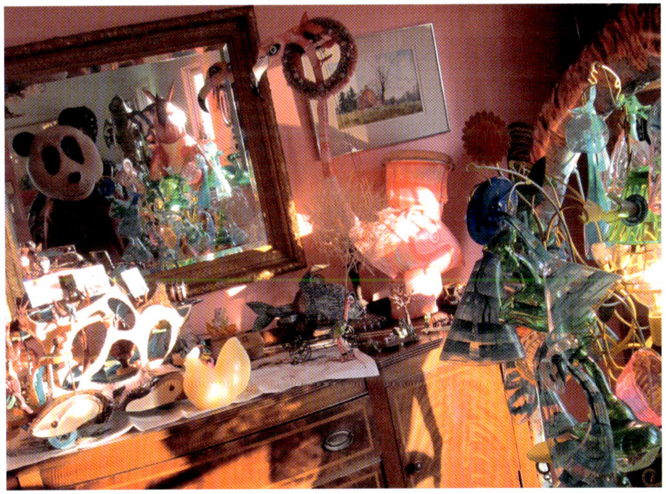

Paula A. Allen

St. Petersburg/ Pass A Grille, Florida

My work is a culmination of my exploration of nature and human nature. It is this dualism that plays an essential role in my creative process. It is the artist's search for balance guiding the viewers to look deeper within themselves. I work in a variety of media: mixed media paintings, sculpture, illustration, watercolor, body art and costume design, and large public artworks I design with children. Some of the visual origins of my work are influenced by a recent trip to India, which blessed me with many life-changing experiences.

The greatest influence on my art, however, has been living in St. Petersburg, Florida, a city known for its large art community. I live on the barrier Island region called Pass A Grille, a beautiful quiet area on the Gulf of Mexico. The Island allows me to be isolated in a small community, but close to St. Petersburg. I am able to work out drawing ideas in the sand on the beach, paint in my courtyard on my easel, paint and draw in my home studio, and take long morning walks along the island's quiet streets. In contrast, when I work on larger art pieces I work in downtown St. Petersburg's warehouse art spaces. In my travels, I have been known to take time out to work in the Adirondacks of New York in a studio that sits right over a lake with dramatic views and the blue cool colors of winter—a wonderful contract to Florida's landscape.

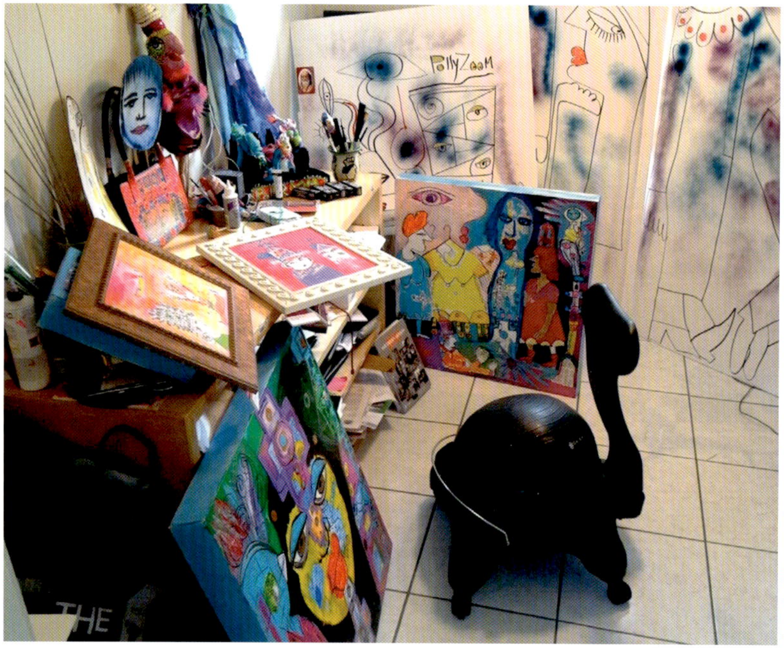

The Pollyzoom Think Tank in St. Petersburg, Florida, is my home studio, where I keep drawings, paintings, runway costumes, wearable art, puppets, and poetry. St. Pete just won another award for being a top city in the arts in the U.S.A.

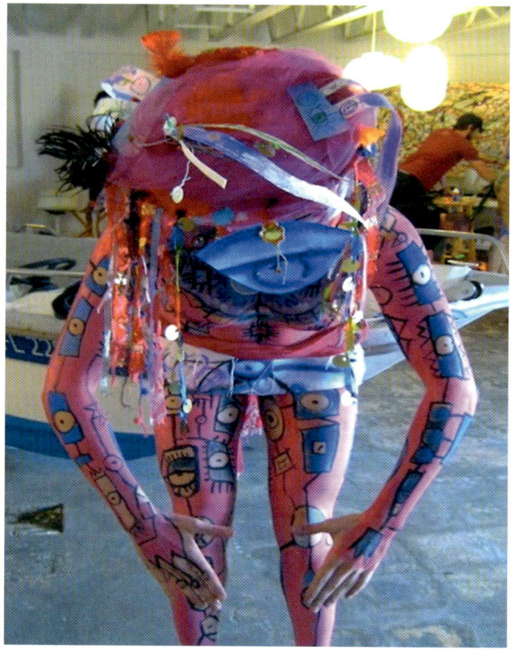

I create larger art forms, costume design, and body art for models such as Anna Rawson on the runway in larger warehouse studios.

The Pass A Grille beach is a wonderful place to get ideas and to draw them in the sand. I work out many ideas along the beach and consider it one of my best studio spaces!

Although most of my art is created in Florida, sometimes I do create art in upstate New York such as at this rustic studio location in the Adirondack Mountains. My grandmother's sewing basket sits on the oak table; the winter sun has set; the lake and mountains come right into the studio. The blue grey color from the winter on this lake is another influence on some of my series of blue watercolors.

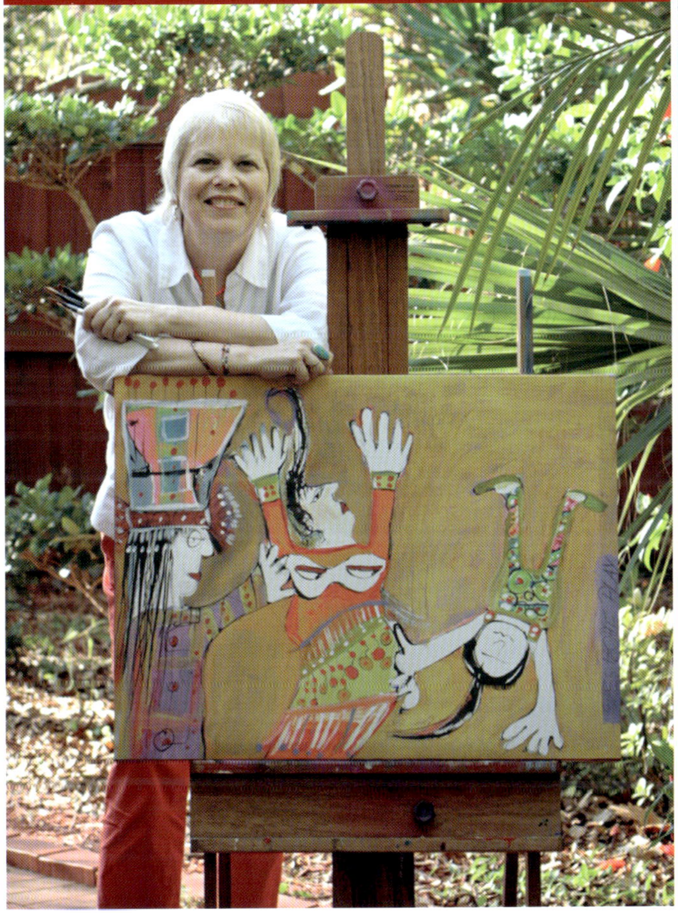

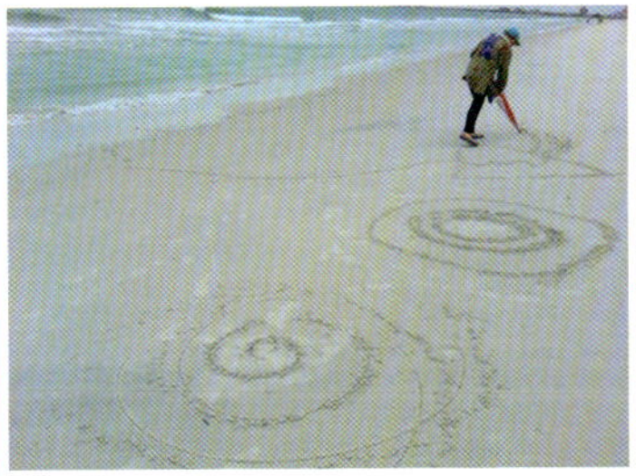

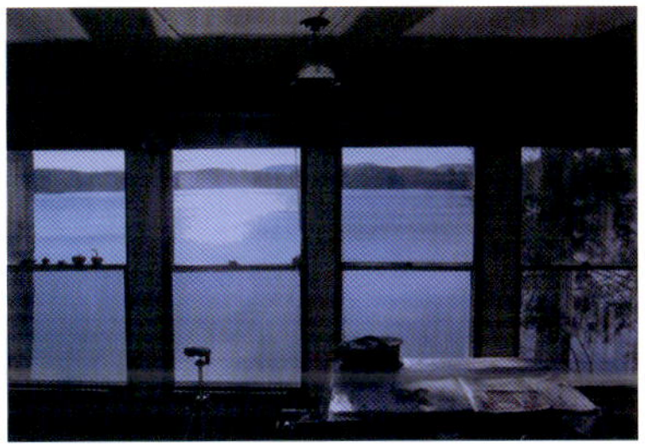

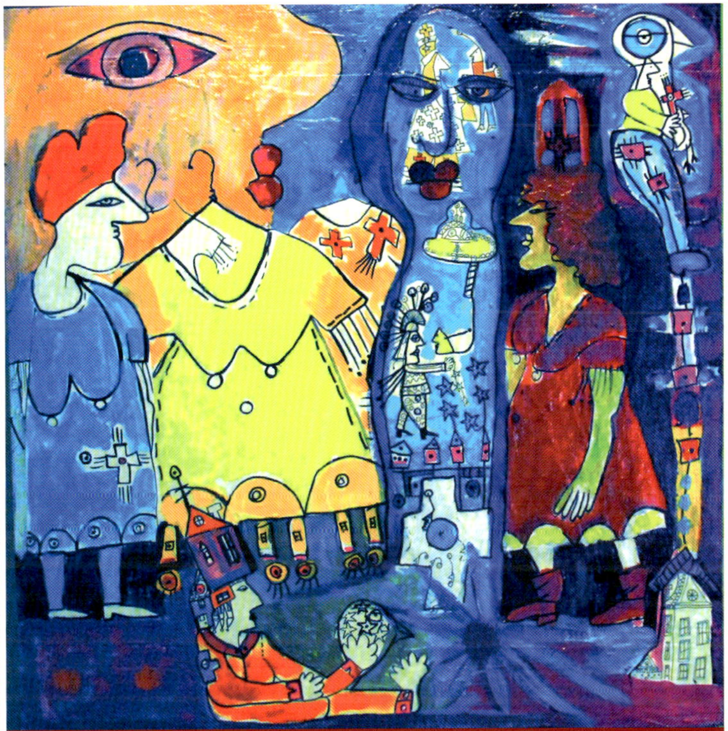

Above: The Yellow Dress. *30 x 30".*

My other Florida studio is Pass A Grille, Florida, with a wonderful outdoor courtyard surrounded with bamboo, flowers, and the nearby gulf. The bright vibrant colors in the courtyard influence my paintings. I created the painting on the easel after returning from a trip to India, which was another color influence. Courtesy of Dylan Marvin.

Agamemnon Otero

London, United Kingdom

The images and tones I work with derive from natural phenomenon. Nature's vivid colors and untamed geometry guide my painting. I distil the physical world that inspires me, staying close to my subject, while invoking its energetic pulse. I am fascinated by the space in-between, the crack amidst the physical and metaphysical.

I have built three studios in the United States and the United Kingdom. I make each place I travel to my own painting space, by designing everything from the furniture to the painting racks to building the foundations with my own hands. I paint my subjects in situ being at "home" (London), or in the highlands of Scotland, the marsh of Maine, a boat in Brazil, or even a mountain shrine in Japan.

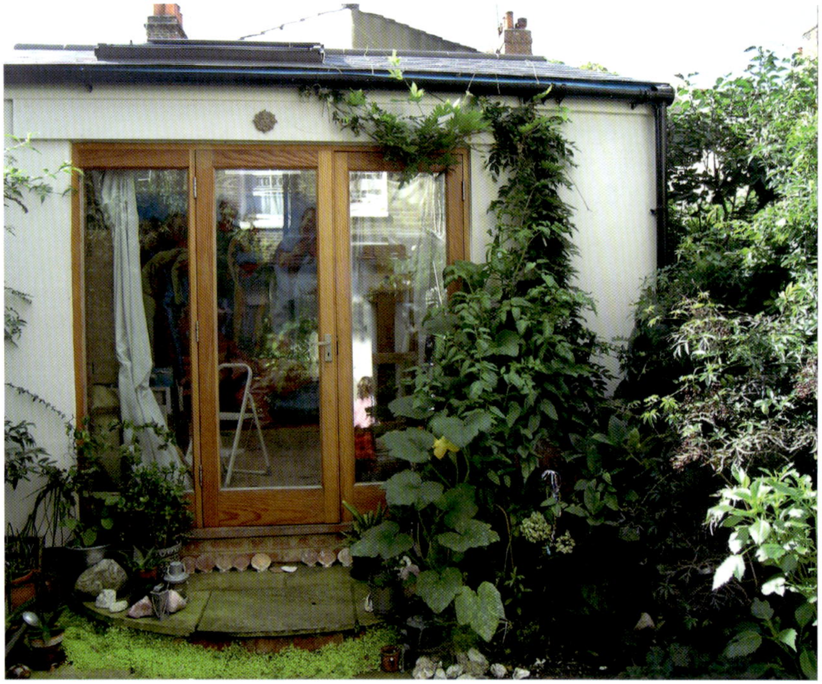

I built my London-based Two Hawks Studio in 2004.

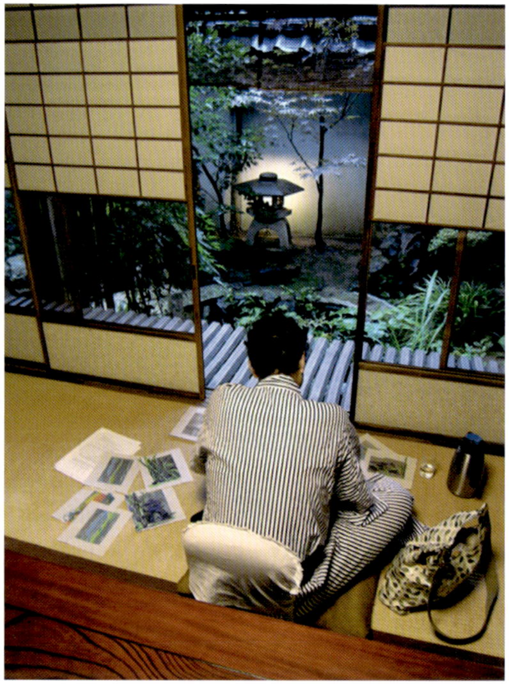

And here I am in Japan.

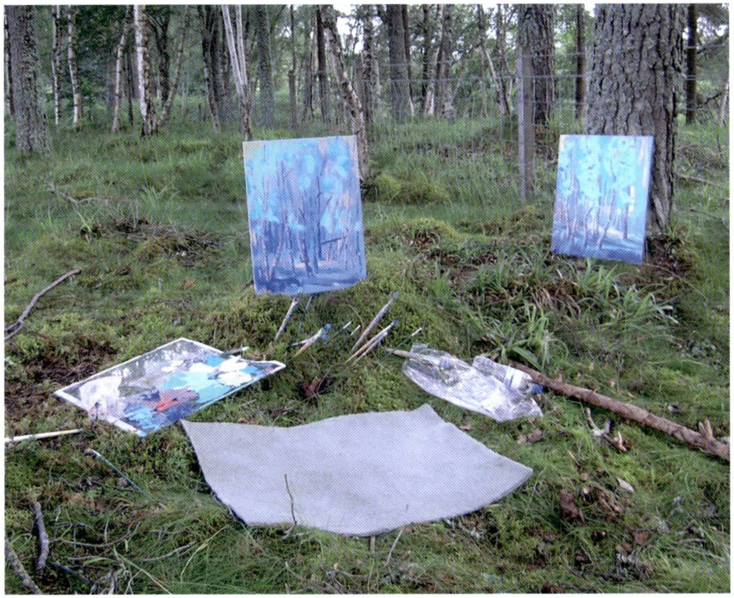

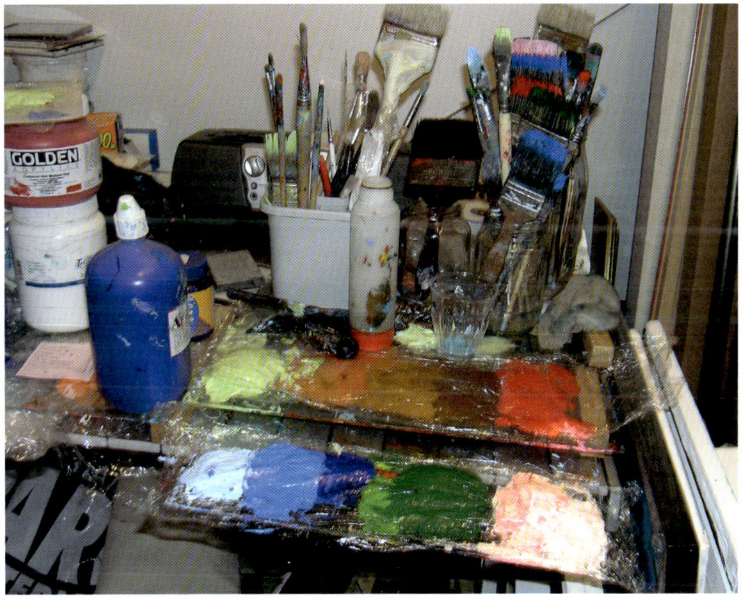

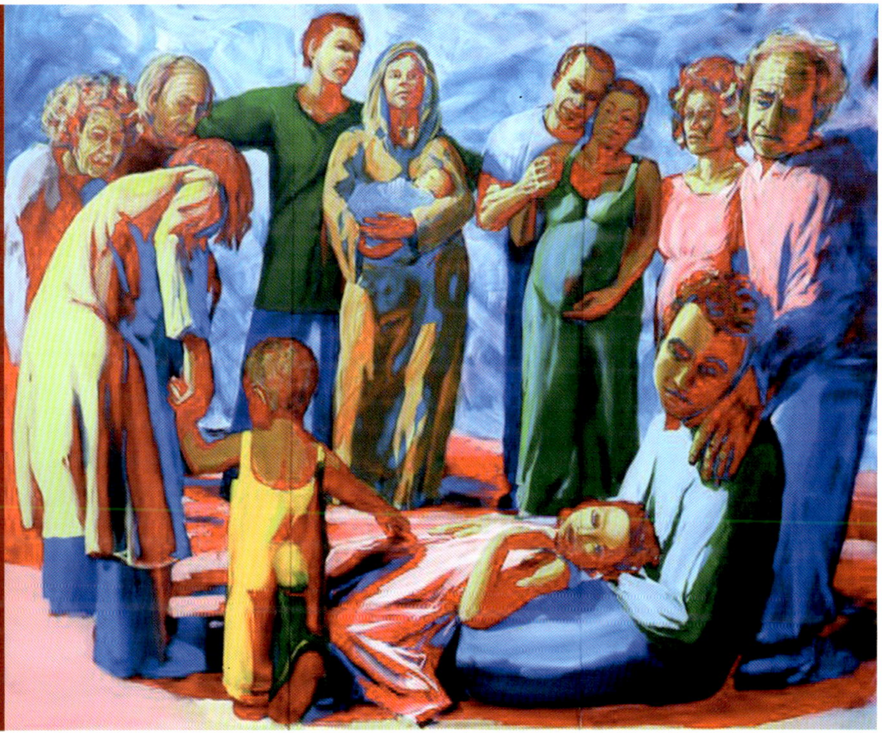

My process has me painting in acrylic in situ (this is in a birch wood in Scotland) to capture the mood and then continuing painting in my studio, playing on larger canvases with different mediums.

My workspace with glass mixing pallets for my ***Circle of Life*** *painting.*

Circle Of Life. *Triptych. Acrylic/canvas. 8'2" x 9'8". 2007.*

Where to Find the Artists' Work

Mary Lou Alberetti
www.maryloualberetti.com

Steven Alexander
www.stevenalexanderstudio.com

Shown at:

David Findlay Jr. Gallery
New York, NY 10019

Gremillion & Co Fine Art
Houston, TX 77005

David Richard Gallery
Santa Fe, NM 87501

Jamie Allen
www.jamierallen.com

Shown at:

Cade Tompkins Projects
Providence, RI 02906

Fine Art Associates
Honolulu, HI 96814

Halele a Gallery
Poipu, Kauai, HI 96756

Paula Allen
www.pollyzoom.com

Shown at:

Artpool Gallery
St. Petersburg, FL 33712

Davidson Fine Art
St. Petersburg, FL 33701

Morean Arts Center
St. Petersburg, FL 33701

Sandy Askey-Adams, PSA
www.sandyaskeyadams.com

Shown at:

Bucks County Gallery
of Fine Art
New Hope, PA 18938

Hardcastle Gallery
Centreville, DE 19807

www.hardcastlegallery.com

Morgan Gallery of Fine Art
Blakeslee, PA 19610

www.morgangalleryonline.com

William Ris Gallery
Stone Harbor, NJ 08246

and Avalon, NJ 08202

Alice G. Ballard
www.aliceballard.com

Shown at:

Blue Spiral 1
Asheville, NC 28801

Hodges Taylor Art
Consultancy
Charlotte, NC 28202

Tao Evolution, Hong Kong

Stephanie Barenz
www.stephaniebarenz.com

Shown at:
www.plaidtuba.com

Helmut Barnett
www.hbarnettartist.com

Shown at:

Corbett vs Dempsey Gallery
Chicago, IL 60622

David Dike
Dallas, TX 75201

Wally Workman Gallery
Austin, TX 78703

Nicole Beck
www.nicolebeck.com

Keith Berr
www.keithberrfineart.com
www.keithberr.com

Shown at:
Joseph Saxton Gallery
Canton, Ohio 44702

Alan Binstock
www.alanbinstock.com

Shown at:

Causey Contemporary
Brooklyn, NY 11211

Stewart Fine Art
Boca Raton, FL 33431

The Wit Gallery
Lenox, MA 01240

Tom Block
www.tomblock.com

Maureen K. Brookfield
www.mkbart.com

Shown at:

Framers Edge Gallery
Braintree, MA 02184

Ropewalk Gallery
Mattapoisett, MA 02739

Russell Gallery
Plymouth, MA 02360

South Street Gallery
Hingham, MA 02043

South Shore Art Center
Cohasset, MA 02025

Sheryl Budnik
www.sherylbudnik.com

Shown at:

Grace Chosy Gallery
Madison, WI 53711

Richard App Gallery
Grand Rapids, MI 49506

Gary Chapman
www.garychapmanart.com
www.garychapmanart.blogspot.com

Shown at:
Grace Chosy Gallery
Madison, WI. 53711

Lydon Contemporary
Chicago, IL 60654

www.lydonfineart.com

Mark Gallery
Englewood, NJ 07631

Tory Folliard Gallery
Milwaukee, WI. 53202

Wantoot Gallery
Mineral Point WI 53565

Terrence James Coffman
www.terrencecoffmanstudio.com

Shown at:
Grace Chosy Gallery
Madison, WI 53711

Lydon Contemporary
Chicago, IL 60654

Mark Gallery
Englewood, NJ 07631

Tory Folliard Gallery
Milwaukee, WI 53202

Wantoot Gallery
Mineral Point, WI 53565

Cynthia F. Cooley
www.cynthiacooley.com

Shown at:
Borelli-Edwards Galleries
Pittsburgh, PA 15201

Pittsburgh Center for the Arts
Pittsburgh, PA 15232

Leila Daw
www.LeilaDaw.com

Shown at:
A.I.R. Gallery
Brooklyn, NY 11201

Atrium Gallery
St Louis, MO 63108

Michelle DeMarco
www.michelledemarco.com

Murray Dewart
www.dewartsculpture.com

Shown at:
Boston Sculptors Gallery
Boston, MA 02118

Mill Brook Gallery and Sculpture Garden
Concord, NH 03301

Wade Eldean
www.eldean.com/art

Clark Ellefson
www.lewisandclarklamps.com

Lewis+Clark
Columbia, SC 29201

Rob Evans
www.robevansart.net

Catherine Eyde
www.CatherineEyde.com

George Fellner
www.gfellnerphotography.com

Shown at:
Nature Genetics
New York, NY 10013

Yale School of Medicine
New Haven, CT 06510

Kat Fitzpatrick
www.katfitzpatrick.com

Shown at:
The Garden District Gallery
New Orleans, LA 70130

The Caron Gallery
Tupelo, MS 38804

Snowbird Mountain Lodge
Robbinsville, NC 28771

The Mockingbird Cafe and Gallery
Bay St. Louis, MS, 39520

Scott Fraser
www.sfraser.com

Shown at:
Gallery 1261
Denver, CO 80204

J. Cacciola Gallery
New York, NY 10001

Jenkins Johnson Gallery
San Francisco, CA 94108

Pismo Gallery at Aspen
Aspen, CO 81611

Debra Fritts
www.debrafritts.net

Shown at:
Echt Gallery
Chicago, IL 60654

Gallery One
Nashville, TN 37205.

Pacini Lubel
Seattle, WA 98104

Signature Gallery
Atlanta, GA 30305

Nancy Gaucher-Thomas, NWS
www.gaucher-thomas.com

Dimitri Gerakaris
dg@art-metal.com
www.art-metal.com
www.wallrelief.com

Shown at:

Architectural and Sculptural Metalsmithing
Canaan, NH 03741

Ken and Julie Girardini
www.girardinidesign.com

Shown at:
Zenith Gallery
Washington, DC 20012

Allison Gildersleeve
www.allisongildersleeve.com

Shown at:
Asya Geisberg Gallery
New York, NY 10011

Cynthia-Reeves
Hanover, NH 03755

Galleri Andersson/Sandstr m
Aktrisgr nd 34, 903 64 UME..., Sweden

Robischon Gallery
Denver, CO. 80202

Jeanie Gooden
Shown at:

Craighead-Green Gallery
Dallas, TX 75207

M.A. Doran Gallery
Tulsa, OK 74105

Tinney Contemporary
Nashville, TN 37219

Karen Hackenberg
www.karenhackenberg.com

Shown at:
Simon Mace Gallery
Port Townsend, WA 98360
Smith and Vallee Gallery
Edison, WA 98232
Vermillion Gallery
Seattle, WA 98122

Hanrahan Meyers Architects
www.hanrahanmeyers.com

New York, NY 10038
Email: info@hanrahanmeyers.com

Stephen Hansen
www.stephenhansen.com

Shown at:
Water Street Gallery
Saugatuck, MI 49406
waterstreetgallery.com
William & Joseph Gallery
Santa Fe, NM 87501
Zenith Gallery
Washington, DC 20012

Ann Harwell
www.annharwell.com

Shown at:
Artspace
Raleigh, NC 27602
Piedmont Craftsmen
Winston-Salem, NC 27101

Martha Hayden
www. Marthahayden.com

Shown at:
Central Booking
Brooklyn, NY 11201
Peltz Gallery
Milwaukee, WI 53202

Karen Hibbs
www.hibbsartglass.com

Gayla Hodson
www.galahodson.com

Shown at:
Editions Limited Gallery of Fine Art
Indianapolis, IN 46220

Cheryl Holz
www.CherylHolz.com

Shown at:
Art Advisory Ltd.
Chicago, IL 60659
Art Resources
Minneapolis, MN 55405
Corporate Artworks
Arlington Heights, IL 60005
Health Environment Art Services
Arlington Heights, IL 60005
McGrill Art Associates
Minneapolis, MN

Frank Hyder
www.frankhyder.com

Shown at:
Butters Gallery
Portland, OR 97209
Galeria Medicc
Caracas, Venezuela
Ode to Art Contemporary
Singapore 179109
Patrick International Fine Art
Toronto, Ontario, M5R 1J2
Projects Gallery
Philadelphia, PA 19123
and Miami, FL 33127
Rebecca Hossack Art Gallery
London, W1T 6BA
and New York, NY 10012
Walter Wickiser Gallery
New York, NY 10001

Gale Jamieson
www.galejamieson.com

Dale Kennington
www.dalekennington.com

Shown at:
Corporate Art Source
Montgomery, AL 36106

Kathleen Kinkopf
www.kathleenkinkopf.com
Email: kathleenkinkopf@comcast.net

Helen R. Klebesadel
www.Klebesadel.com

Shown at:
ArtfulHome.com
Grace Chosy Gallery
Madison, WI 53711

Barbara Krupp
www.barbarakrupp.com

Shown at:
Dabbert Gallery
Sarasota, FL 34236
Darby Fine Art
Vero Beach, FL 32960
Frame of Mind Gallery
Toronto, Ontario, Canada M5M 4A6
Pennello Gallery
Cleveland, OH 44106
Nestology Gallery
King of Prussia, PA 19406
Rice Gallery
Leawood, KS 66211

Kevin Lyles
www.kevinlyles.com.

Anne Marchand
www.annemarchand.com

Shown at:
Emerge Fine Art
Cary, NC 27511
Porter Contemporary
New York, NY 10001
Zenith Gallery
Washington, DC 20040

Karla Matzke
www.matzkefineart.com

Shown at:
Matzke Fine Art Gallery
and Sculpture Park
Camano Island, WA 98282
Museum of Northwest Art
La Conner, WA 98257
Schack Art Center
Everett, WA 98201

John McConnell
www.johnmcconnellartist.com

Elizabeth Miller McCue
www.elizabethmccue.com

Shown at:
art4business
Philadelphia, PA 19127
Highlands Art Gallery
Chester, NJ 07930
New Hope Arts, Inc.
New Hope, PA 18938
New Hope Sidetracks Art Gallery
New Hope, PA 18938
New York Sculptors Gallery
Brooklyn, NY 11201

Margie McDonald
www.margiemcdonald.com

Kelly Milukas

Shown at:

The Art Stable Gallery
Westport, MA 02790

Bow House Studio
Tiverton, RI 02878

Ann Morris
Sculpture Woods, Lummi Island, WA

www.annmorrisbronze.com

Shown at:
Arroyo
Santa Fe, NM 87501

Lisa Harris Gallery
Seattle, WA 98101

Lucia Douglas Gallery
Bellingham, WA 98225

Stonington Gallery
Seattle, WA 98104

Dorothy Netherland
www.dorothynetherland.com

Shown at:
Barbara Archer Gallery
Atlanta, GA 30307

If ART Gallery
Columbia, SC 29201

Matthew Campbell Gallery
Greenville, SC 29601

Lynn O Brien
www.lynnobrienart.com

Shown at:
Harris Stanton Gallery
Akron, OH 44313

Carol Oldenburg
www.caroloIdenburg.com

Shown at:
Marketview Arts
York, PA 17401

Agamemnon Otero
www.agamemnonotero.com

Shown at:
Bayview Gallery
Camden, ME 04843

Ralli Museum
Punta Del Este, Uruguay

Royal Infirmary of Edinburgh
Main Atrium Hall, UK EH1645A

Stockwell Studio
London, UK SW4 6QU

Transistor Gallery
Bristol, UK BS6 6AY

Two Hawks Studio
London, UK

Tere Pastoriza
www.terepastoriza.com

Kate Pond
www.katepond.com

Barbara Purchia
http://home.comcast.net/~glasscoop/

Florence Putterman
www.florenceputterman.com

Shown at:
Basisden Gallery
Tampa, FL 33606

Dancing Crane Gallery
Bradenton, FL 35205

Projects Gallery
Philadelphia, PA 19123

Walter Wickiser Gallery
New York, NY 10001

Mario Quilles
www.marioquilles.com
www.airstudio-nm.net

www.artgraze.com
Email: airstudio@copper.net

Mel Rea
www.melrea.com

Shown at:
Bennett Gallery
Nashville, TN 37215

Muse Gallery
Columbus, OH 43206

Shain Gallery
Charlotte, NC 28209

Bill Reid
www.beebomb.com

Shown at:
Ann Nathan Gallery
Chicago, IL 60654

Tory Folliard Gallery
Milwaukee, WI 53202

Amanda Richardson
www.amandarichardson.co.uk

Shown at:
Human Arts Gallery
Ojai, CA 93023

Waterworks Gallery
Friday Harbor, WA 98250

Zenith Gallery
Washington, DC 20040

Ellen Rolli

Shown at:
Copley Society of Art
Boston, MA 02116

Galerie Sono
South Norwalk, CT 06854

Hutson Gallery
Provincetown, MA 02657

Onessimo Fine Art
Palm Beach Gardens, FL 33418

Barton Rubenstein
www.RubensteinStudios.com

Kenneth G. Ryden
www.rydenarts.com

Shown at:
Editions Limited Gallery of Fine
Indianapolis, IN 46220

Renee Sage

Shown at:
Adelaide Central Gallery
South Australia,
Australia 5067

Arts in Health at Flinders
Medical Centre
South Australia,
Australia 5042

Paul Santoleri
www.paulsantoleri.com

Shown at:
Galerie Ligne 13
Paris, France

Projects Gallery
Philadelphia, PA 19123

Ebeth Scott-Sinclair
www.ebethscottsinclair.com

Shown at:
Hughes Gallery
Boca Grande, FL 33921

Monty Stabler Galleries
Homewood, AL 35209

Greg Spitzer
www.sculpturebyspitzer.com
Medford, MA 02155

Shown at:
L Attitude Gallery
Boston, MA 02116

Powers Gallery
Acton, MA 01720

The Walsingham Gallery
Newburyport, MA 01950

Stephanie Standish
www.FeatherWeightPress.com

Melinda Stickney-Gibson
www.melindastickneygibson.com

Shown at:
Butters Gallery
Portland, OR 97209
Darnell Fine Art
Santa Fe, NM 87501
Elena Zang Gallery
Woodstock, NY 12409
Kouros Gallery
Ridgefield, CT 06877
Littlejohn Contemporary
New York, NY 10001
Thomas Masters Gallery
Chicago, IL 60610

Robert Swedroe
www.robertswedroe.com

Shown at:
American Institute of Architects
Miami, FL 33132
Bakehouse Gallery
Miami, FL 33127
Conrad Miami 1
Miami, FL 33131
Contessa Gallery
Cleveland, OH 44124
Hecht, Amdur, Havenick Art Gallery
Temple Beth Sholom
Miami Beach, FL 33140
Kelley Roy Gallery
Miami, FL 33137
Sacco Gallery
Miami, FL 33138
Sagamore Hotel
Miami Beach, FL 33139
Sardinas Gallery at St. Thomas University
Miami Gardens, FL 33054
Scope Fair Miami
Miami, FL 33138

Tracey Tarling
www.traceytarling.com

Shown at:
BAU-XI Galleries
Vancouver V6H339
and Toronto M571G5, Canada
Whistler Village Art Gallery
Whistler, BC VON 1B4
www.whistlerart.com

Pringle Teetor
www.flambeauxart.com

Shown at:
Cedar Creek Gallery
Creedmoor, NC 27522
Hillsborough Gallery of Arts
Hillsborough, NC 27278
North Carolina Crafts Gallery
Carrboro, NC 27510
Saxapahaw Artists Gallery
Saxapahaw, NC 27340

W. Gerome Temple
www.gerometemple.com

Claudia G. Thomas
Shown at:
Art Affair Gallery
Sanford, FL 32771
The FL Frame House Gallery
Winter Park, FL 32789

Tjelda vander Meijden
www.tjelda.com
www.palettepressprints.com

Shown at:
Cavaliero Fine Arts
New York, NY 10021
Palette Press Studio
Brookside, NJ 07926

Graceann Warn

Shown at:
River Gallery
Chelsea, MI 48118
Hoadley Gallery
Lenox, MA 01240
Left Bank Gallery
Wellfleet, MA 02667
Miller Gallery
Cincinnati, OH 45208
Modern Arts Midwest
Lincoln, NE 68508
Snyderman-Works Gallery
Philadelphia, PA 19106
Sopa Fine Arts
Kelowna, BC V141V9

Nina Weiss
Nina Weiss/Art Endeavors Studio

Highland Park, IL 60035

Shown at:
Button-Petter Gallery
Saugatuck, MI 49406
Editions Limited Gallery
Indianapolis, IN 46202
Illinois Artisans Shop
Chicago, Il 60601
Southern Illinois Art &
Artisan Center
Whittington, IL 62897

Kathleen Westkaemper
www.kathleenwestkaemper.com

Shown at:
43rd Street Gallery
Richmond, VA 23225
Artspace
Richmond, VA 23224
Atelier Gallery
Charleston, SC 29401
Crossroads Art Center
Richmond, VA 23230
Glave Kocen Gallery
Richmond, VA 23220

Judy Youngblood
www.judyyoungblood.com

Shown at:
William Campbell Contemporary Art
Fort Worth, TX 76107

Resources

Alabama

Corporate Art Source
2960-F Zelda Rd.
Montgomery, AL 36106

Monty Stabler Galleries
1811 29th Ave. South
Homewood, AL 35209
www.montystablergalleries.com

California

Human Arts Gallery
246 East Ojai Ave.
Ojai, CA 93023
www. humanarts.com

Jenkins Johnson Gallery
464 Sutter St.
San Francisco, CA 94108
www.jenkinsjohnsongallery.com

Colorado

Gallery 1261
1261 Delaware St.
Denver, CO 80204
www.gallery1261.com

Pismo Gallery at Aspen
433 E. Cooper Ave.
Aspen, CO 81611
www.pismoglass.com

Robischon Gallery
1740 Wazee St.
Denver, CO 80202
www.robischongallery.com

Connecticut

Galerie Sono
123 Washington St.
South Norwalk, CT 06854
www.sonogalerie.com

Kouros Gallery
150 Mopus Bridge Rd.
Ridgefield, CT 06877
www.Kourosgallery.com

Yale School of Medicine
Brady Memorial Lab
310 Cedar St.
New Haven, CT 06510

Delaware

Hardcastle Gallery
5714 Kennett Pike
Centreville, DE 19807
www.hardcastlegallery.com

Florida

American Institute of Architects
Miami, Fl 33132
www.aiamiami.org

Art Affair Gallery
112 East 1st St.
Sanford, FL 32771
www.artaffairgallery.com

Artpool Gallery
2030 Central Ave.
St. Petersburg, FL 33712

Baisden Gallery
422 Grand Central Pkwy.
Suite 100
Tampa, FL 33606

Bakehouse Gallery
561 NW 32nd St.
Miami, FL 33127
www.bacfl.org/

Conrad Miami 1
395 Brickell Ave.
Miami, FL 33131

Dabbert Gallery
76 So. Palm Ave.
Sarasota, FL 34236
www.dabbertgallery.com

Dancing Crane Gallery
1019 10th Ave. W
Bradenton, FL 34205

Darby Fine Art
1902 14th Ave.
Vero Beach, FL 32960

Davidson Fine Art Gallery
1100 First Ave. North
St. Petersburg, FL 33701

Effusion Gallery
1130 Ocean Drive
Miami Beach, FL 33139
www.effusiongallery.com/

The Florida Frame House Gallery
444 W New England Ave.
Suite 118
Winter Park, FL 32789
www.floridaframehouse.net

Hecht, Amdur, Havenick Art Gallery Temple Beth Sholom
4144 Chase Ave.
Miami Beach, FL 33140

Hughes Gallery
333 Park Ave.
Boca Grande, FL 33921
www.hughesgallery.net

Kelley Roy Gallery
50 Northeast 29th St.
Miami, FL 33137
www.kelleyroygallery.com

Morean Arts Center
719 Central Ave.
St Petersburg, FL 33701

Onessimo Fine Art
4530 PGA Blvd. Suite 101
Palm Beach Gardens, FL 33418
www.onessimofineart.com

Sacco Gallery
6444 Biscayne Blvd.
Miami, FL 33138

Sagamore Hotel
1671 Collins Ave.
Miami Beach, FL 33139
www.sagamorehotel.com

Sardinas Gallery at St. Thomas University
16401 NW 37th Ave.
Miami Gardens, FL 33054

Stewart Fine Art, Gallery Center
Banyan Trai
Boca Raton, FL 33431
www.sfaglass.com

Wynwood Lofts
#208, 250 NW 23rd St.
Miami, FL 33127
www.projectsgallery.com

Georgia

Barbara Archer Gallery
280 Elizabeth St. #A012
Atlanta, GA 30307
www.barbaraarcher.com

Signature Gallery
3267 Roswell Rd. NE
Atlanta, GA 30305
www.signaturegallery.com

W. Gerome Temple
PO Box 9304
Savannah, GA 31412
www.gerometemple.com

Hawaii

Fine Art Associates
1020 Auahi St. Suite 401
Honolulu, HI 96814
www.fineartassociates.com

Halele'a Gallery
2829 Ala Kalanikaumaka Suite k-159
Poipu, Kauai, HI 96756
www.haleleagallery.com

Illinois

Ann Nathan Gallery
212 W. Superior St.
Chicago, IL 60654
www.annnathangallery.com

Art Advisory Ltd.
5836 N. Christiana Ave.
Chicago, IL 60659
www.artadvisoryltd.com

Art Resources
International Market Square
Suite 166, 275 Market St.
Minneapolis, MN 55405
www.artresourcesgallery.com

Corbett vs. Dempsey Gallery
1120 N. Ashland Ave.
3rd Floor
Chicago, Illinois 60622
www.corbettvsdempsey.com

Corporate Artworks
76 West Seegers Rd.
Arlington Heights, IL 60005
www.corporateartworks.com

Echt Gallery
222 W. Superior St.
Chicago, IL 60654
www.echtgallery.com

Health Environment Art Services
76 West Seegers
Arlington Heights, IL 60005
www.healtheart.com

Illinois Artisans Shop
James R. Thompson Center
100 W. Randolph Suite 10-610
Chicago, Il 60601
www.facebook.com/illinoisartisans

Lydon Contemporary
230 W. Superior St.
Chicago, IL 60654
www.lydonfineart.com

Nina Weiss/Art Endeavors Studio
3150 Skokie Highway
Suite #12
Highland Park, IL 60035
www.ninaweiss.com

Southern Illinois Art & Artisan Center
14967 Gun Creek Trail
Whittington, IL 62897
www.museum.state.il.us

Thomas Masters Gallery
245 West North Ave.
Chicago, IL 60610
www.thomasmastersgallery.com

Indiana

Editions Limited Gallery
838 East 65th St. # B
Indianapolis, IN 46220
www.editionsltd.com

Kansas

Rice Gallery
11535 Ash St.
Leawood, KS 66211
www.thericegallery.com

Louisiana

The Garden District Gallery
1332 Washington Ave.
New Orleans, LA 70130
www.gardendistrictgallery.com

Maine

Bayview Gallery
33 Bayview St.
Camden, ME 04843
and
58 Maine St.
Brunswick, ME 04011
www.bayview.com

Maryland

Adah Rose Gallery
3766 Howard Ave.
Kensington, MD 20895
Email:
adahrosegallery@gmail.com

Massachusetts

The Art Stable Gallery
865 Main Rd.
Westport, MA 02790
www.artstablegallery.com

Boston Sculptors Gallery
486 Harrison Ave.
Boston, MA 02118
www.bostonsculptors.com

Copley Society of Art
158 Newbury St.
Boston, MA 02116
www.copleysociety.org

Hoadley Gallery
21 Church St.
Lenox, MA 01240
www.hoadleygallery.com

Hutson Gallery
432 Commercial St.
Provincetown, MA 02657
www.hutsongallery.net

L Attitude Gallery
211 Newbury St.
Boston, MA 02116
www.lattitudegallery.com

Left Bank Gallery
25 Commercial St.
Wellfleet, MA 02667
www.leftbankgallery.com

Powers Gallery
144 Great Rd.
Acton, MA 01720
www.powersgallery.com

Ropewalk Gallery
33 Country Rd.
Mattapoisett, MA 02739
www.ropewalkgallery.com

Russell Gallery
Plymouth Art Guild
11 North St.
Plymouth, MA 02360
www.plymouthguild.org

Sculpture By Spitzer
236 Boston Ave
Medford, MA 02155
www.sculpturebyspitzer.com

South St. Gallery
149 South St.
Hingham, MA 02043
www.southSt.gallery.com

South Shore Art Center
119 Ripley Rd.
Cohasset, MA 02025
www.ssac.org

The Walsingham Gallery
47 Merrimac St.
Newburyport, MA 01950
www.thewalsinghamgallery.com

The Wit Gallery
27 Church St.
Lenox, MA 01240
www.thewitgallery.com

Michigan

Button-Petter Gallery
161 Blue Star Highway
Saugatuck, MI 49406
www.buttonpettergallery.com

Richard App Gallery
910 Cherry St.
Grand Rapids, MI 49506

River Gallery
120 S Main St.
Chelsea, MI 48118
www.chelsearivergallery.com

Water Street Gallery
98 Center St.
Douglas, MI 49406
www.waterstreetgallery.com

Minnesota

McGrill Art Associates
Minneapolis, MN
www.mcgrillartassociates.com

Mississippi

The Caron Gallery
122 W. Main St.
Tupelo, MS 38804
www.thecarongallery.com

The Mockingbird Cafe and Gallery
110 S 2nd St.
Bay St. Louis, MS 39520
www.mockingbirdcafe.com

Missouri

Atrium Gallery
4814 Washington Ave.
St Louis, MO 63108
www.atriumgallery.net

Nebraska

Modern Arts Midwest
800 P St. Suite 300
Lincoln, NE 68508
www.modernartsmidwest.com

New Hampshire

Architectural and Sculptural Metalsmithing
69 Upper Gates Rd.
Canaan, NH 03741

Cynthia-Reeves
57 South Main St.
PO Box 187
Hanover, NH 03755
www.cynthia-reeves.com

Mill Brook Gallery and Sculpture Garden
236 Hopkinton Rd.
Concord, NH 03301
www.themillbrookgallery.com

New Jersey

Highlands Art Gallery
Chester Village Square
54 Main St. Suite 3
Chester, NJ 07930
www.highlandsartgallery.com

Mark Gallery
11 Grand Ave.
Englewood, NJ 07631
www.mark-gallery.com

Palette Press Studio
31 West Main St. Box 119
Brookside, NJ 07926
Email: palettepressllc@aol.com

William Ris Gallery
94 Second Ave.
Stone Harbor, NJ 08246
and
271 21st St.
Avalon, NJ 08202
www.williamris.com

New Mexico

Arroya Gallery
200 Canyon Rd.
Santa Fe, NM 87501
www.arroyosantafe.com

Darnell Fine Art
640 Canyon Rd.
Santa Fe, NM 87501
www.darnellfineart.com

David Richard Gallery
544 South Guadalupe St.
Santa Fe, NM 87501

Karan Ruhlen Gallery
225 Canyon Rd.
Santa Fe, NM 87501
www.karanruhlen.com

William & Joseph Gallery
727 Canyon Rd.
Santa Fe, NM 87501

New York

Asya Geisberg Gallery
537B West 23rd St.
New York, NY 10011
www.asyageisberggallery.com

Cavaliero Fine Arts
190 East 72nd St.
New York, NY 10021
www.cavalierofinearts.com

Central Booking
111 Front St. #210
Brooklyn, NY 11201
www.centralbookingnyc.com

Causey Contemporary
111 Front St., Suite 212-14
Brooklyn, NY 11211
www.causeycontemporary.com

David Findlay Jr. Gallery
728 Fifth Ave.
New York, NY 10019

Elena Zang Gallery
3671 Route 212
Woodstock, NY 12409
www.elenazang.com

hanrahan Meyers architects
6 Maiden Lane
Suite 510
New York, NY 10038
www.hanrahanmeyers.com

J. Cacciola Gallery
537 W. 23rd St.
New York, NY 10011
www.j.cacciolagallery.com

Littlejohn Contemporary
547 West 27th St.
New York, NY 10001
www.littlejohncontemporary.com

Nature Genetics
USA Headquarters
75 Varick St.
New York, NY 10013

New York Sculptors Gallery
55 Washington St.
Suite 256
Brooklyn, NY 11201
www: sculptorsguild@gmail.com

Pierogi Gallery
177 N. 9th St.
Brooklyn, NY 11211
www.pierogi2000.com

Porter Contemporary
548 West 28th St.
New York, NY 10001
www.portercontemporary.com

Walter Wickiser Gallery
210 11th Ave. #303
New York, NY 10001
www.walterwickisergallery.com

North Carolina

Artspace
201 E. Davie St
Raleigh, NC 27601
www.artspacenc.org

Blue Spiral 1
38 Biltmore Ave.
Asheville, NC 28801
www.bluespiral1.com

Cedar Creek Gallery
1150 Fleming Rd.
Creedmoor, NC 27522
www.cedarcreekgallery.com

Emerge Fine Art
200 S. Academy St.
Cary, NC 27511
www.emergefineart.com

Hillsborough Gallery of Arts
121 N. Churton St.
Hillsborough, NC 27278
www.hillsboroughgallery.com

Hodges Taylor Gallery
401 North Tryon
Charlotte, NC 28202
www.hodgestaylor.com

North Carolina Crafts Gallery
212 W. Main St.
Carrboro, NC 27510
www.nccraftsgallery.com

Piedmont Craftsmen Gallery
601 North Trade St.
Winston Salem, NC 27101
www.Piedmontcraftsmen.org

Saxapahaw Artists Gallery
1610 Jordan Drive
Saxapahaw, NC 27340
www.saxapahawartists.com

Shain Gallery
2823 Selwyn Ave.
Charlotte, NC 28209
www.shaingallery.com

Snowbird Mountain Lodge
4633 Santeetlah Rd.
Robbinsville, NC 28771
www.snowbirdlodge.com

Ohio

Contessa Gallery
24667 Cedar Rd.
Cleveland, Ohio 44124
www.contessagallery.com

Harris Stanton Gallery
2301 West Market St.
Akron, OH 44313
www.harrisstantongallery.com

Keith Berr
1420 East 31st Street
Cleveland OH 44114
www.keithberr.com

Joseph Saxton Gallery
520 Cleveland Ave. NW
Canton, OH 44702

Miller Gallery
2715 Erie Ave.
Cincinnati, OH 45208
www.millergallery.com

Muse Gallery
188 E. Whittier St.
Columbus, OH 43206
www.amusegallery.com

Pennello Gallery
12407 Mayfield Rd.
Cleveland, OH 44106
www.pennellogallery.com

Oklahoma

JRB Art at the Elms
2810 North Walker Ave.
Oklahoma City, OK 73103
www.jrbartgallery.com

M.A. Doran Gallery
3509 South Peoria
Tulsa, OK 74105
www.madorangallery.com

Oregon

Butters Gallery
520 N.W. Davis, Second floor
Portland, OR 97209
www.buttersgallery.com

Pennsylvania

art4business
161 Leverington Ave.
Suite 101
Philadelphia, PA 19127
www.art4business.com

Borelli-Edwards Galleries
3583 Butler St.
Pittsburgh, PA 15201
www.begalleries.com

Bucks County Gallery of Fine Art
77 W. Bridge St.
New Hope, PA 18938
www.buckscountygalleryart.com

Marketview Arts
37 W. Philadelphia St.
York, PA 17401
www.marketviewarts.com/contact

Morgan Gallery of Fine Art
Rte. 940, P.O. Box 226
Blakeslee, PA. 19610
www.morgangalleryonline.com

Nestology Gallery
King of Prussia Mall
King of Prussia, PA 19406

New Hope Arts, Inc.
2 Stockton Ave.
New Hope, PA 18938
www.newhopearts.org

New Hope Sidetracks Art Gallery
2A Stockton Ave.
New Hope, PA 18938
www.sidetracksart.com

Pittsburgh Center for the Arts
6300 Fifth Ave.
Pittsburgh, PA 15232
www.pittsburgharts.org

Projects Gallery
629 North Second St.
Philadelphia, PA 19123

Snyderman-Works Gallery
303 Cherry St.
Philadelphia, PA 19106
www.snyderman-works.com

Rhode Island

Cade Tompkins Projects
198 Hope St.
Providence, RI 02906
www.cadetompkins.com

Kelly Milukas Home Gallery
Bow House Studio
355 Neck Rd.,
Tiverton, RI 02878
www.kellymilukas.com

South Carolina

Atelier Gallery
153 King St.
Charleston, SC 29401
www.theateliergalleries.com

Lewis+Clark
1221 Lincoln St.
Columbia, SC 29201
www.lewisandclarklamps.com

If ART Gallery
1223 Lincoln St.
Columbia, SC 29201
www.ifartgallery.blogspot.com

Matthew Campbell Gallery
28 West North St.
Greenville, SC 29601
www.matthewcampbellgallery.com

Tennessee

Bennett Gallery
2104 Crestmoor Rd.
Nashville, TN 37215
www.bennettgalleriesnashville.com

Gallery One
5133 Harding Pike, Suite 1A
Nashville, TN 37205
www.galleryone.biz

Tinney Contemporary
237 5th Ave. North
Nashville, TN 37219
www.sarah@tinneycontemporary.com

Texas

Craighead Green Gallery
1011 Dragon St.
Dallas, TX 75207
www.craigheadgreengallery.com

David Dike
2613 Fairmount
Dallas, TX 75201
www.daviddikefineart.com

Gremillion & Co Fine Art
2501 Sunset Blvd
Houston, TX 77005

Wally Workman Gallery
1202 W. 6th St.
Austin, TX 78703
www.wallyworkman.com

William Campbell Contemporary Art
4935 Byers Ave.
Fort Worth, TX 76107
www.
williamcampbellcontemporaryart.com

Virginia

43rd St. Gallery
1412 W. 43rd St.
Richmond, VA 23225
www.43rdstgallery.com

Artspace
00 East Fourth St.
Richmond, VA 23224
www.artspacegallery.org

CrossRoads Art Center
2016 Staples Mill Rd.
Richmond, VA 23230
www.crossRd.sartcenter.com

Glave Kocen Gallery
1620 West Main St.
Richmond, VA 23220
www.glavekocengallery.com

Washington

Lisa Harris Gallery
1922 Pike Place
Seattle, WA 98101
www.lisaharrisgallery.com

Lucia Douglas Gallery
1415 13th St.
Bellingham, WA 98225
www.luciadouglas.com

Matzke Fine Art Gallery and Sculpture Park
2345 Blanche Way
Camano Island, WA 98282
www.matzkefineart.com

Museum of Northwest Art
121 1st St.
La Conner, WA 98257
www.museumofnwart.org

Pacini Lubel
207 2nd Ave. South
Seattle, WA 98104
www.pacinilubel.com

Sculpture Woods
3851 Legoe Bay Rd.
Lummi Island, WA
www.annmorrisbronze.com

Schack Art Center
2921 Hoyt Ave.
Everett, WA 98201
www.schack.org

Simon Mace Gallery
236 Taylor St.
Port Townsend, WA 98360
www.simonmacegallery.com

Smith and Vallee Gallery
5742 Gilkey Ave.
Edison, WA 98232
www.smithandvallee.com

Stonington Gallery
119 South Jackson St.
Seattle, WA 98104
www.stoningtongallery.com

Vermillion Gallery
1508 11th Ave.
Seattle, WA 98122
www.vermillionseattle.com

Waterworks Gallery
35 Argyle St.
Friday Harbor, WA 98250
www.waterworksgallery.com

Washington, D.C.

Zenith Gallery
PO Box 55295
Washington DC 20040
www.zenithgallery.com

Wisconsin

Grace Chosy Gallery
1825 Monroe St.
Madison, WI 53711
www. gracechosygallery.com

Peltz Gallery
1119 East Knapp St.
Milwaukee, WI 53202

Tory Folliard Gallery
233 N. Milwaukee St.
Milwaukee, WI. 53202
www.toryfolliard.com

Wantoot Gallery
Mineral Point, WI 53565

INTERNATIONAL

Canada

BAU-XI Galleries
3045 Granville St.
Vancouver BC V6H3J9
and
340 Dundas St. West
Toronto ON M57aG5
www.bau-xi.com

Patrick International Fine Art
190 Davenport Rd.
Toronto, Ontario, M5R 1J2
www.patrickinternationalfineart.com

Sopa Fine Arts
2934 South Pandosy St.
Kelowna, BC V141V9
www.sopafinearts.com

Whistler Village Art Gallery
4293 Mountain Square
Whistler, BC
www.whistlerart.com

Australia

Adelaide Central Gallery
45 Osmond Terrace,
Norwood
South Australia, Australia 5067
www.acsa.sa.edu.au/gallery

Arts in Health at Flinders Medical Centre
Flinders Drive,
Bedford Park
South Australia, Australia 5042
www.flinders.sa.gov.au/artsinhealth

France

Galerie Ligne 13
33 Rue Condamine
Paris, France

United Kingdon

Rebecca Hossack Art Gallery
2a Conway St.
Fitzroy Square, London, W1T 6BA, UK
and
262 Mott St.
New York, NY 10012
www.r-h-g.co.uk

Royal Infirmary of Edinburgh Main Atrium Hall,
Edinburgh, UK EH164S/T
www.nhslothian.scot.nhs.uk

Stockwell Studio
London, UK SW4 6QU

Transistor Gallery
Bristol, UK BS6 6AY

Hong Kong

Tao Evolution
12 Circular Pathway
Sheung Wan
Hong Kong, + 852 2805 1112
http://taogallery.com

Singapore

Ode to Art Contemporary
252, North Bridge Rd.
Raffles City Shopping Centre
#01-36E/F, Singapore 179109
www.odetoart.com

Sweden

Galleri Andersson/Sandström
Hudiksvallsgatan 6, 113 30
Stockholm, Sweden
Aktrisgränd 34, 903 64 UME..., Sweden
www.gsa.se

Uruguay

Ralli Museum
Punta Del Este, Uruguay

Venezuela

Galeria Medicci
Calle Par s con Nueva York
Edf. Themis Mari, PB
Las Mercedes, Caracas
Venezuela
www.medicci.com

Index of Artists